THE MESSIAH IN THE PSALMS

Discovering Christ in Unexpected Places

1-72

Bro. Hall,
May God bless you!
Daniel Musgraves

THE MESSIAH IN THE PSALMS

Discovering Christ in Unexpected Places

1-72

Daniel L. Segraves

WAP Academic
A Division of Word Aflame Press
8855 Dunn Road, Hazelwood, MO 63042
www.pentecostalpublishing.com

The Messiah in the Psalms

by Daniel L. Segraves

© 2007 Word Aflame Press
Hazelwood, MO 63042

All Scripture quotations, unless otherwise indicated, are taken from the New King James Version®, Copyright © 1982 by Thomas Nelson, Inc. Used by permission. All rights reserved.
Scripture quotations marked NIV are taken from the HOLY BIBLE, NEW INTERNATIONAL VERSION®. NIV®. Copyright © 1973, 1978, 1984 by International Bible Society. Used by permission of Zondervan Publishing House. All rights reserved.
Scripture quotations marked NLT are taken from the Holy Bible, New Living Translation, copyright © 1996, 2004. Used by permission of Tyndale House Publishers, Inc., Wheaton, Illinois 60189. All rights reserved.

All rights reserved. No portion of this publication may be reproduced, stored in an electronic system, or transmitted in any form or by any means, electronic, mechanical, photocopy, recording, or otherwise, without the prior permission of Word Aflame Press. Brief quotations may be used in literary reviews.

Printed in United States of America

WAP ACADEMIC
A Division of Word Aflame Press
8855 Dunn Road, Hazelwood, MO 63042
www.pentecostalpublishing.com

Library of Congress Cataloging-in-Publication Data

Segraves, Daniel L., 1946-
  The Messiah in the Psalms : discovering Christ in unexpected places / Daniel L. Segraves.
    p. cm.
  Includes bibliographical references.
  ISBN-13: 978-1-56722-706-2
  1. Bible. O.T. Psalms—Criticism, interpretation, etc. 2. Messiah—Prophecies. 3. Typology (Theology) I. Title.
BS1430.52.S44 2006
223' .2064--dc22   2006101048

Table of Contents

Preface 7

Introduction 9

CHAPTER 1
The Book of Psalms. 13

CHAPTER 2
Book One, Psalms 1-41. 25

CHAPTER 3
Book Two, Psalms 42-72. 151

APPENDIX 1
Canonical-Compositional Hermeneutics 325

APPENDIX 2
The Use of Psalms in the New Testament 331

APPENDIX 3
David's Explanation of the Psalms. 343

Notes 349

Preface

I well remember the turning point that revolutionized my interest in the Book of Psalms. Before this time, I certainly believed that the Psalter was inspired, and I saw it as something like a hymnal for ancient Israel. It contained wonderfully uplifting poems to be read when one was discouraged, looking for comfort, or in need of wisdom and direction. But I did not recognize the psalms' pervasive focus on the Messiah.

Then I enrolled in the course "The Messiah in the Psalms and Daniel," taught by Dr. John H. Sailhamer at Western Seminary. I had heard good reports about Dr. Sailhamer's courses and looked forward to being in his class, but I'll have to admit that I signed up for the course primarily because I needed the credits toward the Master of Theology degree.

I had not listened to Dr. Sailhamer long, however, before I realized that I knew very little about the Psalter, and I became increasingly enthralled with the discovery that the essential focus of this Old Testament poetic book was on the coming One, the Messiah, Jesus Christ. Since then, my interest in the Book of Psalms has only increased. From December 31, 2000, to May 11, 2003, I taught a series of eighty-nine lessons on the Psalter in the weekly Bible class at Christian Life Center in Stockton, California. In this book, you will read the results of my preparation for the first eighty of those lessons. The rest of the work I have done will be published in a second volume when I finish my research on all 150 psalms.

In addition to teaching from the Book of Psalms nearly every week for two and one-half years, I have been introducing the messianic content of this book to students enrolled in the

Poetic Books class at Christian Life College and to students at Urshan Graduate School of Theology in Studies in Psalms. Because of my intense interest in this book, my preaching is also frequently flavored with its message.

Any attempt to interpret the Scriptures relies on some hermeneutical (interpretive) method. The approach used in this treatment of Psalms is that of canonical-compositional hermeneutics, a brief explanation of which is included in Appendix 1.

I would like to express my appreciation to those who were involved in bringing this work to its present shape. This includes Robert Fuller, the editor in chief of the Division of Publications of the United Pentecostal Church International. He has been a friend for many years, and I appreciate his thoughtful suggestions which have improved this volume. Margie McNall, who is also a friend of long standing to my wife and me, has applied her diligent and excellent skills to prepare the manuscript for publication. I would like to thank the college and seminary students who have read this material and whose interaction with me in class has sharpened my thinking. I am especially grateful to my sweet wife, Judy, for her encouragement to get this work into print and for her patience with me during long hours of research and writing. Above all, I want to express my gratitude to our Lord and Savior, Jesus Christ, for granting me the desire and opportunity to do this work. One of my favorite verses is found in Paul's letter to the Philippians: "[F]or it is God who works in you both to will and to do for His good pleasure" (Philippians 2:13).

I take full responsibility for any errors that may be in this work. It may not be perfect, but I have certainly enjoyed the experience of discovering the Messiah in unexpected places.

Daniel L. Segraves

Introduction

The Psalms have been widely used as devotional literature, giving comfort and hope to those who are in difficult circumstances. Many people have favorite psalms they love to quote or to meditate on, like Psalm 1, 8, 23, or 91. The beautiful words and well-timed cadences of the Psalter soothe troubled hearts. They assure us that we are walking on a path others have trod before us and that, if we trust in our Lord, there is the promise of a better day.

But there is something in the Psalms that goes far beyond this. According to Jesus, Peter, Paul, and the consistent use of the psalms by the New Testament church, the Psalter is first and foremost a book about the Messiah. This does not mean only that there are a few "messianic" psalms scattered throughout the book. The entire Psalter, from beginning to end, testifies of the Messiah. When read as a messianic book, Psalms takes on a dynamic dimension beyond that of devotional literature. It is no longer a section of the Bible that we turn to only when we are searching for encouragement or wisdom; it is a book we turn to in order to know Jesus better. This does not eliminate its devotional value; it enhances it. Now we see that the one with whom we identify in suffering and victory is not just David or other human authors; it is our Lord Jesus Christ.

For many years the first-century church existed without a New Testament. Until the first New Testament book was written, which was at least about fifteen years after the church was founded on the Day of Pentecost, the only Bible Christians had was the Old Testament. From the time that the books that now make up our New Testament began to be written, it was almost another half century before the last book was completed. How could the New Testament church exist without a New Testament? This was possible because the gospel message is deeply rooted in the Hebrew Scriptures. The first apostles found everything they preached in the Old Testament.

During His final days on earth, Jesus explained to His disciples everything in the Old Testament that concerned Him. (See Luke 24:27.) He said, "[A]ll things must be fulfilled which were written in the Law of Moses and the Prophets and the Psalms concerning Me" (Luke 24:44). By explaining the Christ-centered content of the Old Testament, Jesus "opened their understanding, that they might comprehend the Scriptures" (Luke 24:45). He taught them, from the only inspired Scripture that existed at that time, about the sufferings of the Messiah, His resurrection on the third day, "and that repentance and remission of sins should be preached in His name to all nations, beginning at Jerusalem" (Luke 24:46-47).

On the Day of Pentecost, Peter's Bible was the Old Testament. He quoted extensively from Joel and Psalms to explain the events of that day. Twelve verses of Peter's Pentecostal message were either direct quotes from Psalms or explanations and applications of those quotes. It was Peter's use of Psalms that led his hearers to ask, "Men and brethren, what shall we do?" (Acts 2:37).

To read the Book of Acts is to recognize the fundamental place of the Old Testament Scriptures in the mission and message of the first-century church. For example, to explain his message and ministry that led to the healing of the man at the Beautiful Gate, Peter said, "Yes, and all the prophets, from Samuel and those who follow, as many as have spoken, have also foretold these days" (Acts 3:24). Since Peter had already identified David as a prophet (see Acts 2:30), this means that Peter believed David foretold the events that were occurring in the life of the early church. This understanding was not limited to the apostles. The church at large understood that the Book of Psalms foretold the treatment of Jesus by Herod, Pontius Pilate, and the Romans. (See Acts 4:24-28.)

Paul declared that what he believed was that which was written in the Law and the Prophets (Acts 24:14). He had done nothing offensive against the law of the Jews or the Temple (Acts 25:8). He was called before Agrippa "for the hope of the promise made by God to [the] fathers" (Acts 26:6). In a very clear appeal to the Hebrew Scriptures for his message, including the inclusion of Gentiles equally with the Jews, Paul told Agrippa that he said nothing other than those things "which the prophets and Moses said would come—that the Christ would suffer, that He would be the first to rise from the dead, and would proclaim light to the Jewish people and to the Gentiles" (Acts 26:22-23). Rather than claiming innovation for his message, Paul insisted that he said nothing new.[1] After arriving in Rome, Paul told the Jewish community there that he had done nothing against the Jewish people or the fathers (Acts 28:17). Instead, he was bound "for the hope of Israel" (Acts 28:20). He "explained and solemnly testified of the kingdom of God, persuading them concerning Jesus from both the Law of Moses and the Prophets" (Acts 28:23).

The New Testament quotes from, alludes to, or paraphrases the Old Testament in nearly 800 verses.[2] The book most frequently appealed to is Psalms, which is referred to 206 times in the New Testament. Psalm 110:1 is the verse most frequently referred to out of the entire Old Testament; it is quoted, alluded to, or paraphrased twenty times in the New Testament. Jesus Himself quoted Psalm 110:1, confounding the Pharisees. (See Matthew 22:43-44.)

In the Book of Psalms, we discover that Christ, the promised Messiah, is the Son of God. He is, at the same time, the Son of Man and, specifically, the Son of David. The fact that He is the Son of God does not mean that He is in any way less than God. The Messiah is God Himself in human existence. The psalms foretell the Messiah's birth, important events in His life—including things not found in the New Testament, His betrayal, His sufferings, His death, His resurrection, His ascension, His second coming, and the Millennium. The Psalter foretells the proclamation of the gospel, the Messiah's bride, and the gifts given to the New Testament church upon His ascension.

When our eyes are opened to the primary focus of the Book of Psalms, we begin to understand why this book was such a major part of the preaching of the first-century believers. And we come to know that through the reading of the Psalter, we will "grow in the grace and knowledge of our Lord and Savior Jesus Christ" (II Peter 3:18).

CHAPTER 1

The Book of Psalms

Why Do We Call Them Psalms?

The Book of Psalms takes its English title from the Septuagint title *Psalmoi*, a word that means "hymns" sung to musical accompaniment.[1] Although the Hebrew *mizmor*, meaning "a song sung with musical accompaniment," appears fifty-seven times in the Book of Psalms, the actual title of the book in the Hebrew text is *Tehillim*, meaning "praises."

In addition to the title *Tehillim*, a portion of the book is identified as "the prayers (*tefillot*) of David." (See Psalm 72:20.) This is an ancient title for a book comprised of Psalms 3-72. The word *mizmor* always appears in the superscription of psalms. (See, for example, Psalm 3.) In the Hebrew text, the superscription is actually the first verse. Those labeled *mizmor* in the section comprising the *tefillot* may be prayers intended to be sung.

Who Wrote the Psalms?

Ninety-nine of the psalms identify the author or authors in the superscription. Although some question the authenticity and validity of the superscriptions—they are set apart from the psalms as a kind of heading and not numbered with the

verses—the superscriptions are included in the Hebrew text as the first verse. It has been suggested that we should accept the superscriptions as authoritative for the following reasons:
1. Biblical poets typically identified themselves with their work. (See II Samuel 22:1; 23:1; Isaiah 38:9; cf. Psalm 18.)
2. Not all of the psalms have superscriptions. This seems to suggest the authenticity of the superscriptions, for if they had been added after the psalms were originally written, it seems that superscriptions would have been added to all of the psalms.
3. The Septuagint indicates that those who translated from Hebrew to Greek in the third century BC knew little about the meaning of the musical terms in the superscriptions. If this were so, the terms in the superscriptions must have substantially predated the Septuagint.
4. Jesus' use of what is now included as superscription indicated that He viewed the words as authoritative and authentic. (See Matthew 22:43-45.)

The superscriptions indicate the following authors for the Psalms:

Moses

The superscription of Psalm 90 reads, "A Prayer of Moses the man of God." (See also Exodus 15:1; Deuteronomy 31:19, 30; 32:1; 33:1.) Moses was a writer of psalms. Although we cannot know when Psalm 90 was written and when it was added to the Book of Psalms, it is no doubt the oldest psalm in the book, dating possibly from about 1500 BC.

David

Seventy-three psalms are identified as having been written by David. (See Psalms 3-9, 11-32, 34-41, 51-65, 68-70, 86, 101, 103, 108-110, 122, 124, 131, 133, 138-145.) These psalms would have been written in the tenth century BC. Psalm 18 is apparently the same psalm of David recorded in II Samuel 22.

Solomon
Two psalms are attributed to Solomon. (See Psalms 72, 127.)

Asaph
Asaph, son of Berechiah, a Levite and a chief musician of David, was appointed by David as the chief minister before the ark of the covenant. (See I Chronicles 16:4-5.) He is identified as the author of twelve psalms. (See Psalms 50, 73-83.) On the day that David appointed Asaph, a cymbalist, and other musicians, he delivered to the musicians a psalm, a portion of which is included in the Book of Psalms as Psalm 105:1-15. (See I Chronicles 16:7-22.)

The Sons of Korah
The children of Korah survived their father's rebellion against Moses. (See Numbers 26:9-11.) Korah, whose father was Izhar, was a grandson of Kohath and great-grandson of Levi. (See Exodus 6:16-21.) Heman was the head of the Kohathites in David's day. He and his sons were responsible to minister with songs and music. (See I Chronicles 6:33; 15:16-17, 19; 16:41-42; 25:1-7.) Heman and his sons continued their service under Solomon (II Chronicles 5:11-14), Jehoshaphat (II Chronicles 20:19), Hezekiah (II Chronicles 29:14-19), and Josiah (II Chronicles 35:15-18).

Eleven psalms are attributed to the sons of Korah. (See Psalms 42, 44-49, 84-85, 87-88.)

Ethan the Ezrahite
Ethan was the name of a wise man who lived during Solomon's time. (See I Kings 4:31.) The name also appeared among the Levitical musicians during David's time. (See I Chronicles 15:17, 19.) We know little about Ethan, but he was

probably not the one who was contemporaneous with David, since the disastrous events of Psalm 89:38-45 did not occur until after David's and Solomon's reigns. Some are of the opinion that Ethan and Jeduthun were one and the same.[2]

How Psalms Are Structured

We refer to Psalms as one of the poetic books because it consists of poetry. The word "poem," from the Greek *poiema*, means "a creation" or "a work." A poem is "an arrangement of words in a particular order to express ideas in a style more imaginative and powerful than that of ordinary speech."[3] The arrangement of words in Hebrew poetry follows the poetic conventions of the ancients. The three basic features of ancient poetry are parallelism, meter, and figurative images. To be considered as poetry, two out of three of these characteristics must be present.

Parallelism
With parallelism, a single idea is expressed in two balanced and related lines. The characteristic of Hebrew poetry is sets of double lines (*bicola*). Each set expresses a single idea. An example may be seen in Psalm 33:6-12:

(6) By the word of the LORD the heavens were made,
And all the host of them by the breath of His mouth.
(7) He gathers the waters of the sea together as a heap;
He lays up the deep in storehouses.
(8) Let all the earth fear the LORD;
Let all the inhabitants of the world stand in awe of Him.
(9) For He spoke, and it was done;
He commanded, and it stood fast.
(10) The LORD brings the counsel of the nations to nothing;
He makes the plans of the peoples of no effect.

(11) The counsel of the LORD stands forever,
The plans of His heart to all generations.
(12) Blessed is the nation whose God is the LORD,
The people He has chosen as His own inheritance.

In Psalm 33:6-12, the parallelism features two lines with the same thought expressed in both lines in different words. This is synonymous parallelism. It is also possible for the parallelism to consist of two lines with a different thought expressed in each line. This is antithetical parallelism.

Psalm 33:6-12 is synonymous parallelism. To further illustrate, here are additional examples:

Psalm 92:12:
The righteous shall flourish like a palm tree,
He shall grow like a cedar in Lebanon.

Psalm 46:1:
God is our refuge and strength,
A very present help in trouble.

Psalm 19:7:
The law of the LORD is perfect, converting the soul;
The testimony of the LORD is sure, making wise the simple.

Psalm 30:11:
You have turned for me my mourning into dancing;
You have put off my sackcloth and clothed me with gladness.

Here are some examples of antithetical parallelism, with each line expressing a different thought:

Proverbs 3:5:
Trust in the LORD with all your heart,
And lean not on your own understanding.

Proverbs 27:6:
>   Faithful are the wounds of a friend,
>   But the kisses of an enemy are deceitful.

Psalm 30:5:
>   For His anger is but for a moment,
>   His favor is for life;
>   Weeping may endure for a night,
>   But joy comes in the morning.

Proverbs 14:11:
>   The house of the wicked will be overthrown,
>   But the tent of the upright will flourish.

Psalm 32:10:
>   Many sorrows shall be to the wicked;
>   But he who trusts in the LORD, mercy shall surround him.

A third form of parallelism has been called synthetic parallelism. In this form, the lines following the first line develop the theme expressed in the first line. An example may be seen in Psalm 1:1:

>   Blessed is the man
>   Who walks not in the counsel of the ungodly,
>   Nor stands in the path of sinners,
>   Nor sits in the seat of the scornful.[4]

A fourth form of parallelism may be called climactic parallelism. With this form, the first line is incomplete, and the second line repeats the idea in the first line, then completes it. An example may be seen in Psalm 96:7:

>   Give to the LORD, O families of the peoples,
>   Give to the LORD glory and strength.

A fifth form of parallelism is known as emblematic parallelism. In the first line is a figure of speech, and the lines following explain or expand the meaning of the figure. An example may be seen in Psalm 1:3-4:

> He shall be like a tree
> > Planted by the rivers of water,
> > That brings forth its fruit in its season,
> > Whose leaf also shall not wither;
> > And whatever he does shall prosper.

All forms of parallelism give full expression to an idea. Synonymous parallelism does this by expressing in the second line a meaning similar to the meaning of the first line, further developing the idea in the first line by means of vivid imagery. Antithetical parallelism does this by expressing in the second line a meaning opposite to the meaning in the first line. Even though both lines in antithetical parallelism are opposite in meaning, they express a single idea that is further expanded by means of the second line. Synthetic parallelism gives full expression to an idea by developing the theme of the first line in the following lines; climactic parallelism does this by completing the thought of the first line; emblematic parallelism fully expresses the idea by expanding or explaining the meaning of a figure of speech found in the first line.

Another purpose for parallelism is to contribute to the biblical idea of meditation. The word translated "meditate" (*hagah*) means to read over and ponder what is written. The idea is to read and reread the verse of Scripture. With parallelism, the reader reads the first line, holds that thought, reads the second line, then returns to the first line.

Meter

Another feature of biblical poetry is meter. This has to do with the balance existing between two parallel lines. Although it may not be seen in translation, the first line and the second line of Hebrew poetry are usually three words in length. The lament, a special kind of meter, commonly has three words in the first line and two words in the second line.

Figurative Language

It is characteristic of poetry to use figurative language featuring comparison. The comparison can be explicit, as in a simile: "He eats *like* a horse." Or the comparison can be implicit, as in a metaphor: "He champed at the bit." The simile states that someone is like a horse in some way. The metaphor assumes comparison of someone with a horse by describing the person with characteristics of a horse.

Here are examples of similes:

Psalm 33:7a:
>He gathers the waters of the sea together *as* a heap.

Psalm 72:16:
>And those of the city shall flourish *like* grass of the earth.

Psalm 92:10:
>But my horn You have exalted *like* a wild ox.

Psalm 92:12:
>The righteous shall flourish *like* a palm tree,
>He shall grow *like* a cedar in Lebanon.

Metaphors are more common than similes. Here are some examples of metaphors, where the comparison is implied:

Psalm 33:7b:
>He lays up the deep in storehouses.

Here, the waters of the ocean are compared with grain kept in storehouses. The metaphor pictures God as a farmer who gathers His grain and stores it.

Psalm 92:5b:
> Your thoughts are very deep.

This is a comparison of the Lord's thoughts with a deep valley.

Psalm 92:13:
> Those who are planted in the house of the LORD
> Shall flourish in the courts of our God.

Psalm 92:14:
> They shall still bear fruit in old age;
> They shall be fresh and flourishing.

In Psalm 92:13-14, righteous people are compared to trees planted in the courtyard of the Temple. They bear fruit and are green and full of sap.

The Structure of the Book of Psalms

Since the Psalter is a collection of psalms by a variety of authors, the structure of the book as we now have it is not original with any of the authors whose psalms appear in the book. Its structure is, rather, the result of the inspired efforts of a composer who did his work after all of the individual psalms were completed. There were earlier collections, some smaller and some larger, but the final result was a book intentionally shaped to serve a theological purpose.[5]

Traditional View

The traditional view of the structure of the Psalter sees the Book of Psalms divided into five smaller books.

The first book extends from Psalm 3 through Psalm 41, concluding with these words: "Blessed be the LORD God of Israel from everlasting to everlasting! Amen and Amen" (Psalm 41:13).

The second book extends from Psalm 42 through Psalm 72, concluding with these words: "Blessed be the LORD God, the God of Israel, who only does wondrous things! And blessed be His glorious name forever! And let the whole earth be filled with His glory. Amen and Amen" (Psalm 72:18-19).[6]

The third book extends from Psalm 73 through Psalm 89, concluding with these words: "Blessed be the LORD forevermore! Amen and Amen" (Psalm 89:52).

The fourth book extends from Psalm 90 through Psalm 106, concluding with these words: "Blessed be the LORD God of Israel from everlasting to everlasting! And let all the people say, 'Amen!' Praise the LORD!" (Psalm 106:48).

The fifth book extends from Psalm 107 through Psalm 150. All of Psalm 150 is in praise to the Lord, but since the book obviously comes to an end with Psalm 150:6, there is no need for "Amen."

A common explanation for this five-book structure is to say that it is intended to provide a way to read the psalms together with the Pentateuch. Psalms 1-41 would be read in conjunction with Genesis; Psalms 42-72 with Exodus; Psalms 73-89 with Leviticus; Psalms 90-106 with Numbers; and Psalms 107-150 with Deuteronomy.

A similar structure may be seen in I Chronicles 16:7-36. Here, a collection drawn from three psalms (Psalm 96; 105:1-15; 106:1, 47-48), concludes with the words "Blessed be the LORD God of Israel from everlasting to everlasting! And all the people said, 'Amen!' and praised the LORD" (I Chronicles 16:36).

The similarity of these sections indicates some kind of intentional structure, but more recent scholarship questions whether these are the most significant structural features of the Psalter and whether the New Testament writers viewed the five-book division of the Psalms as significant for their purposes.[7]

Recent Views

Thematic. The thematic approach to the structure of the psalms was suggested by Franz Delitzsch and further developed by Christoph Barth. The idea is that the psalms are linked together not only by key words, but also by broad themes.

Structural. As suggested by P. Auffret, this approach sees a chiastic structure within the Psalter, specifically within Psalms 15-24. A chiasm is a kind of reverse, inverted outline. Auffret bases the chiasm on several key words.

Redactional. This is the idea that the current shape of the Psalter is a revision of an earlier shape, with the current shape intended to serve certain theological purposes, but not necessarily one purpose.

Canonical. Brevard Childs suggests that we can dispense with any discussion about any previous shape of the Psalter and focus on its present shape and structure. We do not need to be concerned with how the present shape came to be; all we need to be concerned with is that this is the shape found in the canon.

Compositional. The compositional approach sees the current shape of the Psalter as reflecting an inspired work bringing together previously existing materials in a form intended to advance a specific theological purpose. One compositional approach sees the Psalter as a collection of prayers for the Jewish people in exile, functioning as a replacement for Temple worship.

A compositional/canonical approach seems most satisfying, because it recognizes the obvious facts concerning the variety of authors and evidence of previous collections now reshaped into the current canonical form. The following points seem evidently true:

1. The Psalter is a composition with a specific purpose and literary strategy.
2. The Psalter is composed for individuals, not for the community.[8]
3. The Psalter is composed for those in exile or tribulation as a source book for hope and divine comfort.[9]
4. The framework of the Psalter is messianic: It focuses on Zion theology and the kingdom of God, by which we

mean the physical restoration of Davidic hope, the ultimate fulfillment of the promise God made to David that the Messiah would descend physically from him to rule on David's throne in Zion. Within this framework, the individual psalms "are a collection of the prayers and praises of Israel['s] great leaders, intended to provide a means for those in the present to identify with God's help of those in the past."[10] The selection and arrangement of the psalms are intended to explore the relationship between the law of Moses and Israel's hope for the future, or, as we might say from the Christian perspective, the relationship between law and grace. The final form of the Psalter is also intended to explore the meaning of the Davidic covenant in view of the apostasy and exile of the house of David.

CHAPTER 2

Book One
Psalms 1-41

Psalms 1-2

The placement of Psalm 1 makes it an obvious introduction to the entire Psalter. It pronounces a blessing on "the man who walks not in the counsel of the ungodly, nor stands in the path of sinners, nor sits in the seat of the scornful" (Psalm 1:1), implying that walking in the counsel to be found in the Book of Psalms is the source of blessing.

Psalm 1 is known as a Torah, or law, psalm, because it describes the blessed man as one who delights "in the law of the LORD" and who meditates "in His law . . . day and night" (Psalm 1:2). The word *torah* means "instruction," and it is used (as is its New Testament equivalent, *nomos*) with a variety of meanings. Here, it is apparently not a reference to the law of Moses, but to the psalms themselves. In other words, Psalm 1:2 does not mean that the reader would be better off meditating in the law of Moses than in the psalms! The psalms offer wise instruction and godly counsel.

Psalm 1, a Torah psalm, is connected conceptually with Psalm 2, a royal, messianic psalm. This is a pattern in the Psalter. Psalm 19, another Torah psalm (see Psalm 19:7-8), is connected with Psalms 20-21, royal, messianic psalms (see Psalm 20:6). Psalm 119, a Torah psalm (see Psalm 119:1 [the word "law" appears in

Psalm 119 twenty-five times]), is connected to the section of psalms known as Songs of Ascents (Psalms 120-134), with their royal, messianic focus (see Psalm 132:10-18). For the Torah psalms to be attached to royal, messianic psalms in this way follows an ancient method of interpretation by attachment. In other words, to attach the messianic psalm to the Torah psalm serves to provide interpretation for the Torah psalm. The concept of law must be interpreted in connection with the concept of the Messiah.

Psalm 1 begins by pronouncing a blessing upon the person who delights in the law (*torah*, "instruction," a reference here to Scripture) of the Lord (Psalm 1:2); Psalm 2 ends by pronouncing a blessing on all who put their trust in the Son, the Messiah (Psalm 2:12b). The idea presented here is that meditation upon the Scripture leads to trust in the Messiah.[1] The word translated "trust" (*chasah*) is used in the Old Testament with the same essential meaning as the New Testament words "faith" and "believe." The meaning of *chasah* is "to take refuge." This helps us understand the New Testament *pistis* ("faith") and *pisteuo* ("I believe"), which are used essentially as synonyms for the Old Testament "trust." Both New Testament words have to do with trust.

Contrary to a view that arose during the twentieth century, biblical faith is not about some kind of mental perspective, manipulation, or gymnastics by which one cajoles God into fulfilling one's desires. Faith is not, in the strictest sense, a way of thinking. It is trust in God in the sense of taking refuge in Him in time of trouble and believing Him to be who He claims to be and to do what He promises to do.

The "counsel of the ungodly . . . the path of sinners . . . the seat of the scornful" (Psalm 1:1) is a series of terms further described in Psalm 2:1 as plotting "a vain thing." The "counsel of the ungodly" is seen in Psalm 2:2 as "the rulers take counsel together, against the LORD and against His Anointed [the Messiah]." It is ungodly counsel that leads kings and rulers to say, "Let us break Their bonds in pieces and cast away Their cords from us" (Psalm 2:3).

Psalm 1 declares of the ungodly that they are "like the chaff which the wind drives away. Therefore the ungodly shall not stand in the judgment, nor sinners in the congregation of the righteous. . . . the way of the ungodly shall perish" (Psalm 1:4-6). According to Psalm 2, this happens because "He who sits in the heavens shall laugh; the LORD shall hold them in derision. Then He shall speak to them in His wrath, and distress them in His deep displeasure" (Psalm 2:4-5). The Messiah will "break them [the nations that follow ungodly counsel] with a rod of iron . . . [and] dash them to pieces like a potter's vessel" (Psalm 2:9).[2] The Son will be angry with those who do not kiss Him—as an act of respect and homage—and they will "perish in the way, when His wrath is kindled but a little" (Psalm 2:12).

The person who rejects the ungodly counsel that encourages people to cast off loyalty to the Lord and His Messiah and who instead delights and meditates in the Scripture will, in contrast to the fate of those who rebel, "be like a tree planted by the rivers of water, that brings forth its fruit in its season, whose leaf also shall not wither" (Psalm 1:3). The wise man is like a healthy, fruitful, enduring tree. The man who follows ungodly counsel is like chaff. The wind will drive him away; he will perish. (See Psalm 1:6; 2:12.)

The response of the Lord to those who follow ungodly counsel is to laugh and to hold them in derision (Psalm 2:4). In wrath, He will speak to them and distress them. The distressing proclamation the Lord makes to those who seek to rebel is this: "Yet I have set My King on My holy hill of Zion" (Psalm 2:6). In their desire to cast off the authority of the Lord and His Messiah, the people are plotting "a vain thing" (Psalm 2:1). It is vain because God has set His king, the Messiah, on Zion. The plotting of the ungodly will do nothing to change that. He will not neglect the covenant He made with David. (See II Samuel 7:8-17; Psalm 89:34-37.)

The Messiah says, "I will declare the decree: The LORD has said to Me, 'You are My Son, today I have begotten You. Ask of Me, and I will give You the nations for Your inheritance, and the ends of the earth for Your possession. You shall break them with a rod of iron; You shall dash them to pieces like a potter's vessel' " (Psalm 2:7-9).

The idea of the Messiah as the "begotten Son" is an important theme in the New Testament. In some cases, the New Testament quotes Psalm 2:7 directly (Acts 13:33; Hebrews 1:5; 5:5), but there are allusions to Psalm 2:7 as well (John 1:14, 18; 3:16, 18; I John 4:9). If the words of Psalm 2 were ever used in conjunction with the ascension of one of David's descendants to the throne, that merely human king would have, in that context, been considered "the anointed" and the "begotten son." But the purpose for the placement of this psalm in the Psalter was not to preserve ascension formulas, but to point to the ultimate anointed One, the Son of God.

The only wise response for the rulers of the earth was to "be instructed . . . serve the LORD with fear, and rejoice with trembling" and to "kiss the Son" (Psalm 2:10-12). They should abandon their vain attempt to rebel and should rather put their trust in the Messiah. If they would abandon their ungodly counsel and meditate in Scripture, this was what they would do.

Psalms 1-2 introduce the contrast between the "righteous" (*tsaddiq*) and the "ungodly" (*rasha*) that continues throughout the Psalter.

The early church saw Psalm 2 as being fulfilled in the actions of Herod, Pontius Pilate, and the unbelieving Gentiles and Jews. (See Acts 4:24-28.)

Psalms 3-7

Following the introduction to the Psalter in Psalms 1-2, in which a royal, messianic psalm (Psalm 2) was attached to a Torah (law) psalm (Psalm 1), showing that meditation on Scripture led to trust in the Messiah, Psalms 3-7 formed a unit showing that God's messianic promise to David would be fulfilled, even in the face of the rebellion of David's descendants. Specifically, even though Absalom rebelled against his father David, attempting to usurp the throne by his own cleverness, God's promise would be kept.

Psalm 3

The superscription of Psalm 3 reads, "A Psalm of David when he fled from Absalom his son." This is the opening bracket of a collection of five psalms on the topic of rebellion within the Davidic family and its threat to the fulfillment of the promise God made to David that Solomon would sit on his throne. (See II Samuel 7:12-16; I Chronicles 22:6-10; 28:5-10; I Kings 1:17-35.) The closing bracket is Psalm 7, which is composed of the words David sang to the Lord when he heard from Cush the news of Absalom's death. (See the superscription of Psalm 7.)

Absalom was David's third son. (See II Samuel 3:3.) At Absalom's command, his servants killed his oldest brother, Amnon (see II Samuel 3:2), because Amnon raped Absalom's sister, Tamar, Amnon's half-sister. (See II Samuel 13:1-29.) These events resulted in the estrangement of David and Absalom. (See II Samuel 13:30-39; 14:1-20.) Finally, after a restoration of sorts (see II Samuel 14:21-33), Absalom devised a scheme to steal the throne from his father. (See II Samuel 15:1-12.) The scheme seemed to work for a time; David fled from Jerusalem with his servants. (See II Samuel 15:13-37; 16.) Through palace intrigue, however, Absalom's plot failed (see II Samuel 17), and he was killed by Joab, David's military leader. (See II Samuel 18.)

With this backdrop, the words of Psalm 3 become meaningful. Many joined Absalom in his rebellion against David (verse 1; compare II Samuel 15:6, 11-13; 17:1, 11; 18:7). Many thought David's situation was hopeless (verse 2). David, on the other hand, knew that the Lord was his shield, his glory, and the One who lifted up his head (verse 3). Rather than giving in to despair, David cried to the Lord, who heard him (verses 4, 7). Therefore, David lay down fearlessly and slept, sustained by the Lord (verses 5-6). Because David had complete confidence that God would fulfill His promise to perpetuate his throne through Solomon, regardless of the bleakness of the circumstances, he said, "Salvation belongs to the Lord. Your blessing is upon Your people" (verse 8).

In verse 2, a form of the word *yeshua'* ("deliverance" or "salvation") is used in the phrase, "there is no help for him in God." David believed there was help in God, however, for he prayed, "Save me, O my God!" (verse 7). Here, the Hiphil imperative form of *yeshua'* is translated "save me." The same word appears in the phrase, "salvation belongs to the LORD" (verse 8). It may have appeared, from all circumstances, that David was helpless, but the certainty of the promise God made to David meant there was help. If God made a promise, He would fulfill it regardless of the vain plotting of men. (See Psalm 2:1-6.) The throne of David would be perpetuated, no matter how impossible it may have looked at that point.

As it was placed in the Psalter, Psalm 3 was intended to show David's confidence that God would fulfill His promise to place the Messiah on David's throne. (See Psalm 89:3-4, 34-37; Isaiah 9:6-7; Jeremiah 23:5-6; Luke 1:32-33.) This would give the Jewish readers of this psalm, who read the Psalter in this order after the destruction of Jerusalem by the Babylonians, confidence that the messianic promise would yet be fulfilled. If David was confident in the face of the apparent hopelessness associated with Absalom's rebellion, they could continue to be confident, even though they too experienced trouble. They were driven into exile, but David himself had, in a sense, also experienced exile. Since he had been restored to the throne, they could have hope that one day the throne of David would be occupied again by the promised seed.

The "lifting of the head" is a Hebrew figure of speech expressing confidence in the Lord.[3] The striking of enemies on the jaw signifies humiliation, and the "metaphor of the breaking of teeth likens the enemies to wild animals whose strength is taken away when their teeth are crushed."[4]

At this point, we are not certain of the meaning of *Selah*. (See verses 2, 4, 8.) Although it appears seventy-one times in thirty-nine psalms, it is never found in a superscription. It also appears three times in Habakkuk 3. "Among the suggestions for its meaning is 'interlude,' indicating a break in the text or performance. It is also possible that it is a cue for the choir to repeat a litany or affirmation of a statement in the psalm or for a particular instrument, possibly a drum, to be beaten to keep the rhythm or emphasize a word."[5]

Psalm 4

The superscription of Psalm 4 does not identify the circumstances surrounding the origin of the psalm. It has been suggested that the psalm is connected with the time of Saul's pursuit of David, or with the time of Absalom's rebellion, or with an unnamed king, or even with a time of harvest failure.[6] As it relates to its placement in the Psalter, the original circumstances may not be significant, because it finds its place in the section concerning Absalom's rebellion with the apparent intent of further developing the theme begun in Psalm 3.

Within the context, the prayers of Psalm 4 continued the theme of the prayers of Psalm 3. Because of rebellion within his kingdom, there seemed to be a threat to the messianic promise connected with David's throne. David represented the dynasty of God's covenanted loyalty.[7] Those who had rebelled against him had turned his "glory to shame" (verse 2a). They "[loved] worthlessness and [sought] falsehood" (verse 2b). But David knew that "the LORD [had] set apart for Himself him who [was] godly" (verse 3a). This was an apparent reference to David himself, for he immediately declared, "The LORD will hear when I call to Him" (verse 3b).

To those who questioned the future of the Davidic promise, the psalm counseled, "Stand in awe, and sin not: commune with your own heart upon your bed, and be still" (verse 4, KJV). The word translated "sin" (*chata*) had to do with "missing the mark." It would certainly miss the mark if anyone allowed the circumstances to cause him to cast away his confidence in God's promise. Rather than missing the mark, one should stand in awe (of God), meditate on his bed, and be still (verse 4b). Like David, one could lie down and sleep. (See verse 8 and Psalm 3:5.) Rather than being distracted by the upheaval in the kingdom and questioning whether any good could come out of it (verse 6a), one should offer the sacrifices of righteousness and put his trust in the Lord (verse 5).

David confessed that God had relieved him in his distress and put gladness in his heart (verses 1, 7). He prayed for mercy (verse 1). In response to the hopelessness that seemed to infect many, David prayed, "LORD, lift up the light of Your countenance upon us" (verse 6). This allusion to the priestly benediction of Numbers 6:24-26 was a request for God to make His covenant blessings evident.[8] The connection between Psalm 3:5 ("I lay down and slept; I awoke, for the LORD sustained me") and Psalm 4:8 ("I will both lie down in peace, and sleep; for You alone, O LORD, make me dwell in safety") is evident.

Psalm 4 continues the theme of Psalm 3. Within the context of Psalms 3-7, Psalm 4 further develops the theme of the certainty of the Davidic covenant with its messianic hope in the midst of political turmoil.

Psalm 5

The superscription of Psalm 5 does not identify the circumstances of its writing, but its placement within the framework of Absalom's rebellion (see comments on Psalm 3) indicates that it should be read as a further development of that theme.

David prayed that God would hear his prayer and consider his meditation (verses 1-2a, 3). He identified God as his King (verse 2b). There was recognition here that God was the ultimate King. In the face of human rebellion—specifically Absalom's rebellion—against a human king, God was the ultimate King who sat "in the heavens" (Psalm 2:4) and who would tolerate no challenge. Although the kings of the earth had set themselves in opposition to the Lord and His anointed One (Psalm 2:2)—and at this time Absalom had proclaimed himself to be king—God had set His king on His holy hill of Zion (Psalm 2:6). By rebelling against

David, Absalom was ultimately rebelling against the Messiah, for had Absalom's plan succeeded, God's plan would have failed.

Verses 4-6 and 9-10 addressed the problem David faced with the rebellion of Absalom. Absalom's act of rebellion was wicked and evil. This meant it did not please God and that it would not succeed (verse 4). Absalom's boastful work of iniquity assured its own failure and provoked God's hatred (verse 5). Since Absalom was a bloodthirsty and deceitful man who spoke falsehood, he was abhorred by the Lord and would be destroyed (verse 6). The words spoken by Absalom and those who joined him in his rebellion were unfaithful (i.e., untrustworthy), characterized by flattery. (See II Samuel 15:1-6.) This reflected their inner corruption (verse 9).

Because of their rebellion, David prayed that God would pronounce them guilty, let them fall as a consequence of their own counsel, and cast them out from the place they had usurped. Although Absalom's rebellion was immediately against David, it was ultimately against God (verse 10).

In contrast to Absalom, David declared that he would approach God on the basis of mercy and in fear (verse 7). He prayed that God would lead him in His righteousness, making His way straight before him, because of his enemies (verse 8). His most immediate enemies were, of course, Absalom and those associated with him.

David put his trust in the Lord, even in the midst of disappointment and instability. He loved the name of the Lord.[9] He knew God would defend him from Absalom's attempt to cast him from the throne. This was cause for joy (verse 11).

The final verse of Psalm 5 is quite similar to the final verses of Psalms 1, 2, and 3. According to Psalm 1:6, the Lord knows the way of those who are righteous, which means they will endure while the ungodly perish. According to Psalm 2:12, those who put their trust in the Son are blessed. According to Psalm 3:8, the blessing of the Lord is upon His people. Although the final verse of Psalm 4 is not as specific, it implies the blessing of the Lord in

David's ability to "lie down in peace, and sleep" safely (Psalm 4:8). This is a direct consequence of the fact that "the LORD has set apart for Himself him who is godly" (Psalm 4:3).

As it was originally written, Psalm 5 may have addressed other enemies and circumstances, but as the psalm was placed in the Psalter, it seems evident it was intended to further develop the problem of Absalom's challenge to David's throne and thus to the Davidic covenant and its messianic promise, and it further described David's confidence that God's promise would prevail. To those who read these words after the destruction of Jerusalem by Babylon, when David's throne may have seemed permanently vacated, the message would be to continue to trust God to keep His promise to raise up the Messiah on David's throne. David's throne had been vacated once before, only to be restored. If the attempt to thwart God's purpose in the days of Absalom had failed, they could be certain any other attempt was doomed. The people of Israel might find themselves, so to speak, in the same situation as David when he was in exile, but they would one day be restored in conjunction with the restoration of the throne to David's greatest Son. (See Psalm 2:7, 12.)

Psalm 6

The previous psalms in the collection concerned with Absalom's rebellion (Psalms 3, 4, 5) reflected David's joyous confidence that Absalom's plot would fail and that he would be vindicated and restored to the throne. (See Psalms 3:3-8; 4:3, 7-8; 5:11-12.) But in real life, those who are challenged by circumstances to question the certainty of God's promise are not always quite so optimistic. Psalm 6 reveals the heart of a man who knew that God would come to his rescue, but who was nevertheless troubled over the apparent delay.

Like Psalms 4 and 5, Psalm 6 does not identify its circumstances in the superscription. But although we may not know its original circumstantial context, it is placed here in a purposeful context to further develop the theme of the certainty of God's covenantal promise to David in the face of its first challenge: Absalom's rebellion.

David knew he should simply wait on the Lord to deliver in His time, so he prayed that God would not be angry with him for asking, "How long?" (See verses 1-3.) The reason he was struggling with God's timing was that he was weak (verse 2a), troubled physically (2b) and spiritually (3a).

David prayed for deliverance, for salvation, for the sake of the mercies of the Lord (verse 4). David's appeal to the mercies (*chesed*, "loyal love") of the Lord was an apparent reference to the Davidic covenant, characterized by mercy. (See II Samuel 7:15; 22:51; I Kings 3:6; 8:23; II Chronicles 6:42; Nehemiah 1:5; 9:32; Isaiah 55:3; Acts 13:34.)

David knew Absalom was determined to kill him (see II Samuel 17:1-14), but he knew that if Absalom's plans were successful, he would be unable to continue to testify to the mercies of the Lord on this earth.[10] In other words, if Absalom succeeded in killing David, it would indicate the covenant God made with David had failed. If David did not survive this challenge, he could not celebrate the mercies of the Lord as seen in the Davidic covenant (verse 5).

David's previous discussion of sleep had described it as peaceful (see Psalms 3:5; 4:8). But people of faith are not always able to avoid the distress that accompanies those circumstances that arise when those around them rebel against God. So here, David confessed that he was not always able to rest in peace (verse 6). The grief associated with Absalom's rebellion seemed to hasten the aging process (verse 7).

David wished for all those who were "workers of iniquity"— an apparent reference to Absalom and his cohorts—to depart from him (verse 8a). He knew the Lord had heard his prayer (verses 8b, 9a) and that He would answer (9b). When He did answer, David's enemies would "be ashamed and greatly troubled" (verse 10a). They would be turned back from their plot suddenly (verse 10b).

Psalm 6 is comforting to believers in any situation where they are opposed and it seems God's promises are delayed. We may be able in many cases to continue to rejoice in God's promises even in the midst of devastating circumstances, but there are times when all of us wonder just how much longer it will take for God to intervene. At times such as these, the words of Psalm 6 can be prayed with the assurance that God's purpose will prevail—in His time.

Psalm 7

The superscription of Psalm 7 reads, "A Meditation of David, which he sang to the LORD concerning the words of Cush, a Benjamite." This indicates that Psalm 7 is the conclusion of the unit beginning with Psalm 3, which is a "Psalm of David when he fled from Absalom his son" (see the superscription of Psalm 3). Psalm 3 opens a series of five psalms concerned with the rebellion of Absalom against his father David, the first significant attempt to thwart God's messianic purpose announced in Psalm 2. Psalm 7 was David's response when he heard of Absalom's death from Cush.

Even in the face of Absalom's rebellion, David commanded Joab to "deal gently . . . with the young man Absalom" (II Samuel 18:5). But when Absalom's head was caught in the boughs of a tree, Joab thrust three spears into him, and Joab's ten young armor bearers finished killing him. (See II Samuel 18:9-18.) After Absalom's death, Joab told Cush, "Go, tell the king what you have seen" (II Samuel 18:21).

When Cush reached David, he said, "There is good news, my lord the king! For the LORD has avenged you this day of all those who rose against you" (II Samuel 18:31).

David asked, "Is the young man Absalom safe?" (II Samuel 18:32a).

"May the enemies of my lord the king, and all who rise against you to do harm, be like that young man!" answered Cush (II Samuel 18:32b).

"O my son Absalom—my son, my son Absalom," David wept, "if only I had died in your place! O Absalom my son, my son!" (II Samuel 18:33).

Although David was distressed with Absalom's rebellion, he loved him as his son, and his initial response to the news of his son's death was grief. Like many fathers upon hearing the news of the death of a son, David wished he could have died in his son's place. But as he moved past the initial grief, David's prayer reflected his larger awareness of the fact that Absalom's rebellion against him was actually rebellion against God, and that Absalom's death was a consequence of his own sin.

The opening words of David's prayer affirmed his trust in the Lord even in the midst of persecution. There were those who would have liked to tear David "like a lion" and rend him in pieces. He prayed for deliverance from such people. (See Psalm 7:1-2.)

In Psalm 7:3-5, David declared his innocence in the matter of Absalom's death. The iniquity was not in his hands (verse 3). He had not "repaid evil to him who was at peace" with him (verse 4a). David had not "plundered [his] enemy without cause" (verse 4b). David was so certain of his innocence in this matter that he prayed that if he was at fault, the enemy would pursue him and overtake him, trampling his life to the earth and laying his honor in the dust (verse 5).

David prayed that the Lord would arise in His anger and lift Himself up because of the rage of David's enemies. He prayed that the Lord would rise up on his behalf and carry out judgment. (See verse 6.)

David believed that if God would judge those who had rebelled against him, the congregation would "surround" the LORD. This seems to imply that the innocent bystanders who had not been involved in the rebellion of Absalom and who were thoroughly confused and disoriented by the events associated with this attempted coup would align themselves with God's purposes as seen in the Davidic covenant when they observed the judgment of God on the rebels. For the sake of these people, therefore, David prayed that God would rise up from His throne to carry out judgment. (See verse 7 and II Samuel 19:2-10.)

Not only did David want the Lord to judge others, he invited the Lord to judge him "according to [his] righteousness" and "according to [his] integrity" (verse 8). Only a man who was completely sure of his innocence in a matter would boldly ask to be judged in this way.

David prayed that the rebellion instigated by Absalom would come completely to an end (although Absalom was dead by this time, many had joined him in his rebellion and needed to be dealt with) and that God would "establish the just" (verse 9a), a reference to himself and to those who had remained loyal to him. God saw not only one's deeds; He "[tested] the hearts and minds" (verse 9b). The words translated "hearts" and minds" meant literally "hearts" and "kidneys." It was customary among the Hebrews to use the inner organs of the body as metaphors for the innermost person. This was seen also in the New Testament in references to the heart and intestines (translated "bowels" in the KJV [see Philippians 1:8; 2:1; Colossians 3:12; Philemon 1:7, 12, 20; I John 3:17]).

In the modern English-speaking world, of course, the heart is still used as a metaphor for the inner person. Because of the biblical use of these terms, it would be a mistake to try to make fine distinctions between the meanings of words used to represent the inner man (e.g., when Jesus said that we are to love God with all of our heart, soul, mind, and strength [Mark 12:30], He did not imply that to love God with the heart was one thing and to love Him with the mind was another thing; He meant that we are to love God with everything within us).

David realized he was completely dependent upon God for his defense from Absalom's uprising. God is the One who saves the upright. (See verse 10).

The anger of God with those who rebel against Him is a theme found elsewhere in this section. (See verse 11; Psalm 3:7; 5:4-6). God's anger is not, however, the basis of His judgment. He is a just (*tsaddiq*, "righteous") judge.

If the wicked do not turn from their wickedness, God prepares His weapons to use against them (verses 12-13).

The wicked—like Absalom in his rebellion against God's purposes—produce iniquity. They conceive trouble and falsehood. (See verse 14.)

It is typical with the wicked, and it was certainly the case with Absalom, to fall into their own pit. The trouble they plan for others comes back upon them. (See verses 15-16; Proverbs 26:27; Ecclesiastes 10:8.)

David concluded this psalm by stating his intention to praise the Lord. For the connection between the Lord and His name, see note 9 on page 350. The challenge to David's throne, and thus to the Davidic covenant with its messianic focus, had concluded with failure, and David—once troubled by the apparent delay in the defeat of Absalom's plan (see Psalm 6)—now sang in praise to the Lord (verse 17).

The intentional arrangement of the psalms may be seen in that this section concludes with David's stated intention to "sing praise to the name of the LORD Most High," and the next psalm begins with praise to the name of the Lord (Psalm 8:1). The purposeful placement of the next psalm is also evident in that it is a messianic psalm celebrating the genuineness of the Messiah's humanity, His solidarity with humankind.

Psalm 8

This psalm is intentionally placed here—although the superscription offers no information as to the circumstances of its writing—to advance the messianic theme of the Psalter. Psalms 3-7, which track the ill-fated attempt of Absalom to usurp his father's throne, conclude with his defeat and David's announcement that he "will sing praise to the name of the LORD Most High" (Psalm 7:17). Psalm 8 begins with this praise, flowing naturally out of the conclusion of Psalm 7.

Psalm 8, with its focus on the Son of Man, should be read as a messianic psalm, for that is how it is interpreted in the New Testament. (See Hebrews 2:6-9.) The Son of Man is the same One to whom the Lord has said, "You are My Son, today I have begotten You" (Psalm 2:7). He is the King who is placed by the Lord upon His holy hill of Zion (Psalm 2:6), whose inheritance is the nations, whose possession is the ends of the earth (Psalm 2:8), and who must be kissed by the kings and judges of the earth lest He be angry (Psalm 2:12). He is the anointed One, the Messiah (Psalm 2:2).

David began the psalm with a declaration of the excellence of the name of the Lord, who had set His glory "above the heavens" (verse 1). (For a discussion of the significance of the name of the Lord, see note 9 on page 350.) The background of this praise was the defeat of Absalom by the Lord. (See Psalms 3:7-8; 5:10; 7:11-13.)

Verse 2 was connected by Jesus with the praise of the Messiah by children. (See Matthew 21:15-16.) As the children in the Temple cried out, "Hosanna to the Son of David!" in the words of Psalm 118:25 ("Hosanna" was transliterated from the Hebrew words translated "save now" in Psalm 118:25), thus identifying Jesus as the messianic Son of David in the words of a messianic psalm (Psalm 118), Jesus connected their praise with the words of Psalm 8:2. When the chief priests and scribes protested the children's identification of Jesus as the Messiah, Jesus justified the children's praise by pointing the chief priests and scribes to Psalm 8:2.

The point here is that Psalm 8:2 has to do with the Messiah and with the fact that young children would recognize Him as the Messiah and proclaim Him to be so even in the face of God's enemies who would reject His anointed One. The faith of children would "silence the enemy and the avenger." This is precisely what happened in the Temple as recorded in Matthew 21:15-16. The chief priests and scribes who rejected Jesus as the Messiah were silenced by the proclamation of faith made by children.

As David contemplated the marvels of the creative work of God as seen in the heavens, he asked, "What is man that You are mindful of him, and the son of man that You visit him?" (verse 4). The poetic form of verse 4 indicates that the emphasis is not on human beings as a whole, but on one specific human being, the Son of Man. The first line of the verse asks a general question that is further specified in the second line.[11]

David's question should not be thought to demean the Son of Man, for although He had been made "a little lower than the angels," He had been "crowned . . . with glory and honor" (verse 5). He had been given dominion over the entire created realm (verses 6-8). David's question was a legitimate question, because he knew this Son of Man would be a human being descended from him. (See Psalm 132:11.) In view of the incredible majesty of the created realm, how could a descendant of David be exalted to the place of dominion over the created realm? How could a human being be clothed with glory and honor? (See verse 5.) We know now, of course, that the reason is that this Son of Man was not only the Son of Man; He was also the Son of God.

The crowning of the Son of Man with glory and honor occurred as a consequence of His death. (See Hebrews 2:9.) Since He was a human being, made a little lower than the angels, He could "taste death for everyone" (Hebrews 2:9). This was made possible by the grace of God (Hebrews 2:9).

Although Psalm 8 did not address the death of the Son of Man, the superscription of Psalm 9 identified it as "to the tune of 'Death of the Son.'" (The words *'l muth labben* translate, "Concerning the death of the Son."[12]) This connects Psalm 8 with Psalm 9.

David concluded this psalm as it began, by ascribing excellence to the name of the Lord (verse 9). The first major challenge to the messianic promise was past; the Son of Man would rise above His enemies because He was given dominion over all of the works of the hands of the Lord (verse 6).

Psalms 9-10

The rendering of the superscription of Psalm 9 in the KJV leaves mysterious the meaning: "To the chief Musician upon Muthlabben, A Psalm of David." The phrase translated "upon Muthlabben" (*'l muth labben*) is translated by the NKJV as "to *the tune of* 'Death of the Son.' " The words "the tune of" are supplied by the translators; they are not in the Hebrew text. The idea suggested by the NKJV translation is that this psalm is to be sung to the tune of another psalm titled "Death of the Son."

In view of the contextual and canonical emphasis on a Son that begins in Psalm 2 (verses 7, 12), a Son who is the Anointed, the Messiah (Psalm 2:2), continuing through Psalms 3-7, where the son (Absalom) is a rebel against his father (David), but more significantly against the anointed Son,[13] to the return to the Son of Man in Psalm 8, it is better to translate the superscription "concerning the death of the Son." The preposition *'l*, translated "upon" by the KJV and "to" by the NKJV, also means "concerning." *Muth* means "death," and *labben* means "of the son."

The superscription identifies the psalm as a psalm of David.

The significance of Psalm 9 being about the death of the Son may be seen in the identification of Psalm 8 as a messianic psalm in Hebrews 2:6-8. In the context in Hebrews, the Son is "crowned with glory and honor" as a consequence of His death, which He experienced "for everyone" (Hebrews 2:9). Although Psalm 8 declares that the Son of Man has been "crowned . . . with glory and honor" (Psalm 8:5), it does not discuss His death. The idea of the death of the Son of Man is found in the superscription of the next psalm, Psalm 9.

The linkage of Psalm 9 with Psalm 8 by means of the "Son" motif actually provides a linkage all the way back to Psalm 2 and ahead to Psalm 10, because Psalms 9 and 10 were apparently one psalm in an earlier form. The evidence for this is as follows:

First, when Psalms 9 and 10 are placed together, they form an acrostic. Psalm 9 takes us through exactly half of the Hebrew alphabet; Psalm 10 takes us through the second half.[14]

Second, the Septuagint puts the two together as one. Thus, Psalm 11 in the English translation is Psalm 10 in the Septuagint.

Third, only Psalm 9 has a superscription. If the two are not to be read as one, Psalm 10 is the only psalm without a superscription between Psalm 3 and Psalm 32.

Where the acrostic is irregular, it seems to be because of an emphasis on "the wicked one." (See footnote 14.) This indicates an intentional emphasis on the contrast between "the righteous" and "the wicked one" (*rasha*) that begins in Psalm 1 (verses 1, 4, 5, 6), where a form of *rasha* is translated "ungodly." (See Psalm 9:5, 16-17; 10:2, 3, 4, 13, 15.)

Psalm 9 is a psalm of thanksgiving, describing the Lord coming to aid those who are in distress. Psalm 10 is a psalm of lament, but at the points where the acrostic is interrupted in Psalm 10, the lament is changed back into the defeat of the enemy. Psalm 10 has to do with the eschatological judgment of God upon all the nations, as found in Daniel 7 and Ezekiel 38.

Psalm 9 declares the eternality of the reign of the Lord. (See Psalm 9:4b-5, 7-8, 11, 15-17, 19-20.) The Lord will not only judge the wicked nations; He will deliver the righteous. (See Psalm 9:9-10, 12, 18.)

David began Psalm 9 by praising the Lord (verses 1-2).[15] He was certain that his enemies would be defeated (verse 3) because God had "maintained [his] right and [his] cause" (verse 4). It is not difficult to see here a lingering reference to Absalom's rebellion and failure. (See comments on Psalms 3-7.) But God's concern to perform the Davidic covenant (see II Samuel 7) goes beyond Absalom; it reaches out to embrace any nation of the world that might seek to rebel against the Anointed of the Lord (verses 5-6). (See comments on Psalm 2.) The Lord endures forever; so does

His throne (verses 7-8). His judgment results not only in the destruction of the wicked (verse 5), but also in justice for the oppressed who trust Him (verses 9-10).[16]

In Psalm 9:11 David continued his praise to the Lord, calling attention to His deeds, including the fact that when the Lord took vengeance on the wicked He did not forget "the cry of the humble" (verse 12). In Psalm 9:13 David cried for mercy, crediting the Lord with rescuing Him from death—which was perhaps another allusion to the Absalom challenge—and asking God to consider his trouble from those who hated him. David promised to declare the praise of the Lord, including His deliverance, in Zion (verse 14).

Just as Absalom "made a pit and dug it out," only to fall "into the ditch which he made" (Psalm 7:15), so the nations who rebelled against the Lord and His Messiah (Psalm 2:2) had "sunk down in the pit which they made" (verses 15-16). The destiny of all who forgot God was to be "turned into hell" (verse 17). But the needy—those who trusted the Lord—would not experience that kind of destiny (verse 18).

David concluded Psalm 9 by praying that the Lord would arise (see Psalm 7:6), refuse to let the rebels prevail, and judge the nations (verse 19). The judgment of the Lord would convince the rebels that they were only men; they had no claim to deity (verse 20).

In contrast to Psalm 9, which is a psalm of praise to the Lord, Psalm 10 is a psalm of lament. This establishes a general pattern, which is followed up to and including Psalm 41. Although hope is certainly found in this group of Davidic psalms, it is hope against the backdrop of trouble.

The psalm opens with the plea, "Why do You stand afar off, O LORD? Why do You hide in times of trouble?" (verse 1). David knew that the Lord heard "the desire of the humble" (verse 17) and that He would "do justice to the fatherless and the oppressed" (verse 18), but his cry reflected the reality of his emotional condition. In view of the apparent—although temporary—success of the wicked, it seemed that God was distant and uninvolved. Similarly, the words of Psalm 22:1, spoken by Jesus on the cross, reflected the emotional feeling of forsakenness: "My God, My God, why have You forsaken Me?" This should not be interpreted to mean that God actually had forsaken the Messiah, any more than Psalm 10:1 should be interpreted to mean that the Lord actually was "afar off" and hiding in times of trouble. Psalm 22, a messianic psalm, vividly described the suffering of Christ on the cross. The rest of Psalm 22:1 clarified the fact that Jesus' suffering was not the result of abandonment by God, but a consequence of His destiny: "Why are You so far from helping Me, and from the words of My groaning?" The prayer continued, "O My God, I [cried] in the daytime, but You [did] not hear; and in the night season, and [was] not silent" (Psalm 22:2).

This prayer of Jesus fit the description of Hebrews 5:7: "Who, in the days of His flesh, when He had offered up prayers and supplications, with vehement cries and tears to Him who was able to save Him from death, and was heard because of His godly fear." The prayers of Jesus were heard by God, but the answer was not to save Him from death. It was Jesus' destiny to learn "obedience by the things which He suffered" (Hebrews 5:8) that He might be perfected and become "the author of eternal salvation to all who obey Him" (Hebrews 5:9).[17] The point is that the fact that our prayer is not answered as we had hoped, or in the time frame for which we had hoped, is no indication that our prayer is not heard. It seemed to David that God was standing afar off, hiding in the time of trouble, but that was perception, not reality.

Verses 2-11 describe the characteristics of "the wicked one." He is proud, and one of the symptoms of pride is persecution of the poor (verse 2). He is boastful and self-indulgent, blessing (i.e., adoring or approving) those who are greedy and renouncing the Lord (verse 3). Another symptom of pride is that the wicked one does not seek God; he does not even think of God (verse 4). The wicked one seems to prosper (see Psalm 73), gives no thought to God's judgments, and sneers at his enemies (verse 5). He thinks he is immovable and that he will never experience adversity (verse 6). His words are characterized by cursing, deceit, oppression, trouble, and iniquity (verse 7). The wicked one lurks in secret places to murder those who are helpless and innocent (verses 8-10). He convinces himself that God has forgotten him and that He is unaware of his wicked deeds (verse 11).

As in Psalms 7:6 and 9:19, David prayed that the Lord would arise from His throne to come to the aid of the humble (i.e., those who trust in Him [compare with Psalm 9:12]). David wondered why the wicked one would renounce God and think that God would not bring him to account (verse 13).

The wicked one was mistaken to think that God was not aware of his sins against the helpless, such as the fatherless (verse 14 [compare with verse 8]). God had seen the trouble and grief caused by the wicked one, and He would repay him for his evil (verse 14).

David prayed that God would "break the arm of the wicked and the evil man" (verse 15). The arm was a symbol of strength. He prayed that God would discover all of the wickedness, overlooking none (verse 15).

Although Psalm 10 is a psalm of lament, it concludes in hope in view of the fact that "the LORD is King forever and ever" and that "the nations have perished out of His land" (verse 16). This is an allusion to the Davidic covenant with its divinely ordained king who is actually reigning on behalf of the Lord and to the promise of land made to Abraham, Isaac, and Jacob. (See Genesis 15:18-21.)

Although it may have seemed that the Lord was distant and hidden (verse 1), He actually "heard the desire of the humble" (verse 17 [compare with verse 12]). Since He heard their desire, He would "prepare their heart" (i.e., comfort them) (verse 17).

God would "do justice to the fatherless and the oppressed, that the man of the earth may oppress no more" (verse 18).

Although Absalom's challenge to the throne of David, and thus to the messianic promise, was over, there would be other challenges. In the midst of these challenges it may have seemed that the wicked were prospering, that their plot would succeed, and that God was uninvolved. This certainly seemed to be the case in conjunction with the death of the Son—the theme of Psalms 9 and 10. But in His time, God would rise up and judge the wicked one, bringing his rebellion to nothing.

Psalm 11

Psalm 11 continues the theme begun in Psalm 10. The house of David was troubled by "the wicked" (verses 2, 5, 6). (Compare with Psalm 10:2-4, 13, 15.) The wicked ones are contrasted with the righteous ones (verses 3, 5).

The theme of trust in the Lord, introduced in verse 1, continues the motif begun in Psalm 2:12: trust in the Son, the Messiah.

In this psalm, David was either in a conversation with his advisors, or he was consulting with himself. He asked, "How can you say to my soul, 'Flee as a bird to your mountain'?" (verse 1b). Either he was being counseled to flee from the wicked, like a bird flies away from a snare, or he was considering flight. (Compare with Psalm 55:6; 124:7.) The point is, how can flight be considered when one is trusting in the Lord?

If his advisors were counseling David, they justified their counsel to flee by saying, "For look! The wicked bend their bow, they make ready their arrow on the string, that they may shoot secretly at the upright in heart. If the foundations are destroyed, what can the righteous do?" (verses 2-3).

It is common in Psalms and elsewhere to describe the words of those who are wicked metaphorically as deadly weapons. (See Psalm 37:14-15; 57:4; 64:3-4; Proverbs 12:18; Isaiah 54:17; Jeremiah 9:8.)

The "foundations" refer in a metaphor to the social order established by God.[18] (See Psalm 75:3; 82:5; Ezekiel 30:4.) The idea here is that a challenge to David was a challenge to the Davidic covenant and ultimately to the Messiah's rule. The "foundation" of Israel, and ultimately of the world, was the throne of David, occupied by the Messiah.

David's answer was confident: "The LORD is in His holy temple, the LORD'S throne is in heaven; His eyes behold, His eyelids test the sons of men" (verse 4). There was no need to flee from the challenge of the wicked; God was in control. He was completely aware of the attempts of the "nations . . . kings . . . and . . . rulers" (Psalm 2:1-2) to thwart His messianic purpose, but they would fail.

The idea of the Lord testing the righteous suggests a comparison to testing gold to determine its purity. This testing may be connected with the challenge mounted by the wicked. In other words, when someone rebels against the Lord and His anointed One, the righteous are tested to see whether they will identify with the rebels or be faithful. But the Lord hates those who rebel; they can hope to carry out their rebellion only by violence. Violence would be required to dethrone the Lord (verse 5).

The fate of the wicked, the rebels, is compared to the destruction of Sodom and Gommorah (verse 6). They will be destroyed.

The Lord is righteous, and He loves those who are righteous, that is, those who do right. These are the upright, and His countenance beholds them. This phrase could be translated, "The upright beholds His countenance" (verse 7). Either way, the idea is that God delivers the upright, in contrast to the destruction of the wicked.

Psalm 11 acknowledges a challenge to God's messianic purpose, a challenge that is doomed. Regardless of the efforts of those who are wicked, God is still on His throne, and that means His purposes will be accomplished on earth.

Psalm 12

Like Psalm 11, Psalm 12 continues the theme of trouble for the house of David. The words of those who are unfaithful are contrasted with the words of the Lord. Although nothing specifically is said about the Lord's reign, there is a focus on His faithfulness to keep and preserve those who trust in Him.

Like Psalm 10, Psalm 12 begins with a bleak cry: "Help, LORD, for the godly man ceases!" (verse 1a). The word translated "ceases" (*gamar*) indicates that the godly are no more. As the second half of the verse indicates, "the faithful disappear from among the sons of men" (verse 1b). In other words, it is not "help" that ceases, but it is those who are faithful, or godly, who cease to be.

This is certainly hyperbole, but it accurately expressed David's concern for the apparent success of those who were unfaithful, as also seen in Psalms 10-11. It seemed as if the number of the unfaithful was overwhelming the faithful. This is something that believers of all eras have experienced. To this day, there are believers who are convinced that things are worse than they have ever been, that people of true faith are vanishing, and that unbelievers are proliferating. There is certainly some truth to the idea that unbelievers have a very high profile in most any society, but if believers focus on that problem exclusively, they are missing the divine assurances of God's faithfulness and the ultimate victory of His purposes.

Those who are unfaithful are characterized by their words: their words are idle (compare with Matthew 12:36), they practice flattery (compare with Proverbs 20:19; 28:23; 29:5), and they speak with a double heart[19] (verse 2). This description resurrects the image of Absalom turning the hearts of the people of Israel with his flattery and insincere words. (See II Samuel 15:2-6.)

David prayed that the Lord would "cut off all flattering lips, and the tongue that speaks proud things" (verse 3). The pride of the unfaithful was evident in their words: "With our tongue we will prevail; our lips are our own; who is lord over us?" (verse 4). In a sense, these rebels against God's authority seemed to be convinced that they could create their own reality by their words. Like today's practitioners of various forms of shamanism—who believe there is some kind of creative magic in words—or even pseudo-Christian positive confessionism, these unfaithful people believed they would prevail with their words. They denied any responsibility to surrender to the will of any external authority.

The Lord responded to "the oppression of the poor" and "the sighing of the needy" by promising to "set him in the safety for which he yearns" (verse 5). He would not allow the rebels to succeed. The Lord would "arise," in answer to the prayers of David. (See Psalms 3:7; 7:6; 9:19; 10:12.) Even though Psalm 12 did not specifically mention the reign of the Lord or His throne, it was indirectly referred to here with the idea that the Lord would arise from His throne to respond to the threat of the wicked ones. For the Lord to arise meant He was seated on His throne; the rebels had been unsuccessful in their efforts to unseat Him.

In contrast to the idle, flattering, proud words of the unfaithful, the "words of the LORD are pure words, like silver tried in a furnace of earth, purified seven times" (verse 6).

The promise of the Lord was that He would "keep them" (the poor and needy [verse 5]) and "preserve them from this generation forever" (verse 7). He will not allow the wicked ones to carry out their threats.[20]

When "vileness is exalted among the sons of men," it results in wicked ones prowling "on every side" (verse 8). The implication seems to be that where there is a general trend in a society to surrender to the Lord, those who are wicked tend to be more secret with their rebellion.

Psalm 13

Continuing the theme of trouble in the house of David, Psalm 13 begins, "How long, O LORD? Will You forget me forever? How long will You hide Your face from me?" (verse 1). The general tenor of this lament is very much like the sentiments expressed in Psalms 6:3; 7:1-2; 10:1; 12:1. The apparent success of the wicked ones caused David to feel forgotten by God. (Compare the emotional turmoil of the Messiah in Psalm 22.)

Four times David asked, "How long?" "How long shall I take counsel in my soul, having sorrow in my heart daily? How long will my enemy be exalted over me?" (verse 2). The idea expressed in the phrase, "How long shall I take counsel in my soul" is translated by the NIV as, "How long must I wrestle with my thoughts?" It seemed at times to David that his enemy—and thus God's enemy—was winning. How long would this go on?

David prayed that God would "consider" and "hear" him, enlightening his eyes (restoring his health [see Psalms 6:7; 38:10]) and sparing him from death (verse 3). Unless God did this, David's enemy would say, "I have prevailed against him" (verse 4a). It was the intention of those who troubled David to rejoice when he was moved. The word translated "moved" (*mot*) implied tottering or slipping. It seemed clear that David's enemy desired to usurp his throne. Thus, the enemy desired to thwart God's messianic purpose.

Coming back again to the theme of trust established in Psalm 2:12, David asserted, "But I have trusted in Your mercy; my heart shall rejoice in Your salvation" (verse 5). The word translated "mercy" (*chesed*) continued the theme of God's loyal love that characterized the Davidic covenant. (See II Samuel 7:15 and comments on Psalm 6:4.) The reference to "salvation" advances an emphasis seen in Psalm 3:8. The word translated "salvation" is a form of *yeshua'*, which finds its fullest significance in the name given to the Messiah.

Although Psalm 13 begins with a plaintive cry of forsakenness, it concludes with these hopeful words: "I will sing to the LORD, because He has dealt bountifully with me" (verse 6). When David turned away from a focus on his enemy and refocused on the mercy and salvation of the Lord, his hope was restored and worship overcame complaints. Even in the face of the challenges of his enemy, David recognized that the Lord had been exceedingly good to him.

Psalm 14

The words of this psalm are quite similar to the words of Psalm 53.[21] One significant difference may be seen by comparing Psalm 14:5-6 with Psalm 53:5.

> There they are in great fear, for God is with the generation of the righteous. You shame the counsel of the poor, but the LORD is his refuge. (Psalm 14:5-6).

> There they are in great fear where no fear was, for God has scattered the bones of him who encamps against you; you have put them to shame, because God has despised them. (Psalm 53:5).

What is the purpose of having two psalms with such great similarity? Both of these psalms are intentionally placed where they are within their immediate contextual relationship with the psalms around them and within the contextual form of the entire Psalter. Each serves an intended purpose in advancing the theme of the Book of Psalms.

Psalm 14 underscores the theme established in Psalms 1-2. Here, the ungodly person—the wicked one—is identified as "the fool." To characterize the fool as saying in his heart, "There is no God" (verse 1a) is probably not intended to indicate that this fool is an atheist. The point of Psalm 14 is not to attempt to prove the existence of God. Atheism was not typical of the ancient milieu in which the psalms were composed. Rather, the fool was one who thought God would never call him into account for his deeds. In the context here, the fool was someone like Absalom or those who identified with him in his rebellion; they lived as if they would never give an account to God.

These fools were corrupt; their deeds were abominable (detestable). None of those who denied human accountability to God were doing good (verse 1b).

Fools were mistaken to think that God would never call them into account. Even as they made this claim, the Lord was looking "down from heaven upon the children of men, to see if there [were] any who [understood], who [sought] God" (verse 2). What He saw was that "they [had] all turned aside, they [had] together become corrupt; there [was] none who [did] good, no, not one" (verse 3).

This, like previous poetic hyperbole (see Psalm 12:1), painted a bleak picture of the situation in David's day. The popularity of challenges to David's throne, beginning with Absalom, made it look as though all Israel had abandoned the true God and His anointed king. The situation seemed similar in Elijah's day. (See I Kings 19:10, 18.) We should not be disturbed by exaggeration used as a literary device; this is typical of human communication, as typical as any metaphor. We should read this as it was intended to be read and as the first readers would have understood it. Hyperbole is intended to express the depth of emotional trauma experienced by the author. This is, after all, inspired hyperbole!

In Romans 3:10-18, Paul quoted from Psalm 14:1-3, together with Psalms 5:9; 10:7; 36:1; 140:3; and Isaiah 59:7-8, to demonstrate the universal sinfulness of humans.

Now David asked, "Have all the workers of iniquity no knowledge, who eat up my people as they eat bread, and do not call on the LORD?" (verse 4). In their rebellion against God, fools behaved as if God had not spoken, as if there was no divine revelation. Indeed, they acted as if the Davidic covenant was nonexistent. Their abuse of those who were faithful ("my people") and their refusal to "call on the LORD" was the kind of behavior expected of those who were ignorant of God.

But ignorance is not bliss, at least not when it is ignorance of God and His revealed will. The self-assurances fools give themselves (e.g., "there is no God") do not prevent them from knowing the truth: "There they are in great fear" (verse 5a). Their fear is a consequence of a fact they cannot deny: "For God is with the generation of the righteous" (verse 5b). Although the majority may, in some cases, side with those who rebel against God, that does not bring the outcome of their rebellion into question. God is with those who are faithful to Him. Numbers are insignificant at this point. God will prevail; His purposes will be accomplished.

Those who rebel against God may "shame the counsel ['frustrate the plans,' NIV] of the poor, but the LORD is his refuge" (verse 6). The poor here represent those who trust in the Lord. (See Matthew 5:3.) Those who rebel against God will attempt to thwart those who are faithful to God, but their misguided efforts will not succeed. Those who trust the Lord take refuge in Him; He protects them.

Verse 7 is apparently an inspired addition to the psalm from the era of the Exile: "Oh, that the salvation of Israel would come out of Zion! When the LORD brings back the captivity of His people, let Jacob rejoice and Israel be glad."[22] The word translated "salvation" (*yeshua'*) carries the meaning of "deliverance" and finds its ultimate fulfillment not in the return from exile, but in the person of the Messiah, *Yeshua'*, transliterated into Greek as *Iesous* and into English as "Jesus."

Psalm 15

In view of the deliverance from captivity promised in Psalm 14:7, David asked, "LORD, who may abide in Your tabernacle? Who may dwell in Your holy hill?" (verse 1).

The words "tabernacle" and "holy hill" are intended to focus on the divine presence connected with the ark of the covenant that was returned to Mount Zion by David. (See II Samuel 6:2, 12-18.) The questions, "Who may abide . . . who may dwell," are not about the *identity* of those who could enter God's presence, but about their *character*.[23]

Here are the requirements to enter into God's presence:
1. To walk uprightly [with integrity] (verse 2a).
2. To work righteousness [to do the right thing] (verse 2b).
3. To speak the truth in his heart [to sincerely hold to truth] (verse 2c).
4. To refrain from backbiting [slander] (verse 3a).

5. To refrain from doing evil to others (verse 3b).
6. To refrain from taking up a reproach against a friend [to cast "no slur on his fellowman," NIV] (verse 3c).
7. To despise a vile person (verse 4a).
8. To honor those who fear the Lord (verse 4b).
9. To refuse to change, even if he has sworn to his own hurt [to keep his word, even if it is difficult] (verse 4c).
10. To refrain from usury (verse 5a).
11. To refuse bribes (verse 5b).

These eleven traits characterize people of faith, people who will be permitted to enjoy the presence of the Lord. This kind of person will "never be moved" (verse 5c). The same word translated "moved" here (*mot*) is also used in Psalm 13:4. David's enemies wanted him to be removed from the throne; but those who are people of character will never be moved.

The list of character qualities required of those who will abide and dwell in the presence of the Lord is antithetical to Absalom's character traits. He violated most of these requirements, and the consequence was death. He aspired to sit on the throne of David, but his character prevented him from invading the presence of the Lord on the "holy hill."

Psalm 16

Both Peter and Paul saw Psalm 16 as a messianic psalm. On the Day of Pentecost, Peter quoted extensively from the Septuagint translation of Psalm 16:8-11: "For David says concerning Him: *'I foreseen the LORD always before my face, for He is at my right hand, that I may not be shaken. Therefore my heart rejoiced, and my tongue was glad; moreover my flesh also will rest in hope. For You will not leave my soul in Hades, nor will You allow Your Holy One to see corruption. You have made known to me the ways of life; You will make me full of joy in Your presence'* " (Acts 2:25-28).

Peter pointed out that David was not talking about himself, for "the patriarch David . . . is both dead and buried, and his tomb is with us to this day" (Acts 2:29). In other words, David had seen corruption, so the psalm was not about him. In this context, Hades was a reference to the abode of the righteous dead—represented by the grave—as they awaited resurrection. Again, since David was "both dead and buried," he was still in this place awaiting resurrection; therefore, he was not writing about himself. Instead, "being a prophet, and knowing that God had sworn with an oath to him that of the fruit of his body, according to the flesh, He would raise up the Christ to sit on his throne, he, foreseeing this, spoke concerning the resurrection of the Christ, that His soul was not left in Hades, nor did His flesh see corruption" (Acts 2:30-31).

As further evidence that Psalm 16 was not about David, Peter said, "For David did not ascend into the heavens" (Acts 2:34). Whoever Psalm 16 was about was someone who would not stay in the grave long enough for His body to corrupt; He would be resurrected shortly after burial. This was, of course, Jesus Christ.

This was not Peter's opinion only. Paul, who was not taught messianic truths by any human being (see Galatians 1:15-24; 2:1-2, 6-10), also saw Psalm 16 as being about the Messiah. As he preached at Antioch, Paul said, "Now when they had fulfilled all that was written concerning Him, they took Him down from the tree and laid Him in a tomb. But God raised Him from the dead. . . . And that He raised Him from the dead, no more to return to corruption, He has spoken thus: *'I will give you the sure mercies of David.'* Therefore He also says in another Psalm: *'You will not allow Your Holy One to see corruption'* " (Acts 13:29-30, 34-35). Paul did not think that David was speaking of himself: "For David, after he had served his own generation by the will of God, fell asleep, was buried with his fathers, and saw corruption; but He whom God raised up saw no corruption" (Acts 13:36-37).

Should we read all of Psalm 16 as a reference to the Messiah? In view of the fact that Peter specifically identified

Psalm 16:8-11 as being about the Messiah, there seems to be no reason to understand Psalm 16:1-7 any differently. Peter said, "For David says concerning Him," before quoting the final section of the psalm. Throughout the psalm, the speaker seems to be the same person. There was no obvious change of speakers between verses 7 and 8.

In verse 1, the Messiah prayed a prayer similar to other messianic prayers, recorded both in the Psalter and in the Gospels: "Preserve me, O God, for in You I put my trust." (Compare to Psalm 22:1-2, 8, 11, 19-21.)

The prayer continued in verse 2: "O my soul, you have said to the LORD, 'You are my Lord, my goodness is nothing apart from You.' " In the New Testament, the Messiah, Jesus, often clearly indicated His complete dependence on the Father: "Then Jesus answered and said to them, 'Most assuredly, I say to you, the Son can do nothing of Himself, but what He sees the Father do; for whatever He does, the Son also does in like manner. For the Father loves the Son, and shows Him all things that He Himself does; and He will show Him greater works than these, that you may marvel' " (John 5:19-20). (See John 5:21-32.) Jesus also indicated His oneness with the Father: "I do not pray for these alone, but also for those who will believe in Me through their word; that they all may be one, as You, Father, are in Me, and I in You; that they also may be one in Us, that the world may believe that You sent Me" (John 17:20-21). "I and My Father are one" (John 10:30). When viewed through the lens of the New Testament, it does not seem strange to hear the Messiah say to the Lord: "My goodness is nothing apart from You." The Messiah was a genuine human being who was completely dependent on God for all things. This did not detract from the Messiah's deity, but it underscored the genuineness of the Incarnation and the fact that in humbling Himself, Jesus laid aside His divine prerogatives, not His divine nature. (See Philippians 2:5-11.)

References to the "earth" (*'eretz*) in the Psalter should be understood in terms of the "land" promised to Abraham, Isaac, and Jacob. In the overall context of the Psalter, the "saints" who were on the land, the Promised Land, were those who were faithful to God's covenant, including the Davidic covenant. "They are the excellent ones, in whom is all my delight" (verse 3).

On the other hand, those who "[hastened] after another god" would find that "their sorrows [would] be multiplied" (verse 4a). The Messiah would not participate in the worship of any false god: "Their drink offerings of blood I will not offer, nor take up their names on my lips" (verse 4b).

If it is thought strange that the Messiah would make such a statement, we should remember that one of His first temptations was the temptation to worship Satan. (See Matthew 4:8-10.) He responded, "Away with you, Satan! For it is written, *'You shall worship the LORD your God, and Him only you shall serve'*" (Matthew 4:10). As a genuine human, the Messiah was confronted with the choice to worship a false God or the true God. He chose, of course, to worship the true God. (See Psalm 22:22; Hebrews 2:11-13.)

In verses 5-6, the Messiah continued, "O LORD, You are the portion of my inheritance and my cup; You maintain my lot. The lines have fallen to me in pleasant places; yes, I have a good inheritance." The words "portion" and "cup" represented God's supply. (See Psalm 23:5.) The "lot" was a reference to what God had given His Servant. The "lines" represented the Messiah's inheritance in terms of the language of the conquest of Canaan; they were the "boundary lines."[24]

The New Testament represented the Messiah as the heir of God. (See Hebrews 1:2.) Believers are joint heirs with Christ. (See Romans 8:17.)

The Messiah blessed the Lord who had given Him counsel (verse 7a). His heart instructed Him in the night seasons (verse 7b). It is interesting to note, in view of Peter's quote from the Septuagint, that the Septuagint translates the latter half of verse 7,

"My reins too have chastened me even till night." If we accept this translation, it presents a picture of the Messiah similar to that of the Book of Hebrews, where the Son learned "obedience by the things which He suffered" and "having been perfected, He became the author of eternal salvation to all who obey Him" (Hebrews 5:8-9).

We know because of their inspired use in the New Testament that verses 8-11 have to do specifically with the Messiah, and there is nothing to prevent verses 1-7 from joining in this messianic theme. Even if verses 1-7 are not specifically about the Messiah, the psalm is included here to present David as a figure of the coming One.

Psalm 17

Both Peter and Paul saw Psalm 16:9-10 as a reference to the resurrection of the Messiah. Although there may not be a specific quote from Psalm 17 in the New Testament, it seems clear that it is intentionally placed at this point in the Psalter to advance the concept of the Resurrection: "As for me, I will see Your face in righteousness; I shall be satisfied when I awake in Your likeness" (verse 15).

Sailhamer points out that to "the extent that the composer of the book of Psalms [the person who arranged the psalms in the order they appear in Scripture, under the inspiration of the Holy Spirit] sees David as a messianic figure, his words in this psalm give expression to the hope of the resurrection of the Messiah found in the previous psalm."[25]

Although the circumstances under which David wrote this psalm are uncertain, because of its placement in the Psalter and its content, it seems appropriate to view it as a messianic psalm. If we view the psalm this way, it begins with a prayer of the Messiah: "Hear a just cause, O LORD, attend to my cry; give ear to my prayer, which is not from deceitful lips" (verse 1). As we noted in the discussion of Psalm 16:1, this prayer seems appropriate as a messianic prayer when compared with other prayers of the Messiah recorded in the Psalter and in the New Testament.[26] On several occasions, the Gospels note that Jesus prayed without recording the content of the prayer. We know there were occasions He prayed the words of the Old Testament (e.g., compare Matthew 27:46 with Psalm 22:1; Hebrews 10:5-7 with Psalm 40:6-8 [Septuagint; in this case we do not know precisely when the Messiah prayed this prayer]).

In verse 2 the prayer continued: "Let my vindication come from Your presence; let Your eyes look on the things that are upright." In view of the challenge to the Davidic covenant by those who rebelled against David, these words would be appropriate on David's lips. But they would also be appropriate on the lips of the Messiah in view of His rejection by first-century unbelievers.

It would be somewhat difficult to see the words of verse 3 as limited to a prayer of David: "You have tested my heart; You have visited me in the night; You have tried me and have found nothing; I have purposed that my mouth shall not transgress." The phrase "You have tried me and found nothing" would be perfectly appropriate in a messianic prayer. Jesus endured temptation without sin.

There were those who wished to destroy the Messiah before the appointed hour of the cross (see Luke 4:28-30; John 5:18; 8:37, 59; 10:31-33), but He escaped early death: "Concerning the works of men, by the word of Your lips, I have kept away from the paths of the destroyer. Uphold my steps in Your paths, that my footsteps may not slip" (verses 4-5).

The prayer continued, "I have called upon You, for You will hear me, O God; incline Your ear to me, and hear my speech" (verse 6). Compare this with the prayer of Jesus recorded in John 11:41-42: "Father, I thank You that You have heard Me. And I know that You always hear Me."

The words of verse 7 would be appropriate as a prayer of David as he considered those who rose up against him, beginning with Absalom, but they were also appropriate for the

Messiah: "Show Your marvelous lovingkindness by Your right hand, O You who save those who trust in You from those who rise up against them."

The figures of speech in verse 8 describe close relationship with God. In Deuteronomy 32:10-11 they are metaphors for God's loving care.[27] "Keep me as the apple of Your eye; hide me under the shadow of Your wings" (verse 8).

The theme of the "wicked" appeared again in verse 9. David certainly was oppressed by the wicked, but so was the Messiah: "From the wicked who oppress me, from my deadly enemies who surround me."

The description of the enemies as having "fat hearts" in verse 10 apparently should be understood as "callous" hearts; the phrase indicated their rebellion. Their rebellion was seen in that they had closed their hearts and that they spoke proudly.

In a description similar to Psalm 22:13, 21, the enemies were described as a lion: "They have now surrounded us in our steps; they have set their eyes, crouching down to the earth, as a lion is eager to tear his prey, and like a young lion lurking in secret places" (verses 11-12). The use of this imagery may further indicate that this psalm was to be understood as pointing to the Messiah.

Now the prayer called for deliverance from the enemy in language similar to previous psalms: "Arise, O LORD, confront him, cast him down; deliver my life from the wicked with Your sword" (verse 13). (See comments on Psalms 3:7; 7:6; 9:19; 10:12; 12:5.)

Verse 14 presents difficulties in translation.[28] The best understanding seems to be the idea of continued judgment on those who are "of the world who have their portion in this life." The general idea seems to be captured by the NLT: "Save me by your mighty hand, O LORD, from those whose only concern is earthly gain. May they have their punishment in full. May their children inherit more of the same, and may the judgment continue to their children's children."[29]

Verse 15 is a wonderful anticipation of the Resurrection: "As for me, I will see Your face in righteousness; I shall be satisfied when I awake in Your likeness." Together with Psalm 16:9-10 (as interpreted by Peter in Acts 2:26-27 and Paul in Acts 13:35), this seems to be intended as a reference to the resurrection of the Messiah.

The approach we are taking in reading the psalms is that, although they may have originally referred to David or others, they were selected by the inspiration of the Holy Spirit and placed in the Psalter in an intentional arrangement to point to the Messiah. In this view, it may be possible to understand specific psalms or portions of psalms as possibly applying to David or the Messiah, but where they can be understood as referring to the Messiah, they should be. Jesus did say, "All things must be fulfilled which were written in the Law of Moses and the Prophets and the Psalms concerning Me" (Luke 24:44b). In view of this, it seems appropriate to look for the Messiah in the psalms, although we do not wish to force a messianic meaning on a clearly nonmessianic text.

Psalm 18

An unusual feature about this psalm is that it is also found in II Samuel 22. The superscription over the psalm is little changed from the wording of II Samuel 22:1. The question that arises immediately is why the words of this psalm are recorded twice in Scripture.

The biblical view of the origin of Scripture means that this psalm is included in both places by inspiration. But to discover how we are to understand the words, we must look beyond the words of the psalm itself to the context in which the words are found. The context in II Samuel 22 is not the same as the context in the Psalter. The context immediately preceding II Samuel 22 seems to point to reading the psalm as a poetic description of David's deliverance from Saul, as indicated in II Samuel 22:1. The context has to do with David's exploits and experiences, and this is one of them. However, II Samuel 23:1-7 hints that David's words have meaning that extends beyond himself to the Messiah.[30]

The context of Psalm 18 indicates, however, that the psalm is intended to be read differently here. In the Psalter, we are to understand the words as referring in some way to the Messiah. The final verse in Psalm 18 suggests its messianic intent, especially as it is compared with the larger context of the Psalter: "Great deliverance He gives to His king, and shows mercy to His anointed, to David and his descendants forevermore" (Psalm 18:50). These words can be understood as referring to David, as God's anointed king, and to all of David's descendants who would sit on his throne. But given the right context, they can also be understood as referring to the Messiah. Jesus is the King of kings: "These will make war with the Lamb, and the Lamb will overcome them, for He is Lord of lords and King of kings; and those who are with Him are called, chosen, and faithful" (Revelation 17:14; see also Revelation 1:5; 19:16).

In the phrase "shows mercy to His anointed," the word translated "anointed" is from *Meshiyach*, which is translated into English as Messiah and into Greek as *Christos*, or Christ. Although this terminology is used in many places in the New Testament, it is especially interesting in view of our present study to see its use in Revelation 11:15: "Then the seventh angel sounded: And there were loud voices in heaven, saying, 'The kingdoms of this world have become the kingdoms of our Lord and of His Christ, and He shall reign forever and ever!' " This kind of expression, which is found in Psalm 2:2, is echoed in references like Psalm 18:50. In one sense, David was the Lord's anointed, but the Messiah was the ultimate anointed One of whom David was only a type, although David was His physical ancestor: "I, Jesus, have sent My angel to testify to you these things in the churches. I am the Root and the Offspring of David, the Bright and Morning Star" (Revelation 22:16). In the Psalter, when the anointed One is in view, we are to understand Him as the Son of God. (See Psalm 2:2, 7, 12.) This idea is contained in

Psalm 18:50 and, because of the significant influence of the Psalter on New Testament Christology, in references like Revelation 11:15.

The phrase "to David and his descendants" (translated "to David, and to his seed" by the KJV) can also be understood as referring in this context to His ultimate and greatest descendant, Jesus Christ. The word translated "descendants" is a singular form of *zera'*. Although it is appropriate to translate it in the plural form when it has reference to many descendants (see, e.g., Genesis 15:5, where the singular form of the word is used to refer to the numerous descendants of Abraham), in the christological sense of the word in the New Testament, a point is made about the word being singular: "Now to Abraham and his Seed were the promises made. He does not say, 'And to seeds,' as of many, but as of one, *'And to your Seed,'* who is Christ" (Galatians 3:16). In other words, when the word "seed" is used in reference to Christ, we should note the singularity of the word: In the truest and final sense, there is only one Messiah, one Christ, one anointed One. He is not just part of the seed of Abraham and David; He is not just one among many. He is *the* promised seed, the specific and singular offspring in view in the messianic texts.

It seems that Paul saw a messianic theme in Psalm 18, for he quoted Psalm 18:49 in his letter to the saints at Rome: "Now I say that Jesus Christ has become a servant to the circumcision for the truth of God, to confirm the promises made to the fathers, and that the Gentiles might glorify God for His mercy, as it is written: *'For this reason I will confess to You among the Gentiles, and sing to Your name'* " (Romans 15:8-9). In a context composed of quotes from Psalms (Psalm 18:49; 117:1), from the Law (Deuteronomy 32:43), and from the Prophets (Isaiah 11:10), Paul invested Psalm 18 with messianic content. The One who would give thanks to the Lord and sing praises among the Gentiles was none other than the Messiah. This should not be thought strange in view of the fact that the Messiah declared the name of the Lord among His brethren (the people of Israel) and sang praise to God "in the midst of the assembly [the congregation of Israel]" (see Psalm 22:22; Hebrews 2:12), and in view of the fact that this is what the Messiah actually did during His life on earth. (See Matthew 4:12-17; 12:14-21; Luke 2:27-32; Acts 26:19-23; Galatians 3:14.) What He has done for the Jews, He has done also for the Gentiles.

Sailhamer points out that in Psalm 18:20-50, David was cast "as a figure of the promised messianic King, God's 'anointed' (v. 50), seeing in his own divinely wrought victories a portrait of his eternal descendant (v. 50b)."[31] The following claims were especially appropriate for the Messiah: "The LORD rewarded me according to my righteousness; according to the cleanness of my hands He has recompensed me. For I have kept the ways of the LORD, and have not wickedly departed from my God. For all His judgments were before me, and I did not put away His statutes from me. I was also blameless before Him, and I kept myself from my iniquity. Therefore the LORD has recompensed me according to my righteousness, according to the cleanness of my hands in His sight. With the merciful You will show Yourself merciful; with a blameless man You will show Yourself blameless; with the pure You will show Yourself pure; and with the devious You will show Yourself shrewd" (Psalm 18:20-26). It would be one thing for David to talk about "my righteousness" and "the cleanness of my hands" and about being "blameless," but it was certainly another thing for these words to reflect the sinlessness of the Messiah. (See Hebrews 4:15.) It may seem strange to think of the Messiah saying, "I kept myself from my iniquity," but the word translated "iniquity" (*'avon*) can have reference to guilt. In other words, if we read this as a reference to the Messiah, He had no guilt. All of the statements in verses 20-26 could have reference to David only in a very limited way; they find their full significance in Christ.

Verses 27-48 described the Messiah's victory over His enemies. Again, these words meant one thing when placed in a Davidic context of his deliverance from Saul, but they meant quite another when placed in a messianic context of His deliverance from those who rejected Him. His deliverance was most clearly portrayed in His resurrection from the dead. (See Psalm 16:9-10; 17:15.) Paul connected the identity of Jesus as the anointed One, the Son of God, and David's offspring with His resurrection from the dead (Romans 1:3-4).

But it is also possible to see the Messiah in Psalm 18:1-19. As in other psalms, the Messiah prayed for deliverance from His enemies[32] and from death (verses 1-6). God's answer mirrored closely the actual events that occurred as Jesus hung on the cross. Notice the following comparisons:

"Then the earth shook and trembled; the foundations of the hills also quaked and were shaken" (Psalm 18:7); "Then, behold, the veil of the temple was torn in two from top to bottom; and the earth quaked, and the rocks were split" (Matthew 27:51).

"He bowed the heavens also, and came down with darkness under His feet. . . . He made darkness His secret place; His canopy around Him was dark waters and thick clouds of the skies" (Psalm 18:9, 11); "Now from the sixth hour until the ninth hour there was darkness over all the land" (Matthew 27:45).

". . . the foundations of the world were uncovered at Your rebuke, O LORD, at the blast of the breath of Your nostrils" (Psalm 18:15b); ". . . the earth quaked, and the rocks were split, and the graves were opened. . . . And behold, there was a great earthquake" (Matthew 27:51b-52a; 28:2a).

"He sent from above, He took me; He drew me out of many waters. He delivered me from my strong enemy, from those who hated me, for they were too strong for me. . . . He also brought me out into a broad place; He delivered me because He delighted in me" (Psalm 18:16-17, 19); "And behold, there was a great earthquake; for an angel of the Lord descended from heaven, and came and rolled back the stone from the door, and sat on it. His countenance was like lightning,[33] and his clothing as white as snow. And the guards shook for fear of him, and became like dead men. But the angel answered and said to the women, 'Do not be afraid, for I know that you seek Jesus who was crucified. He is not here; for He is risen, as He said' " (Matthew 28:2-6a).

When considered in its context, in view of its use in the New Testament, in view of its themes that appear elsewhere in the Psalter and in the New Testament in reference to the Messiah, and in view of its poetic description of the events surrounding the crucifixion and resurrection of Jesus Christ, it seems certain that Psalm 18 is intended to advance the messianic theme of the Book of Psalms. The words of this psalm are appropriate for David in II Samuel 22, but they are even more appropriate and more richly fulfilled in the Messiah and in His victory over all who opposed Him.

Psalm 19

One of the ways meaning was imputed in ancient literature was interpretation by attachment. By one piece of literature being attached to another, the pieces served to provide meaning to one another. The Hebrew word for this was *samuk*, which meant to "lean, lay, rest," or "support." The idea was that one piece of literature leaned against another, or supported another.

This is seen in three significant places in the Psalter. Psalms 1-2 are interpreted by their attachment to one another, Psalms 19-21 by their attachment to one another, and Psalms 119-134 by their attachment to one another. In each case, the first psalm in the group extols the Word of God, and the attached psalms extol the Messiah. The idea is that meditation on the Word leads to faith in the Messiah.

In the case of Psalm 19, verses 1-6 address God's revelation in creation. Verses 7-14 address His revelation in Scripture.

God's revelation in creation, commonly referred to as general revelation (as opposed to special revelation, as in Scripture), is seen as universal in scope. The specific aspect of God's creation in view is that which is extra-terrestrial: the heavens, the firmament [sky] (verse 1), and the sun (verses 4-6). God's creation declares His glory and shows His handiwork (verse 1). It communicates with human beings, revealing knowledge in a universal language (verses 2-4). According to Paul, creation revealed the invisible attributes of God, including His eternal power and Godhead (Romans 1:19-20). Paul revealed a Hebrew perspective on the revelatory nature of creation when He told the people in Lystra, "Nevertheless He did not leave Himself without witness, in that He did good, gave us rain from heaven and fruitful seasons, filling our hearts with food and gladness" (Acts 14:17). The rain from heaven, resulting in fruitful seasons, was a witness to God. Ethan wrote concerning the throne of David, "It shall be established forever like the moon, even like the faithful witness in the sky" (Psalm 89:37).

But as marvelous as the witness of creation was, written revelation was required for the fullest unveiling of the Messiah. That is what David turned to in Psalm 19:7-14. Under a series of words used as poetic synonyms, David discussed the effect and the nature of written revelation. He referred to it as the law, the testimony, the statutes, the commandment, and the judgments of the Lord. As to its nature, Scripture was perfect and sure (verse 7), right and pure (verse 8), true and righteous (verse 9), and sweet (verse 10). As to its effect, Scripture converted the soul, made wise the simple (verse 7), caused the heart to rejoice, enlightened the eyes (verse 8), and provided warning and great reward (verse 11). Scripture exposed human error and cleansed those who valued it from secret faults (verses 12). It prevented its readers from coming under the dominion of presumptuous sins, leaving them blameless and innocent (verse 13). In the midst of the discussion about the nature and effects of Scripture, David wrote, "The fear of the LORD is clean, enduring forever" (verse 9a). The idea was that Scripture led to the fear of the Lord.

Because of the nature and effects of the Scriptures, they were more desirable and valuable than gold (verse 10a).

In the final verse of the psalm, a link may be seen with Psalm 1: "Let the words of my mouth and the meditation of my heart be acceptable in Your sight, O LORD, my strength and my

Redeemer" (verse 14). The counterpart to this in Psalm 1 is verse 2: "But his delight is in the law of the LORD, and in His law he meditates day and night." The idea here, as Psalm 19 is followed by Psalms 20-21, is the same as in Psalm 1 as it is followed by Psalm 2: Meditation in Scripture leads to faith in the Messiah.

Psalm 20

Just as Psalm 2, a messianic psalm, follows Psalm 1, a Torah [law] psalm, so Psalms 20-21 are messianic psalms following a Torah psalm (Psalm 19). A link may be seen between Psalm 20 and Psalm 2: "The kings of the earth set themselves, and the rulers take counsel together, against the LORD and against His Anointed [His Messiah]" (Psalm 2:2); "Now I know that the LORD saves His anointed [His Messiah]; He will answer him from His holy heaven with the saving strength of His right hand" (Psalm 20:6).

In the context of the Psalter, the first five verses of Psalm 20 form a blessing on behalf of the anointed king of the house of David, with this king representing the ultimate King, the Messiah. This blessing anticipates a day of trouble when the Lord will answer and defend the Messiah (verse 1). He will send help "from the sanctuary" and strength "out of Zion" (verse 2; compare with Psalm 18:6).

The Lord would remember the Messiah's offerings and sacrifice (verse 3). This verse would certainly mean one thing as it pertained to David, but quite another when David was a symbol of the Messiah. Although there is no reason to think that Jesus did not participate fully in Temple worship when He walked on this earth, His ultimate offering and sacrifice was the offering of Himself. (See Hebrews 10:1-10.)

The Lord would grant the Messiah the desire of His heart, fulfilling all His purpose (verse 4).

The Messiah joined His brethren in rejoicing in the Lord's deliverance. (Compare this with Psalm 18:49; 22:22.) All of the Messiah's petitions will be fulfilled. (Compare with verse 4.)

The Lord delivered His anointed One, His Messiah. He would answer Him from heaven "with the saving strength of His right hand," a figure of speech referring to the power of God (verse 6).

In the midst of military challenges—like those of Absalom—those who rejected the authority of David's throne trusted in horses and chariots. But those who remembered the promise God made to David (see II Samuel 7) trusted in the name of the Lord (verse 7). The Messiah trusted in God also in the midst of all of the challenges to His right to the Davidic throne.

Those who rejected the throne established by God were defeated, but those who recognized the divine authority of the Davidic throne survived every challenge (verse 8).

The words "save, LORD" (verse 9) capture the essence of the promise that "whoever calls on the name of the LORD shall be saved" (Joel 2:32; see also Acts 2:21; Romans 10:13). The words "may the King answer us when we call" (verse 9) are significant when applied to David, but even more significant when the king in view is the Messiah, the King of kings.

Psalm 21

Psalm 21 contains direct links back to Psalm 20 and conceptual links to preceding psalms. Sailhamer points out that the "purpose of such links is to elevate the portrait of the 'king' taken up from the preceding psalms to a much higher plane."[34]

The king rejoices in the Lord's deliverance, or salvation (verse 1). This links Psalm 21 conceptually with Psalm 20:1-2, 5-9.

The words of verse 2 reflect the hope of Psalm 20:4: "You have given him his heart's desire, and have not withheld the request of his lips" (verse 2); "May He grant you according to your heart's desire, and fulfill all your purpose" (Psalm 20:4).

Psalm 20 expresses the hope for deliverance; Psalm 21 expresses its fulfillment: "For You meet him with the blessings of goodness; You set a crown of pure gold upon his head" (verse 3).

The crown of pure gold vividly described this king as the only legitimate king. In his vision of Armageddon, John described the Son of Man, the Messiah, as having "on His head a golden crown" (Revelation 14:14).

That this is no ordinary, mortal king may be seen in verses 4-6: "He asked life from You, and You gave it to him—length of days forever and ever. His glory is great in Your salvation; honor and majesty You have placed upon him. For you have made him most blessed forever; you have made him exceedingly glad with Your presence."

This King, the Messiah, trusted in the Lord, and "through the mercy of the Most High he [would] not be moved" (verse 7). (Compare this with Psalm 20:7.)

Sailhamer points out that "by addressing the king directly in vv. 8-12, the psalm connects the idea of God's future judgment (v. 9b) with the coming of the 'king' (v. 9a). The king is thus not one of David's historical descendants but rather the messianic king promised to David. In this way Ps 21 plays an important role within this book by focusing the reader's attention on the future of the house of David instead of on its past."[35]

Psalm 21 concludes with a wish for the exaltation of the Lord and a commitment to sing and praise in proclamation of His power (verse 13).

Psalm 22

To read Matthew 27:33-46 and Psalm 22:1-22 together is to see the evident connection between these texts. Psalm 22 has long been viewed as a messianic psalm fulfilled in the sufferings of Jesus on the cross, and this is certainly supported by a reading of Matthew.

Matthew wrote, "Then they crucified Him, and divided His garments, casting lots, that it might be fulfilled which was spoken by the prophet: *'They divided My garments among them, and for My clothing they cast lots'* " (Matthew 27:35). The prophet

Matthew had in mind was David (see Acts 2:29-30), who wrote, "They divide My garments among them, and for My clothing they cast lots" (Psalm 22:18).

The Crucifixion was accomplished by driving nails through the hands and feet of Jesus to fasten Him to the cross. (See Luke 24:39-40; John 20:25, 27.) David wrote, "For dogs have surrounded Me; the congregation of the wicked has enclosed Me. They pierced My hands and My feet" (Psalm 22:16).

Matthew wrote, "And those who passed by blasphemed Him, wagging their heads and saying, 'You who destroy the temple and build it in three days, save Yourself! If You are the Son of God, come down from the cross.' Likewise the chief priests also, mocking with the scribes and elders, said, 'He saved others; Himself He cannot save. If He is the King of Israel, let Him now come down from the cross, and we will believe Him. He trusted in God; let Him deliver Him now, if He will have Him; for He said, "I am the Son of God" ' " (Matthew 27:39-43). David wrote, "All those who see Me ridicule Me; they shoot out the lip, they shake the head, saying, 'He trusted in the LORD, let Him rescue Him; let Him deliver Him, since He delights in Him!' " (Psalm 22:7-8).

Matthew wrote, "Now from the sixth hour until the ninth hour there was darkness over all the land" (Matthew 27:45). This meant that from noon until 3:00 PM night interrupted the day. David wrote, "O My God, I cry in the daytime, but You do not hear; and in the night season, and am not silent" (Psalm 22:2).

Matthew wrote, "And about the ninth hour Jesus cried out with a loud voice, saying, 'Eli, Eli, lama sabachthani?' that is, *'My God, My God, why have You forsaken Me?'* " (Matthew 27:46). David began the psalm, "My God, My God, why have You forsaken Me?" (Psalm 22:1).

Another aspect of fulfillment was recognized by John, who wrote, "After this, Jesus, knowing that all things were now accomplished, that the Scripture might be fulfilled, said, 'I thirst!' " (John 19:28). This was an apparent reference to Psalm 22:15, where David wrote, "My strength is dried up like a potsherd, and My tongue clings to My jaws; You have brought Me to the dust of death."

In Psalm 22:1-21a, the suffering Messiah was speaking, describing His experiences on the cross. In Psalm 22:21b He proclaimed that His prayer for deliverance had been answered. We know, from the New Testament account, that His prayer was answered not by sparing Him from the suffering of the cross, but by the Resurrection. In Psalm 22:22, the Messiah declared His intent to declare the name of the Lord to His brethren and to praise Him in the midst of the assembly.[36] (See Hebrews 2:11-12.)

In Psalm 22:23-24, David spoke to the congregation, to those who "[feared] the LORD," about the suffering of the Messiah.

In Psalm 22:25-27, David spoke to the Messiah.

In Psalm 22:30-31, David looked to the future and declared that the events of Psalm 22 would be recognized by "a people who [would] be born" to be the work of the Lord. This "posterity [would] serve Him."[37]

Some have thought that Jesus' plaintive cry, "My God, My God, why have You forsaken Me?" indicated that at the moment of His greatest need, God abandoned Jesus. This was not the case. Instead, Jesus' words indicated the genuine depth of the emotional trauma He experienced; His suffering was not just physical; it affected every aspect of His being, materially and immaterially. In the same way that any human being in the midst of the horrors of painful circumstances might cry out, "God, where are you?" (see Psalm 10:1), so Jesus on the cross cried out of His experience of aloneness and the feeling of being forsaken.

When Jesus uttered the words of Psalm 22:1a, He acknowledged the messianic import of the psalm. Although we have no record that He prayed all of the words in Psalm 22:1-22, we should understand His use of the first words as representative of His entire experience. This is how the psalm was understood by the writers of the gospels.[38]

Jesus' feeling of being forsaken was further developed in the words, "Why are You so far from helping Me, and from the words of My groaning?" (verse 1b). Although Jesus prayed, and His prayer was heard (see Hebrews 5:7), the answer was not to deliver Him from the experience of death. His prayer was answered by means of the Resurrection. (See Psalm 22:21b-22.)[39]

Because the light of day was interrupted by the darkness of night for three hours, from noon until 3:00 PM, Jesus cried out to God "in the daytime" and "in the night season" (verse 2). There was no answer from God at that time; God's answer would come with resurrection. (See Romans 1:4.)

On the cross, Jesus acknowledged the holiness of God, which was demonstrated by His enthronement "in the praises of Israel" (verse 3). The phrase "praises of Israel" was a figure of speech used as a "confessional reference to God's rule,"[40] as seen between the cherubim on the ark of the covenant. (See Psalms 80:1; 99:1.) This made very significant the tearing of the curtain separating the Holy Place from the Most Holy Place in the Jerusalem Temple at the time of Christ's death. (See Matthew 27:51.) The tearing of this veil represented the access into God's presence that is now available to all people of faith on the basis of Christ's death. (See Hebrews 10:19-22.)

In Psalm 22:4-8, the Messiah contrasted His experience on the cross with the experiences of the "fathers"[41] who trusted in God and were delivered (verses 4-5). In contrast to those who were delivered, He said, "But I am a worm, and no man; a reproach of men, and despised by the people" (verse 6). The first part of this verse was, of course, a figure of speech intended to describe the extent of the reproach Jesus experienced on the cross.[42]

The extent of the way the unbelievers despised Jesus could be seen in their ridicule of Him (verse 7). They denied that God had any interest in the events of the cross (verse 8).

The Messiah acknowledged the genuineness of His human existence and His dependence on God since His birth (verses 9-10).

The words of verse 11 were similar to those of verse 1b. Although His prayer was heard, the answer was not deliverance from death. The answer was resurrection from death. (See comments on verse 1b.)

In Bashan, a fertile region east of the Jordan River known for its sheep and plump cattle, "a breed of ferocious undomesticated cattle roamed free."[43] The imagery of danger was vividly presented in the words, "Many bulls have surrounded Me; strong bulls of Bashan have encircled Me. They gape at Me with their mouths, like a raging and roaring lion" (verses 12-13).

The Messiah described His physical condition in verses 14-15. He was "poured out like water" and His heart was like "wax." These were metaphors expressing formlessness and His inner feelings of anguish; He could no longer function as a human being. Like a dried-out and useless potsherd, He had exhausted his resilience and was unable to cope with the trauma.[44] On the cross, He cried out, "I thirst" (John 19:28). Not only did Jesus experience dehydration; His bones were out of joint; He was brought "to the dust of death."

Although dogs were domesticated at this time, "they still lived as scavengers, often roaming in packs on the outskirts of town (Ps 59:6, 14) and scavenging in town itself (1 Kings 14:11). For these reasons the term *dog* [was] often one of derision and contempt in the Bible."[45]

The Messiah described those who were involved in His crucifixion as "dogs" (verse 16). They pierced His hands and feet.[46]

On the cross, the Messiah endured the shame of nakedness: All of His bones could be counted; the onlookers stared at Him (verse 17).

His garments were divided among those who participated in His crucifixion. They cast lots for His robe (verse 18). (See Matthew 27:35.)

The Messiah's prayer in verses 19-21a recapitulated the danger He faced on the cross. He prayed that the Lord would not be far from Him (19a; see verses 1b and 11a). He prayed for help

(19b; see verse 1b). He prayed for deliverance from the sword, the chief weapon used by the Roman military (verse 20a). (See Romans 13:4.) He returned to the imagery of the dog, the lion, and the oxen, or bulls (verses 20b-21a; see verses 12-13, 16.)

Finally, the sufferings were past. The Messiah declared, "You have answered Me. I will declare Your name[47] to My brethren; in the midst of the assembly I will praise You" (verses 21b-22). The writer of Hebrews saw Psalm 22:22 as being connected with the death of the Messiah and occurring after His death. The phrase "crowned with glory and honor" indicated that it occurred after the Resurrection. (See Hebrews 2:9-12.)

Beginning in Psalm 22:23, David spoke to those who feared the Lord. He encouraged them to praise, glorify, and fear the Lord. The reason for this, according to verse 24, was that the Lord did not despise the Messiah in His afflictions, regardless of the assessment made by those who participated in His crucifixion (verses 6-8), nor did He hide His face from the Messiah, even though the Messiah felt forsaken (verses 1-2).

In verse 25 David spoke to the Messiah, declaring that he would praise the Messiah in the congregation of believers and that he would make public payment of his vows.

The Messiah's victory over death brought blessings for the poor. Those who sought the Lord would have reason to praise Him; their hearts would enjoy abundant life forever (verse 26).

The death and resurrection of the Messiah would have universal impact. He would be worshiped by "the ends of the world" and "all the families of the nations" (verse 27).

The resurrection of the Messiah further proved the universality and eternality of the rule of the Lord (verse 28). In the larger context of Psalms, it was evidence of the certainty of the Davidic covenant.

Those who would worship the Messiah included the prosperous and the suffering (verse 29). His rule would be universal.

The worship of the Messiah would not end with the generation that saw the experiences of Psalm 22. He would be served by their posterity (verse 30). People yet to be born would hear of His righteousness and of the work accomplished on the cross (verse 31).

If Psalm 22 is a messianic psalm, we would expect the superscription to make some contribution to the messianic theme. The KJV offers a partial translation and transliteration: "To the chief Musician upon Aijeleth Shahar, A Psalm of David." The NKJV offers a translation: "To the Chief Musician. Set to 'The Deer of the Dawn.' A Psalm of David." Why, then, does the LXX translate the superscription as "For the end, concerning the morning aid, a Psalm of David"?

Kidner's comments are helpful:

> This may be a tune-name . . . but is better explained as a glimpse of the theme, and translated . . . 'On the help of (*i.e.*, at) daybreak'. The word *'ayyelet* ('Hind', RSV) is very close to the rare word *'eyalut*, 'help' (19, Heb. 20), and could be vocalized to coincide with it, if it is not indeed a feminine form of *'eyal* (help), Psalm 88:4 (Heb. 5). So the title draws attention to the deliverance which will light up the final verses of the psalm.[48]

If this is the way we should read the superscription, the psalm begins by pointing to the resurrection of Christ: This was His aid or help on the morning of the first day of the week.[49]

Psalm 22 is not the only Old Testament reference to the events Jesus experienced in His suffering on the cross, but it is certainly a clear and sustained prophecy of the event that brought redemption for the human race.

Psalm 23

The words of Psalm 23 give great comfort to believers who experience painful and difficult circumstances in life. But as it is placed in the Psalter, following Psalm 22 with its content focused on the death of the Messiah and preceding Psalm 24 with its "King of Glory" content, Psalm 23 should be read as a reference to the Messiah's hope as he walked "through the valley of the shadow of death" (verse 4).

Even though He experienced the deepest agony, including a feeling of being forsaken by God (see Psalm 22:1), the Messiah confessed that the Lord was His shepherd, supplying all that He needed (verse 1), providing green pastures—to say that sheep were made to "lie down" meant that they had eaten their fill; the sheep stood to eat—and still waters—sheep were frightened by rapidly running waters and would not drink from them (verse 2).

For the sake of His name (for His reputation), the Lord restored the Messiah's soul (compare to Psalm 22:20, 29 [the Hebrew *nephesh*, "soul" or "life" appears in both verses as well as here in Psalm 23:3]). Also for the sake of His reputation, the Lord led the Messiah in paths of righteousness, or right paths (verse 3). The idea that the Lord did this for the sake of His reputation was tied with His promise to David that He would raise up the Messiah as David's descendant to sit on David's throne. (See II Samuel 7:12-16; Psalm 132:10-11; Acts 2:30-32; Revelation 22:16.) Had the soul (*nephesh*, "life") of the Messiah not been restored, it would have meant that the Lord had not kept His promise to David and it would have reflected negatively on His character.

The Messiah's experience on the cross was described as "the valley of the shadow of death" (verse 4). Even in the midst of this experience, the Messiah would fear no evil for the Lord was with Him, comforting Him with His rod and staff. In the shepherd/sheep relationship, the rod and staff represented the shepherd's presence, protection, and guidance.[50]

In the presence of His enemies—a reference to His experience on the cross (see Psalm 22:7-8, 11-13, 16-18, 20-21)—the Lord prepared a table for the Messiah, anointed His head with oil, and caused His cup to run over (verse 5). The table was a symbol of provision and blessing, as was the overflowing cup (see Psalm 16:5). The statement "You [anointed] my head with oil" referred to the Messiah as the anointed One, although a different Hebrew word (*dashan*) was translated "anoint" than was ordinarily used in connection with royal anointing. The same word is translated "prosperous" (NKJV) or "fat" (KJV) in Psalm 22:29, perhaps providing a verbal link between the two psalms.[51] *Dashan* did have to do with generous anointing with oil, so in this context it was appropriate to apply it to the Messiah.

Having passed through the valley of the shadow of death and having experienced the restoration of His soul ("life"), the Messiah testified that goodness and mercy would follow Him all the days of His life (verse 6). The word translated "follow" (*radaph*) meant "pursue" or "chase." Goodness and mercy would not be passive in relation to the Messiah; His life would be characterized by the presence of these virtues.

The "house of the LORD" was the Temple in Jerusalem. The Temple was not built when David was alive, so Psalm 23 could not have had its ultimate fulfillment with David.

To translate the Hebrew *yashab* as "dwell" is to follow the Septuagint, Syriac, Targum, and Vulgate. The Hebrew text reads "I will return to the house of the LORD."[52] As this is read regarding the Messiah, the "psalm looks forward to the time when the Anointed One returns to the temple."[53] This messianic image is seen elsewhere in the Old Testament. (See Zechariah 9:8-9; Malachi 3:1.) In the most immediate context, this prepares the reader for Psalm 24, wherein the King of Glory, the Messiah, enters the "everlasting doors" into His holy place on the hill of the Lord. (See Psalm 24:3, 7, 9.)

The Messiah will dwell in the house of the Lord forever, further signifying that Psalm 23 does not have its ultimate fulfillment in David.

Psalm 24

As it pertains to the Messiah, Psalm 24 celebrates His return to Jerusalem, the hill of the Lord, and His holy place through the gates of the city and the "everlasting doors" of the Temple. The psalm also identifies those who will be permitted to fellowship with the Messiah upon His return.

In the larger context of the Old Testament, the Messiah returned to His house. (See comments on Psalm 23:6.) As He entered His house, He was identified as the King of glory, the Lord of hosts (verses 7-10). In other words, the Messiah was God, as identified elsewhere. (See Psalm 45:6; Hebrews 1:8; Isaiah 9:6.)

The Messiah's kingdom was universal in scope: "The earth is the LORD's, and all its fullness, the world and those who dwell therein" (verse 1). Indeed, the Messiah was the Creator Himself (verse 2).

Verse 3 posed a question: "Who may ascend into the hill of the LORD? Or who may stand in His holy place?" The hill of the Lord was Mount Zion. His holy place was the Temple. Since the Messiah was entering His holy place, the question had to do with the qualifications of those who could fellowship with Him there.

Verse 4 answered the question: "He who has clean hands and a pure heart, who has not lifted up his soul to an idol, nor sworn deceitfully." This had to do with external and internal purity, faithfulness in worship, and integrity.

The person who met the qualifications of verse 4 would be blessed with salvation and righteousness (verse 5).

Jacob, in the context of verse 6, represented all those who sought the Lord, as defined by verse 4.

Those who sought the Lord sang to the gates of Jerusalem and to the doors of the Temple to open for the King's entrance (verses 7-9). He was the King of glory (i.e., the glorious King), the strong and mighty Lord, victorious in battle. He was the Lord of hosts (i.e., angelic hosts).

The good news of Psalm 24, as it is read in conjunction with Psalms 22-23, was that the crucified Messiah would not stay in the grave. He would come forth in great glory and power, returning to rule the world from His holy place on the hill of the Lord. Those who were faithful to Him would be privileged to fellowship with Him in His victorious reign.[54]

Psalm 25

Psalm 25 seems intentionally placed to focus on the hope that consumed Israel in the days following the Exile and during the time that the Psalter was being arranged in its final shape, the hope of the return of God's people to the holy city in conjunction with the reign of the Messiah on His holy hill.[55] Psalm 24 sees the King of glory, the Messiah, entering the gates of Jerusalem and returning to the house of the Lord. (See comments on Psalm 23:6.) The psalm also answers the question of who is qualified to ascend into the hill of the Lord and to stand in His presence. (See Psalm 24:3-4.)

Psalm 25 is an acrostic with some irregularities. Two verses begin with *resh*, *waw* and *qoph* are missing, and the last verse begins with *peh*, suggesting an addition in the process of composition.[56]

Israel's hope for the return of the Lord to His Temple was kindled by prophecies such as that given by Isaiah, who wrote before the exile of Judah: "Now it shall come to pass in the latter days that the mountain of the LORD's house shall be established on the top of the mountains, and shall be exalted above the hills; and all nations shall flow to it. Many people shall come and say, 'Come, and let us go up to the mountain of the LORD, to the house of the God of Jacob; He will teach us His ways, and we shall walk in His paths.' For out of Zion shall go forth the law, and the word of the LORD from Jerusalem" (Isaiah 2:2-3; see also Micah 4:1-5). Zechariah, who wrote during the Exile, further advanced this hope: "Thus says the LORD of hosts: 'Peoples shall yet come, inhabitants of many cities; the inhabitants of one city shall go to another, saying, "Let us continue to go and pray before the LORD, and seek the LORD of hosts. I myself will go also." Yes, many peoples and strong nations shall come to seek the LORD of hosts in Jerusalem, and to pray before the LORD.' Thus says the LORD of hosts: 'In those days ten men from every language of the nations shall grasp the sleeve of a Jewish man, saying, "Let us go with you, for we have heard that God is with you"'" (Zechariah 8:20-23).

Prophecies such as these looked ahead to the millennial era, but they sparked hope in the hearts of the Jewish people that their fulfillment was imminent. Under the inspiration of the Holy Spirit, Psalm 25 was placed to illustrate the kind of prayers that would be prayed when the King of glory came in through the lifted gates and the everlasting doors (Psalm 24:7-9) to take up His abode on the "hill of the LORD" (Psalm 24:3). As God answered these prayers, He was showing people His ways and teaching them His paths. Notice the comparison between Psalm 25:4 and Isaiah 2:3:

> Show me Your ways, O LORD; teach me Your paths. (Psalm 25:4)

> He will teach us His ways, and we shall walk in His paths. (Isaiah 2:3)

Psalm 25 envisioned the Lord as having returned to His Temple, where He heard the prayers of His people. This was a psalm of David, who lived and died before the first Temple was built, but his words took on new significance as they were placed in a messianic context.

The psalm expresses confidence and trust that the Lord will not allow the enemy to gain the victory (verses 1-2). No one who "waits on" (i.e., trusts in [verse 2]) the Lord will suffer the shame of being defeated; only those who "deal treacherously" (i.e., who take matters into their own hands rather than trusting in the Lord) will suffer the shame of defeat (verse 3).

The prayer recognizes the inadequacy of human understanding with the appeal to be shown the ways of the Lord, to be taught His paths, and to be led and taught in His truth (verses 4-5a). God is the deliverer (i.e., salvation), and a person of faith will "wait [on Him] all the day" (verse 5b), as opposed to those who "deal treacherously without cause" (verse 3b).

The prayer continues its focus on human inadequacy with an appeal to the tender mercies and lovingkindnesses of the Lord and for forgiveness from youthful sins (verses 6-7). The appeal for mercy and forgiveness is based on the Lord's "goodness," just as it is later based on His "name" (verses 7b, 11). If God refuses to forgive, it will reflect negatively on any idea of His "goodness." His goodness is bound up with His forgiveness. (See Psalm 23:6.)

Because the Lord is "good and upright," "He teaches sinners in the way" (verse 8; compare with verse 4). The sinners He teaches are those who are humble, and the way in which He guides them is the way of justice (verse 9).

The Lord's paths (i.e., His ways) are characterized by mercy and truth, but only those who "keep His covenant and His testimonies" enjoy His paths (verse 10). In the larger messianic context of the Psalter, the idea of keeping the Lord's covenant and testimonies should not be seen as a focus on the law of Moses but on the life of faith. Although the law of Moses was in effect when the individual psalms were written and when the Psalter found its final shape, it was recognized that the rituals of the law did not bring delight to God. (See Psalm 51:16.) His delight was, instead, in "a broken and a contrite heart," a heart of faith (Psalm 51:17). (Compare Psalm 32:1-2 with Romans 4:4-8.) Even Abraham, who lived four centuries before the law of Moses was given (see Galatians 3:17), was described by the Lord as a man who "obeyed My voice and kept My charge, My commandments, My statutes, and My laws" (Genesis 26:5). This was not because Abraham had some advance notice of the contents of the law of Moses (see Deuteronomy 5:3), but because he was a man of faith. (See Genesis 15:6.) The point is that the law of Moses was intended to bring a stiff-necked and rebellious people to a place of faith in the Messiah. (See Deuteronomy 9:6-7; Galatians 3:22-25.) But those who were not stiff-necked and rebellious were counted as righteous on the basis of their faith in God. They had in this sense kept His covenant, for they had already embraced the faith to which the covenant was intended to lead.

Just as verse 7 appeals to the mercy of the Lord on the basis of His goodness, so verse 11 appeals for pardon on the basis of His name. To say "for Your name's sake" means "for the sake of Your reputation." (See comments on Psalm 23:3.) Since the Lord promises to pardon the iniquity of those who confess their sins, it will reflect negatively on His reputation if He does not do so. Of course, we may be sure this will never happen. He will always pardon our iniquity, even though it is great, for the sake of His name.

The person who will be taught the way of the Lord is not only humble (verse 9), but also one who fears the Lord (verse 12). The reward of walking in the way of the Lord is prosperity;[57] specifically, the person who walks in the way of the Lord will receive the covenant promises like the inheritance of the land promised to Abraham (verse 13). Another reward of fearing the Lord is to know His "secret," defined here as His covenant (verse 14). The covenant is not for those who do not fear the Lord; it is kept secret from them.

Although this psalm, as it is placed in the Psalter, is intended to demonstrate the kind of instruction the Messiah will give when He returns to His millennial house, that return had not actually occurred when the psalms were arranged in their final form, and it had certainly not occurred when David first wrote this psalm. At the time the psalm was written, David's throne was still under challenge, and at the time the Psalter was arranged most of the Jewish people were still dispersed from the Promised Land. This was demonstrated in the prayers for deliverance. This was the portion of the psalm that identified it as a psalm of lament.

The psalm expressed exclusive hope in the Lord, based on the knowledge that He would spare His people from the net or snare of the enemy (verse 15). An appeal was made for the Lord to turn to those who were desolate and afflicted and to have mercy on them (verse 16). Emotional troubles had increased for David, and he prayed to be brought out of his distresses (verse 17). He wished for God to observe his affliction and pain and to forgive his sins (verse 18). Many enemies had cruel hatred for him, and David wanted God to consider them (verse 19). The phrase translated "keep my soul" by the NKJV meant something like "guard my life" (NIV); this is connected with a prayer for deliverance (verse 20a). The prayer "let me not be ashamed," first appearing in verse 2, was repeated, as was the confession of trust in the Lord (verse 20b). The idea was "let me not be put to shame" (NIV). David prayed to be preserved by integrity and uprightness (verse 21). The confession that he was waiting for the Lord was repeated from verse 3. Thus the psalm drew to a conclusion on the same note as it began.

The final prayer was for the redemption of Israel "out of all their troubles" (verse 22). This took the psalm beyond being merely an expression of David's personal concern to the larger scope of the troubles experienced by the entire nation. The connection of the psalm with the millennial hope took the psalm even further in its application; it was relevant for all who trusted in the Lord (verses 2, 20), who humbled themselves before Him (verse 9), and who feared the Lord (verse 12). In the final analysis, Israel would be delivered from all troubles by believing in the Messiah at the time of the Second Coming.

Psalm 26

Following the focus on the house of the Lord, the Temple, begun in Psalm 23 and continued through Psalms 24 and 25, this psalm addresses David's love for the Lord's house, the place where His glory dwells (verse 8). In the larger context of the Psalter, this should be viewed as pointing to the day when the Messiah will rule the nations from His holy hill. (See comments on Psalms 23:6; 24:3-4, 7-10; 25:4.) David lived, of course, before Solomon's Temple was built. During his day, the Tabernacle was located at Gibeon, about five and one-half miles north of Jerusalem. (See I Chronicles 16:39; 21:29; II Chronicles 1:3, 13.)

Psalm 26 is linked to Psalm 25 also by the themes of integrity (compare Psalm 26:1 with Psalm 25:21), trust in the Lord (compare Psalm 26:1 with Psalm 25:2, 20), and a plea for vindication in the face of the enemy (compare Psalm 26:1 with Psalm 25:2, 19-20).

The appeal to be examined and proved by the Lord and for the Lord to try the mind and heart (verse 2) evokes a connection with the qualifications required to "ascend into the hill of the LORD" and to "stand in His holy place" (Psalm 24:3). In order to do so, one must have "clean hands" and a "pure heart" (Psalm 24:4).

Verses 3-5 contain similar ideas to those found in Psalms 1 and 25. The words, "I have walked in Your truth" and "I have not sat with idolatrous mortals, nor will I go in with hypocrites" and "I have hated the assembly of evildoers, and will not sit with the wicked" (verses 3-5) express the same ideas as found in Psalm 1: "Blessed is the man who walks not in the counsel of the ungodly, nor stands in the path of sinners, nor sits in the seat of the scornful; but his delight is in the law of the LORD, and in His law he meditates day and night" (Psalm 1:1-2). The words, "I have walked in Your truth" reflect the prayer of Psalm 25:5: "Lead me in Your truth and teach me" and the statement of Psalm 25:10: "All the paths of the LORD are mercy and truth." The statement, "For Your lovingkindness is before my eyes" (Psalm 26:3) evokes the prayer, "Remember, O LORD, Your tender mercies and Your lovingkindnesses" (Psalm 25:6). The prayers of Psalm 25 are portrayed as having been answered in Psalm 26.

The statement "I will wash my hands in innocence" (verse 6) further connects Psalms 26 and 24. In Psalm 24:4, the person who ascends into the hill of the Lord and who stands in His holy place is the person who "has clean hands" (Psalm 24:4). Clean or innocent hands qualify one to approach the altar of the Lord (Psalm 26:6), which is located on the hill of the Lord in conjunction with His holy place. (See Psalm 24:3-4.)

Verse 7 indicates that those who approach the house of the Lord during the millennial era will not be coming only to pray for vindication. They will offer prayers of thanksgiving for the "wondrous works" of the Lord.

The house of the Lord is the place where His glory dwells (verse 8). Because God lives there, people of faith love His house (verse 8).

Verses 9-11 also connect Psalm 26 with Psalm 1 and with intervening psalms that have to do with sinister sinners who are "bloodthirsty." The prayer, "Do not gather my soul with sinners" (verse 9), sounds very much like, "Blessed is the man who walks not in the counsel of the ungodly, nor stands in the path of sinners" (Psalm 1:1). The prayer, "Do not gather . . . my life with bloodthirsty men" (verse 9) connects with the statement, "The LORD abhors the bloodthirsty and deceitful man" (Psalm 5:6). Bloodthirsty men are characterized by sinister schemes and the practice of bribery to achieve their purposes.

Psalm 26 comes to a close as it opened, with a focus on integrity. (Compare verse 11 with verse 1.) The plea for mercy and redemption further connects the psalm with Psalm 25. (See Psalm 25:6, 7b, 10, 16, 22.)

To say, "My foot stands in an even place" (verse 12a) indicates standing on level ground. This "level ground" is defined contextually as "the hill of the LORD" and "His holy place" (Psalm 24:3). It is a place of security and stability.

The final statement, "In the congregations I will bless the LORD" (verse 12b) seals the connection of Psalm 26 with Psalm 1:5 ("Therefore the ungodly shall not stand in the judgment, nor sinners in the congregation of the righteous"), Psalm 22:22 ("I will declare Your name to My brethren; in the midst of the assembly I will praise You"), and Psalm 22:25a ("My praise shall be of You in the great assembly"). Since the Psalm 22 references are identified in the New Testament as messianic texts (see comments on Psalm 22:22, 25), there is a strong indication that Psalm 26 should be understood in the same way. This would require reading the words "redeem me" (verse 11) as "deliver me" or "rescue me," both of which are legitimate translations of *pedaniy*.

Psalm 27

This psalm continues the theme established in Psalm 23 concerning the Lord's return to His Temple.[58] A thematic link may be seen immediately by comparing verse 4 with Psalm 23:6.

> . . . That I may dwell in the house of the LORD all the days of my life . . . (Psalm 27:4)

> . . . And I will dwell in the house of the LORD forever. (Psalm 23:6)

The emphasis on the house of the Lord, the Temple, may be seen in verses 4-6: "One thing I have desired of the LORD, that will I seek: that I may dwell in the house of the LORD all the days of my life, to behold the beauty of the LORD, and to inquire in His temple. For in the time of trouble He shall hide me in His pavilion; in the secret place of His tabernacle He shall hide me. . . . therefore I will offer sacrifices of joy in His tabernacle" (Psalm 27:4-6). (See comments on Psalms 23:6; 24:3, 7-9; 25:4; 26:6, 8.)

Further thematic links may be seen by comparing verse 11 with Psalm 25:4:

> Teach me Your way, O LORD, and lead me in a smooth path . . . (Psalm 27:11a)

> Show me Your ways, O LORD; teach me Your paths. (Psalm 25:4)

These verses link this section of Psalms with the millennial prophecy concerning the house of the Lord in Isaiah 2:3: "Many people shall come and say, 'Come, and let us go up to the mountain of the LORD, to the house of the God of Jacob; He will teach us His ways, and we shall walk in His paths.' " The psalms of David were written before Isaiah, of course, but they were intentionally placed to develop the theme of the Messiah's return to the Temple of the Lord from whence He will rule and to which the nations of the earth will come to pay Him homage.

A description of the millennial Temple may be seen in Ezekiel 40-47:12. The significance of the connection between this section of Psalms and the Messiah's entry into the millennial Temple is seen by comparing Psalm 24:7-10 with Ezekiel 43:1-2, 4, 7; 44:1-2:

> Lift up your heads, O you gates! And be lifted up, you everlasting doors! And the King of glory shall come in. Who is this King of glory? The LORD strong and mighty, the LORD mighty in battle. Lift up your heads, O you gates! Lift up, you everlasting doors! And the King of glory shall come in. Who is this King of glory? The LORD of hosts, He is the King of glory. (Psalm 24:7-10)

> Afterward he brought me to the gate, the gate that faces toward the east. And behold, the glory of the God of Israel came from the way of the east. His voice was like the sound of many waters; and the earth shone with His glory. . . . And the glory of the LORD came into the temple by way of the gate which faces toward the east. . . . And He said to me, "Son of man, this is the place of My throne and the place of the soles of My feet, where I will dwell in the midst of the children of Israel forever. No more shall the house of Israel defile My holy name. . . ." Then He brought me back to the outer gate of the sanctuary which faces toward the east, but it was shut. And the LORD said to me, "This gate shall be shut; it shall not be opened, and no man shall enter by it, because the LORD God of Israel has entered by it; therefore it shall be shut." (Ezekiel 43:1-2, 4, 7; 44:1-2)

As the relevant texts in Psalms are compared with the relevant texts in Ezekiel, the significance of the cry "lift up your heads, O you gates! And be lifted up, you everlasting doors! And the King of glory shall come in" may be seen. The glory of the God of Israel enters the Temple by the eastern gate.[59] The Temple is the place of His throne and where He will dwell. After He enters the eastern gate, it is shut so that no one else can enter by it.

Further connections may be seen by comparing Psalm 24:3 with Ezekiel 43:12:

> Who may ascend into the hill of the LORD? Or who may stand in His holy place? (Psalm 24:3)

> This is the law of the temple: The whole area surrounding the mountaintop is most holy. Behold, this is the law of the temple. (Ezekiel 43:12)

The architectural details of the millennial Temple that Ezekiel described differed significantly from the Tabernacle of Moses and from Solomon's Temple. The service itself differed. Although there were similarities, Ezekiel took great pains to distinguish the millennial Temple from previous forms of the house of the Lord. One reason for this may have been to clearly indicate that the building of a Temple for the millennial era will not signal a return to the law of Moses. The Millennium is about the New Covenant; it is not a revival of the Old Covenant. (See, e.g., Jeremiah 31:31-34; Isaiah 2:1-5; 11:1-10.)

Still another thematic thread may be seen by comparing Psalm 27:14 with Psalm 25:3, 21:

> Wait on the LORD; be of good courage, and He shall strengthen your heart; wait, I say, on the LORD! (Psalm 27:14)

> Indeed, let no one who waits on You be ashamed. . . . Let integrity and uprightness preserve me, for I wait for You. (Psalm 25:3, 21)

Psalm 27 began with recognition of the reality of enemies.[60] There was, however, no need to fear the darkness, for the Lord was light; there was no need to fear defeat, for the Lord was salvation (i.e., deliverance); there was no need to fear weakness, for the Lord was strength (verse 1).

David's reference to the stumbling of his enemies in verses 2-3 could have included the Absalom theme of Psalms 3-7.

Rather than giving way to fear, David focused on his desire to dwell in the house of the Lord permanently, to behold the Lord's beauty (i.e., delightfulness), and to inquire of Him in His Temple (verse 4). The nature of this inquiry may be seen in Psalms 25-26.

David knew that protection from his enemies would be found in the Lord's house. To be hidden in the Tabernacle, the secret place, was like being set "high upon a rock" (verse 5).

The consequence of being hidden by the Lord in His house was victory over one's enemies. This victory resulted in David offering a New Covenant kind of sacrifice: shouts of joy and songs of praise (verse 6). (Compare with Hebrews 13:15.)

Verse 7 was a plea for answered prayer; specifically, it was a cry for mercy. This thread of thought connected with Psalms 23:6; 25:6-7, 10, 16.

The Lord called David to seek His face; David's response showed that he was a man after God's own heart (verse 8). (See I Samuel 13:14.)

Verse 9 contained the words of a specific prayer, a plea not to be forsaken by God.

Verse 10 acknowledged that the Lord would not forsake those who sought His face.

The connection between verse 11 and Psalm 25:4 has already been noted, but there is also a connection between verse 11 and Psalm 26:12. The words "even" (Psalm 26:12) and "smooth" ("plain," KJV) are both translated from the Hebrew *miyshor*. The kind of path David prayed to be led in, in Psalm 27:11 was the same kind of place he confessed to stand in, in Psalm 26:12.

David prayed not to be delivered to his adversaries. False witnesses had risen against him, threatening violence (verse 12).

It was extremely significant in the messianic context of the Psalter that David declared that the thing that prevented him from losing heart was faith: "I would have lost heart, unless I had believed that I would see the goodness of the LORD in the land of the living" (verse 13). Here was a connection between the idea of the coming Messiah, the New Covenant Temple, and the centrality of faith. The thing that prevented David from losing heart was not obedience to the law of Moses, but faith in the goodness of the Lord.

Finally, the words of David were used to encourage all who read the psalms to "wait on the LORD." Contextually, this meant "wait in faith."[61] To wait in faith would result in "good courage" and strength of heart.

Psalm 28

As it continues the theme of the Lord's presence in the Temple (verse 2)—a theme established in Psalm 23:6—this psalm identifies the Messiah as the focus of hope (verse 8).[62] The Messiah has been specifically mentioned previously in Psalm 2:2 and Psalm 20:6. He is, as we have seen, the theme of the entire Psalter. This theme is developed by the arrangement of the psalms, and it is enhanced by the subthemes developed around it.

Psalm 28 begins with a prayer that is reminiscent of previous prayers in the Psalter (verse 1). (See Psalms 4:1; 5:1; 17:1; 22:1-2; 25:1; 26:1.) The Lord is identified as a rock, connecting Psalm 28 with Psalm 27:5. The idea of the Lord as a rock is also seen previously in Psalm 18:2, 31, 46.[63] There is remarkable similarity between Psalm 28:1 and Psalm 40:2:

> To You I will cry, O LORD my Rock: do not be silent to me, lest, if You are silent to me, I become like those who go down to the pit. (Psalm 28:1)

> He also brought me up out of a horrible pit, out of the miry clay, and set my feet upon a rock, and established my steps. (Psalm 40:2)

The word translated "pit" (*bowr*) is used here as a metaphor for a place of despair.

The prayer is continued in verse 2, where the reference to the holy sanctuary ties this psalm together with the theme established in Psalm 23:6. (See comments on Psalm 23:6; 24:3, 7-10; 25:4; 26:6, 8; 27:4-6, 11.)

The words of the prayer found in verse 3 are very similar to the words of previous prayers in the Psalter. The word translated "wicked" (*rasha*) is a key word in the Psalter as it is used in contrast with the "righteous."[64] Another term used to describe these same people is "workers of iniquity." The term appears previously in Psalms 5:5; 6:8; 14:4. In Psalm 5:5, the workers of iniquity are those who are boastful. In Psalm 6:8, the workers of iniquity are depicted as enemies (see Psalm 6:10). In Psalm 14:4, the workers of iniquity are described as those who have no knowledge, who devour God's people, and who do not call on the Lord. Here, the workers of iniquity are hypocrites: They "speak peace to their neighbors, but evil is in their hearts" (verse 3). In Psalm 15:3, in a text quite similar to Psalm 24, the qualifications necessary to abide in the Tabernacle and to dwell on the holy hill include refraining from doing evil to one's neighbor. Under that requirement alone, those who are workers of iniquity are unqualified to approach the Temple.

The portion of the prayer recorded in verse 4 is also similar to previous prayers in the Psalter; it asks the Lord to give the wicked what they deserve.[65] Lest we think this ignores God's mercy, we should note that these people have consistently demonstrated their rebellion against God: ". . . they do not regard the works of the LORD, nor the operation of His hands" (verse 5a). Because of this, "He shall destroy them and not build them up" (verse 5b). The idea that the Lord will destroy this kind of person is found also in Psalm 5:6, where He is said to destroy those who speak falsehood. These workers of iniquity do speak falsehood; they "speak peace to their neighbors, but evil is in their hearts" (verse 3b).

David's prayer seems to end with verse 4. Verse 5 provided the rationale for the final part of his prayer and a declaration of the certainty of the destruction of the wicked. In verse 6 David blessed the Lord for hearing his prayers.

The final words of David in this psalm are found in the confession of verse 7. In words similar to those in Psalm 18:2 and 13:5, David declared the Lord to be his strength and shield. His trust in the Lord had not been disappointed; he had been helped. As a consequence, his rejoicing heart expressed its praise in song. Verse 7 captures and brings together several themes seen in the previous psalms. This includes the idea of the Lord as a shield.[66] It includes the idea of the Lord as our strength.[67] Other major themes encapsulated here include trust in the Lord,[68] singing His praises,[69] and rejoicing in Him.[70]

Verses 8-9 were apparently added after the Exile when the psalms were being arranged in their current inspired order. They were written, of course, under the same inspiration as the earlier verses. In these verses, there was "an application of David's words to a specific situation in the life of the people, namely, their waiting for the salvation and blessing of the 'anointed one.' "[71] David declared the Lord to be his strength (verse 7); verse 8 declared that the Lord was "their strength," that is, the strength of His people. David declared that the Lord was his shield (verse 7); verse 8 declared that the Lord was "the saving refuge of His anointed." The word translated "anointed" was a form of the Hebrew *Meshiyach*, which found its way into English by transliteration as "Messiah."

The psalm closed with a prayer for salvation and blessing for the people of God. It included a plea that they would be shepherded (compare with Psalm 23:1) and lifted up forever.

Psalm 29

The thematic focus on the Lord in His Temple continues in Psalm 29: "And in His temple everyone says, 'Glory!' The LORD sat enthroned at the Flood, and the LORD sits as King forever" (9b-10).

It may be that the arrangement of the psalms here is intended to connect Psalm 29 with Psalm 28 not only with the Temple theme but also by identifying Psalm 29:3-11 as the song of praise referred to in Psalm 28:7. The first line of Psalm 28:8 reads, "The LORD is their strength." Psalm 29:11 reads, "The LORD will give strength to His people." In this view, the song itself is conceptually framed by the references to the Lord strengthening His people.[72]

Psalm 29 presents the Lord as king over creation. As originally written, the psalm may have been intended to present a challenge to the Canaanite religion, but that is not the reason for its inclusion at this point in the inspired arrangement of the psalms.[73] The thematic thread here is the Lord ruling from His Temple as the King over all. This points the hope of the postexilic Israelites ahead to another day, a day when the Temple will be rebuilt and when the Lord will dwell in the Temple, sitting "as King forever" (verse 10).

The opening verse contains an imperative, a command: "Give unto the LORD, O you mighty ones, give unto the LORD glory and strength" (verse 1). The word translated "give" (*havu*) means "ascribe." In the strictest sense, created beings cannot give God glory and strength, but they can ascribe these characteristics to Him.

The words translated "mighty ones" (*beney 'eliym*) mean literally "sons of God." This may be a reference to the angels, who are identified as the sons of God in Job 1:6; 2:1; 38:7. This seems to be the meaning of the same term in Psalm 89:6. There is a connection here between the glory of the Lord and His authority over the created realm; the same idea may be seen in Psalm 19:1.

The strength of the Lord is a significant theme in the psalms. (See comments on Psalm 28:7.)

The command to give to the Lord the glory "due to His name" (verse 2) means the glory that is due Him because of His character, identity, and works. Contextually, this has to do with His authority over all creation.[74] The command to "worship the LORD in the beauty of holiness" means something like "worship the LORD in the splendor of holiness."[75] The Septuagint translates verse 2: "Bring to the Lord glory, *due* to his name; worship the Lord in his holy court." It may at first seem strange to think that a phrase translated "beauty of holiness" from the Hebrew text would be translated "holy court" from the Greek text. But an examination of other texts where this terminology is used suggests the accuracy of the Septuagint as a dynamic equivalence. I Chronicles 16:29 is similar to Psalm 29:2: "Give to the LORD the glory due His name; bring an offering, and come before Him. Oh, worship the LORD in the beauty of holiness!" This is in the context of the return of the ark of the covenant to the tent that David had prepared for it in Jerusalem (I Chronicles 16:1).

The idea of worshiping the Lord in the beauty of holiness is connected with worshiping the Lord in the proximity of the ark. Another similar text connects the "beauty of holiness" clearly with worshiping in the courts of the Temple: "Give to the LORD, O families of the peoples, give to the LORD glory and strength. Give to the LORD the glory due His name; bring an offering, and come into His courts. Oh, worship the LORD in the beauty of holiness! Tremble before Him, all the earth" (Psalm 96:7-9). The phrase "beauty [or "splendor"] of holiness" is a poetic description of the courtyard of the Temple of the Lord.[76]

Verses 3-9, with poetic richness, declare the authority of the Lord over the waters, thunder, trees, fire, wilderness, and the animal kingdom. As a consequence of His authority over creation, "in His temple everyone says, 'Glory!' " (verse 9b). As if to summarize His authority over creation, verse 10 declares, "The LORD sat enthroned at the Flood, and the LORD sits as King forever."

For the ancients, there was little that was more frightening or uncontrollable than raging floodwaters. Specifically, the flood of Noah was an event of enormous destruction, but even then God was in control: He spared Noah and his family.

Verse 1 commands "the sons of God" to ascribe strength to Him; verse 11a declares that the Lord gives strength to His people. Since He is a God of strength, He imparts strength. Since He is in control of everything in the created realm, He blesses His people with peace (verse 11b). (Compare with Psalm 4:8.) There is no need to fear; God is in control.

On a literary note, it may be that verses 3-9 can give insight as to the significance of the use of "word" (*logos*) in the New Testament. (See John 1:1-5, 14; I John 1:1-2.) In this poetic structure, the "voice" of the Lord is equated with the Lord Himself. A. A. Anderson points out that it "is not impossible that the mention of the voice of Yahweh brought to the minds of the Israelites the concept of the Word of Yahweh, so powerful and diverse."[77] There is no intention in this psalm to suggest that the "voice" of the Lord is something or someone other than the Lord. Similarly, Adam and Eve heard the "voice of the LORD" walking in the garden; this was a reference to the Lord Himself. (See Genesis 3:8, KJV.)

In a context similar to this, Psalm 103:19-20 describes the voice of the LORD as "the voice of His word":

> The LORD has established His throne in heaven, and His kingdom rules over all. Bless the LORD, you His angels, who excel in strength, who do His word, heeding the voice of His word. (Psalm 103:19-20)

The New Testament, though written in Greek, is influenced by the Hebrew Scriptures. The purpose of the references to the "voice" of the Lord in the Old Testament is not to inform us about the nature of the Godhead; the purpose of these texts is to poetically identify the voice of the Lord with the Lord. Likewise,

John's references to the "word" of God are not intended to inform us about the nature of the Godhead; his literary purpose is to identify the "word" with God Himself.

> Greek *Logos* (Aram. *Memra,* used as a designation of God in the Targums, i.e., Aramaic translations of the OT). The Greek word means, (1) *a thought* or *concept;* and (2) *the expression* or *utterance of that thought.* As a designation of Christ, therefore, *Logos* is peculiarly suitable because (1) in Him are embodied all the treasures of the divine wisdom, the collective thought of God (1 Cor. 1:24; Eph. 3:10-11; Col. 2:2-3); and (2) He is, from eternity, but especially in His incarnation, the utterance or expression of the Person and thought of Deity (Jn. 1:3-5, 9, 14-18; 14:9-11; Col. 2:9). In the Being, Person, and work of Christ, Deity is expressed.[78]

Psalm 30

This psalm is apparently placed where it is to continue the theme established in Psalm 23:6 of the "enjoyment of God's presence in the temple."[79] In that sense it is a messianic psalm; the general idea expressed by the arrangement of these psalms during the post-exilic period is that there is a future for Israel. The Temple will be rebuilt, and it will be occupied by the Messiah.

It may be said that the immediate fulfillment of this promise occurred with the building of the second Temple, but something far greater than that is in view in the inspired arrangement of the Psalter.

The superscription of the psalm identifies it as "a song at the dedication of the house of David." We do not know for certain to what "house" this refers. In its original form, this cannot refer to the Temple, because the Temple was not built during the time of David. It may refer to David's personal palace or to the building materials assembled by David that would later be used in the construction of

Solomon's Temple.[80] Whatever it may have meant previously, the psalm is placed here in the post-exilic Psalter to advance the theme of hope associated with the rebuilding of the Temple.

Although the people of Israel had been in captivity, God had not allowed their foes to rejoice over them (verse 1). Instead, when they cried out to the Lord, He healed them (verse 2). That is, He restored them to the Promised Land. He spared the nation from death (verse 3).

In response to their deliverance from Babylonian captivity, the people praised the Lord and gave thanks to Him (verse 4).

God's anger had been seen in allowing the southern kingdom to go into Babylonian captivity (verse 5).[81] But His anger did not endure forever; because of His favor on the people of Israel, they were released from captivity and allowed to return to their land to rebuild the Temple and the city of Jerusalem.[82] The time of Israel's captivity was a time of weeping. (See Psalm 137.) But this weeping was not forever; it terminated in their joyous return.

There was a time, before their captivity, during their times of prosperity, that Israel became very self-reliant and independent of God. During this time they said, "I shall never be moved" (verse 6).

Following their captivity, the Lord by His favor made their "mountain stand strong" (verse 7a). When "mountain" was used symbolically in Scripture, it generally represented strength or authority. It could be said that God restored Israel's strength or their authority as God's chosen people. As it was used here, the mountain in view could even have been the holy mountain, Mount Moriah, upon which the Temple was built. (See II Chronicles 3:1.)[83] Read in this way with its post-exilic emphasis, this was a reference to the rebuilding of the Temple.

When the Lord's face was hidden from the people of Israel during their captivity, they were troubled (verse 7b). But they cried out to the Lord, making supplication to Him (verse 8). He had promised that when they cried out to Him in captivity, He would hear and restore them to their land. (See Deuteronomy 30:1-5.)

Included in their supplication were these words: "What profit is there in my blood, when I go down to the pit? Will the dust praise You? Will it declare Your truth?" (verse 9). The idea here was this: If the nation perished in Babylon, how would that honor and praise God? Who would be left to declare God's truth?[84]

The prayer of Israel in captivity continued, "Hear, O LORD, and have mercy on me; LORD, be my helper!" (verse 10).

When the Lord answered their prayers and restored Israel to the Promised Land with the hope of rebuilding the Temple, their mourning was turned into dancing; their sackcloth was traded for gladness (verse 11).

The phrase translated "to the end that my glory may sing praise to You and not be silent" (verse 12) could be translated, "that my heart may sing to you and not be silent" (NIV). The word translated "glory" by the NKJV and "heart" by the NIV (*kabod*) is used in Psalm 7:5 (translated "honor" by the NKJV) as a virtual synonym for "life." It "frequently refers to the whole human being or existence,"[85] and so it seems here. The people of Israel, restored to the land, wanted their entire lives to sing praise to God. They vowed to give thanks to Him forever (verse 12).

Psalm 31

Psalm 31 continues the theme of the blessings associated with the Lord's presence in His Temple. Specifically, verse 20 reads, "You shall hide them in the secret place of Your presence from the plots of man; You shall keep them secretly in a pavilion from the strife of tongues." This same idea is seen in Psalm 27:5, which shares in advancing the theme begun in Psalm 23:6: "For in the time of trouble He shall hide me in His pavilion; in the secret place of His tabernacle He shall hide me; He shall set me high upon a rock." The Temple is described as His pavilion or as the secret place. (See Psalm 27:4.)

Various ideas connect Psalm 31 with previous psalms. Compare the request "lead me and guide me" of verse 3. (Compare with Psalm 25:4-5, 9; 27:11.) Compare the "wide place" of verse 8 with the "even place" of Psalm 26:12 and the "smooth path" of Psalm 27:11. Also compare verse 17 with Psalm 25:3.

It should be noted that on the cross Jesus prayed the words of Psalm 31:5: "Into Your hand I commit my spirit." (See Luke 23:46.) Similarly, He prayed the words of Psalm 22:1 on the cross. (See Matthew 27:46.) As we compared Psalm 22 with Jesus' experiences on the cross, it became evident that we should read the entirety of Psalm 22 as a messianic psalm, with the possibility that His prayer on the cross may have included most of Psalm 22.[86]

Since Jesus also prayed words from Psalm 31 on the cross, should we view the entire psalm as messianic? In view of the common translation of verses 5 and 10, this may seem problematic: "Into Your hand I commit my spirit; You have redeemed me, O LORD God of truth" (verse 5). In spite of the fact that Jesus prayed the first phrase of this verse on the cross, we may reject the idea that the last phrase has any messianic reference in view of the idea of the redemption of the Messiah. How could the sinless Messiah be redeemed? This problem may vanish, however, in view of the fact that the Hebrew *padah*, translated "redeemed," contains within its range of meaning the idea of "rescue."[87] For this reason, the NLT translates the verse, "I entrust my spirit into your hand. Rescue me, LORD, for you are a faithful God." If we understand the verse to be a plea for rescue, it fits within the context of the prayers of Jesus in the Garden of Gethsemane and on the cross.[88]

Verse 10 may seem to be a problem for reading the entire psalm as a messianic prayer: "For my life is spent with grief, and my years with sighing; my strength fails because of my iniquity." The Messiah had no iniquity. But the word translated "iniquity" (*'avon*) also contains the idea of punishment or ruin. Note the following translations:

> My life is consumed by anguish and my years by groaning; my strength fails because of my affliction, and my bones grow weak (NIV).

> For my life is spent with sorrow, and my years with sighing; my strength fails because of my misery, and my bones waste away (RSV; NRS).

> For my life is wasted with grief: and my years in sighs. My strength is weakened through poverty and my bones are disturbed (DRA).

> For my life is spent with grief, and my years with groanings: my strength has been weakened through poverty, and my bones are troubled (LXX).

Perhaps most significant here is that the LXX translates the Hebrew *'avon* with *ptocheiai*, a Greek word meaning "poverty." If translating verse 10 as a reference to the Messiah's affliction, misery, or poverty is closer to the inspired intent here than to translate it as a reference to someone's iniquity, not only is the problem of verse 10 removed, but the meaning of the verse is in complete harmony with other descriptions of the Messiah's suffering.[89]

As it was originally written as an individual psalm, Psalm 31 was a prayer that David prayed for help from the Lord. But as it was placed here in the post-exilic arrangement of the psalms, it seems to fit the general messianic intent of the arrangement of the psalms, advancing the messianic theme and pointing Israel to a future that will include a suffering Messiah. For that reason, we will read it as a messianic psalm, like Psalm 22.

As He faced the crucifixion, the Messiah put His trust in the Lord (verse 1a). He prayed that He would not be ashamed (compare with Psalm 25:1-3)—that is, that His trust would not be disappointed—and that He would be delivered (verse 1b). This should be compared with Psalm 22:1-5, 8; Matthew 26:39; Hebrews 5:7-8.

The Messiah prayed that His deliverance would be speedy (verse 2). This should be compared with Psalm 22:19.

He proclaimed the Lord to be His rock and fortress, and asked for the Lord to lead and guide Him for the Lord's "name's sake" (verse 3). Compare this with Psalm 22:22; Hebrews 2:12; John 12:28; 17:6.

The Messiah asked to be pulled from the net secretly laid for Him and recognized God to be His strength (verse 4). Compare this with John 5:18; 7:1.

Verse 5 is clearly a prayer of the Messiah: "Into Your hand I commit my spirit." (See Luke 23:46.) Even though Jesus may not have prayed all of the words of Psalm 31 on the cross, or at any other time, just as He may not have prayed all of the words of Psalm 22, the placement of this psalm seems intended to bring the reader to see the psalm as descriptive of the Messiah's experiences and sentiments.

As we have already noted, the last phrase of verse 5 could be read as a plea to be rescued or as a confession, "You have rescued me." Compare this to Psalm 22:20-21.

Verse 6 described the Messiah's hatred of idolatry. He trusted in no one but the Lord. This should be compared with Matthew 4:8-10.

In verses 7-8, the Messiah rejoiced in the Lord's mercy and that His trouble had been considered and His soul known in adversities. Compare this with Psalm 22:22.

Verse 9 was a plea for mercy by One who was in trouble, whose material and immaterial parts "[wasted] away with grief." Compare this with Isaiah 53:3-5, 10, 12.

As we have seen previously, verse 10 described the poverty, affliction, or misery of the Messiah. Compare this with Psalm 22:14-17; Isaiah 52:14; 53:3-8, 10-12; II Corinthians 8:9.

In verse 11, the Messiah described Himself as a reproach among His enemies and His neighbors and as so repulsive to His acquaintances that they fled from Him. Compare this with Psalm 22:6-7.

In verse 12, the Messiah described Himself as "forgotten like a dead man, out of mind . . . a broken vessel." Compare this with Psalm 22:15; Isaiah 53:8-9, 12.

In verse 13, the Messiah recounted the slander and fear accompanying the plans of those who would take His life. Compare this with Psalm 22:12-13, 16; Matthew 17:23; 26:4; Mark 9:31; 10:34; Luke 22:2; John 5:18; 7:1.

The Messiah reaffirmed His trust in the Lord (verse 14). (See comments on verse 1.)

The Messiah confessed that His life was in the hand of the Lord and prayed for deliverance from His enemies who persecuted Him (verse 15). Compare this with Psalm 22:20-21; Matthew 26:39, 42.

In verse 16, He prayed that God's face would shine upon Him, the Servant of the Lord, and that He would be saved ("delivered," *yasha'*). The Messiah was identified as the Servant of the Lord. (See Isaiah 52:13.)

The Messiah reiterated His prayer not to be ashamed (verse 17). (See comments on verse 1.)

He prayed that "lying lips" would be silenced (verse 18). Compare this with Matthew 26:59-61.

The Messiah testified to the greatness of the goodness of the Lord to those who feared and trusted Him (verse 19). Compare with Psalm 22:22-23.

In verse 20, the Messiah acknowledged that the Lord would hide those who feared Him and trusted Him in His "secret place . . . a pavilion." As we have seen, this is a reference to the Temple of the Lord.

The Messiah blessed the Lord for His marvelous kindness "in a strong city" (verse 21). This may have been a reference to the future restoration of Jerusalem and the Temple, as seen in the references to the "secret place" and the "pavilion" in verse 20.

In verse 22, the Messiah acknowledged that He spoke with haste when He said He was "cut off" from the eyes of the Lord, and confessed that the Lord heard His prayer. Compare this with Psalm 22:1-2, 21.

The psalm concludes with a command to love the Lord, who preserves those who are faithful and repays those who are proud (verse 23). The conclusion includes a command to those who hope in the Lord to "be of good courage." The result of obeying this command is that the Lord "shall strengthen your heart" (verse 24).

Read in this way, Psalm 31 is not only a messianic prayer, it is also encouragement from the Messiah for all people of faith, who find God to be faithful even in the midst of the most painful circumstances of life.

Psalm 32

This psalm of David, in which he recounted the confession of his sin and the joy of forgiveness, closes with his words being applied "on behalf of the 'righteous' and 'upright in heart' (v. 11). The 'righteous' are those to whom the book of Psalms as a whole is addressed (cf. 1:6.)"[90] The idea of trusting in the Lord (verse 10) ties the psalm together with Psalm 2 and all intervening references to the value of trust in the Lord.[91] The reference to the "righteous" also connects this psalm with a theme established in the first psalm.[92] The "righteous" are also known as the "upright in heart," another description frequently appearing in the Psalter to describe those to whom this book is written.[93]

Psalm 32:1-2 offers what could be described as New Covenant insight into the nature of justification by faith: "Blessed is he whose transgression is forgiven, whose sin is covered. Blessed is the man to whom the LORD does not impute iniquity, and in whose spirit there is no deceit." Paul quoted this text from the Septuagint as evidence that we were justified by faith apart from works: "Now to him who works, the wages are not counted as grace but as debt. But to him who does not work but believes on Him who justifies the ungodly, his faith is accounted for righteousness, just as David also describes the blessedness of the man to whom God imputes righteousness apart from works: *'Blessed are those whose lawless deeds are forgiven, and whose sins are covered; blessed is the man to whom the LORD shall not impute sin'* " (Romans 4:4-8).[94]

Even though David wrote when the law of Moses was in effect, he did not connect right standing with God with the works of the law. Rather, he connected right standing with God with faith (i.e., trust [verse 10]) in the Lord. Since this was how Paul read the psalm in his inspired use of it, we must read it the same way. Since David's focus was on faith rather than on the law, this psalm was messianic; it pointed ahead to the day when the Messiah would establish the New Covenant. (See Matthew 26:28; II Corinthians 3:6; Hebrews 9:15.)

Before David confessed his sin, when he "kept silent," his "bones grew old" through his "groaning all the day long" (verse 3). Before his confession, God's "hand was heavy" upon him "day and night." His "vitality was turned into the drought of summer" (verse 4). The struggle with his conscience was described in graphic terms of its physical consequences. Sin that is not confessed is troublesome not only to the inner man, but also to the outer man.

All that is required to receive forgiveness, however, is to acknowledge or confess one's sins (verse 5). The placement of this psalm in the Psalter indicates that we are to understand it to mean that forgiveness in the messianic age is not tied to the animal sacrifices of the law of Moses. (See Hebrews 10:1-10.) Even though the Temple would be rebuilt, as indicated in Psalms 23-31, this did not indicate that the law of Moses would be eternally perpetuated. When the Messiah Himself is actually dwelling in His Temple (i.e., during the millennial age [see comments on Psalm 27]), the focus will be on faith in the Messiah, not on animal sacrifices. Although animal sacrifices will be offered during the Millennium, it will not be to effect forgiveness of sins. These sacrifices will apparently be intended as memorials of the work accomplished by Christ on the cross, much as the Lord's Supper involves eating bread and drinking the fruit of the vine, not to effect the remission of sins, but to "proclaim the Lord's death till He comes" (I Corinthians 11:26).[95]

Prayer is an indication of godliness. David's experience with prayer caused him to encourage others to follow his example of confession of sin (verse 6a). Those who pray will find that God will protect them in time of danger (verses 6b, 7).

In verse 8, the Lord said, "I will instruct you and teach you in the way you should go; I will guide you with My eye." This seems intentionally placed here as a divine response to the prayer, "Show me Your ways, O LORD; teach me Your paths" (Psalm 25:4).[96] The thematic connection of Psalm 25:4 with Isaiah 2:3 suggests that all references to "the way" in Psalms point to the Millennium, when, in the words of this verse, the Messiah will be instructing and teaching people of faith in the way they should go. In other words, as with its first two verses, this psalm continues to point to the messianic future.

Verse 9 is an appeal to embrace understanding in contrast to the horse and mule. The point is that horses and mules must be harnessed before they will obey. This may represent a relationship with God characterized by the law of Moses in contrast with a relationship with God characterized by New Covenant faith (i.e., understanding). In contrast with the New Covenant, the law of Moses is described as bondage. It is a yoke, much like a bit and bridle. (See Acts 15:10; Galatians 2:4; 4:3, 9, 24-25; 5:1.) In this sense, the law of Moses did not require understanding; it was not a faith covenant. It required obedience, much like the obedience of the harnessed horse and mule. (See Galatians 3:10-12.) Thus, verse 9 indicates there is a relationship with God superior to a relationship characterized by bits and bridles. This superior relationship is characterized by understanding. This is understanding that results from having been instructed and taught by the Messiah (verse 8). It is a relationship of trust (verse 10), which results in justification by faith (verses 1-2).

Verse 10 contrasts "the wicked" with the one who trusts in the Lord. This contrast begins in Psalm 1; it is thematic in Psalms.[97] The wicked will experience "many sorrows"; the righteous will be surrounded by mercy.

Verse 11 encourages those who are righteous (i.e., those who trust the Lord) to be glad, rejoice, and to shout for joy. The reason for this celebration is the messianic, New Covenant hope to which Psalms points and which is further developed in Psalm 33.

Psalm 33

The author of this psalm is not identified. The intentional placement of the psalm is readily seen by the thematic connection between its first verse and the last verse of Psalm 32: "Be glad in the LORD and rejoice, you righteous; and shout for joy, all you upright in heart!" (Psalm 32:11); "Rejoice in the LORD, O you righteous! For praise from the upright is beautiful" (Psalm 33:1). Both verses command those who are righteous to rejoice. Both verses identify the righteous as those who are upright.

Because of the thematic connection between the psalms, we should read Psalm 33 as a continuation and further development of the themes found in Psalm 32 and all of the previous psalms, even though David is not identified as the author of Psalm 33.[98] Neither is David identified as the author of Psalms 1, 2, and 10.

Psalm 33 is a psalm of praise (verses 1-5), first to the Lord as Creator (verses 6-9), then to Him as the sovereign Lord of all nations (verses 10-19). At the conclusion of the psalm, the people of God respond to the command to rejoice in the Lord, found in verse 1, by saying, "Our soul waits for the LORD; He is our help and our shield. For our heart shall rejoice in Him, because we have trusted in His holy name. Let Your mercy, O LORD, be upon us, just as we hope in You" (verses 20-22). Thus, "[w]ithin the compositional strategy of the book of Psalms, David's words of praise have given expression to the people's hope for future deliverance."[99]

Verses 1-5 develop the command to rejoice in the Lord and to praise Him. The Lord is to be praised with a new song accompanied by skillfully played musical instruments (verses 2-3). (Compare to Psalm 150.[100]) The reason the Lord is to be praised is that His word is right, His work is done in truth (verse 4), He loves righteousness and justice, and the earth is full of His goodness (verse 5).

Verses 6-9 identify the Lord as the Creator. The background of Genesis 1 may be seen in the statements that the heavens were made by the "word of the LORD" and by the "breath of His mouth" (verse 6). This was done as "He spoke" and as "He commanded" (verse 9). These statements together, equating the Lord's "word" with His "breath," form the background of the New Testament texts concerning the "Word." (See John 1:1-14; I John 1:1-3.) The Word (Hebrew, *dabar*; Greek, *logos*) should not be thought of as a person distinct from God. God's Word is connected inseparably with Him to the extent that it is an expression of His person and purpose. (See comments on Psalm 29:3-9.) Since the Word in New Testament terms is the Messiah, we should read verses 6-9 as messianic in that they attribute creation to the Word, just as the New Testament does.

To the ancients, the waters of the sea were frightening, for they were beyond human control. But God's greatness is seen in His control of the waters (verse 7). The proper response to be made to the Lord is to fear Him and stand in awe of Him (verse 8).

Verses 10-19 identify the Lord as the sovereign ruler of all nations.[101] Verse 10 may be seen as a response to Psalm 2:2: "The kings of the earth set themselves, and the rulers take counsel together, against the LORD and against His Anointed" (Psalm 2:2); "The LORD brings the counsel of the nations to nothing; He makes the plans of the peoples of no effect" (verse 10). Any attempt made by human beings to rebel against God will fail.

In contrast to the failed counsel of humans, "The counsel of the LORD stands forever, the plans of His heart to all generations" (verse 11).

Whereas ungodly nations are destroyed, "Blessed is the nation whose God is the LORD, the people He has chosen as His own inheritance" (verse 12). This is a reference to Israel and to the Jewish people.

God is omniscient; He sees everyone, and He knows the hearts and works of all people (verses 14-15).

Deliverance does not come from military might (verses 16-17), but from fearing the Lord and keeping one's hope in His mercy (verses 18-19).

The focus on the Lord's sovereignty over the nations is a messianic focus, because it is through the Messiah that the Lord exercises this rule. (See Psalm 2:8-12.)

In view of the facts of the Lord's praiseworthiness, His creative work, and His sovereignty over all nations, the psalm concludes with a confession of waiting for the Lord—our help and shield—and rejoicing in Him (verses 20-21). To trust in His holy name is to trust in Him (verse 21b).

The psalm closes with an appeal for the Lord's mercy and a confession of hope (verse 22).

Psalm 34

The superscription of this psalm declares it is "a psalm of David when he pretended madness before Abimelech, who drove him away, and he departed." Abimelech was apparently the same person as Achish the king of Gath. (See I Samuel 21:10-15.) It may be that Abimelech was the king's official royal name and that Achish was his personal name. Abimelech meant "my father is king." Achish had a variety of meanings, including "only a man."

David fled from Saul's violent anger (see I Samuel 18-20) to Achish. The servants of Achish recognized David, causing David to fear for his life. (See I Samuel 21:10-15.) So David pretended to be insane, scratching on the gate and drooling. Achish said to his servants, "Look, you see the man is insane. Why have you brought him to me? Have I need of madmen, that you have brought this fellow to play the madman in my presence? Shall this fellow come into my house?" (I Samuel 21:14-15).

David's pretense resulted in Achish having a lack of interest in him, and David was able to escape. He wrote Psalm 34 in thanksgiving to God for his deliverance.

The question before us, however, is this: Is there any sense in which this psalm, which originally had to do with David's deliverance from Abimelech, should be viewed as pointing ahead to the Messiah? The general context of the Psalter would certainly suggest that this, like all previous psalms, is messianic, but is there anything in the psalm itself to advance a messianic theme?

Six points indicate that we are to read this psalm as pointing to the Messiah.

First, it is placed in the Psalter in the context of other psalms that are clearly messianic in intent. If Psalm 34 is not about the Messiah, the continuity that we have seen to this point is broken.

Second, the general content of the psalm, including the blessing of the Lord, praise, deliverance, the righteous, and trust in the Lord, is in harmony with the general content of the previous psalms.

Third, there seems to be an allusion to verse 8 in Hebrews 6:4, where to "[taste] the heavenly gift" is descriptive of the New Covenant, and thus messianic, experience.[102]

Fourth, the Septuagint translation of verse 5a "was early used in the Christian baptismal liturgy (it is probably reflected in 1 Pet. 2:4)."[103] If early Christians used the words of this verse in conjunction with Christian baptism, it meant they read Psalm 34 as a messianic psalm.

Fifth, the psalm is an acrostic. Verse 1 begins with *aleph*, verse 2 with *beth*, and so forth. The *waw*, however, is missing. There are twenty-two letters in the Hebrew alphabet, and the twenty-two verses in this psalm are maintained by the addition of the final verse, which is outside of the acrostic. This final verse connects the psalm to the general theme of the previous psalms as established in Psalm 2:12b: "Blessed are all those who put their trust in Him." Psalm 34:22b reads, "And none of those who trust in Him shall be condemned." The structure of the psalm suggests that in its original form, as written by David to celebrate his escape from Abimelech, there was a verse beginning with *waw*, and the psalm ended with what is now verse 21. When the Psalter was arranged into its present shape during the post-exilic era, an inspired shape that pointed to the Messiah, the verse beginning with *waw* was not included, and the current verse 22 was added. Although this is speculation, it seems reasonable to conclude that the verse beginning with *waw* was not included because it did not advance the messianic intent of the Psalter, and verse 22 was added in order to contribute to the messianic theme.

Sixth, and perhaps most convincing, is the fact that verse 20 was quoted in John 19:36 as being specifically fulfilled in the events surrounding Jesus' death. Verse 20 reads, "He guards all his bones; not one of them is broken." In John's account of Jesus' death, he pointed out that the Jews asked Pilate to have the legs of Jesus and those who were crucified with Him broken so they would die quickly enough to be taken down from the crosses before the beginning of the Sabbath (John 19:31). The soldiers broke the legs of the thieves, but "when they came to Jesus and saw that He was already dead, they did not break His legs" (John 19:33). John wrote, "For these things were done that the Scripture should be fulfilled, *'Not one of His bones shall be broken'* " (John 19:36). This indicated that an inspired writer of a New Testament book viewed Psalm 34 as a messianic psalm. If he did, so should we. Since Psalm 34 is intentionally placed and composed, the entire psalm is messianic, not merely verse 20. As with Psalm 31 (see verse 5) and Psalm 22 (see verses 1-22), Psalm 34 should be read as expressing the sentiments of the Messiah wherever possible. The words that originally expressed David's gladness at being delivered from Abimelech now express the Messiah's gladness at being delivered from death by means of the Resurrection.

The psalm begins with praise and blessing given to the Lord (verse 1). The second verse continues this theme, and introduces the idea that those who are humble will be glad when they hear the Lord exalted. The third verse begins with a command to join in magnifying the Lord and concludes with an invitation to join in the exaltation of His name. (Compare with the messianic intent of Psalm 22:22.)

The reason the Lord is to be praised is that He heard the Messiah when He sought Him and delivered Him from all of His fears (verse 4). It may seem strange to think of the Messiah as praying for deliverance from fear, but this seems quite in keeping with Hebrews 5:7: "[W]ho, in the days of His flesh, when He had offered up prayers and supplications, with vehement cries and tears to Him who was able to save Him from death, and was heard because of His godly fear." If it seems problematic to think of the Messiah as facing fear, we should note that the Septuagint, widely quoted in the New Testament with its messianic intent, translates the Hebrew *meguwrah* [fear] with the Greek *errusato*, which includes the meanings, "to draw out of danger," "to rescue," "to save," and "to deliver."

Those who look to the Lord are "radiant" and "not ashamed" (verse 5). The Septuagint translates this verse: "Draw near to him, and be enlightened: and your faces shall not *by any means* be ashamed."

The Messiah, who was made "poor" that we might be "rich," cried out to the Lord, who heard Him and delivered Him out of all His troubles (verse 6).[104]

The role of angels in ministering to the Messiah may be seen in Matthew 4:11 and Luke 22:43 (verse 7).

Verse 8 offers an imperative to "taste and see that the LORD is good" and promises that the person who trusts in Him (compare with verse 22) is blessed.

Similarly, verse 9 is a command for the saints of the Lord to fear Him, with the promise that those who fear Him will not want (lack). This promise follows a theme seen in Psalm 23:1.

Although young lions may lack, not so those who seek the Lord (verse 10). We should be careful to note that this verse does not promise that those who seek the Lord will never experience physical hunger. The promise is that they will not lack "any good."

As it relates to the law of Moses, there was a promise of plenty on the condition of perfect obedience to all of the commands of the law. (See Deuteronomy 28.) But as it relates to the New Covenant, there must be a willingness to suffer, if necessary, for our faith.

Another imperative is found in verse 11, a command to come and listen and to be taught the fear of the Lord.

If a person wishes to live long and experience good things (verse 12), he must not speak evil or deceit (verse 13), and he must depart from evil, do good, and seek and pursue peace (verse 14).

The Lord sees the righteous (compare with Psalm 1:5-6) and hears their cries (verse 15), but He is against those who do evil. (Compare with Psalm 1:1, 4-6.) They will be forgotten (verse 16).

Again, as in verse 15, the righteous are assured that the Lord hears them when they cry out; He delivers them from all of their troubles (verse 17). This does not mean they will never experience trouble; it means God will not abandon them to their troubles. (See verse 19.)

The Lord values a broken heart and a contrite spirit (verse 18). As seen elsewhere, He resists the proud, but He extends grace to the humble. (See Proverbs 3:34; James 4:6; I Peter 5:5.)

The Lord does not promise that the righteous will not experience afflictions, but He does promise to deliver them (verse 19). (Compare with I Corinthians 10:13.)

As this psalm relates to the Messiah, there is a precise fulfillment in that not one of His bones was broken (verse 20). (See John 19:36.)

The evil in which the wicked engage shall slay them, and those who hate the righteous will be held guilty (verse 21). (See Psalm 7:15-16.)

The final verse, apparently added by inspiration during the post-exilic period, ties this psalm together with all the preceding psalms: "The LORD redeems the soul of His servants, and none of those who trust in Him shall be condemned" (verse 22). (Compare with Psalm 2:12b; 16:9-10.)

In view of the content of Psalm 34, the context in which it is found, the acrostic arrangement with the missing *waw* and the nonacrostic final verse, and the precise messianic fulfillment of verse 20, it seems quite clear that the entire psalm should be viewed as advancing the messianic theme of the Psalter.

Psalm 35

We do not know the circumstances under which David originally wrote this psalm. It was clearly a time of trouble for him, involving enemies, false witnesses, and mockers. His life was in danger. He prayed for vindication and promised to praise the Lord for deliverance. The psalm is sometimes identified as an imprecatory psalm, since it incorporates lament (complaint) and protestations of innocence.[105]

Although this psalm as originally written addressed specific situations in the life of David, there is convincing evidence within the psalm, in addition to the contextual evidence in the Psalter itself, that it is intended to be read as descriptive of the sufferings of the Messiah and as advancing the messianic theme of the Book of Psalms. The entire psalm can be read as a prayer of the Messiah, and there is specific evidence pointing to this messianic link.

First, there is the reference to false witnesses: "Fierce witnesses rise up; they ask me things that I do not know" (verse 11). When Jesus was brought before the Sanhedrin, the chief priests and the entire council listened to many people testify against Him as they sought a reason to put Him to death. They found no authentic reason to kill Him. (See Mark 14:55.) There were many who "bore false witness against Him, but their testimonies did not agree. Then some rose up and bore false witness against Him, saying, 'We heard him say, "I will destroy this temple made with hands, and within three days I will build another made without hands." ' But not even then did their testimony agree. And the high priest stood up in the midst and asked Jesus, saying, 'Do You answer nothing? What is it these men testify against You?' But He kept silent and answered nothing" (Mark 14:56-61a).

As is often the case, there was some truth in this accusation, but the false witnesses misinterpreted what Jesus said. Jesus had said, "Destroy this temple, and in three days I will raise it up" (John 2:19). He was referring, however, to His resurrection from the dead. (See John 2:20-22.) Although no specific New Testament text refers to Psalm 35:11 as being fulfilled in the actions of these false witnesses, the subsequent connections with events in the sufferings of Christ that are more specific suggest that the reference to the false witnesses was intended in the post-exilic arrangement of the Psalter to point to experiences the Messiah would endure.

Second, there is an evident connection between Psalm 35 and Psalm 22. Psalm 22 is without question messianic; the Messiah prayed the words of Psalm 22:1 on the cross, and Psalm 22:1-22 describe His experiences in specific detail.[106] Psalm 35:17 contains a phrase that is virtually identical with Psalm 22:20-21.

> Lord, how long will You look on? Rescue me from their destructions, my precious life from the lions. (Psalm 35:17)
>
> Deliver Me from the sword, My precious life from the power of the dog. Save Me from the lion's mouth. (Psalm 22:20-21a)[107]

Not only are both texts appeals for deliverance; they both use the same vocabulary. Both texts make the subject of deliverance "my precious life." Psalm 22 seeks deliverance from "the dog" and "the lion's mouth"; Psalm 35 seeks deliverance from "the lions." Although there are differences, the similarities are marked.

Another evident connection between Psalm 22 and Psalm 35 follows in both psalms immediately after the prayer for deliverance for "my precious life."

> I will give You thanks in the great assembly; I will praise You among many people. (Psalm 35:18)
>
> I will declare Your name to My brethren; in the midst of the assembly I will praise You. (Psalm 22:22)

Both texts refer to praising the Lord in the "assembly" (*qahal*). Both are contextually connected with the prayer for deliverance for "my precious life." The writer of Hebrews specifically saw Psalm 22:22 as a messianic reference. (See Hebrews 2:12.) If Psalm 22:22 is messianic, it seems reasonable to conclude that Psalm 35:18 is also.

Another possible connection between Psalm 35 and Psalm 22 may be seen in a comparison of Psalm 35:21 and Psalm 22:7:

> They also opened their mouth wide against me, and said, "Aha, aha! Our eyes have seen it." (Psalm 35:21)
>
> All those who see Me ridicule Me; they shoot out the lip, they shake the head. (Psalm 22:7)

Although the wording of these two texts is not precisely the same, the sense is that those who saw the Messiah as He hung on the cross ridiculed Him. A comparison of the immediate context of these verses in both psalms strengthens the idea that there is a connection. (Compare Psalm 35:22-26 with Psalm 22:11-21.)

Third, as is the case with Psalms 22 (verse 1), 31 (verse 5), and 34 (verse 20), there is a definite textual connection between Psalm 35 and the New Testament:

> Let them not rejoice over me who are wrongfully my enemies; nor let them wink with the eye who hate me without a cause. (Psalm 35:19)
>
> But this happened that the word might be fulfilled which

is written in their law, *"They hated Me without a cause."* (John 15:25)

Jesus explained to His disciples that the world's hatred of Him would be mirrored in its hatred of the disciples (John 15:18-25). Since Jesus revealed the Father, those who rejected Jesus had no excuse, no cause for their hatred (John 15:21-25). Jesus saw this hatred as fulfilling the prophecy of Psalm 35:19.[108] Since Jesus Himself viewed the words of Psalm 35 as messianic prophecy, we should read the entire psalm in this way. It would seem strange to think that only one-half of one verse in the psalm pointed ahead to the Messiah. Since the psalms are individual units of thought, it seems reasonable to think that if a portion of a unit has messianic implications, so does the entire unit. When the entire psalm is examined, this seems evident.[109]

The first eight verses of Psalm 35 form a prayer for vindication and deliverance from the Messiah's enemies. This section connects Psalm 35 with Psalms 1, 6, 7, 25, and 31:

> Let them be like chaff before the wind. (Psalm 35:5a)

> The ungodly are not so, but are like the chaff which the wind drives away. (Psalm 1:4)

> Let those be put to shame and brought to dishonor who seek after my life. (Psalm 35:4)

> Let all my enemies be ashamed and greatly troubled; let them turn back and be ashamed suddenly. (Psalm 6:10)

> Let those be ashamed who deal treacherously without cause. (Psalm 25:3b)

> Let the wicked be ashamed; let them be silent in the grave. (Psalm 31:17b)

> For without cause they have hidden their net for me in a pit, which they have dug without cause for my life. Let destruction come upon him unexpectedly, and let his net that he has hidden catch himself; into that very destruction let him fall. (Psalm 35:7-8)

> He made a pit and dug it out, and has fallen into the ditch which he made. His trouble shall return upon his own head, and his violent dealing shall come down on his own crown. (Psalm 7:15-16)[110]

Immediately after asking for deliverance and vindication, the Messiah promised to respond with joy and with proclamations of the Lord's uniqueness (verses 9-10). This is similar to the contextual connection between deliverance and praise in Psalm 7:14-17.

The description of the Messiah as poor connects Psalm 35:10 with Psalm 34:6 and suggests a New Testament connection with II Corinthians 8:9.

The fierce witnesses of verse 11 anticipated the false witnesses against Jesus. (See Mark 14:56-57.) The reference to false witnesses in verse 11 introduced a section of the psalm that extends through verse 26. These people rewarded the Messiah evil for good and brought sorrow to His soul (verse 12). The problem was not simply that they were false witnesses. The problem was that He had done good for them, and they responded by seeking to destroy Him. When they were sick, He humbled Himself and fasted and prayed for them (verse 13). He was as concerned about them as He would have been for a friend or brother (verse 14).

But in the day of the Messiah's adversity, those to whom He had done good rejoiced, gathering against Him and unceasingly tearing at Him (verse 15). They responded to His adversity by feasting, mocking, and gnashing at Him with their teeth (verse 16).

In words that connect Psalm 35 with Psalm 22, the Messiah prayed to be rescued (verse 17), promising to give thanks to the Lord "in the great assembly" (verse 18). (Compare Psalm 35:17-18 with Psalm 22:20-22.) This connects the psalm with its messianic use in the New Testament. (See Hebrews 2:12.)

The false witnesses had no cause for their duplicity (verse 19). According to Jesus, this verse was fulfilled by those who hated Him. (See John 15:25.)

It was deceit, not a desire for peace, that motivated the false witnesses (verse 20). Their ridicule of the Messiah provided another connection between Psalm 35 and Psalm 22. (Compare Psalm 35:21 with Psalm 22:7.)

The Messiah's prayer returned to a plea for vindication against the false witnesses (verses 22-26). This connects Psalm 35 with pleas for vindication in Psalm 17:2 and 26:1.

On the other hand, the Messiah prayed that those who favored His righteous cause would gladly shout for joy and continually say, "Let the LORD be magnified, Who has pleasure in the prosperity of His servant" (verse 27). The idea of the Messiah as the Servant of the Lord connects Psalm 35 with other messianic texts. (See, e.g., Isaiah 42:1; 52:13.)

The psalm concludes with a promise to speak of the Lord's righteousness and praise all the day long (verse 28).

The internal evidence in Psalm 35, its connections with the messianic context of the Psalter, and the use made of the psalm by Jesus indicate that it should be read as advancing the messianic theme of the Book of Psalms.

Psalm 36

The first verse of this psalm of David can be translated in two ways, each of which gives a different focus to the first four verses. Some translations render verse 1 in such a way as to indicate that sin itself, rather than God, is speaking in the heart of the wicked:

> The transgression of the wicked saith within my heart, that there is no fear of God before his eyes (KJV).
>
> Transgression speaks to the ungodly within his heart; there is no fear of God before his eyes (NAS).
>
> Transgression speaks to the wicked deep in his heart; there is no fear of God before his eyes (RSV).
>
> The transgression of the wicked is affirming within my heart, "Fear of God is not before his eyes" (YLT).
>
> The transgressor, that he may sin, says within himself, *that* there is no fear of God before his eyes (LXX).
>
> Sin whispers to the wicked, deep within their hearts. They have no fear of God to restrain them (NLT).

It is possible, however, to translate the verse so that it is a revelation from God concerning those who are wicked:

> An oracle within my heart concerning the transgression of the wicked: There is no fear of God before his eyes (NKJV).
>
> An oracle is within my heart concerning the sinfulness of the wicked: There is no fear of God before his eyes (NIV).

The word translated "oracle" by the NKJV and NIV and "saith" (KJV), "speaks" (NAS; RSV), "affirming" (YLT), "says" (LXX), and "whispers" (NLT) is *ne'um*. Here, it is used in a construct form with *pesha'*, a word that has to do with transgression or rebellion. Although the phrase *ne'um pesha' larasha'* can be translated something like "transgression speaks to the ungodly"

(NAS), *ne'um* is ordinarily used to indicate that God is speaking. The word *ne'um* appears 372 times in the Hebrew text. In approximately 71 percent of the use of the word, it is connected with *Yahweh* in a construct form to indicate that God is speaking. In another 25 percent of the use of the word, it is connected with *Adonai* and *Yahweh*. So in approximately 96 percent of the use of *ne'um*, it has to do with an oracle or divine utterance. In virtually all of the remaining cases, it is clear who is speaking. For example, in Numbers 24, it is used repeatedly to indicate that Balaam is speaking. (See Numbers 24:3, 4, 15, 16.) It is unusual for there to be any uncertainty as to who is speaking, and it would certainly be unusual for an inanimate object or force, like transgression, to be speaking.

Because David was a prophet, or a spokesman for God (Acts 2:30), and because *ne'um* is used to describe God speaking in virtually every use of the word, and because the translation seems to flow more naturally in the context of verses 1-5, we will following the reading, "An oracle within my heart concerning the transgression of the wicked: There is no fear of God before his eyes" (verse 1).

In this case, the first four verses form a word from the Lord as to characteristics of those who are "the wicked" (*rasha*). This forms an immediate connection with all of the psalms beginning with Psalm 1:1, where a form of *rasha* is translated "ungodly." One of the themes of the psalms is the contrast between the wicked and the righteous, and Psalm 36 stands in solidarity with that theme.

Those who are wicked do not fear God (verse 1). They have no regard for the reality of God in their life and in the world.[111] A wicked person "flatters himself" (verse 2); that is, he is a self-centered, egotistical person. He is so blinded by his self-absorption that he cannot see the significance of his sin: "In their blind conceit, they cannot see how wicked they really are" (verse 2, NLT). The words of the wicked person reveal his inner character; they are wicked and deceitful (verse 3a). He has abandoned wisdom and right living (verse 3b). Even in his bed, the wicked person is devising further wickedness (verse 4a). Rather than abhoring evil, he "sets himself in a way that is not good" (verse 4b). This is a further connection with a theme begun in Psalm 1, a theme that contrasts "the way" of the wicked with "the way" of the righteous. (See Psalm 1:1, 6.) The concept of "the way" has to do with how a person actually lives.[112]

Verses 5-9 include a celebration of the Lord's mercy (*chesed*, "loyal love") and faithfulness (verse 5), His righteousness, judgments, and the way He preserves humans and animals (verse 6). Because of His lovingkindness (*chesed*), people put their trust in Him (verse 7). This connects Psalm 36 with another theme originating in Psalm 2:12, the blessing of trusting in the Lord. Those who trust the Lord are "abundantly satisfied with the fullness" of His house (verse 8a). This is still another connection with a theme established earlier in the psalms, the theme of the blessings associated with the house of the Lord. This theme originates in Psalm 23:6. Those who have access to the house of the Lord "drink from the river" of His pleasures (verse 8b). The blessings of trusting in the Lord include life and light (verse 9).

Verses 10-11 form a prayer that God will continue to extend His lovingkindness (*chesed*) to those who know Him (verse 10a) and His righteousness to those who are upright in heart (verse 10b) and that He will prevent those who are proud and wicked from opposing those who trust in Him (verse 11).

The final consequence of being a worker of iniquity is to fall, to be cast down, and to be unable to rise (verse 12).

The question now arises, is there any sense in which Psalm 36 should be understood as advancing the messianic theme of the Psalter? Indications that the psalm is messianic include a number of connections between this psalm and the New Testament and connections with messianic themes within the Psalter.

First, Paul quoted Psalm 36:1b as proof of the universal sinfulness of the human race. (See Romans 3:18.) In its context in Romans, this statement from Psalms was intended to advance the argument that the Old Covenant was insufficient to deal with the sin problem and that the New Covenant did what the Old Covenant could not: "Now we know that whatever the law says, it says to those who are under the law, that every mouth may be stopped, and all the world may become guilty before God. Therefore by the deeds of the law no flesh will be justified in His sight, for by the law is the knowledge of sin. But now the righteousness of God apart from the law is revealed, being witnessed by the Law and the Prophets, even the righteousness of God, through faith in Jesus Christ, to all and on all who believe. For there is no difference" (Romans 3:19-22). Paul's use of Psalm 36 suggested that the psalm was intended to advance the messianic theme of the Psalter because it indicated the universal sinfulness of the human race and its need for a Savior.

Second, Paul alluded to the last phrase of verse 4 in Romans 12:9. One of the characteristics of a wicked person was that he did not abhor evil. Paul counseled the believers at Rome to abhor evil. The idea was that it was the way of the wicked not to abhor evil; it was the way of the righteous to abhor evil. Ultimately, the way of the righteous was the messianic way; it was the way of faith in the Messiah.

Third, Paul alluded to the second phrase of verse 6 ("Your judgments are a great deep") in Romans 11:33: "Oh, the depth of the riches both of the wisdom and knowledge of God! How unsearchable are His judgments and His ways past finding out!" These words were used in a context in Romans that indicated they describe the mystery of the New Covenant, which was bound up with Jews and Gentiles coming to the Messiah on the same basis. Paul understood the phrase in Psalm 36:6 to be connected with New Covenant, messianic truth.

Fourth, the theme of trust in the Lord was introduced to the Psalter in a messianic setting in Psalm 2:12. Here, in verse 7, in the phrase "therefore the children of men put their trust under the shadow of Your wings," everything that had previously been said in the Psalter about trust was gathered up and included. This meant the messianic theme was included in this reference to trust.

Fifth, the statement in verse 8 about the fullness of God's house, a reference to the Temple, also gathered up and included all that had previously been said in the Psalter about this messianic theme, beginning with Psalm 23:6.

Sixth, there is an apparent connection between verse 8b and New Covenant teaching concerning the new birth: "And You give them drink from the river of Your pleasures" (verse 8b); "On the last day, that great day of the feast, Jesus stood and cried out, saying, 'If anyone thirsts, let him come to Me and drink. He who believes in Me, as the Scripture has said, out of his heart will flow rivers of living water' " (John 7:37-38). The messianic context in Psalm 36:7-8 suggests strongly that the reference to the river of God's pleasures is to be understood as a reference to the Holy Spirit in the New Covenant. This is confirmed by verse 9, which contains two New Covenant ideas. First, the phrase "for with You is the fountain of life" bears close affinity with Jesus' words to the Samaritan woman: "If you knew the gift of God, and who it is who says to you, 'Give Me a drink,' you would have asked Him, and He would have given you living water. . . . Whoever drinks of this water will thirst again, but whoever drinks of the water that I shall give him will never thirst. But the water that I shall give him will become in him a fountain of water springing up into everlasting life" (John 4:10, 13b-14). Verse 9 continues with another New Covenant concept: "In Your light we see light." The Messiah is described in the New Testament as not only the life, but also as the light: "In Him was life, and the life was the light of men. And the light shines in the darkness, and the darkness did not comprehend it. . . . That was the true Light which gives light to every man coming into the world" (John 1:4-5, 9).[113]

In view of its connections with themes in other psalms and with New Covenant contexts, it seems evident that Psalm 36 is intended to advance the messianic focus of the Book of Psalms.

Psalm 37

This psalm provides a major advance on the theme of the contrast between the righteous and the wicked, a contrast that begins in Psalm 1. As this theme is developed in Psalm 2, the wicked are those who reject the Messiah; the righteous are those who trust in the Messiah. As Sailhamer points out, "The psalm is . . . a restatement of the central themes of Pss 1-2 and the whole book."[114] (See comments on Psalms 1-2.) The messianic significance of Psalm 37 is seen in the connection between Psalm 2:4 and Psalm 37:13:

> He who sits in the heavens shall laugh; the LORD shall hold them in derision. (Psalm 2:4)

> The Lord laughs at him, for He sees that his day is coming. (Psalm 37:13)

In these verses, as well as in the context that surrounds them in both psalms, there is a connection that ties Psalm 37 together with all of the previous messianic psalms. This connection may also be seen by comparing Psalm 2:12 with Psalm 37:40:

> Kiss the Son, lest He be angry, and you perish in the way, when His wrath is kindled but a little. Blessed are all those who put their trust in Him. (Psalm 2:12)

> And the LORD shall help them and deliver them; He shall deliver them from the wicked, and save them, because they trust in Him. (Psalm 37:40)

In both psalms, the way to deliverance is the way of trusting in the Messiah.

Another evidence that Psalm 37 is intentionally placed and that it seamlessly advances the messianic theme of the Psalter may be seen by comparing the last verse of Psalm 36 and the first two verses of Psalm 37:

> There the workers of iniquity have fallen; they have been cast down and are not able to rise. (Psalm 36:12)

> Do not fret because of evildoers, nor be envious of the workers of iniquity. For they shall soon be cut down like the grass, and wither as the green herb. (Psalm 37:1-2)

Psalm 36 concludes with a discussion of the workers of iniquity; Psalm 37 begins with a discussion of the workers of iniquity. Psalm 36 concludes by saying that the workers of iniquity have been cast down; Psalm 37 begins by saying the workers of iniquity will soon be cut down. Psalm 36 concludes by saying that the workers of iniquity are not able to rise; Psalm 37 begins by saying that the workers of iniquity will wither as the green herb. Thematically, these psalms are one. Since Psalm 36 advances the messianic theme of the Psalter, so must Psalm 37. Although we do not know when David originally wrote either psalm, as they are placed in the Psalter in this intentional arrangement, they are intended to be read as a flowing, uninterrupted progression of thought.

Psalm 37 is an acrostic, which indicates an intentional arrangement of the verses to advance a specific theme. In this case, that theme is the contrast between the wicked and the righteous. In the Hebrew text, verse 1 begins with *aleph*, verse 3 with *beth*, verse 5 with *gimel*, verse 7 with *daleth*, verse 8 with *he*, verse 10 with *waw*, verse 12 with *zayin*, verse 14 with *heth*, verse 16 with *teth*, verse 18 with *yod*, verse 20 with *kaph*, verse 21 with *lamed*, verse 23 with *mem*, verse 25 with *nun*, verse 27 with *samek*, the third phrase (in the NKJV) of verse 28 with *ayin*, verse 30 with *pe*, verse 32 with *tsadde*, verse 34 with *qoph*, verse 35 with *resh*, verse 37 with *shin*, and verse 39 with *tau*. In the English translation, there may seem to be some irregularity here.

Beginning with verse 1, every other verse begins with a succeeding letter of the Hebrew alphabet through verse 7. Then, verse 8 picks up the acrostic which continues with every other verse through verse 20. Without skipping a verse, the acrostic picks up in verse 21 and continues with every other verse through verse 27. Then, partway through verse 28, the acrostic continues with every other verse through verse 34. Verse 35 continues the acrostic, which involves every other verse through verse 39. So at verses 7-8, 20-21, 27-28, and 34-35, the acrostic seems interrupted.

The significant issue is not, however, how this acrostic may appear in an English translation, but how it appears in the Hebrew text. In the Hebrew text, the acrostic begins with verse 1 and continues with every other line to verse 39, with one exception. There are two lines between the lines that begin with *heth* and *teth*. The extra line here appears as verse 15 in our English translations: "Their sword shall enter their own heart, and their bows shall be broken." When the acrostic is interrupted in this way, it is for emphasis. Attention is directed to the point where the acrostic is irregular, somewhat like underlining or highlighting. In this case, the psalm calls attention to the destruction of the wicked. They will experience the destruction they are attempting to perpetrate upon the righteous. This connects Psalm 37 with Psalm 7. Psalm 7, which concludes the section of the Psalter that begins in Psalm 3 and describes Absalom's rebellion, says concerning the wicked, "His trouble shall return upon his own head, and his violent dealing shall come down on his own crown" (Psalm 7:16).

The section of the Psalter dealing with the rebellion of Absalom describes the first attempt to thwart God's messianic purpose. God had promised David that the Messiah would descend from Him, not from Absalom. (See Psalm 132:11.) Absalom's plot failed. The connection of Psalm 37 with Psalm 7 indicates that all such plots will fail. Absalom was not the only wicked person who would attempt to thwart God's promise. There would be many others who would try in a variety of ways to defeat the divinely ordained plan. None would succeed. These vain attempts continued right up to the efforts of

Herod to assassinate the boy Jesus. But the good news of the Psalter is that although the wicked may rise up, they will not prevail.

In Psalm 37, the wicked (*rasha*) are specifically mentioned in thirteen verses (verses 10, 12, 14, 16, 17, 20, 21, 28, 32, 34, 35, 38, 40). The righteous (*tsaddiq*) are specifically mentioned in ten verses (verses 6, 12, 16, 17, 21, 25, 29, 30, 32, 37). The wicked are implied, but not specifically mentioned, in seven verses (verses 1, 2, 9, 13, 15, 22, 36). The righteous are implied, but not specifically mentioned, in twenty-one verses (verses 3-5, 7-9, 11, 14, 18, 19, 22-24, 26-28, 31, 33-34, 37, 40). There are four verses where the wicked and the righteous are specifically mentioned in the same verse (verses 16-17, 21, 32). There are four verses where the wicked are specifically mentioned and the righteous are implied in the same verse (verses 14, 28, 34, 40).

Psalm 37 appears to be structured as follows: Verses 1-11 show "the need for patience in light of the apparent success of the wicked"; verses 12-22 show "the need for patience in light of the final judgment of the wicked"; verses 23-33 provide "encouragement for the righteous in view of the role of the wicked"; verses 34-40 give "a renewed call for patience in view of the apparent success of the wicked."[115]

Be Patient: The Success of the Wicked Is Only Apparent

Those who trust the Lord (see verse 3) are not to worry because of those who do evil, nor are they to envy those who work iniquity (verse 1). The reason for this is that the doom of evildoers is certain (verse 2).

The antidote to worrying about those who do evil is to trust in the Lord, to do what is right, to dwell in the land promised to the patriarchs (by application, this means believers should receive and enjoy God's promises), to be strengthened by God's faithfulness (verse 3), to delight oneself in the Lord (verse 4), to commit one's ways to Him (verse 5), to rest in Him, to wait patiently for him (verse 7), to cease from anger, and to forsake wrath (verse 8). The reward for this is that the Lord will give those who trust in Him the desires of their heart (verses 4-5). He will demonstrate to all that they are in right standing with Him; He will see that justice is done for them (verse 6).

Although it may seem that the wicked are prospering and that they are getting their way (verse 7), they will be "cut off" (verse 9). But those who wait on the Lord will "inherit the earth" (verse 9); that is, they will fully enjoy the promises God has given to them. For the people of Israel, this was connected with the land, promised to Abraham, Isaac, and Jacob.

It will not be long before the wicked cannot be found (verse 10). But the meek can be found, however, for they will inherit the earth and "delight themselves in the abundance of peace" (verse 11). Jesus quoted this verse in the Sermon on the Mount. (See Matthew 5:5.)

Be Patient: The Wicked Will Be Judged

Although the wicked plot against the righteous (verse 12), their efforts will not succeed because the Lord will laugh at their plans in view of their day of judgment (verse 13; compare with Psalm 2:4). When the wicked attempt to destroy the poor and needy who are upright, they seal their own doom (verses 14-15). Though a righteous man may have little, it is better than the riches of the wicked (verse 16). The Lord is on the side of the righteous; He is opposed to the wicked (verse 17). Those who are upright have an eternal inheritance (verse 18). Their trust in God will not be disappointed even in bad times (verse 19). The wicked, on the other hand, will perish like the fading splendor of the meadows or like vanishing smoke (verse 20). The wicked are characterized by their refusal to pay what they owe; the righteous are characterized by showing mercy and by generosity (verse 21). Those who are blessed by God—the righteous—will receive the promise of God; those who are cursed by Him—the wicked—will be cut off (verse 22).

Be Encouraged: The Lord Is For the Righteous

The Lord directs the steps of good people; He delights in

the way of the righteous (verse 23; compare with Psalm 1:6). A righteous man may fall, but the Lord will help him rise (verse 24). This is not the case with the wicked; when they fall, they are not able to rise (Psalm 36:12). At no time in his life had David seen the righteous forsaken by God. He had never seen the descendants of the righteous begging bread (verse 25). The reason for this was that God was a merciful, generous God, who blessed the descendants of the righteous (verse 26).

In order to be righteous, one must depart from evil and do what is right. If one does this, he will be able to dwell permanently in the land promised to Abraham, Isaac, and Jacob (verse 27). (See also verses 3, 9, 11.)

The Lord will see that justice is done for those who trust Him (His saints); He will not forsake them (verse 28; see also verse 6). The Lord will preserve His saints, just as surely as the descendants of the wicked will be cut off (verse 28). The righteous will inherit the land, dwelling in it permanently (verse 29). (Compare with verses 3, 9, 11, 27.)

The words of the righteous are characterized by wisdom and justice (verse 30). This is because "the law of his God is in his heart" (verse 31). (Compare with Psalm 1:2.) As a consequence, "None of his steps shall slide" (verse 31).

Although the wicked look for opportunities to slay the righteous (verse 32), the Lord will not abandon the righteous into the hand of the wicked (verse 33). When the righteous are judged by the wicked, the Lord will not join the wicked in their condemnation (verse 33).

Be Patient: The Lord Will Keep His Promises

The righteous are those who wait on the Lord and keep His way (verse 34). The concept of life as a "way" links Psalm 37 with a theme that begins in Psalm 1:1. (See also Psalms 1:6; 2:12; 5:8; 18:30, 32; 25:8, 9, 12; 27:11; 32:8; 35:6; 36:4; 37:5, 7, 23.) The Hebrew *derek*, translated "way," takes a very practical view of life; it is a way of living. There is a way of living that characterizes the wicked, and there is a way of living that characterizes the righteous. The Lord will exalt those who keep His way by giving them the land promised to Abraham, Isaac, and Jacob as their inheritance (verse 34). The righteous will also see it when the wicked are cut off (verse 34).

The wicked are sometimes perceived to prosper (verse 35), yet their prosperity is temporary (verse 36).

Peace is promised to the person who is blameless and upright (verse 37), but those who transgress the way of the Lord will be destroyed (verse 38).

The Lord will deliver the righteous; He will strengthen them during troubling times (verse 39). Specifically, He will deliver them from the wicked (verse 40). The Lord delivers the righteous because they trust in Him (verse 40). This concluding verse ties Psalm 37 together with the theme of trust in the Messiah, a theme beginning in Psalm 2:12. (See Psalms 4:5; 5:11; 7:1; 9:10; 11:1; 16:1; 17:7; 18:2, 30; 20:7; 25:2, 20; 31:1, 6, 19; 34:22; 36:7; 37:3, 5.)

The evidence indicates that Psalm 37 should be viewed as advancing the messianic theme of the Psalter. It is thematically tied together with previous messianic psalms and has an obviously intentional acrostic shape that emphasizes the fate of the wicked (those who do not trust in the Messiah) as opposed to the righteous (those who trust in the Messiah).

Psalm 38

This psalm is identified as a psalm of lament (complaint); it is also recognized as a penitential psalm, or a psalm of repentance. David recognized he was being chastened by the Lord for his sin (verses 1-2). His sin had resulted in physical illness (verses 3-5, 7)[116] and emotional turmoil (verses 6, 8-10).

Because of the consequences of his sin, even David's friends and relatives avoided him (verse 11). His enemies took advantage of his weakness to plot against him (verse 12). David did not respond (verses 13-14).

David did not respond to the disapproval of his friends and relatives or to the destructive plans of his enemies because his hope was in the Lord; he knew the Lord would hear him (verses 15-16).[117]

David could go no further; he was consumed by sorrow (verse 17), so he did the only right thing to do in a situation like this: he confessed his sin (verse 18).

Repentance did not placate David's enemies, however (verse 19). In fact, now that David had determined to do the right thing, they continued to be his enemies, rendering evil for good (verse 20).

David concluded his prayer with a plea not to be forsaken by God (verse 21). He prayed that the Lord, his Deliverer, would help him quickly (verse 22).

We do not know when David wrote Psalm 38, or what connection, if any, it may have originally had with Psalm 37 or Psalm 36. But the question before us now has to do with why Psalm 38 is placed at this point in the Psalter. The most obvious connection has to do with evil men.[118] The connection between Psalm 36 and Psalm 37 is evident. Psalm 36 ends with a discussion of the workers of iniquity (Psalm 36:12). Psalm 37 begins with a discussion of the workers of iniquity (Psalm 37:1). In Psalm 36:12, David declared that the workers of iniquity had been cast down. In Psalm 37:2, he said that they would "soon be cut down." According to Psalm 36:12, the workers of iniquity are "not able to rise." According to Psalm 37:2, the workers of iniquity would "wither as the green herb."

The message of Psalm 37 is that people who trust in the Lord (who is identified contextually in the Psalter as the Messiah[119]) need not fret because of evildoers. (See Psalm 37:1, 40.) But Psalm 38 "appears to be placed here as a vivid example of David's own 'fretting' over evil men."[120] David wrote, "Those also who seek my life lay snares for me; those who seek my hurt speak of destruction, and plan deception all the day long" (verse 12). He prayed, "Hear me, lest they rejoice over me, lest, when my foot slips, they exalt themselves against me" (verse 16). He complained, "My enemies are vigorous, and they are strong; and those who hate me wrongfully have multiplied. Those also who render evil for good, they are my adversaries, because I follow what is good" (verses 19-20).

We may at first think that David had forgotten his own counsel in Psalm 37:40: "And the LORD shall help them and deliver them; He shall deliver them from the wicked, and save them, because they trust in Him." But although he had temporarily, during a time of great emotional turmoil, slipped into fretting over evildoers, he recovered in the prayer, "Do not forsake me, O LORD; O my God, be not far from me! Make haste to help me, O Lord, my salvation!" (verses 21-22). In Psalm 37:40, David acknowledged that the Lord would help those who trust Him by delivering them from the wicked, and in Psalm 38:22 he called on the Lord for this help, indicating his trust in the Lord.

Psalm 36 advances the messianic theme of the Psalter. Its connections with Psalm 37 mean that Psalm 37 continues that theme. Now, the connections between Psalm 38 and Psalm 37 indicate that the messianic theme continues into Psalm 38: Sin will result in divine rebuke, with physical, emotional, and social consequences (verses 1-14, 16-20), but those whose hope and trust are in the Lord will find deliverance (verses 15, 21-22).

Psalm 39

Like Psalm 38, Psalm 39 is a lament. Immediate comparisons may be seen between the two:

> I said, "I will guard my ways, lest I sin with my tongue; I will restrain my mouth with a muzzle, while the wicked are before me." I was mute with silence, I held my peace even from good; and my sorrow was stirred up. (Psalm 39:1-2)

> But I, like a deaf man, do not hear; and I am like a mute who does not open his mouth. Thus I am like a man who does not hear, and in whose mouth is no response. (Psalm 38:13-14)

In both psalms, David declared his intention to refrain from speaking in response to the threats of his enemies.

> And now, Lord, what do I wait for? My hope is in You. (Psalm 39:7)

> For in You, O LORD, I hope; You will hear, O Lord my God. (Psalm 38:15)

In both psalms, David confessed that his hope is in the Lord.

> Remove Your plague from me; I am consumed by the blow of Your hand. (Psalm 39:10)

> O LORD, do not rebuke me in Your wrath, nor chasten me in Your hot displeasure! For Your arrows pierce me deeply, and Your hand presses me down. (Psalm 38:1-2)

In both psalms, David recognized that God was chastening him for his sin.[121] He prayed for deliverance from this chastening, for he recognized the error of his way.

A distinction between the two psalms is that in Psalm 39 David did not complain about having been rejected by his family and friends (see Psalm 38:11), nor did he focus on his enemies (see Psalm 38:12, 19-20).

In the midst of his sorrow for the consequences of his sin, David made a commitment to silence (verses 1-2). He did this to avoid sinning with his tongue (verse 1). But the longer he remained silent, the angrier his situation made him (verse 3).

"The metaphors 'my heart grew hot' and 'the fire burned' express anger."[122] So David spoke to the Lord.

In Psalm 38, David's focus in his prayer was on this world, but in Psalm 39, his focus shifted to "a new vantage point, the divine viewpoint of eternity."[123] He prayed to know his "end," the measure of his days, and the full scope of his frailty (verse 4). He acknowledged that his days were as "handbreadths"[124] and his age was "as nothing" before the Lord. At his best, man was but "vapor" (verse 5).[125] Even as a man went about living his life, he was "like a shadow" who busied himself "in vain" (verse 6a). The person who "[heaped] up riches . . . [did] not know who [would] gather them" (verse 6b).[126]

In view of the brevity and uncertainty of life, David confessed that his hope was in the Lord (verse 7). He prayed for deliverance from his sins (verse 8a) and that he would not be made "the reproach of the foolish" (verse 8b). The word translated "reproach" (*herpah*) has to do with scornful taunting.

The reason David determined to keep silence was that he recognized his suffering was from the Lord; it was divine discipline (verse 9). He prayed for release from this discipline; he was consumed by it (verse 10).

When God chastened a person for sin, beauty vanished and the brevity of life was underscored (verse 11).

David concluded his prayer by confessing his solidarity with the patriarchs (verse 12). He appealed to his heritage to remind the Lord that he was part of the covenant community. Although he acknowledged his sinfulness, David did not think himself severed from the community of people of faith, reaching all the way back to Abraham, the first stranger and sojourner. Even in the New Testament, those under divine discipline were still part of the believing community. (See I Corinthians 11:27-32; Hebrews 12:5-11; James 5:14-16.)

In his final words in this prayer, David prayed that the Lord would leave him alone so that he could regain strength (verse 13a). Otherwise, he would perish (verse 13b).

It may seem strange for the psalm to end on such a negative note, "but it is important to note that it is followed in the next psalm by an account of God's answer to David's prayer and the reassurance of God's promise to send a deliverer."[127]

Psalm 39 serves the messianic purpose of the Psalter by turning the focus away from the temporal consequences of sin and back to the Lord as the only source of hope. It provides a bridge to the clearly messianic Psalm 40. (Compare Psalm 40:6-8 with Hebrews 10:5-9.)

Psalm 40

This is one of those psalms that is specifically quoted in the New Testament as a reference to the Messiah. The writer of Hebrews tied Psalm 40:6-8 to the Incarnation:

> Therefore, when He came into the world, He said: *"Sacrifice and offering You did not desire, but a body You have prepared for Me. In burnt offerings and sacrifices for sin You had no pleasure. Then I said, 'Behold, I have come—in the volume of the book it is written of Me—to do Your will, O God.'"* (Hebrews 10:5-7)

> Sacrifice and offering You did not desire; my ears You have opened. Burnt offering and sin offering You did not require. Then I said, "Behold, I come; in the scroll of the book it is written of me. I delight to do Your will, O my God, and Your law is within my heart." (Psalm 40:6-8)

Underscoring the messianic significance of the psalm, the writer of Hebrews quoted a second time from Psalm 40:6-8, though in an abbreviated form:

> Previously saying, *"Sacrifice and offering, burnt offerings, and offerings for sin You did not desire, nor had*

> *pleasure in them"* (which are offered according to the law), then He said, *"Behold, I have come to do Your will, O God."* He takes away the first that He may establish the second. By that will we have been sanctified through the offering of the body of Jesus Christ once for all. (Hebrews 10:8-10)

So, altogether, five verses in Hebrews are taken up with the messianic focus of Psalm 40. The point that is made in Hebrews is that the Messiah quoted the words of Psalm 40:6-8 in conjunction with His incarnation, declaring the temporary nature of the law of Moses and its inability to satisfy the righteous requirements of God in regard to sin by means of its sacrificial system. The ultimate and efficacious sacrifice, of which the sacrifices offered according to the law were but a vague shadow (see Hebrews 10:1-4), was the body prepared for the Messiah. When the Messiah fulfilled the will of God by taking upon Himself the sins of the world and dying for those sins (see Hebrews 10:12), the law of Moses was taken away so that the New Covenant could be established (see Hebrews 10:9).[128]

The influence of the Septuagint in Hebrews may be seen by comparing Psalm 40:6a with Hebrews 10:5b:

> Sacrifice and offering You did not desire; my ears You have opened. (Psalm 40:6a)
>
> *Sacrifice and offering You did not desire, but a body You have prepared for Me.* (Hebrews 10:5b)

The reading "a body You have prepared for Me" instead of "my ears You have opened" follows the Septuagint. A literal translation of the Hebrew text would be, "My ears you have digged." This was an apparent reference to the creation of the human body (see Genesis 2:7), in which the various orifices, including the ears, were "digged out."[129] Since the Messiah had a body, He would have ears. It suited the purposes of the writer of Hebrews to quote a form of the Septuagint, because the emphasis was on the body of the Messiah as the sacrifice that did what the sacrifices of the law could not do.[130]

Even though the connection between Hebrews 10 and Psalm 40 indicates the messianic nature of Psalm 40, it may be thought that there is an insurmountable problem in Psalm 40:12 that prevents the entire psalm from being messianic.

> For innumerable evils have surrounded me; my iniquities have overtaken me, so that I am not able to look up; they are more than the hairs of my head; therefore my heart fails me. (Psalm 40:12)

If this verse is to be read as a reference to the speaker's personal sins, it cannot be a reference to the Messiah, who is sinless. (See Hebrews 4:15; 7:26.) In this case, we would have to say that a portion of the psalm, but not all of it, is messianic. But since at least a portion of the psalm is seen as messianic in the inspired New Testament, and since there is no change of speakers throughout the psalm, we may be well advised to seek a way to read the entire psalm as messianic that does justice to biblical and exegetical theology. In other words, if the Messiah could claim verses 6-8 as His own, is there anything that prevents all of the words of the psalm from being His?

In Psalm 31:10, the same word translated "iniquities" in Psalm 40:12 (*'avon*) appears. It is possible, however, to read the verse as messianic, because *'avon* can be a reference to punishment or ruin.[131] In Genesis 4:13, Cain said, "My punishment [*'avon*] is greater than I can bear!" Although Cain was being punished for his sins, his complaint was not about his sins, but about his punishment. In Genesis 19:15, the angels warned Lot to escape "the punishment [*'avon*] of the city."[132] In I Samuel 28:10, Saul promised the witch of Endor that no punishment [*'avon*] would come upon her for her participation in bringing up Samuel.

It is significant that in Isaiah 53:11, it is said that the Messiah will "bear their iniquities [*'avon*]." The word translated "bear" in this verse is *saval*, which means to bear in the sense of carrying. In Isaiah 53:12, where it is said of the Messiah that "He bore the sin of many," the word translated "sin" is *chet'*, not *'avon*, and the word translated "bore" is *nasa'*, not *saval*. *Nasa'* has the meaning "to lift up, to bear up." Although *'avon* and *chet'* share a common range of meaning, as do *nasa'* and *saval*, they also carry possible distinctions of meaning, depending on the context in which they are used. The use of the different vocabulary in Isaiah 53:11-12 seems intentional. Isaiah 53:11 seems to indicate that the Messiah carried the guilt or the punishment for the sins of others; Isaiah 53:12 seems to indicate that He bore their sins away. If we read Psalm 40:12 in view of Isaiah 53:11, messianic intent would be seen in Psalm 40:12.

It should also be noted that the phrase "taken hold of me" ["have overtaken me"] "can be said appropriately of *sufferings*, but not of *sins* (compare Job 27:20, Psalm 69:24). Thus, the difficulties in referring this psalm to Christ, arising from the usual reading of this verse, are removed."[133]

Spurgeon understood verse 12 to refer to the Messiah and wrote,

> For innumerable evils have compassed me about. On every side he was beset with evils; countless woes environed the great Substitute for our sins. Our sins were innumerable, and so were his griefs. There was no escape for us from our iniquities, and there was no escape for him from the woes which we deserved. From every quarter evils accumulated about the blessed One, although in his heart evil found no place. Mine iniquities have taken hold upon me, so that I am not able to look up. He had no sin, but sins were laid on him, and he took them as if they were his. "He was made sin for us." The transfer of sin to the Saviour was real, and produced in

> him as man the horror which forbade him to look into the face of God, bowing him down with crushing anguish and woe intolerable. O my soul, what would thy sins have done for thee eternally if the Friend of sinners had not condescended to take them all upon himself? Oh, blessed Scripture! "The Lord hath made to meet upon him the iniquity of us all." Oh, marvellous depth of love, which could lead the perfectly immaculate to stand in the sinner's place, and bear the horror of great trembling which sin must bring upon those conscious of it. They are more than the hairs of mine head: therefore my heart faileth me. The pains of the divine penalty were beyond compute, and the Saviour's soul was so burdened with them, that he was sore amazed, and very heavy even unto a sweat of blood. His strength was gone, his spirits sank, he was in an agony.[134]

The Darby Translation provides "my punishments" as an alternative translation to "mine iniquities." In this reading, the Messiah took upon Himself, as His own, the punishment for sin.

Bernard E. Northrup interprets verse 12 to mean that the "Messiah has assumed our iniquities as His own."[135]

The *New Living Translation* renders the verse in such a way as to allow verse 12 to be a reference to the Messiah:

> For troubles surround me—too many to count! They pile up so high I can't see my way out. They are more numerous than the hairs on my head. I have lost all my courage. (Psalm 40:12, NLT)

We will read the entire psalm as messianic, since messianic use is made of it in Hebrews 10, since there is no change of speakers throughout the psalm, since it is possible to translate and understand verse 12 as a reference to the Messiah's sufferings on behalf of sinners, and in view of the messianic shape of the entire Psalter.[136]

Psalm 40 was a prayer of the Messiah, just as were Psalms 16; 18:1-19; 22:1-22; 31; 35. In this psalm, the Messiah declared His patience in waiting for the Lord, who inclined to Him and heard Him (verse 1). (Compare with Psalm 22:21; Hebrews 5:7.) In answer to His prayer, the Messiah was delivered from a horrible pit of miry clay, and His feet were set upon a rock (verse 2). (Compare with Psalm 35:7.) The Messiah sang a new song of praise to God; the song would result in many trusting in the Lord (verse 3).

The person who trusted in the Lord, was no respecter of persons, and who did not follow lies was blessed (verse 4). (Compare with Psalm 2:12.) The wonderful works of the Lord and His thoughtfulness toward human beings were numberless (verse 5).

Even though the law of Moses required sacrifices and offerings, this ritualistic system was not God's desired means of atoning for sin, for it did nothing to deal with the sin problem (verse 6). (See Psalm 32:1-2 [with Romans 4:6-8]; 51:16-17; Hebrews 10:1-10.) The sacrifices were intended to remind the people of Israel of their sinfulness (Hebrews 10:3).[137] The only means by which God intended to deal with the sin problem was through the offering of the body of the Messiah. (Compare verses 6-8 with Hebrews 10:5-10.) When the Messiah said, "Behold, I come; in the scroll of the book it is written of me" (verse 7), He indicated that the Torah anticipated His incarnation. (See Genesis 3:15; 49:10-12; Deuteronomy 18:15-18; 34:10.) The Messiah came to do the will of God, and that will was to complete and bring to an end the law of Moses, replacing it with the New Covenant, which would provide sanctification "through the offering of the body of Jesus Christ once for all." (See verse 8; Hebrews 10:9-10.)

The "great assembly" to whom the Messiah "proclaimed the good news of righteousness" and from whom He "[did] not restrain" His lips (verse 9) was the same assembly among whom He praised the Lord. (See Psalm 22:22; 35:18; Hebrews 2:12.) Specifically, it was the assembly of those who believed on the

Messiah. The Messiah declared God's righteousness, faithfulness, salvation, lovingkindness, and truth to this assembly (verse 10).

The Messiah prayed for the mercies of the Lord and to be preserved by His lovingkindness and truth (verse 11). He was surrounded by innumerable evils and overtaken by the iniquities He bore on behalf of others. (See Isaiah 53:11; II Corinthians 5:21.) The effects of being the sin-bearer were such that the Messiah was unable to look up; the evils that surrounded Him outnumbered the hairs of His head, causing His heart to fail Him (verse 12). This painful description underscored the scope and reality of the Messiah's suffering, as reflected also in the other messianic prayers in the Psalter. (See, e.g., Psalm 22:1-22; Matthew 26:38-39, 42; 27:46; Hebrews 5:7.)

The Messiah prayed for hasty deliverance (verse 13). (Compare with Psalm 22:19.) He prayed that those who sought to kill Him would be ashamed and brought to mutual confusion (verse 14a), that those who wished Him evil would be "driven backward and brought to dishonor" (verse 14b), and that those who said, "Aha, aha!" to Him would be shamefully confounded (verse 15). (Compare with Psalms 22:7; 35:21.)

On the other hand, the Messiah prayed that all those who sought the Lord would rejoice and be glad and that those who loved His salvation would continually say, "The LORD be magnified!" (verse 16).

As in Psalm 35:10, the Messiah confessed to being poor and needy (verse 17a). (Compare with II Corinthians 8:9; Philippians 2:5-8.) Even though He was poor, the Lord thought upon Him and helped and delivered Him. The prayer closes with the Messiah asking that God would not delay in delivering Him (verse 17b).

Psalm 41

Although the superscription of Psalm 41 does not indicate the specific event in David's life reflected in the psalm, the evidence suggests it had to do with Ahithophel's betrayal of David in conjunction with Absalom's rebellion. David was concerned with his enemies (verse 5) who conspired against him (verse 7). He said these enemies included "my own familiar friend in whom I trusted, who ate my bread" and who "[had] lifted up his heel against me" (verse 9).

Ahithophel was a trusted counselor of David (II Samuel 15:12). His advice was like the voice of God (II Samuel 16:23). Ahithophel joined Absalom in his rebellion against David (II Samuel 15:31).

As it relates to the messianic shape of the Psalter, it is significant that Jesus saw His betrayal by Judas as being a fulfillment of Psalm 41:9.

> "I do not speak concerning all of you. I know whom I have chosen; but that the Scripture may be fulfilled, *'He who eats bread with Me has lifted up his heel against Me.'* Now I tell you before it comes, that when it does come to pass, you may believe that I am He." . . . When Jesus had said these things, He was troubled in spirit, and testified and said, "Most assuredly, I say to you, one of you will betray Me." Then the disciples looked at one another, perplexed about whom He spoke. Now there was leaning on Jesus' bosom one of His disciples, whom Jesus loved. Simon Peter therefore motioned to him to ask who it was of whom He spoke. Then, leaning back on Jesus' breast, he said to Him, "Lord, who is it?" Jesus answered, "It is he to whom I shall give a piece of bread when I have dipped it." And having dipped the bread, He gave it to Judas Iscariot, the son of Simon. Now after the piece of bread, Satan entered him. Then Jesus said to him, "What you do, do quickly." (John 13:18-19, 21-27)

Because of Jesus' use of the psalm, we are to understand David as a messianic person who prefigured in some way the ultimate Son of David, the Messiah Himself. The events in David's life paralleled at times the events in the life of the Messiah. One of those parallel points had to do with the betrayal of David by Ahithophel and the betrayal of Jesus by Judas.

> When David has to flee for [sic] Absalom and Ahithophel, he crosses the brook Kidron (2 Sam. 15.23); John's passion narrative starts with Jesus crossing the Kidron (Jn 18.1). On the Mount of Olives, David prays God to turn Ahithophel's counsel into foolishness (2 Sam. 15:30-31); on the same mount, Jesus prays his Father to take away from him the cup of the passion (Mk 14:32-42 par.). Ahithophel plans to take the king at night by surprise, so that his men will flee and he can kill the king (2 Sam. 17:1-2); Judas comes at night with a crowd to have Jesus seized, and the disciples flee (Mk 14:43-52 par.). Ahithophel says to Absalom on that occasion: "The man you are looking for means as much as the return of all, and the entire people will be in peace' [sic] (2 Sam. 17:3); according to John, Caiaphas says to the Sanhedrin: 'It is profitable for you that one man dies for the people, and that the whole nation does not perish' (Jn 11.50). When Ahithophel's counsel is not followed, he hangs himself (2 Sam. 17.23), just as Judas does after his repentance (Mt. 27.5). . . . Ahithophel's suicide is the only one in the OT, apart from war incidents; that of Judas is unique in the NT. That Judas is called 'the son of perdition', in Jn 17.12, finds a parallel in the rabbinic view, that Ahithophel has no share in the world to come (e.g. *m. Sanh.* 10.1).[138]

Since the entirety of Psalm 41 cannot refer to the Messiah (see verse 4), and since the psalm as originally written was apparently rooted in Absalom's rebellion,[139] we may ask if verse 9, as originally written by David, had in view the distinct treacheries of both Ahithophel and Judas. If the answer is yes, then we have a verse with more than one meaning. The problem here, as it relates to hermeneutics, is that this might seem to open the entire

Scripture to multiple meanings, casting us adrift on a sea of interpretive uncertainty and putting the text at the mercy of purely human speculation.

One response to this dilemma would be to say that we are justified in seeing more than one meaning only when the New Testament specifically indicates that this is the case, as here.[140] Although this would open the Old Testament text to dual meanings, interpretive control would be provided by the inspired use of such texts in the New Testament.

Another approach would be to see the messianic intent of the Psalter as being tied to the final shape it took in the post-exilic period. If we view this final shape as being an inspired shape, the words of the individual psalms, which originally existed only in the limited context of the individual psalms as they were written independently of each other, were now found in a new and much larger context, a messianic context. In this view, the interpretive control is not found in the words of the individual psalms as they were originally written, but in those same words as they were found in their new and larger context.

That there is an intentional shape of the Psalter can be seen by looking no further than the obvious division of the Psalter into five smaller books, with Book One spanning Psalms 1-41, Book Two Psalms 42-72, Book Three Psalms 73-89, Book Four Psalms 90-106, and Book Five Psalms 107-150. We do not have to embrace the traditional view that these five books are connected in some way with the five books of the Torah to see that there is some kind of intentional design here. Although we might dismiss these divisions as a purely human invention, since the words "Book One," "Book Two," and so forth are not part of the text, we cannot so easily dismiss the ending of each book, which is part of the text:

> Blessed be the LORD God of Israel from everlasting to everlasting! Amen and Amen. (Psalm 41:13)

And blessed be His glorious name forever! And let the whole earth be filled with His glory. Amen and Amen. The prayers of David the son of Jesse are ended. (Psalm 72:19-20)

Blessed be the LORD forevermore! Amen and Amen. (Psalm 89:52)

Blessed be the LORD God of Israel from everlasting to everlasting! And let all the people say, "Amen!" Praise the LORD! (Psalm 106:48)

The first four books share quite similar endings. Blessing is pronounced upon the Lord and "amen" is declared. The fifth book, containing Psalms 107-150, does not have this ending, although it does conclude the Psalter with "Praise the LORD!" (Psalm 150:6), because Psalm 150 obviously ends the entire Psalter, as well as the fifth book within the Psalter.

These endings could not be coincidental, and they were apparently not an original part of the individual psalms to which they were attached. For example, Psalm 72 was a psalm of Solomon, but it ends, "The prayers of David the son of Jesse are ended" (Psalm 72:20). This indicates there was an earlier shape to a collection of psalms that served a different purpose than the shape of the collection we now have in the Psalter. The collection we now have, which originated in the post-exilic era, was inspired not only in its words—including any additions like the endings of these books—but also in its shape. Its shape is messianic, as seen in the use of the Psalter in the New Testament and in the relationship of the individual psalms to each other.

Thus, rather than seeing Psalm 41:9 as having a dual meaning, we should read it as having a singular meaning determined by its current messianic context. This harmonizes with the use made of the verse by Jesus in John 13:18. David's experience with betrayal at the hand of Ahithophel becomes Jesus' experience with betrayal at the hand of Judas. This does not mean that in this case the entire psalm should be understood as a reference to the Messiah, even though that is the case with other psalms. Rather, the focus here is on a specific experience in the life of David and how that experience parallels a specific experience in the life of the Messiah.

When the individual psalms were originally written, they had a specific meaning and purpose. But the Holy Spirit, who inspired them in the first place, further inspired their creative use in a variety of ways and contexts in the canon of Scripture. This may be seen by comparing I Chronicles 16:8-36 with Psalms 96, 105, and 106. Portions of Psalms 96, 105, and 106 are found in I Chronicles 16:8-36. The words of Psalm 105:1-15 are found in I Chronicles 16:8-22, with very slight variation. The words of Psalm 96:1-13a are found in I Chronicles 16:23-33, with somewhat greater variation. The words of Psalm 106:1, 47-48 are found in I Chronicles 16:34-36, with some variation. Though the words found in I Chronicles 16:8-36 represent three different psalms as they are found in the Psalter, they represent one unit as they are found in I Chronicles. David presented them to Asaph and his brethren in this form so they could use these words to thank the Lord (I Chronicles 16:7). The occasion was the placement of the ark of the covenant in the tabernacle David had prepared for it (I Chronicles 16:1). It is possible, then, that the same inspired words may have three different ranges of meaning: First, there was a meaning attached to the psalm as originally written, within its own isolated context; second, there was a meaning attached to the words of the psalm as they were incorporated into worship upon the placement of the ark of the covenant into the tabernacle David prepared; third, there was a meaning attached to the psalms as they were found in the larger context of the Psalter. This does not mean, however, that there are "layers" of meaning in a specific text of Scripture. The meaning, in each case, is determined by the context in which the words are found.

God was concerned about the poor, so He blessed those who shared His concern (verse 1a). The Lord delivered such people from trouble (verse 1b), preserved them, kept them alive, blessed them, and refused to deliver them to their enemies' will (verse 2). The Lord strengthened those who shared His values and sustained them in their illness (verse 3).

David cried out for mercy and healing for his soul, confessing his sins (verse 4). His enemies spoke evil of him, eagerly anticipating his death (verse 5). They lied about David (verse 6), whispering against him, and planning some way to hurt him (verse 7). They said that David had some devilish disease that would kill him (verse 8).[141] Even David's trusted friend betrayed him (verse 9).

David again asked for the Lord's mercy (verse 10a). He prayed to be raised up so that he could repay his enemies (verse 10b). He knew God was pleased with him, because his enemy was unable to triumph over him (verse 11). David declared his integrity; he knew he would always enjoy God's presence (verse 12).

Verses 5-12 seem best understood, as it pertains to their original context, in view of Absalom's rebellion against David.[142]

Verse 9 is best understood, in the context of the Psalter, as a reference to the betrayal of the Messiah.

Verse 13 concludes the psalm with an ending similar to the conclusion of books two, three, and four of the Psalter, marking a turning point in the larger book. This turning point may be seen by comparing the superscriptions of Book One (Psalms 1-41) with the superscriptions of Book Two (Psalms 42-72).

CHAPTER 3

Book Two
Psalms 42-72

Psalm 42 begins Book Two within the Psalter.[1] An immediate distinction can be seen between Book One and Book Two by an examination of the superscriptions. In Book One, thirty-seven out of forty-one psalms are attributed to David. Those not attributed to David are Psalms 1, 2, 10, and 33. But of these, Psalm 10 is to be read together with Psalm 9 as one psalm, and Psalm 33 is to be read together with Psalm 32 as one psalm. Therefore, only two psalms are not connected with David, Psalms 1 and 2. These are, of course, introductory to the entire Psalter, introducing the messianic theme that is continued by the selection and arrangement of the Davidic psalms through Book One.

Book Two, on the other hand, includes psalms by a variety of authors. Although David is identified as the author of most of them,[2] seven are attributed to the sons of Korah,[3] one to Asaph,[4] and one to Solomon.[5] There are four anonymous psalms,[6] one of which is apparently by David.[7] Psalm 43, though anonymous, is intended to be read together with Psalm 42 as one psalm. This identifies Psalm 43 with the sons of Korah.

The conclusion of Book Two reads, "The prayers of David the son of Jesse are ended" (Psalm 72:20). Since twelve of the psalms preceding this conclusion of Book Two are not prayers of David, this indicates an earlier shape of this portion of the Psalter that included exclusively the prayers of David. The new inspired purpose to which these psalms were put in the post-exilic era included the insertion of psalms by the sons of Korah, Asaph, Solomon, and an unknown author or authors into the collection of psalms by David. Psalm 72:20 provides closure for the large section of the Psalter beginning with Psalm 3, the first of David's prayers, and extending through Book One and Book Two. Psalm 72:20 indicates that "all these psalms [Psalms 3-72] are to be read as prayers on behalf of God's promise of a Messiah."[8] The more specific closure of Book Two comes at Psalm 72:19, with an ending similar to the endings of Book One (see Psalm 41:13), Book Three (see Psalm 89:52), and Book Four (see Psalm 106:48).

Of the seventy-eight psalms remaining in the Psalter in Books Three, Four, and Five, only eighteen are attributed to David.[9] These were apparently not originally included in the collection that spans Books One and Two.

Psalms 42-43

The superscription of Psalm 42 indicates that it is "a contemplation of the sons of Korah." The superscriptions of Psalms 44-49 also connect them with the sons of Korah. Psalm 43, however, has no superscription. The content of Psalms 42-43 indicates that they are to be read as one psalm. Thus, Psalm 43 is also seen as connected with the sons of Korah.

The Korathites first appeared in Numbers 26:58 in a listing of the families descended from Levi. They were identified as gatekeepers for Solomon's Temple in I Chronicles 26:1. In II Chronicles 20:19, they were associated with praising the Lord God of Israel "with voices loud and high."[10]

The children of Korah survived their father's rebellion against Moses. (See Numbers 26:9-11.) Korah, whose father was Izhar, was a grandson of Kohath and great-grandson of Levi. (See Exodus 6:16-21.) Heman was the head of the Kohathites in David's day. He and his sons were responsible to minister with songs and music. (See I Chronicles 6:33; 15:16-17, 19; 16:41-42; 25:1-7.)

Heman and his sons continued their service under Solomon (II Chronicles 5:11-14), Jehoshaphat (II Chronicles 20:19), Hezekiah (II Chronicles 29:14-19), and Josiah (II Chronicles 35:15-18).

In view of the lack of a superscription in Psalm 43 and the parallel themes between Psalms 42 and 43, the two should be read as one.

> Why are you cast down, O my soul? And why are you disquieted within me? Hope in God, for I shall yet praise Him for the help of His countenance. (Psalm 42:5)

> Why are you cast down, O my soul? And why are you disquieted within me? Hope in God; for I shall yet praise Him, the help of my countenance and my God. (Psalm 42:11)

> Why are you cast down, O my soul? And why are you disquieted within me? Hope in God; for I shall yet praise Him, the help of my countenance and my God. (Psalm 43:5)

The only difference among these three verses is in the final phrase. The final phrase of Psalm 42:5 reads, "For the help of His countenance." The final phrase of both Psalm 42:11 and Psalm 43:5 reads, "The help of my countenance and my God." But in the Septuagint, the Syriac, and some Hebrew manuscripts, the text of Psalm 42:5 conforms to the text of Psalm 42:11 and Psalm 43:5.[11]

Another parallel may be seen:

> Why do I go mourning because of the oppression of the enemy? (Psalm 42:9b)

> Why do I go mourning because of the oppression of the enemy? (Psalm 43:2b)

As these psalms were originally written, "the psalmist was isolated from temple worship. He may have been a refugee, but it is more likely that he had been exiled to Aram, Assyria, or Babylon and was in the hands of taunting captors (vv.3, 10)."[12] There, he yearned for the presence of God (Psalm 42:1-2), facing the continual taunt, "Where is your God?" (Psalm 42:3). The psalmist remembered when he used to participate in the worship associated with the Temple in Jerusalem (Psalm 42:4). But even in the midst of his despair, he had hope in God and declared his intent to praise Him (Psalm 42:5, 11; Psalm 43:5). He remembered the Promised Land (Psalm 42:6-7) and knew that in spite of his exile the Lord would continue to love him and to provide him with a song (Psalm 42:8). At the same time, the oppression he experienced and the mocking by his enemies made him feel forgotten by God (Psalm 42:9-10).

The psalmist cried out for vindication against the ungodly nation that held him captive (Psalm 43:1). The oppression of the enemy made him feel cast off (Psalm 43:2). He yearned to return to Jerusalem, the place of the holy hill and the Tabernacle (Psalm 43:3). He would experience again the joy of visiting the altar and praising God on the harp (Psalm 43:4).

But why are these psalms placed here, together? Do they advance the messianic theme of the Psalter? In view of the major messianic concepts developed in Book One, they do. They are intended to advance these concepts in the minds of the Jewish people in conjunction with their return to the Promised Land after their exile. Jerusalem was destroyed, as was the Temple. Like the psalmist, the returning Israelites longed for the presence of God. They had long lived with the taunts of their captors. If their God was the true God, why was their holy city destroyed? Why were they in captivity? Had their God forgotten them?

But Psalms 42 and 43 offered hope (Psalm 42:5, 11; 43:5). The Temple would be rebuilt and they would enjoy the worship of the Lord once again (Psalm 42:4; 43:3-4). They would be restored to the Promised Land (Psalm 42:6; Psalm 43:1, 3-4).

The ultimate Temple would be the one to which the Messiah would return.[13] Hope sprang from the "help" of God's countenance. The Hebrew *yeshua'*, a form of which was translated "help," became the name of the Messiah.

Psalm 44

Like Psalms 42-43, Psalm 44 is a psalm of lament. It is also a "contemplation of the sons of Korah."[14] Psalm 44 is different from Psalms 42-43, however, in that it is a psalm of national lament, whereas Psalms 42-43 are psalms of personal lament.

Psalm 44 begins, "We have heard with our ears, O God, our fathers have told us, the deeds You did in their days, in days of old" (verse 1). This is the voice of the congregation.[15] Plural pronouns may also be seen in verses 5, 7-14, 17-20, 22, and 24-26. Singular pronouns are found in verses 4, 6, and 15.

One way to explain the use of both the first person plural and the first person singular is to say that it is "a literary convention rather than a liturgical alternation between people and king. . . . Thus the corporate reflection is personalized at critical points in the literary structure."[16] In this case, there is no interpretive significance to the change in pronouns from plural to singular.

As the psalm opens, the members of the congregation were remembering what their ancestors had told them about their initial possession of the Promised Land (verse 1). The people of Israel were able to inhabit the land ("them You planted") when God drove out the Gentiles ("heathen" or "nations") (verse 2). The ancestors of the people of Israel did not gain possession of the land by their own efforts but by God's "right hand," "arm," and "the light" of God's countenance (verse 3).

At verse 4, the pronoun is singular: "You are my King, O God; command victories for Jacob."

The plural pronoun returns in verse 5, with the congregation asserting that it would conquer its enemies through God and through His name.

In verse 6, the pronoun is singular, with the psalmist declaring that he would not trust in his bow or sword to be saved.

With verse 7, the plural pronoun is restored. The congregation declared that God had saved them from their enemies, shaming those who hated them. They boasted in God, praising His name (verse 8).[17]

The lament began in verse 9, with the congregation complaining that God had cast them off and put them to shame. He had not accompanied their armies when they went out to battle. They had to retreat before their enemies (verse 10a). They were plundered by those who hated them (verse 10b). God had given them up, and they were scattered among the nations (verse 11). God had sold His people into slavery, but He made no profit from it (verse 12). The people of Israel had been made a reproach to those around them; they were the object of scorn and derision (verse 13). Among the nations where they were scattered, they were a byword; people shook their heads at them (verse 14).

In verse 15, the pronoun is singular again. The psalmist was continually dishonored and ashamed. This shame and dishonor was a consequence of the reproaches and reviling of the enemy and avenger (verse 16).

The plural pronoun returns in verse 17. The congregation claimed innocence; they did not see a connection between their experiences and sin. They claimed not to have forgotten God nor to have "dealt falsely" with His covenant. Their heart, they said, had "not turned back," nor had their steps departed from God's way (verse 18). In spite of their professed innocence, God had "severely broken" them; the "shadow of death" loomed over them (verse 19).

Because they insisted they had not forgotten the name of God nor worshiped false gods—they recognized that these sins would have merited their painful experiences—the congregation viewed their suffering as being for the sake of the Lord (verses 20-22). In other words, they had done nothing to deserve it; it was simply the will of the Lord.

The congregation cried for the Lord to awake and to restore them (verse 23). It seemed to them that God was hiding His face from them and forgetting their affliction and oppression (verse 24). Their lives were almost gone (verse 25).[18] Appealing to God's mercy, they cried out for redemption (verse 26).

The connection of Psalm 44 to the messianic theme of the Psalter is seen in that Psalm 45 answers the cry for redemption; the Redeemer is the anointed King, the Messiah, who is in some marvelous way God Himself. (See Psalm 45:1-7; compare with Hebrews 1:8-9.)

But the questions remain: Is the alternation between plural and singular pronouns merely a literary device, and are the members of the congregation accurate in their protestations of innocence?

The people admitted that they had been defeated and plundered by the enemy (verses 9-10). They were "scattered . . . among the nations" (verse 11). This is precisely the fate about which they were warned if they were not perfectly obedient to the law of Moses:

> But it shall come to pass, if you do not obey the voice of the LORD your God, to observe carefully all His commandments and His statutes which I command you today, that all these curses will come upon you and overtake you: . . . The LORD will cause you to be defeated before your enemies; you shall go out one way against them and flee seven ways before them; and you shall become troublesome to all the kingdoms of the earth. Your carcasses shall be food for all the birds of the air and the beasts of the earth, and no one shall frighten them away. . . . You shall be only oppressed and plundered continually, and no one shall save you. . . . The LORD will bring you and the king whom you set over you to a nation which neither you nor your fathers have known, and there you shall serve other gods—wood and stone. And you shall become an astonishment, a proverb, and a byword among all nations where

> the LORD will drive you.... Then the LORD will scatter you among all peoples, from one end of the earth to the other, and there you shall serve other gods.... (Deuteronomy 28:15, 25-26, 29b, 36-37, 64)[19]

The precise parallel between the consequences for disobedience and the experiences of the people as described in Psalm 44 suggests that they were not as innocent as they claimed. From this perspective, the alternation between the plural pronouns—many of which involve these protests of innocence—and the singular pronouns is significant.

At key points, the person who penned this psalm on behalf of the congregation inserted his personal confession, a confession that contrasted with the claims of the congregation.

> It should be noted that in the midst of these reflections, the psalmist inserts his personal thoughts into the words of the congregation, thus providing an explanation of God's past help: "You are my King and my God, who decrees victories for Jacob" (v. 4), and "I do not trust in my bow, my sword does not bring me victory" (v. 6). These two insertions prove helpful in explaining the unusually strong complaint against the Lord in the remainder of the psalm (vv.9-26)....
>
> ... [I]f we read their complaint in light of the ... acknowledgment of the psalmist, "I do not trust in my bow" (v.6), we are led to the conclusion that, though outwardly obedient, they still lacked trust in God. When the psalmist says, "I do not trust in my bow" (v.6), rather than "we do not trust in our bows" (v.6), he implies that the congregation has yet to learn this lesson. In this respect the sense of the psalm is similar to that of 51:16-17, that what pleases God is not just outward obedience to his commandments, but also "a broken and contrite heart" (51:17b).[20]

Where plural pronouns appeared in the psalm, the general tenor was that the people believed they were suffering innocently. Where singular pronouns appeared, the idea was that of the writer's personal trust in God (verses 4, 6) and remorse for sin (verses 15-16).

Read this way, Psalm 44 fits with the exile theme of Psalms 42-43. If the people were not in exile, we can only speculate as to the time of the writing of the psalm.[21] And if they were innocent, as they claimed, we can only speculate as to why God dealt with them as though they were not. It is possible, of course, to suffer innocently, as did Job. But the precise parallels between the predicted punishment for disobedience and the actual experiences of the people of Israel as reflected in this psalm suggest that their claims of innocence were overstated.

However, regardless of the guilt or innocence of the congregation and the significance or lack of it of the alternating plural and singular pronouns, Psalm 44 does conclude with a cry for redemption, a cry that is answered in Psalm 45 with the promise of the coming Messiah.

Psalm 45

Like the previous three psalms,[22] Psalm 45 is "a contemplation of the sons of Korah" addressed to the "Chief Musician." Unlike the previous three psalms, Psalm 45 is "set to 'The Lilies.' " The only other psalm set to precisely this tune is Psalm 69. Psalm 60 is set to "Lily of the Testimony," and the superscription of Psalm 80 can be translated "to the tune 'Lilies of the Covenant' " (NLT).[23]

The superscription of Psalm 45 further identifies it as "a song of loves." This is connected to the wedding theme of the psalm. In the psalm, the marriage of an idealized king is portrayed.[24] It is typical to view Psalm 45 as "a *royal psalm* [that] functioned as a *wedding song* at the occasion of the wedding of a royal couple."[25]

Our chief concern, however, is not with the use that may have been made of this psalm as it was originally composed in isolation from other psalms, but with the use it is given in its new context in the Psalter. This is connected with the remarkable use made of Psalm 45 in the New Testament.

As it relates to its immediate context in the Psalter, Psalm 45 is the answer to the cry for redemption that concludes Psalm 44: "Arise for our help, and redeem us for Your mercies' sake" (Psalm 44:26).[26] In Psalm 45, the divine King arises to defeat the enemy. (See Psalm 45:3-6.)

The messianic connection of Psalm 45 with the New Testament may be seen by comparing verses 6-7 with Hebrews 1:8-9:

> Your throne, O God, is forever and ever; a scepter of righteousness is the scepter of Your kingdom. You love righteousness and hate wickedness; therefore God, Your God, has anointed You with the oil of gladness more than Your companions. (Psalm 45:6-7)

> But to the Son He says: *"Your throne, O God, is forever and ever; a scepter of righteousness is the scepter of Your kingdom. You have loved righteousness and hated lawlessness; therefore God, Your God, has anointed You with the oil of gladness more than Your companions."* (Hebrews 1:8-9)

The writer of Hebrews, in a discussion of the superiority of Jesus Christ to the angels, appealed to Psalm 45:6-7 to demonstrate both the deity and humanity of the Son. The angels were inferior to Him. They were not Sons of God in the sense that the Messiah was. (See Hebrews 1:4-5.) They worshiped the Son. (See Hebrews 1:6.) They were serving spirits. (See Hebrews 1:7.) The Son, on the other hand, was identified as the God and Lord who created all things. (See Hebrews 1:8, 10-12.)

Since the New Testament reads Psalm 45:6-7 as being about the Messiah, and since the person addressed in these verses is the subject of the entire psalm, we should read the entire psalm as being about Him in some way.

Following the superscription, Psalm 45 begins, "My heart is overflowing with a good theme; I recite my composition concerning the King; my tongue is the pen of a ready writer" (verse 1). The words translated "a good theme" (*dabar tov*) mean literally, "a good word." In view of the messianic connection between this psalm and the New Testament, it may be appropriate to read "a good word" as a reference to the gospel message. The gospel is, by definition, "good news." The same letter that connects Psalm 45 with the Messiah—the Book of Hebrews—identifies New Testament believers as those who have "tasted the good word of God" (Hebrews 6:5). Since the theme of Psalm 45 is "the King" (verse 1), and since the King is God (verse 6), it seems reasonable to understand the psalm as a poetic description of events surrounding the proclamation of the gospel message. (The contrastive connection with Psalm 44 is remarkable. Psalm 44, a psalm of national lament, cries for the Lord to awaken and redeem the people. Psalm 45 declares the means of this redemption; it is the "good word.")

The King, the Messiah, was "fairer than the sons of men" (verse 2a). As the "Son of man," He was the most excellent of all men.[27] Grace was "poured upon" His lips (verse 2b). When Jesus ministered in Nazareth, the people marveled "at the gracious words which proceeded out of His mouth" (Luke 4:22). John wrote that "the law was given through Moses, but grace and truth came through Jesus Christ" (John 1:17). The Messiah was eternally blessed of God (verse 2c).

The Messiah, identified as the "Mighty One," prepared for battle against His enemies by girding His sword upon His thigh (verse 3a). The word translated "Mighty One" (*gibbor*) may be compared with Isaiah 9:6, where the Messiah was identified as the "Mighty God" (*'el gibbor*). The Messiah was girded not only with a sword, but also with glory and majesty (verse 3b).[28] (See Jude 25.)

In His majesty, the Messiah was pictured as a conquering king on a steed, riding "prosperously because of truth, humility, and righteousness" (verse 4a). In other words, His military campaign would succeed because He was characterized by truth, humility, and righteousness. A parallel may be seen in Revelation 19:11: "Now I saw heaven opened, and behold, a white horse. And He who sat on him was called Faithful and True, and in righteousness He judges and makes war." (See Revelation 19:12-16.) In the New Testament, humility was connected with faithfulness. (Compare Micah 6:8 with Matthew 23:23.)

The "right hand" metaphor is connected with the military imagery (verse 4b). The "right hand" symbolizes military strength, and the phrase could be translated, "Then your right hand will accomplish mighty acts!"[29] (Compare with Psalm 2:9; Revelation 2:27; 19:15.)

The military imagery continues in verse 5: "Your arrows are sharp in the heart of the King's enemies; the peoples fall under You." (Compare with Revelation 19:15; I Corinthians 15:24-25.) This picks up and continues the theme of the Messiah's conquest of those who rebelled against Him. (See Psalm 2:7-9; 110:1-2, 5-6.)

The use of verses 6-7 in Hebrews 1:8-9 indicates that Psalm 45 has definite messianic content. According to the writer of Hebrews, the words of verses 6-7 were "to the Son" (Hebrews 1:8). The words "Your throne . . . is forever and ever" reflected the promise of the Davidic covenant. God promised David, "When your days are fulfilled and you rest with your fathers, I will set up your seed after you, who will come from your body, and I will establish his kingdom. He shall build a house for My name, and I will establish the throne of his kingdom forever. . . . And your house and your kingdom shall be established forever before you. Your throne shall be established forever" (II Samuel 7:12-13, 16). As it related to David's purely human descendant, Solomon, there was an additional promise and warning: "I will be his Father, and he shall be My son. If he commits iniquity, I will chasten him with the rod of men and with the blows of the sons of men. But My mercy shall not depart from him, as I took it from Saul, whom I removed from before you" (II Samuel 7:14-15). If David's descendants through Solomon were unfaithful to God, they would be punished, but their disobedience would not invalidate the covenant God made with David. (See Psalm 89:20-37.)

Wickedness among Solomon's descendants reached a low point with Coniah, also known as Jeconiah. He was so wicked that his removal from the throne was the beginning of the Babylonian captivity of Judah. Jeremiah declared, "Thus says the LORD: 'Write this man down as childless, a man who shall not prosper in his days; for none of his descendants shall prosper, sitting on the throne of David, and ruling anymore in Judah' " (Jeremiah 22:30). This precipitated Israel abiding "many days without king or prince, without sacrifice or sacred pillar, without ephod or teraphim" (Hosea 3:4). But for Israel to be without a king was not to be a permanent situation: "Afterward the children of Israel shall return and seek the LORD their God and David their king. They shall fear the LORD and His goodness in the latter days" (Hosea 3:5).

The ultimate fulfillment of the Davidic covenant would come through a human descendant of David: "The LORD has sworn in truth to David; He will not turn from it: 'I will set upon your throne the fruit of your body' " (Psalm 132:11). But how could this be, in view of Coniah's unfaithfulness and the fact that none of his descendants would continue the Solomonic lineage from David?

The precise fulfillment of God's promise to David came through the Incarnation, wherein the virgin Mary conceived and brought forth the Son of God, who was at the same time the Son of David. (See Luke 1:31-35.) Mary was a descendant of David through David's son Nathan, not through Solomon. (See Luke 3:23-31.[30]) Joseph was a descendant of David through Solomon. Thus, Jesus' legal claim to David's throne came through His legal father, Joseph. If Joseph had been Jesus' physical father, Jesus would not have qualified to sit on David's throne due to Coniah's defilement. But this defilement was avoided because Mary was also David's descendant, but through Nathan. God's promise to David that the Messiah would descend physically from him to sit on his throne was thus fulfilled. (See Acts 2:29-31.)

As it was originally written in isolation from the Psalter, Psalm 45 may have been a royal psalm functioning as a wedding song at a royal wedding.[31] But as it was included in the Psalter, in its new messianic context, it functioned to declare the deity of the Messiah and the eternality of His throne. Verse 6 identified the Son, the One on the throne, as *Elohim*. His rule was characterized by righteousness.

Verse 7, however, declared that the divine King was somehow human: "You love righteousness and hate wickedness; therefore God, Your God, has anointed You with the oil of gladness more than Your companions." First, this divine King had "companions" (*habar*). *Habar* indicates a real equality of some kind.[32] As quoted in Hebrews 1:9, the Greek *metochous* also indicated a real sharing, partaking, partnership, participation, and fellowship. The context in Hebrews indicated that the Messiah's companions were human beings; since He was human, He stood in solidarity with humanity.[33] Second, God was the God of this divine King. In order for this to be true, the divine King must be not only divine, but also human.

The Messiah was "anointed . . . with the oil of gladness more than" His companions (verse 7b). All of Israel's merely human kings were anointed, but the anointing of the divine-human King exceeded their anointing. (Compare I Samuel 16:1, 13 with Luke 4:16-21.)

At verse 8, the psalm turned to a discussion of the preparations for the wedding of the King and His bride. The King's garments were "scented with myrrh and aloes and cassia" (verse 8). The phrase translated "out of the ivory palaces, by which they have made You glad" could be translated "from the luxurious palaces comes the music of stringed instruments that makes you happy."[34]

Verse 9 addressed the members of the wedding party that included the bride, the queen, and her attendants. The queen's adornment included "gold from Ophir." Ophir was known as the source of fine gold.[35] In conjunction with its messianic theme, this should be compared to Revelation 19:7-9.

The queen seemed to be from a foreign country; she was urged to forget her own people and her father's house (verse 10).[36] This may have been intended to foreshadow the fact that the Messiah's bride would not be characterized by a prescribed ethnicity. (See Galatians 3:28; Colossians 3:11.) If this was the case, the bride was not exclusively Jewish. Thus, it was not the nation of Israel. It may have been, however, that verse 10 merely indicated that the bride was to forsake her own family as she joined the king's family.[37]

The King would "greatly desire" His bride's beauty. But He was more than her husband; He was her Lord, and she was to worship Him (verse 11). This "strongly [suggested] that she [was] to be taken as a figure of the congregation's faithful trust in the King."[38]

The facts that the "daughter of Tyre will come with a gift" and that the "rich among the people will seek" the bride's favor (verse 12) evoke prophecies found elsewhere concerning the universal homage that will be paid to the Messiah and thus to His royal court. (See Isaiah 60:3; Zechariah 14:16-17; Revelation 21:24-26.)

The queen's beautiful clothing is described in verses 13-14a. This may be compared with Revelation 19:7-8.[39]

The queen's companions, the members of the wedding party who accompanied her, were brought before the King "with gladness and rejoicing" (verses 14b-15). These may have been the wise virgins to whom Jesus referred in Matthew 25:1-13. They may also be in view in Revelation 19:9 as those who "are called to the marriage supper of the Lamb."

Where the Messiah's human ancestors have previously reigned, His sons will share in His reign as princes (verse 16). (See Romans 5:17; II Timothy 2:12; Revelation 5:10; 20:4-6.)

The Messiah's name will "be remembered in all generations" and the people shall praise Him forever and ever (verse 17).

Psalm 46

Psalm 46 advances the theme of Zion theology.[40] Specifically, this psalm "helps us to visualize God—the Creator of earth, mountains, and sea—among his people, elevated on a high mountain with a mountain stream—representative of his blessings—flowing throughout his kingdom (46:1-4)."[41] Zion theology, with its focus on "the city of God, the holy place of the tabernacle of the Most High" (verse 4), is essentially the theology of the Davidic covenant. (See II Samuel 7:12-16.) The Davidic covenant/Zion theology theme is the motif that holds the Psalter together. (See, e.g., Psalms 48, 76, 89, 132.) The ultimate expression of this theme has the Messiah sitting on the throne of David, ruling the nations of the world from Mount Zion. The fulfillment begins with the Millennium (Revelation 19; 20:1-6) and extends into eternity. (See Isaiah 9:6; Luke 1:33; Revelation 11:15; 21:1-3, 10, 22-26; 22:1, 3, 16.)

The contextual link between Psalms 45 and 46 is that Psalm 45 portrays "the coming of the ideal King" and that Psalm 46 follows with "a description of the King's city, Jerusalem, at the time of his coming."[42]

Psalm 46 is punctuated by *selah* in three places. (See verses 3, 7, 11.) This provides a natural division of the psalm into three major sections. The first section, consisting of verses 1-3, elaborates on the idea of God as "a very present help in trouble" (verse 1b). The second section, consisting of verses 4-7, describes God as present among His people. (See verse 7a.) The third section, consisting of verses 8-11, "encourages God's people to look forward to the final establishment of the kingdom of God on earth."[43]

Like Psalms 42-45, Psalm 46 is connected with the sons of Korah.[44] Unlike these psalms, Psalm 46 is a "Song for Alamoth." *Alamoth* is the plural form of the Hebrew *Almah*, which means "a young woman." It may be that this phrase in the superscription means that the psalm is to be sung "to the voice of young women," or perhaps in a soprano voice.[45]

It is "virtually impossible to identify the original life situation"[46] of Psalm 46. For our purposes, this is relatively insignificant. The question before us has to do with the function of Psalm 46 within its current context in the Psalter. Why does it follow Psalm 45? Why does it precede Psalm 47?

In Psalm 46, the divine King of Psalm 45, who conquered His enemies (Psalm 45:3-5), occupied the eternal throne (Psalm 45:6), and wedded "the royal daughter" (Psalm 45:13), was present to help His people in trouble (Psalm 46:1-3), occupied the "city of God" (Psalm 46:4-7), and was destined to be exalted throughout the earth (Psalm 46:8-11).

Psalm 47 continues the theme "of the previous psalms by portraying God's reign as King in Jerusalem as extending beyond that of his own chosen people to include all the earth."[47] (See Psalm 47:8.)

A specific connection with the messianic theme established in Psalm 2 may be seen in Psalm 46:

> Why do the nations rage, and the people plot a vain thing? The kings of the earth set themselves, and the rulers take counsel together, against the LORD and against His Anointed, saying, "Let us break Their bonds in pieces and cast away Their cords from us." He who sits in the heavens shall laugh; the LORD shall hold them in derision. Then He shall speak to them in His wrath, and distress them in His deep displeasure. (Psalm 2:1-5)

> The nations raged, the kingdoms were moved; He uttered His voice, the earth melted. . . . He makes wars cease to the end of the earth, He breaks the bow and cuts the spear in two; He burns the chariot in the fire. (Psalm 46:6, 9)

The nations' challenge to the rule of the Messiah is described in Psalm 2, as is their defeat. That theme is woven throughout all of the following psalms in a variety of ways up to and including Psalm 46.

The people of God find Him to be their "refuge and strength," a "very present help in trouble" (verse 1). The cosmic turmoil described in verses 2-3 seems to represent the vain efforts of the unbelieving nations to cast off divine restraint. Zion theology includes the idea that in the last days "the mountain of the LORD'S house shall be established on the top of the mountains, and shall be exalted above the hills; and all nations shall flow to it" (Isaiah 2:2). (See also Isaiah 2:3-4.) Mountains, when used symbolically, seem to represent nations or kingdoms. (See Daniel 2:35, 44-45; Revelation 17:9-11.) In the day of the ultimate conflict between the Messiah and those who reject Him, the "mountains" will shake (verse 3) and "be carried into the midst of the sea" (verse 2).

When all nations are subdued by the Messiah (verses 6-7), there will be "a river whose streams shall make glad the city of God, the holy place of the tabernacle of the Most High" (verse 4). This river, described more fully in Ezekiel 47:1-12, Zechariah 14:8-9, and Revelation 22:1-2, represents the healing influence of the presence of the Lord in the city of God, Jerusalem, after the defeat of the nations. (See Revelation 19:11-21; 20.)

The people are invited to behold the Lord's victory over His enemies (verses 8-9). They need to do nothing to bring about His victory: "Be still, and know that I am God" (verse 10a). All the people need to do is to trust Him (verse 2a).

The Messiah will be exalted throughout the entire earth (verse 10b). (See Isaiah 60:3; Zechariah 14:16-17; Revelation 21:24-26.) His rule will be universal. (See Psalm 47:7-8.)

Twice in Psalm 46 these words appear: "The LORD of hosts is with us; the God of Jacob is our refuge. Selah" (verses 7, 11). These words evoke the promise of the first verse: "God is our refuge and strength, a very present help in trouble." During the millennial era, when the Messiah is ruling from Jerusalem, there will be no need to fear. The presence of the Lord renders all threats meaningless.

Psalm 47

The Zion theology/Davidic covenant theme continues into Psalm 47. The rule of the "great King" (verse 2), emanating geographically from "the city of God" (Psalm 46:4), Jerusalem, extends "over all the earth" (verse 2). "The peoples" and "the nations" are subdued (verse 3). "God is the King of all the earth" (verse 7). He reigns "over the nations [*goyim*, or "Gentiles"]" (verse 8).

These were encouraging words for people whose land had been ravaged by Babylon and whose holy city had been reduced to rubble. Things would not always be as they were. A brighter day was coming. They may have labored in exile and under the heel of a foreign oppressor, but in the midst of this traumatic experience, they had hope of deliverance. The tables would be turned. Even those who now had them in captivity would one day acknowledge Israel's God as the "great King over all the earth" (verse 2).

In view of the fact that it was the Lord who was the universal King, the appropriate response was for all the peoples, including Gentiles, to clap their hands and "shout to God with the voice of triumph!" (verse 1).

Those who worshiped false gods had held the people of Israel captive, but Israel's God, the Lord Most High (*Yahweh Elyon*) was "awesome." "He is a great King over all the earth" (verse 2). He was King even over those who destroyed the holy city and took the people of Israel captive.

The people of Israel, even in captivity, could take comfort in the fact that their God would "subdue the peoples under" them; He would subdue the nations under their feet (verse 3).

It may be that the Babylonians had forcibly removed God's people from the land promised to their fathers, but it was certain that the great King would choose Israel's inheritance (verse 4a). A Gentile king would not make this choice. God had promised the land to Abraham, Isaac, and Jacob. In this case, Jacob represented all of the fathers and their descendants. God made this promise because He loved "Jacob," the people of Israel. The land promised to Israel was "the proud possession of Jacob's descendants" (verse 4, NLT).

When the certainty of the fulfillment of God's promise was considered (verse 5), it was appropriate to sing praises to God, the King of all the earth (verses 6-7). Those with understanding knew that the captivity of Israel was temporary (verse 7b); when God went up "with a shout" and with "the sound of a trumpet" (verses 5), the end of captivity was near and the fulfillment of His promise was at hand.

Even as Israel labored in captivity, God was sitting on His holy throne, reigning over the nations (verse 8). Even their captivity was according to His divine plan. (See comments on Psalm 44:9-26.)

"The people" in this psalm represented the Gentiles. The day was coming when the Gentile princes would gather with "the people of the God of Abraham" (verse 9a). Submission to the Lord would be universal, for "the shields of the earth belong to" Him (verse 9b). (See Isaiah 60:3; Zechariah 14:16-17; Revelation 21:24-26.) His universal exaltation continued the theme from Psalm 46. (Compare Psalm 46:10 with Psalm 47:9c.)[48]

Psalm 47 continues and contributes to the messianic theme of the Psalter. The "King over all the earth" (verse 2b) is identified in Psalm 2 as the Messiah. (See Psalm 2:2-9.)

Psalm 48

Psalm 48 makes a rich contribution to the Zion theology/Davidic covenant theme of the Psalter. The psalm begins with the theme of praise due to the Lord, connecting Psalm 48 with Psalm 47. (Compare Psalm 47:6-7 with Psalm 48:1a.)

Praise is to begin in "the city of our God," Jerusalem, in "His holy mountain," Mount Zion (verse 1). (Compare with Psalm 46:4.)

Jerusalem, sitting on Mount Zion, is "beautiful in elevation, the joy of the whole earth" (verse 2). The idea that Mount Zion sits "on the sides of the north" indicates, for theological purposes, that it enjoys the highest elevation on earth.[49]

God dwells in Jerusalem's "palaces" (verse 3a). The word translated "palaces" (*'armown*) includes within its range of meaning "citadel" and "fortress." In view of the final phrase in verse 3—"He is known as her refuge"—it is probably best to understand it here in the sense of "fortress." Because of God's presence in Jerusalem, He Himself is her refuge or fortress. (Compare with Psalm 46:1, 7, 11.)

The assembly of the kings (verse 4) reflected the rebellion of the nations in Psalm 2:1-3. But as the kings of the earth beheld Jerusalem, they marveled, were troubled, and "hastened away" (verse 5). The invulnerability of Jerusalem, because of God's presence, caused fear to take "hold of them there, and pain, as of a woman in birth pangs" (verse 6). Just as the anointed One would break the rebellious nations "with a rod of iron" and "dash them to pieces like a potter's vessel" (Psalm 2:9), so He could "break the ships of Tarshish with an east wind" (verse 7). (See Ezekiel 27:25-26.) The ships may have had a majestic appearance as they sailed the sea, but the east wind could break them to pieces.

To see the city of Jerusalem was to realize that all one had heard about it was true (verse 8a). It was the city of the Lord of hosts, the city of our God (verse 8b). God would establish this city forever (verse 8c). Regardless of the efforts of those who rebelled against God, Jerusalem would endure.

The lovingkindness—or loyal love (*chesed*)—of God was the meditation of those in His Temple (verse 9). The Temple sat on Mount Zion.

The phrase translated "according to Your name, O God" (verse 10a) means something like "as your name deserves, O God" (NLT). Reflecting the Hebrew theology of name, the name of God represents God Himself.[50] God deserves to be praised to the ends of the earth (verse 10b). The "right hand" of God represents His universal rule, which is characterized by righteousness (verse 10c).

The Lord's judgments were cause for rejoicing on Mount Zion among the "daughters of Judah" (verse 11). The Lord's judgments were "the ways in which he [established] his kingdom by bringing defeat and subjugation to the opposing forces."[51] (See, e.g., Exodus 7:4.)

Zion theology was richly illustrated in the invitation to "walk about Zion, and go all around her. Count her towers; mark well her bulwarks; consider her palaces; that you may tell it to the generation following" (verses 12-13). Not only were the people to be thoroughly acquainted with the city, they were to pass on to their descendants their intimate knowledge of the city and its central place in their faith.

The KJV translates verse 14 more literally than some more recent translations: "For this God is our God for ever and ever: he will be our guide even unto death." The God who dwelt in Jerusalem (see verses 1-3) was the eternal God. He was God not only during one's life span on earth, but "to death." Death was not the end, however. Psalm 48:14 was linked with the promise of the resurrection found in Psalm 49:15.

Psalm 48 continues the messianic theme of the Psalter; the great King who dwells on Mount Zion is the anointed One of Psalm 2:2-6.

Psalm 49

Psalm 49 is classified as a wisdom psalm in that it communicates wisdom (verse 3a) and understanding (verse 3b) by means of a proverb (verse 4a) and a "dark saying" ["riddle," NIV] (verse 4b). (Compare Proverbs 1:5-7.) It is addressed not just to the Jewish community but to "all peoples," "all inhabitants of the world" (verse 1), regardless of economic or social status (verse 2).

The connection between Psalm 49 and Psalm 48 may be seen in that Psalm 48 closes with the promise that God is "our guide even to death" (Psalm 48:14), and Psalm 49 declares, "But God will redeem my soul from the power of the grave, for He shall receive me" (Psalm 49:15). Psalm 49 points out that everyone dies—whether rich or poor, foolish or wise—and that the only hope is in God. (See verses 5-20 and Hebrews 9:27.)

Although Psalm 49 is a wisdom psalm, its opening follows the prophetic model: "Hear this, all peoples; give ear, all inhabitants of the world" (verse 1).[52] (Compare with Micah 1:2.)

The psalm is addressed to all people, as indicated in verse 1, but verse 2 specifies that this includes everyone, regardless of social or economic status. What this psalm is about—the universality of death—pertains to everyone.

In verse 3, wisdom and understanding are virtual synonyms, as are the proverb and dark saying of verse 4. Understanding is the only way to avoid hopelessness in the face of death. (See verse 20.)

A person who has understanding has no reason to fear "in the days of evil," or in the day when death threatens (verse 5).

On the other hand, those who trust in money (verse 6) will find that money will not help them avoid death (verse 7). (See Mark 4:13-20; 10:17-27; I Timothy 6:11-19.) "No payment is ever enough" to ransom a life (verse 8, NIV). That is, no payment of money is ever enough. No one, regardless of his or her financial wealth, can buy eternal life and avoid death (verse 9).

Not only will money not enable a person to avoid death; neither will wisdom. Wise men die just as do fools (verse 10a). (See Psalm 39:4-6.) No matter who a person is or what kind of a person he is, when one dies he leaves his wealth to others (verse 10b).

The foolish think they will live forever (verse 11a). They indicate their belief in their immortality by naming lands after themselves (verse 11b). But regardless of the honor a man may enjoy in this life, he will not live forever (verse 12a). Like a beast, he will die (verse 12b).

The foolish are characterized by their belief that they are immortal; their foolish descendants agree (verse 13). But, regardless of what they think, the foolish die and, like sheep, are buried (verse 14a). In the resurrection, those who are upright will rule over those who are foolish (verse 14b). Whatever beauty the foolish may have possessed will "decay in the grave, far from their princely mansions" (verse 14c, NIV).

Money cannot redeem a life from death (verses 6-9), but God can: "But God will redeem my soul from the power of the grave, for He shall receive me" (verse 15). (See I Peter 1:18-19.)

There is no need for those who trust God to "be overawed when a man grows rich" (verse 16a, NIV) and "when the glory of his house is increased" (verse 16b), because whatever glory the rich may have in this life will not follow him in death (verse 17b). Material goods cannot be taken from this life into the next (verse 17a). (Compare with Job 1:21.)

The rich may "consider themselves fortunate" (verse 18a, NLT) while they are alive, and others will commend them for their success (verse 18b). But, like their ancestors, the rich will die (verse 19a). In death, they "shall never see light" (verse 19b). This is not a denial of the resurrection: It has already been pointed out that "the upright shall have dominion over" the foolish "in the morning," or in the resurrection (verse 14b). Rather, death for the foolish "is described . . . as a place of absolute darkness, where not a ray of light (hope) penetrates ever."[53]

Even though a man may be honored in this life, if he does not have understanding, his death will be as hopeless as the death of a beast (verse 20). In this psalm, understanding is the "key to life."[54] (See Psalm 119:1-4; Proverbs 4:5-7; 16:16.)

Psalm 49 advances the messianic theme of the Psalter with its focus on the hope of redemption (verses 7-8) and resurrection (verses 14-15). Money cannot redeem from death, but God can. The promise that the upright will have dominion over the foolish in the resurrection (verse 14) looks ahead to the day when the upright will share with the Messiah His rule over all the earth. (See Daniel 7:18; I Corinthians 6:2; Revelation 2:26-27; 3:21; 20:4, 6.)

Psalm 50

This is the first of twelve psalms attributed to Asaph, son of Berechiah, a Levite and a chief musician of David. (See also Psalms 73-83.) Asaph was appointed by David as the chief minister before the ark of the covenant. (See I Chronicles 16:4-5.) On the day that David appointed Asaph, a cymbalist, and other musicians, he delivered to the musicians a psalm, a portion of which is included in the Book of Psalms as Psalm 105:1-15. (See I Chronicles 16:7-22.)

Psalm 50:1-15 was addressed to the people of Israel who participated in the covenant established at Sinai. Psalm 50:16-23 was addressed to the wicked, who had no part in this covenant.[55]

A connection with the Zion theology of previous psalms is seen in verse 2: "Out of Zion, the perfection of beauty, God will shine forth."[56] The Zion theology/Davidic covenant theme identifies Psalm 50 with the messianic theme of the entire Psalter. The final verse of the psalm—promising salvation to the person who praises God and "who orders his conduct aright" (verse 23)—connects the psalm with the one following, David's prayer of repentance "after he had gone in to Bathsheba" (Psalm 51, superscription).[57]

The distilled message of Psalm 50 was that God would accept the sacrifices of the Sinaitic covenant from those who offered them with thanksgiving (verse 14), trust (verse 15), and praise (verse 23), even though He did not need them. But He would not accept them from the wicked, who disregarded His commandments and participated in sin (verses 16-22).

The Lord called the earth (verse 1) and the heavens (verse 4) as witnesses as He judged His people. (Compare with Deuteronomy 32:1; I Chronicles 16:31; Isaiah 1:2; 44:23.) His call to the earth "extends far beyond Israel to the whole earth,"[58] "from the rising of the sun to its going down" (verse 1b). To call the earth indicates that He rules the earth; His rule is not limited to Israel.

Zion is identified as "the perfection of beauty" out of which "God will shine forth" (verse 2). As elsewhere in the Psalter, Zion is seen as the center of the earth, God's headquarters, so to speak.

When God comes, it will be to rebuke the wicked. (Compare verses 3 and 21.) In conjunction with His coming, "A fire shall devour before Him, and it shall be very tempestuous all around Him" (verse 3b). It seems that Paul drew on this imagery when he wrote, concerning the revelation of "the Lord Jesus . . . from heaven with His mighty angels" that it would be "in flaming fire taking vengeance on those who [did] not know God, and on those who [did] not obey the gospel of our Lord Jesus Christ" (II Thessalonians 1:7b-8). The conceptual connection between Psalm 50 and II Thessalonians 1 seems to continue:

> Our God shall come, and shall not keep silent; a fire shall devour before Him, and it shall be very tempestuous all around Him. He shall call to the heavens from above, and to the earth, that He may judge His people: "Gather My saints together to Me." (Psalm 50:3-5)

> . . . to give you who are troubled rest with us when the Lord Jesus is revealed from heaven with His mighty angels, in flaming fire taking vengeance on those who do not know God, and on those who do not obey the gospel of our Lord Jesus Christ. These shall be punished with everlasting destruction from the presence of the Lord and from the glory of His power, when He comes, in that Day, to be glorified in His saints. . . . (II Thessalonians 1:7-10a)

If indeed Psalm 50 was in Paul's mind as he wrote to the church of the Thessalonians, the messianic shape of the Psalter was further demonstrated, for the God who will come and devour the wicked is none other than the Messiah, the Lord Jesus Christ.

In its immediate context, the saints who were to be gathered to the Lord were "those who have made a covenant" with Him "by sacrifice" (verse 5). The sacrifice by which the Mosaic covenant was established is described in Exodus 24:4-8.

To call on the heavens and the earth to be involved in some way as God judged His people was to recognize that the entire created realm testified to the Lord as a righteous Judge (verse 6). (Compare Psalm 19:1; 89:37; 97:6; Acts 14:17; Romans 1:20.)

It may be that verse 7 was not so much a rebuke, as the translation often indicates (i.e., "I will testify against you"), but a simple testimony to the people of Israel. The Septuagint translates the phrase, "I will testify to thee." The Hebrew text can be translated either way. But in view of the statement, "I will not rebuke you for your sacrifices" (verse 8a), it may be best to render the phrase as does the Septuagint.

Although God would not rebuke the people of Israel for the sacrifices they offered in conjunction with the Mosaic covenant (verse 8), He wanted them to know that He did not need their sacrifices, for every creature belonged to Him (verses 9-11). They should not think, as the heathen did, that He needed the sacrifices to eat (verses 12-13).[59]

God wanted the Israelites to know that He did not need the animal sacrifices, but He did value thanksgiving (verse 14). He wanted them to trust Him and to demonstrate their trust by calling on Him when they were in trouble (verse 15a). He promised to deliver those who called on Him so that they could glorify Him (verse 15b).

To the wicked, God said, "What right have you to declare My statutes, or take My covenant in your mouth?" (verse 16). Adherence to the sacrificial system would be of no help to them, because they hated and rejected God's instruction (verse 17). They participated in thievery and adultery (verse 18).

They spoke evil, deceitful words (verse 19), even against their own brothers (verse 20).

Because God had not moved quickly to judge these sinners, they thought He never would (verse 21). Many rebels against God think that the lack of immediate judgment indicates that judgment will never come. Actually, when God delays judgment, it is because He is hoping for repentance. (See Romans 2:4.)

If these rebels did not change, they would be torn in pieces. No one would be able to deliver them (verse 22). In order for a person to be saved, he must offer praise and live right (verse 23). The writer of Hebrews may have had this text in mind when he wrote,

> Therefore by Him let us continually offer the sacrifice of praise to God, that is, the fruit of our lips, giving thanks to His name. But do not forget to do good and to share, for with such sacrifices God is well pleased. Obey those who rule over you, and be submissive, for they watch out for your souls, as those who must give account. Let them do so with joy and not with grief, for that would be unprofitable for you. (Hebrews 13:15-17)

Here we have all of the elements of Psalm 50:23. We are to offer sacrifices of praise. We are to live right. If we do these things, we will be saved; that is, those who rule over us will be able to give a joyous, profitable account.[60] If indeed Hebrews is influenced by Psalm 50:23, the messianic theme of the Psalter is further demonstrated, for the central message of Hebrews has to do with the superiority of the New Covenant over the Old Covenant, seen most vividly in the superiority of Jesus Christ over the angels who were involved in the giving of the law of Moses (Hebrews 1-2), over Moses himself (Hebrews 3:1-6), and over the Aaronic priesthood (Hebrews 4:14-16; 5; 6:19-20; 7; 8:1-6).

Psalm 51

This psalm is identified as a "Psalm of David when Nathan the prophet went to him, after he had gone in to Bathsheba" (superscription). (See II Samuel 11; 12:1-15.) The psalm provides the detail of David's confession, which the account in II Samuel 12:13 limits to the words, "I have sinned against the LORD." Following David's confession, Nathan said to him, "The LORD also has put away your sin; you shall not die. However, because by this deed you have given great occasion to the enemies of the LORD to blaspheme, the child also who is born to you shall surely die" (II Samuel 12:13b-14). Although the eternal consequences of David's sin were removed, temporal consequences remained. The death of the son born of the adultery committed by David and Bathsheba would demonstrate to the "enemies of the LORD" the severe consequences of sin.

Psalm 51 contributes to and advances the messianic theme of the Psalter by its connection with Psalm 50 (compare verses 16-17 with Psalm 50:9-13, verse 15 with Psalm 50:23, and verse 18 with Psalm 50:2) and by David's plea for a clean heart, a plea that looks ahead to the New Covenant. (Compare verse 10 with Deuteronomy 30:6; Jeremiah 31:31-34; Ezekiel 36:24-27.) Paul quoted from the psalm to demonstrate God's New Covenant faithfulness in the face of unbelief. (Compare verse 4 with Romans 3:4.)

David cried out for mercy, taking full responsibility for his sin (verse 1a). He appealed to God's "lovingkindness" (*chesed,* "loyal love") and to the "multitude" of His "tender mercies" (verse 1b). His prayer was that his transgressions might be blotted out (verse 1c). Even in conjunction with the giving of the law to Moses, the Lord assured Moses that the forgiveness of iniquity and transgression was based upon His mercy. (See Exodus 34:6-7.) There was never an idea, even during the law's tenure, that forgiveness was purchased by the blood of animals. (See Acts 13:39; Romans 3:20, 28; Hebrews 10:1-4.)

There is no need to attempt to distinguish between "transgressions" (*pesha‘* [verses 1, 3]), "iniquity" (*‘avon* [verse 2]), and "sin" (*hata'ah* [verse 2]). "The variety of words for sin is for poetic reasons, as they express the seriousness of sin."[61]

David prayed to be washed thoroughly from his iniquity and cleansed from his sin (verse 2). He acknowledged his transgressions; he was unable to escape from the fact of his sin (verse 3).

David declared that his sin was against God only (verse 4a). This may sound strange, in view of the indication elsewhere that it is possible to sin against another human. (See, e.g., Matthew 18:15.) But "Herbert Haag argues persuasively that sin in the biblical sense is only against God. We may hurt our fellowman, but we sin against God."[62] Ultimately, although we may wound another person and in that sense sin against that person, it is God who defines right and wrong, determining the definition of sin. Thus, at the end, sin is against God.

The evil David had done in God's sight meant that when God spoke words of judgment, He would be just and blameless (verse 4b). David's sin justified the pronouncement of judgment upon him.

After a discussion of universal sinfulness, which included both Jews and Gentiles, Paul wrote, "For what if some [Jews] did not believe? Will their unbelief make the faithfulness of God without effect? Certainly not! Indeed, let God be true but every man a liar" (Romans 3:3-4a). At this point, Paul quoted the Septuagint translation of Psalm 51:4b: "As it is written: *'That You may be justified in Your words, and may overcome when You are judged'* "(Romans 3b). Contextually, the point seems to be that the unbelief of the Jewish people would not cause God to renege on the promised New Covenant. He would be justified in judging those who rejected Him. If this is the point, a New Covenant link is provided with Psalm 51.

Verse 5 is often appealed to as evidence of the universal sinfulness of humankind: "Behold, I was brought forth in iniquity, and in sin my mother conceived me." The universal impact of the Fall is declared in many texts. (See, e.g., Romans 5:12-21; Ephesians 2:1-3.) But that may not be the point here. Elsewhere, David expressed quite a different sentiment: "For You formed my inward parts; You covered me in my mother's womb. I will praise You, for I am fearfully and wonderfully made; marvelous are Your works, and that my soul knows very well" (Psalm 139:13-14 [see also verses 15-16]). It does not seem in harmony with the general teaching of Scripture to view conception or childbirth as sinful. Children are the heritage of the Lord (Psalm 127:3). In order to enter the kingdom of heaven, one must become like a little child (Matthew 18:3). Jesus seems to have disavowed the claim of the Pharisees that it was possible to sin in the womb (John 9:2-3).

David may have referred here to an event in his ancestry that, according to the law of Moses, disqualified him for entry into the congregation of the Lord. David was precisely the tenth generation from the incestuous relationship between Judah and his daughter-in-law Tamar. (See Genesis 38; Ruth 4:17-22.) The law declared that one "of illegitimate birth shall not enter the assembly of the LORD; even to the tenth generation none of his descendants shall enter the assembly of the LORD" (Deuteronomy 23:2). This ban was "probably restricted to the religious community. Most likely this law did not exclude one from residence in areas where Israel was to live but rather from the benefits of full-fledged citizenship and most particularly (and maybe only) from participation in religious rites in the homes and at the tabernacle and later at the temple."[63]

It may seem strange to think that God chose as king one whose genealogy was tarnished in this way. It may be that this was intended to demonstrate God's interest in genuine faith rather than in a relationship determined by rituals. As seen in this psalm, David was certainly one who grasped the significance of the inner man. He recognized that relationship with God was not determined by the rituals of the law (see verse 16) but by the condition of one's heart (see verses 6, 10, 17).

David acknowledged that God was concerned with the inner man. He desired "truth in the inward parts" (verse 6a). But David also recognized that the only way this desire could become reality was for God to make one to know wisdom "in the hidden part" (verse 6b).

David prayed for cleansing from his sin in words that reflected the rituals of the law, but he used the words metaphorically: "Purge me with hyssop, and I shall be clean; wash me, and I shall be whiter than snow" (verse 7). David did not think hyssop, a small shrub, could cleanse him from sin. (See I Kings 4:33.) Hyssop was used as a kind of application device for the sprinkling of blood and water for ritual purification under the law. (See Leviticus 14:1-7; Numbers 19:1-19.)

It is significant that David would ask God to purge him with hyssop, for it was the duty of the priests to use hyssop in ritual purification. Thus, David asked God to be his priest by performing this priestly function.[64] This contributed to the messianic theme of the Psalter by anticipating a priestly Messiah. (See Hebrews 5:1-10:18.) David knew that when God cleansed him, he would be "whiter than snow."

Cleansing from sin resulted in the restoration of joy and gladness (verse 8a). David used metaphor to describe the consequences of his sin as having his bones broken by God (verse 8b). (Compare with Psalm 35:9-10.) But these "broken bones" would "rejoice." That is, they would be fully healed. They would be strong again.

Rather than casting about for external causes for his sin, David recognized the problem was internal; it was, so to speak, a heart problem. He needed a clean heart and "a steadfast spirit" (verse 10). These blessings could come only from God.

Although David had sinned grievously, he valued the presence of God—the Holy Spirit—more than sin's pleasure (verse 11). In the poetry of verse 11, the Holy Spirit was identified as the presence of God.

David understood the depth of his transgression, but he prayed for full restoration of the joy of salvation (verse 12a). He was not deceived to think that he could avoid sin and do better in the future by sheer willpower; he must be upheld by the "generous Spirit" of God (verse 12b).

David not only wanted to be forgiven and restored to fellowship with God; he also committed to teach God's ways to other sinners so that they too would be converted (verse 13).

In that he ordered the innocent Uriah's death (see II Samuel 11:14-25), David carried the "guilt of bloodshed" (verse 14a). David understood that deliverance from guilt resulted in the ability to sing of God's righteousness (verse 14b). When guilt was removed, the proper response was to praise the Lord (verse 15). (Compare verse 15 with Psalm 50:23.)

David's keen insight into New Covenant realities may be seen in his awareness that God did not desire animal sacrifices or delight in burnt offerings (verse 16). The kinds of sacrifices God desired were brokenness and contriteness (verse 17). (See Micah 6:8.) Rather than being concerned with external rituals, God was concerned with internal character.

The final two verses of Psalm 51 were apparently added to the psalm in the final composition of the Psalter during the Exile.[65] The verses were written when the walls of Jerusalem needed to be rebuilt: "Do good in Your good pleasure to Zion; build the walls of Jerusalem" (verse 18). The walls were not broken down during David's day, but Zedekiah's. (See II Kings 25:8-10.) Verses 18-19 offered hope for the restoration of the exiled people of Israel to their homeland. God's "good pleasure" would be done in Zion when the walls of Jerusalem were built. As in previous psalms, Zion theology prevailed.[66]

Because the rebuilding of Jerusalem and of the Temple would be at God's behest, He would be pleased with the "sacrifices of righteousness," the animal sacrifices offered there (verse 19).

The final two verses of the psalm should not be thought to negate David's previous emphasis on God's disinterest in animal sacrifices. (See verses 16-17.) God would be interested in these sacrifices only as they reflected "a broken and a contrite heart" (verse 17). The portion of the psalm written by David looked ahead to a day when animal sacrifices for sin would end altogether; the verses added in the inspired final composition looked to the more immediate future featuring the second Temple and the restoration of the sacrificial system. Jeremiah prophesied that the Babylonian captivity would last only seventy years (Jeremiah 25:11-12). The people of Israel and Judah would return from their captivity. (See Jeremiah 30-31.) The city of Jerusalem would be rebuilt (Daniel 9:25). This reconstruction project would include the sanctuary, or the Temple (Daniel 9:26). The rebuilding of the walls of Jerusalem was the focus of the Book of Nehemiah; the rebuilding of the Temple was the focus of the Book of Ezra.

Psalm 52

The superscription identifies this psalm as a "contemplation of David when Doeg the Edomite went and told Saul, and said to him, 'David has gone to the house of Ahimelech.' " In view of the occasion for the writing of this psalm, it would be appropriate to review the background of the event in I Samuel.

Having been warned by his friend Jonathan, Saul's son, of Saul's intent to kill him (see I Samuel 20), David went to Nob, where it seems the Tabernacle had been located after being returned to Israel following the destruction of Shiloh, the Tabernacle's first location.[67] When Ahimelech the priest met David, he was afraid and asked, "Why are you alone, and no one is with you?" (I Samuel 21:1). David answered, "The king has ordered me on some business, and said to me, 'Do not let anyone know anything about the business on which I send you, or what I have commanded you' " (I Samuel 21:2). David had sent his young men elsewhere (I Samuel 21:2b).

David then asked Ahimelech for bread (I Samuel 21:3). The priest answered, "There is no common bread on hand; but there is holy bread, if the young men have at least kept themselves from women" (I Samuel 21:4). David assured Ahimelech that he and his young men had been kept from women for about three days (I Samuel 21:5). Ahimelech "gave him holy bread; for there was no bread there but the showbread which had been taken from before the LORD" (I Samuel 21:6a).

The text points out that there was "a certain man of the servants of Saul . . . there that day, detained before the LORD. And his name was Doeg, an Edomite, the chief of the herdsmen who belonged to Saul" (I Samuel 21:7).

After obtaining the showbread, David took Goliath's sword from its place of safekeeping and fled to Achish, the king of Gath. (See I Samuel 21:8-10.)

Later, Doeg informed Saul of what had happened at Nob. (See I Samuel 22:9-10.) Saul sent for Ahimelech and all of the priests at Nob (I Samuel 22:11) and asked Ahimelech, "Why have you conspired against me, you and the son of Jesse, in that you have given him bread and a sword, and have inquired of God for him, that he should rise against me, to lie in wait, as it is this day?" (I Samuel 22:13).

Ahimelech protested his innocence: "And who among all your servants is as faithful as David, who is the king's son-in-law, who goes at your bidding, and is honorable in your house? Did I then begin to inquire of God for him? Far be it from me! Let not the king impute anything to his servant, or to any in the house of my father. For your servant knew nothing of all this, little or much" (I Samuel 22:14-15).

Saul was unmoved: "You shall surely die, Ahimelech, you and all your father's house!" (I Samuel 22:16). The king ordered his guards to kill the priests, but they "would not lift their hands to strike the priests of the LORD" (I Samuel 22:17). So Saul said to Doeg, "You turn and kill the priests!" (I Samuel 22:18a). Doeg obeyed, slaughtering eighty-five priests (I Samuel 22:18). He then went to Nob and, with a sword, killed men, women, children, nursing infants, oxen, donkeys, and sheep (I Samuel 22:19). One of Ahimelech's sons, Abiathar, escaped and fled to David to inform him about these events (I Samuel 22:20-21). David said, "I knew that day, when Doeg the Edomite was there, that he would surely tell Saul. I have caused the death of all the persons of your father's house" (I Samuel 22:22).

David wrote Psalm 52 upon hearing that Doeg had reported to Saul the events at Nob. Doeg was described as a mighty man who boasted in evil (verse 1), as one whose "tongue [devised] destruction, like a sharp razor, working deceitfully" (verse 2). He was one who loved evil more than good and lying rather than righteousness (verse 3). Doeg was a man of deceit who loved "devouring words" (verse 4).

God would destroy Doeg, removing him from his home and taking his life (verse 5). Doeg's destruction would be seen by the righteous, who would fear God and laugh at Doeg, saying, "Here is the man who did not make God his strength, but trusted in the abundance of his riches, and strengthened himself in his wickedness" (verse 7).

In spite of Doeg's treachery, David wrote, "But I am like a green olive tree in the house of God; I trust in the mercy of God forever and ever. I will praise You forever, because You have done it; and in the presence of Your saints I will wait on Your name, for it is good" (verses 8-9). When David expressed his trust in the mercy of God "forever and ever," it anticipated the establishment of the Davidic covenant, wherein God promised, "But My mercy shall not depart from him [David's descendant], as I took it from Saul, whom I removed from before you. And your house and your kingdom shall be established forever before you. Your throne shall be established forever" (II Samuel 7:15-16).

Psalm 52 advances the messianic theme of the Psalter by portraying Doeg as one who sought to frustrate God's messianic purpose through David. If Saul had been successful in killing David—and Doeg's treachery was intended to contribute to that end—the Davidic covenant with its messianic promise would have been circumvented. Doeg was unsuccessful. Even though he boasted in evil, "The goodness of God [endured] continually" (verse 1b). God's goodness overwhelmed Doeg's evil. In the end, Doeg was dead, but David was like "a green olive tree in the house of God" (verse 8).

When Jesus was questioned by the Pharisees because His disciples plucked heads of grain while passing through grainfields on the Sabbath, He referred to David's visit to Nob and how David "ate the showbread, which is not lawful to eat except for the priests, and also gave some to those who were with him" (Mark 2:26). Jesus' point was that the preservation of human life was higher on the biblical hierarchy of values than the rituals of the law of Moses. (See Mark 2:27.) It may also be seen in this use of the account by Jesus that what God intended to accomplish through the Davidic covenant was more important than the law of Moses. That is, the preservation of David's life and thus of the messianic promise outweighed the law's rituals.

Sailhamer sees further evidence of the psalm's messianic theme:

> The note about Doeg is probably intended to bring David's words into the larger messianic picture of the fall of the house of Edom at the hands of the house of David (cf. Nu 24:18). It had long been an important part of the messianic hope of Israel that the Messiah's coming would be marked by the destruction of Israel's enemies, principally, the Edomites (e.g., Am 9:12; Ob 18). Edom was particularly singled out, not because they were excessively evil, but for what was in fact a literary reason: "Edom," similar to the Hebrew word for humankind ("Adam"), was used in order to form a wordplay. Hence, in speaking of the defeat of Edom (v.5), the psalmist naturally calls to mind God's judgment of all humanity. It is only natural, then, that the next psalm focuses on God's universal judgment of humankind.[68]

It is not unusual for the Edomites, the Gentile descendants of Esau, to serve the literary purpose of representing all of the descendants of Adam. In Amos 9:11-12, "Edom" is rendered "mankind" by the Septuagint. This translation is authenticated by James in Acts 15:16-17. In Obadiah 18, the coming of the Messiah (verse 17) is described in terms of the victory of the house of Jacob (and thus of the Davidic lineage) over the house of Esau (i.e., Edom [verse 1]).

Psalm 53

Psalm 53 is very much like Psalm 14.[69] There are, however, significant differences between the two psalms. One difference is that Psalm 14 uses not only "God" (*Elohim*) to identify Israel's God, but it also uses "LORD" (*Yahweh*). (See Psalm 14:2, 4, 6, 7.) Psalm 53 uses *Yahweh* not at all. It consistently uses *Elohim* not only where *Elohim* is used in Psalm 14, but *Elohim* is also used where *Yahweh* is used in Psalm 14.

A difference such as this is apparently intentional. In the general context of Psalm 14, the focus is on Israel's covenant relationship with *Yahweh*. In the immediate context of Psalm 53 (i.e., Psalm 52 and Psalm 54), the focus is on God's judgment of Gentiles. It is significant that Paul, in a series of quotes from the Old Testament to demonstrate the sinfulness of the Jewish people, quoted from the Septuagint version of Psalm 14:3, not from Psalm 53:3. (See Romans 3:12.)[70]

Psalm 53 is intentionally placed in the Psalter immediately after Psalm 52 to demonstrate the judgment of God upon the Gentile world. In order for it to serve its literary purpose, the psalm was amended by inspiration to identify God exclusively as *Elohim* rather than *Yahweh*, God's covenant name by which He revealed Himself to Moses in conjunction with the deliverance of the people of Israel from Egypt. (See Exodus 3:14-15; 6:1-7.) Together with this development, other changes were made to effect a change of the psalm's focus. These changes can be seen as follows:

> There they are in great fear, for God is with the generation of the righteous. You shame the counsel of the poor, but the LORD is his refuge. (Psalm 14:5-6)

> There they are in great fear where no fear was, for God has scattered the bones of him who encamps against you; you have put them to shame, because God has despised them. (Psalm 53:5)

In Psalm 14, Gentiles were in great fear because God was with Israel (e.g., the righteous). These Gentiles may have sought to "frustrate the plans" (NIV) of the poor (e.g., Israel), but *Yahweh* was the refuge of the poor. Psalm 53 revealed a subtle but significant difference: A new fear had gripped the hearts of the Gentiles. It was not just because God was on the side of Israel, but because God was aggressive in destroying the Gentiles. He scattered the bones of those who sought to destroy Israel. Whereas in Psalm 14 the Gentiles shamed Israel, in Psalm 53 Israel shamed the Gentiles. Indeed, God despised them.

In both psalms Israel and the Gentiles appear. But in Psalm 14 the focus is on God's covenant with Israel; in Psalm 53 the focus is on God's universal authority over the entire world of unbelievers.

Both psalms conclude with a nearly identical focus on Zion theology:

> Oh, that the salvation of Israel would come out of Zion! When the LORD brings back the captivity of His people, let Jacob rejoice and Israel be glad. (Psalm 14:7)

> Oh, that the salvation of Israel would come out of Zion! When God brings back the captivity of His people, let Jacob rejoice and Israel be glad. (Psalm 53:6)

The only difference between these two verses is that Psalm 14 identifies God as *Yahweh* whereas Psalm 53 identifies Him as

Elohim. Thus, Psalm 14 focuses on the return of Israel from captivity from the perspective of the covenant God had with Israel. Psalm 53 focuses on the return from the perspective of God's universal authority over all peoples of the world, including those who had held Israel captive.[71]

Regardless of the perspective, salvation comes out of Zion. This ties Psalm 53 together with the messianic theme of the Psalter. Salvation (*yeshuʻat*) comes only when *Yeshuaʻ* arrives.

Psalm 54

Like Psalm 52, Psalm 54 reflects David's contemplation in response to a specific event when he was betrayed to Saul. In this case, the psalm is "a contemplation of David when the Ziphites went and said to Saul, 'Is David not hiding with us?'" (superscription). The details of the event are found in I Samuel 23. Another similar betrayal by the Ziphites is recorded in I Samuel 26.

As David fled from Saul's wrath, he "stayed in strongholds in the wilderness, and remained in the mountains in the Wilderness of Ziph" (I Samuel 23:14a). Saul attempted to locate David daily, but "God did not deliver him into his hand" (I Samuel 23:14b).

While David was in a forest in the Wilderness of Ziph (I Samuel 23:15), "Jonathan, Saul's son, arose and went to David in the woods and strengthened his hand in God" (I Samuel 23:16). Jonathan said to David, "Do not fear, for the hand of Saul my father shall not find you. You shall be king over Israel, and I shall be next to you. Even my father Saul knows that" (I Samuel 23:17).

Jonathan and David "made a covenant before the LORD. And David stayed in the woods, and Jonathan went to his own house" (I Samuel 23:18).

At this point "the Ziphites came up to Saul at Gibeah, saying, 'Is David not hiding with us in strongholds in the woods, in the hill of Hachilah, which is on the south of Jeshimon? Now therefore, O king, come down according to all the desire of your soul to come down; and our part shall be to deliver him into the king's hand' " (I Samuel 23:19-20).

Saul answered, "Blessed are you of the LORD, for you have compassion on me. Please go and find out for sure, and see the place where his hideout is, and who has seen him there. For I am told he is very crafty. See therefore, and take knowledge of all the lurking places where he hides; and come back to me with certainty, and I will go with you. And it shall be, if he is in the land, that I will search for him throughout all the clans of Judah" (I Samuel 23:21-23).

When the Ziphites returned home, David and his men "were in the Wilderness of Maon, in the plain on the south of Jeshimon" (I Samuel 23:24). But when Saul and his men went to seek David, someone informed David. Therefore David "went down to the rock, and stayed in the Wilderness of Maon. And when Saul heard that, he pursued David in the Wilderness of Maon" (I Samuel 23:25). At one time during this episode, Saul and his men were quite close to David and his men: "Saul went on one side of the mountain, and David and his men on the other side of the mountain. So David made haste to get away from Saul, for Saul and his men were encircling David and his men to take them" (I Samuel 23:26).

At this point, "a messenger came to Saul, saying, 'Hurry and come, for the Philistines have invaded the land!' " (I Samuel 23:27). At this news, "Saul returned from pursuing David, and went against the Philistines" (I Samuel 23:28a). Because of David's deliverance, "they called that place the Rock of Escape" (I Samuel 23:28b).

With this background, we can understand David's prayer as recorded in Psalm 54. David prayed not only for salvation (i.e., deliverance) but also for vindication (verse 1). He was innocent in the conflict with Saul. Later, in another event of betrayal to Saul by the Ziphites, David and Abishai actually entered Saul's camp while Saul and his three thousand chosen military men slept. They were able to reach the very spot where Saul lay sleeping with his spear stuck into the ground by his head. Abishai knew he could kill Saul with his own spear by thrusting it through him right into the earth, and he asked David's permission to do so. But David said, "Do not destroy him; for who can stretch out his hand against the LORD's anointed, and be guiltless?" (I Samuel 26:9). David was willing to let the Lord deal with Saul: "As the LORD lives, the LORD shall strike him, or his day shall come to die, or he shall go out to battle and perish. The LORD forbid that I should stretch out my hand against the LORD's anointed" (I Samuel 26:10-11a).

David and Abishai did take the spear and jug of water so they could verify to Saul that they had been within striking distance without harming him (I Samuel 26:11-16).

After asking that God would hear him (verse 2), David said, "For strangers have risen up against me, and oppressors have sought after my life; they have not set God before them" (verse 3). These strangers were, of course, the Ziphites. Although they may have belonged to David's own tribe,[72] they were cast in the same role here as the Gentile Doeg in Psalm 52.[73] They may have been David's brethren, but they were treating him as an alien. And just as Psalm 53 was intentionally positioned to identify Doeg as a "fool [who had] said in his heart, 'There is no God,' " so was it positioned to identify the Ziphites as the same kind of fools. This denial of God was probably not intended to suggest that these "fools" were atheists; atheism was unknown in the world of that time.[74] It meant, rather, that they did not think they would ever answer to God for their actions.[75]

In spite of the efforts of Saul and the Ziphites, David confessed, "Behold, God is my helper; the Lord is with those who uphold my life" (Psalm 54:4). He knew he was on the right side in this conflict, and he knew that God would protect him. He knew his destiny; Samuel had anointed him as king. (See I Samuel 16.)

David would not take personal vengeance, but he knew God would repay his enemies for their evil (verse 5).

In the midst of his trial, David declared his intention to "freely sacrifice" to the Lord and to praise His good name (verse 6).

Even before his deliverance was fully accomplished, David testified that God had delivered him "out of all trouble" and that his eye had "seen its desire upon [his] enemies" (verse 7).

Psalm 54 advances the messianic theme of the Psalter in much the same way this theme is advanced by Psalm 52. It refers to yet another attempt—somewhat like the attempts of Absalom and Doeg—to thwart God's messianic purpose through David. In the case of Absalom, the attempt came from within David's family. In the case of Doeg, it came from a Gentile. In the case of the Ziphites, it came from those of David's tribe who were treating him like an alien.[76] But the origin of the threat did not matter; none would succeed.

Psalm 55

Psalm 55 is a lament psalm, but the occasion is not identified. It has been suggested that the psalm reflects David's disappointment with his son Absalom, with his former counselor Ahithophel, who played the traitor in abandoning David for Absalom, or with Saul.[77]

In view of the messianic context provided this psalm by the entire Psalter, it would be possible to see in the psalm references to the betrayal of Christ by Judas. (See, e.g., verses 12-14, 20-21, 23.) VanGemeren points out that "some have seen in the psalmist's experience a reflection of that of our Lord as he was betrayed by Judas. This appears to be an ancient tradition, as a MS of Jerome's Latin Version has the title 'The voice of Christ against the chiefs of the Jews and the traitor Judas.' "[78] It is VanGemeren's view that Psalm 55, like the clearly messianic Psalm 22, expresses "the anguish of the human soul in which our Lord Jesus shared (Heb 2:17-18)."[79]

The editors of *The Nelson Study Bible* hold that the psalm "speaks prophetically of the experience of the Savior Jesus."[80]

C. H. Spurgeon was of the opinion that as it relates to David's life, the psalm has to do with his betrayal by Ahithophel, but that in a spiritual sense it also presents the Messiah's betrayal by Judas.

> It would be idle to fix a time, and find an occasion for this Psalm with any dogmatism. It reads like a song of the time of Absalom and Ahithophel. It was after David had enjoyed peaceful worship (Psalm 55:14), when he was or had just been a dweller in a city (Psalm 55:9-11), and when he remembered his former roamings in the wilderness. Altogether it seems to us to relate to that mournful era when the King was betrayed by his trusted counsellor. The spiritual eye ever and anon sees the Son of David and Judas, and the chief priests appearing and disappearing upon the glowing canvas of the Psalm.[81]

Our perspective on the Psalter to this point is influenced by the use made of the psalms by Jesus, the apostles, and the first-century church. It is also influenced by David's claims concerning his writings and by immediate and larger contexts in which each psalm is found. When a psalm identifies the occasion with which it is connected, that is helpful. But we are not concerned only with the occasions for which the psalms were originally written; we are concerned with why each psalm is placed as it is within the Psalter. What are the connections between the psalm and the psalms before and after it? What common themes do we see? If the Psalter is to be viewed as advancing messianic hope, how does a specific psalm participate in this purpose?

In addition to the general messianic shape of the Psalter that may be seen beginning with Psalms 1 and 2 and that has been seen to develop consistently up to this point, our understanding of Psalm 55 is influenced by its immediate context. Psalm 52 has to do with David's betrayal to Saul by Doeg. Psalm 54 has to do with his betrayal to Saul by the Ziphites. Psalm 56 has to do with David being captured by the Philistines in Gath. Psalm 57 has to do with David fleeing from Saul into a cave. In the midst of these accounts of treachery, Psalm 53 indicates that all of those who seek to destroy David are fools. The larger picture of the Psalter is that they were fools because they sought to thwart God's messianic purpose through David.

In view of this immediate context, it seems clear that Psalm 55 is connected with a specific episode of betrayal in the life of David. But the psalm itself does not identify that specific betrayal, and it is not necessary to know the specifics in order to see the connection between Psalm 55 and its context. In this section of the Psalter, the focus is on failed efforts to frustrate God's messianic purpose through David. In other words, if David could be destroyed, God would be unable to fulfill His unconditional promise to David concerning the establishment of David's house, kingdom, and throne. (Compare II Samuel 7:16 with Luke 1:32-33.)

By virtue of inspiration, David's writings about his own experiences serve a much more significant purpose than as a kind of glorified personal diary. They take on a new and much larger purpose in that they point ahead to the coming of the Messiah. (See II Samuel 23:1-7.[82]) We will, therefore, read Psalm 55 as looking ahead to the betrayal of Christ by Judas. Although we cannot point to a specific quotation from this psalm by Jesus, there is some intertextual evidence that it should be read as a prayer of the Messiah, perhaps in Gethsemane. There is also some evidence that Peter read the psalm as having to do with Jesus' betrayal by Judas.

First, the intertextual evidence is seen by comparing Psalm 55:12 with Psalm 35:26:

> For it is not an enemy who reproaches me; then I could bear it. Nor is it one who hates me who has exalted himself against me. (Psalm 55:12)

> Let them be ashamed and brought to mutual confusion
> who rejoice at my hurt; let them be clothed with shame and
> dishonor who exalt themselves against me. (Psalm 35:26)

Psalm 35 is definitely a messianic psalm; Jesus Himself understood it to pertain to His experiences. Parallel terminology between Psalm 55 and Psalm 35 would suggest then, especially in view of the conceptual parallels between the two psalms, that Psalm 55 should also be read as having to do with the Messiah.

Second, Peter was apparently influenced by the Septuagint version of Psalm 55:

> Cast your burden on the LORD, and He shall sustain you;
> He shall never permit the righteous to be moved. But
> You, O God, shall bring them down to the pit of destruction; bloodthirsty and deceitful men shall not live out half
> their days; but I will trust in You. (Psalm 55:22-23)

> Casting all your care upon Him, for He cares for you. Be
> sober, be vigilant; because your adversary the devil walks
> about like a roaring lion, seeking whom he may devour.
> Resist him, steadfast in the faith, knowing that the same
> sufferings are experienced by your brotherhood in the
> world. (I Peter 5:7-9)

Although there is no precise quote here, Peter apparently drew from Psalm 55:22. The word translated "burden" by the Septuagint appears here as "care" (*merimna*). In addition to the clear parallels between "cast your burden on the LORD, and He shall sustain you" and "casting all your care upon Him, for He cares for you," there are conceptual parallels between the rest of the texts. David's "He shall never permit the righteous to be moved" became the admonition to resist the devil with the unspoken promise that those who resisted him would be sustained by the Lord. David's reference to bloodthirsty and deceitful men who would be brought "down to the pit of destruction" became connected in Peter's mind to those who did not resist the devil. David's "I will trust in You" became Peter's idea of being "steadfast in the faith."

Judas was one, of course, who did not "humble [himself] under the mighty hand of God" and who did not resist the devil. (See I Peter 5:6-9.) Indeed, his betrayal of Jesus involved Satan entering into him. (See Luke 22:3.)

It is speculation to suggest that Jesus may have prayed the prayer recorded in Psalm 55 in Gethsemane, but if He did pray these words, it seems the occasion would have followed Judas' departure from the Last Supper to accomplish his deed. The accounts of Jesus' prayers in Gethsemane indicate they were lengthy, and few of His words seem to be recorded. (See Matthew 26:36-46; Luke 22:39-46; John 18:1.) Matthew's account included Jesus saying to His disciples, "Watch and pray, lest you enter into temptation. The spirit indeed is willing, but the flesh is weak" (Matthew 26:41). The idea expressed in these words was the same as in Peter's admonition to be "sober, be vigilant; because your adversary the devil walks about like a roaring lion, seeking whom he may devour" (I Peter 5:8). Could it be that at some point during the Gethsemane episode Peter heard the words of Psalm 55:22 on Jesus' lips? Apparently Peter, James, and John were quite close to Jesus—closer than the other disciples—as He prayed. (Compare Matthew 26:36-39, 41 with Luke 22:40-41.) Although the disciples did sleep while Jesus prayed, they doubtless fell asleep at some point after His prayer began, not before it began. It seems that Peter, James, and John were close enough to hear the words that Jesus prayed in deep distress (Matthew 26:37) when, in agony, "He prayed more earnestly," to the extent that "His sweat became like great drops of blood falling down to the ground" (Luke 22:44).

In verse 1, the Messiah prayed that God would hear His prayer and that He would not hide Himself from His supplication. These words are similar, at least, to Jesus' prayer on the cross:

"My God, My God, why have You forsaken Me?" (Matthew 27:46b). These words are drawn directly from Psalm 22:1, indicating that Psalm 22 should be read as a prayer of the Messiah.

In verse 2, the Messiah again prayed to be heard by God and described Himself as "restless" and moaning "noisily." The writer of Hebrews described the Messiah as praying with "vehement cries and tears" (Hebrews 5:7).

The Messiah referred to those who were wicked oppressors, who brought trouble upon Him, and who, in their wrath, hated Him. They were his enemies (verse 3). As one manuscript of the Latin Vulgate indicated, this could have extended beyond Judas to include the religious rulers of the Jewish people in the first century.

The Messiah described His severe internal pain and the terror of death that had fallen upon Him, with its overwhelming fearfulness, trembling, and horror (verses 4-5). To minimize the emotional agony of Christ in the face of the death of the cross would be a great error. He was "sorrowful and deeply distressed" (Matthew 26:37) and said to His disciples, "My soul is exceedingly sorrowful, even to death. Stay here and watch with Me" (Matthew 26:38). Jesus yearned for the emotional support of His friends as He faced His betrayal and crucifixion. The depths of His emotional agony even led Him to pray to be spared from the experience that loomed before Him, if at all possible: "He went a little farther and fell on His face, and prayed, saying, 'O My Father, if it is possible, let this cup pass from Me; nevertheless, not as I will, but as You will' " (Matthew 26:39). Twice more after this prayer, Jesus prayed, "O My Father, if this cup cannot pass away from Me unless I drink it, Your will be done" (Matthew 26:42 [see verse 44]). Luke described Jesus as being in agony and praying so earnestly that "His sweat became like great drops of blood falling down to the ground" (Luke 22:44). He was so weakened that it was necessary for an angel from heaven to strengthen Him at this time. (See Luke 22:43.)

The writer of Hebrews twice described the depth of the emotional pain Jesus experienced in conjunction with His betrayal and death. First, He was described as offering up "prayers and supplications, with vehement cries and tears," with the implication that He wished to be saved from death. (See Hebrews 5:7.) Next, Jesus was described as enduring "the cross, despising the shame" (Hebrews 12:2). He "endured such hostility from sinners against Himself" (Hebrews 12:3).

In view of the description of Jesus' emotional agony in the New Testament, it does not seem inappropriate to view Psalm 55:4-5 as also describing that agony. This is especially the case in view of the descriptions of His agony in Psalm 22.

Although the Messiah prayed for deliverance from betrayal and death (verses 6-8), He submitted to the will of His Father. (See Matthew 26:39, 42.)

The Messiah prayed for the destruction of those who were responsible for the violence and strife in the city of Jerusalem (verse 9). They were responsible for the iniquity and trouble that seethed in the city that John would later describe as being the spiritual equivalent of Sodom and Egypt (verses 10-11). (See Revelation 11:8.)

The Messiah did not view the person who betrayed Him as an enemy, but as a friend with whom He had counseled and worshiped (verses 12-14). When Judas kissed Jesus, indicating the affection that had previously characterized their relationship (i.e., this would not have been the first time Judas had kissed Him), Jesus said, "Friend, why have you come?" (Matthew 26:50).

The Messiah prayed for the death of those who sought to destroy Him (verse 15). This was not because of His personal animosity toward them, but because of their destructive influence on the spiritual climate in first-century Israel. (See verses 9-11.) As long as they lived, they would continue to point the people away from faith in the Messiah. (See verse 19.) Since they did not fear God, they fell into the category of other fools who thought they would never answer to Him for their actions. (See comments on Psalm 53:1.)

Verses 16-18 harmonize with the descriptions of Jesus' prayers elsewhere in both testaments. (See Psalm 22; Hebrews 5:7.)

Jesus and His disciples were at peace with Judas, but he "put forth his hands against" them, breaking his covenant with them (verse 20). Though his words were "smoother than butter," "war was in his heart." "His words were softer than oil, yet they were drawn swords" (verse 21). It is significant that although Judas said to Jesus, "Greetings, Rabbi!" when he kissed Him, the great multitude that came with Judas were armed with swords and clubs. (See Matthew 26:47-49.)

Even in the midst of betrayal, those who cast their burden on the Lord would find that He would sustain them (verse 22a). The promise that the Lord would never permit the righteous to be moved (verse 22b) seems to be connected with the idea that the promised Messiah would never be thrust from His throne. (See comments on Psalm 13:4; 15:5; 16:8; 21:7.)

God would destroy those who rejected the Messiah (verse 23a). Those who sought His life "[should] not live out half their days" (verse 23b). This aptly described Judas's fate. But in the face of treachery and deceit, the Messiah placed His trust in the Lord (verse 23c). (Compare Hebrews 2:13 with Isaiah 8:17.)

Psalm 55 serves well as a prophecy of the Messiah's betrayal and of His trust in God regardless of the efforts of those who would destroy Him. But even if Psalm 55 should not be read as a prayer of the Messiah, it still advances the messianic theme of the Psalter by describing the failed efforts of those who would destroy David.

Psalm 56

The superscription of Psalm 56 suggests that the psalm was to be sung to the tune of *yownath 'elem rechokiym*. This phrase could be translated something like "a silent, distant dove." The NKJV translates the phrase, "The Silent Dove in Distant Lands." The NLT renders it, "Dove on Distant Oaks." To translate the phrase piques our interest in the tune; the title is provocative. Unfortunately, nothing is known about the tune.

The occasion for the writing of Psalm 56, according to the superscription, was when the Philistines captured David in Gath. This was the second psalm to focus on this event.[83] Like Psalms 52, 54, 57, and 59, Psalm 56 reflected a threat on David's life. Any threat on David's life was seen, in the context of the Psalter, as an attempt to thwart God's messianic purpose through David. All of these attempts failed.

When David left Nob on his flight from Saul (see comments on Psalm 52), he went to Achish, the king of Gath. (See I Samuel 21:10.) Apparently, David thought he would find refuge there. But when David heard the servants of Achish saying, "Is this not David the king of the land? Did they not sing of him to one another in dances, saying: 'Saul has slain his thousands, and David his ten thousands'?" (I Samuel 21:11), he feared for his life. (See I Samuel 21:12.) David must have expected anonymity among the people of Gath. When he realized he was recognized, he must have feared either that he would be captured and returned to Saul or that the people of Gath might make an attempt on his life. Anyone who could defeat someone who had slain "ten thousands" would certainly be held in awe.

In order to avoid the consequences of capture or death, David "changed his behavior before them, pretended madness in their hands, scratched on the doors of the gate, and let his saliva fall down on his beard" (I Samuel 21:13). When Achish saw this, he said to his servants, "Look, you see the man is insane. Why have you brought him to me? Have I need of madmen, that you have brought this fellow to play the madman in my presence? Shall this fellow come into my house?" (I Samuel 21:14-15). David's pretense enabled him to escape. (See I Samuel 22:1.)

The words of Psalm 56 described vividly the anguish of a man whose life was threatened. He called out to God for mercy in the face of constant danger (verse 1a). It seemed to David that he would be "swallowed up" by the ceaseless and oppressive fighting of his enemies (verse 1b).

David's enemies were many, and they hounded him all day (verse 2).

David admitted his fear (see also I Samuel 21:12), but he did not wallow in it. Instead, his fear served as a catalyst for him to trust in God (verse 3).[84] He knew that God was as good as His word; He would keep His promises (verse 4a). Since this was so, David could trust God rather than being consumed by fear (verse 4b). Since he knew God was faithful to His word, David knew that the effort to destroy him was futile (verse 4c). God had promised the throne of Israel to David (see I Samuel 16:1, 12-13), and that promise was yet unfulfilled. Therefore, although the circumstances were bleak, there was no reason to fear. God's word would come to pass.

There were those who, for their own reasons, wanted to prevent David from ascending to the throne of Israel. They twisted David's words, thinking only evil against him (verse 5). Those who shared the ambition to get David out of the picture gathered together, hid, carefully noted his movements, and lay in wait to kill him (verse 6).

David prayed that his enemies would experience the consequences of their sins (verse 7).

His enemies were not the only ones who noted David's movements; so did God (verse 8a). David prayed that God would put all his tears into His bottle; he knew God had made a record of them in His book (verse 8b). The practice of catching one's tears in a wineskin was a way to preserve a record of suffering.

Although David was in enemy territory, feeling threatened by the people of Gath, he knew that his enemies would turn back when he cried out to God (verse 9a). They might be against him, but God was for him (verse 9b). Paul echoed this confidence. (See Romans 8:31.)

In verses 10-11, David reiterated his confidence in the word of the Lord. He put his trust in God; why should he be afraid? Nothing that any man could do could thwart God's faithful promise.

Not only was David absolutely confident that God would keep His word; he intended to keep his promises to God (verse 12a). Apparently, one of the vows David had made was to praise God regardless of the circumstances (verse 12b).

Though David felt that his life was threatened, God delivered his soul from death and kept his feet from falling (verse 13a). God spared David so that he could walk before Him (verse 13b). In other words, David would live to see the fulfillment of the promise God had made to him.

Psalm 56 continues the messianic theme of the Psalter by demonstrating again that no threat could prevent God from keeping His promise to place David on Israel's throne. The fact that David ascended to the throne in the face of repeated attempts to stop his ascent demonstrates that the Messiah, David's greatest descendant, will also sit on David's throne, regardless of all attempts to prevent this from happening. (See Psalm 132:11; Acts 2:30.)

Psalm 57

Like Psalms 52, 54, 56, and 59, Psalm 57 was written by David in conjunction with a specific event during the time his life was threatened by Saul and others. In this case, the event was when David "fled from Saul into the cave" (superscription). The psalm is set to the tune of "Do Not Destroy" (*Al-tashcheth*). Four psalms are set to this tune (see also Psalms 58, 59, and 75), but nothing more is known about it.[85]

The details of the event that gave birth to this psalm may be seen in I Samuel 24. After God spared David from Saul following David's betrayal by the Ziphites (see I Samuel 23:13-29; Psalm 54), David went to the Wilderness of En Gedi. (See I Samuel 23:29; 24:1). This was located on the western shore near the center of the Dead Sea, some eighteen miles southeast of Hebron. En Gedi meant "spring of the young goat, and the specific site [was] a fresh water and hot springs oasis. The reference to En Gedi in Song of Solomon 1:14 [indicated] the romantic beauty of the site."[86]

David was not at the oasis, however, but in the Wilderness of En Gedi. Specifically, David and his men were staying deep in a cave in an area known as the Rocks of the Wild Goats. (See I Samuel 24:2-3.)

When Saul heard that David was in the Wilderness of En Gedi, he took three thousand men and pursued David. When he came to an area where there were sheepfolds by the road, Saul went into a cave to attend to his needs. This was the same cave where David and his men were located.

David's men encouraged him to take advantage of Saul, telling him that the Lord had delivered Saul into his hand. David did nothing more, however, than cut off a corner of Saul's robe. (See I Samuel 24:4.)

Even though he had not touched Saul, David's heart was troubled because he had cut Saul's robe. (See I Samuel 24:5.) He said to his men, "The LORD forbid that I should do this thing to my master, the LORD's anointed, to stretch out my hand against him, seeing he is the anointed of the LORD" (I Samuel 24:6). The men with David would have attacked Saul, but David restrained them with his words, allowing Saul to escape. (See I Samuel 24:7.)

Later, David left the cave and called after Saul. When Saul looked back, David bowed and said, "Why do you listen to the words of men who say, 'Indeed David seeks your harm'?" (I Samuel 24:9). David told Saul what had happened in the cave and held up the corner of cloth he had cut from Saul's robe to demonstrate that he did not seek to kill Saul. (See I Samuel 24:10-15.) Saul wept, saying, "You are more righteous than I; for you have rewarded me with good, whereas I have rewarded you with evil" (I Samuel 24:17). At Saul's request, David swore that he would not cut off Saul's descendants after him and that he would not destroy Saul's name from his father's house. At that, Saul returned home, and David and his men returned to the stronghold. (See I Samuel 24:21-22.)

The question that arises now is why Psalm 57 is included at this point in the Psalter. Is it to be read only as the prayer of a man who hid in a cave? If this is the case, the psalm would certainly have usefulness in demonstrating trust in God during difficult situations. But does the psalm have a larger purpose to serve? Are we to read it as advancing the messianic theme of the Psalter?

As Sailhamer points out, "The book of Psalms can be read as a single book, with each individual psalm intentionally arranged within the book in a meaningful way. The underlying arrangement of these songs encourages us to view them as pointing to the Messiah."[87] The agenda and central theme is set for the Psalter by Psalms 1-2. These psalms, by their relationship with each other, indicate that meditation on the Scriptures leads to faith in the Messiah. Psalm 2 reflects the inauguration of the Davidic covenant in II Samuel 7. Then, Psalm 3 is identified in its superscription as the words of David when he fled from Absalom, his son. The relationship of these psalms with each other indicates that the Davidic covenant would be challenged, a theme that continues throughout much of the Psalter. But the Psalter includes psalms to demonstrate that, in the face of continued challenges, the Davidic covenant, with its messianic promise, will prevail.

> Both 2 Samuel and the book of Psalms show David's confidence and faith in God's promise, even in the face of the failure of his own household to live up to the expectations of that promise. Second Samuel does this by narrating the events of David's life that show his confidence in God's promise; Psalms does this by recounting the words of David's prayers and praise, especially his assurance and hope in the coming Messiah. Thanks to the superscriptions, we see that although these psalms are the words of David and recount incidents in his life, they are, in fact, about the Messiah and David's assurance of God's faithfulness to send him.[88]

Psalm 57, typically identified as a psalm of lament,[89] begins with a plea for mercy. This is typical of the lament psalms. (See, e.g., Psalms 6:2; 51:1; 56:1.) David confessed his trust in God.[90] He took refuge under the wings of God as he waited for his calamities to pass (verse 1). The wing imagery is found consistently in the Psalter. (See Psalms 17:8; 36:7; 61:4; 63:7; 91:4.) The picture is that of a mother bird protecting her young. The word "wing" (*kanaph*) is a feminine noun. Jesus used a similar metaphor when He prayed over the city of Jerusalem. (See Matthew 23:37; Luke 13:34.)

David confessed his intention to "cry out to God Most High [*'elohim 'elyon*]" (verse 2a). The Canaanites viewed El as "the creator, the supreme deity of the Canaanite pantheon."[91] But it was revealed to the Israelites that only Yahweh was truly El, and He was El Elyon, God Most High. (See Genesis 14:22; Psalms 83:18; 97:9.) The writers of the psalms often used Elyon in reference to Yahweh.[92] In a similar fashion, theists today may refer to their deity, whatever the name, as "god." Christians also use the word "God," but they use the word in reference to the God of the Bible, as it is found in the translations. For David, the "God Most High" was the "God who [performed] all things for me" (verse 2b). David needed no other God.

"God Most High" was the God who dwelled in heaven (verse 3a). He would "send from heaven and save" David (verse 3a). As in Psalm 56:1, it seemed to David that he was in danger of being swallowed up (verse 3b). This would not happen, however, because God would reproach the person who attempted to do this, and He would "send forth His mercy and His truth" (verse 3c).

David's sense that his soul was "among lions" (verse 4a) connected Psalm 57 thematically with Psalm 22, where the Messiah prayed, "They [gaped] at Me with their mouths, like a raging and roaring lion," and, "Save Me from the lion's mouth" (Psalm 22:13, 21).[93] This, together with the reference to teeth like spears and arrows (verse 4b), connects Psalm 57 with the theme of messianic suffering found elsewhere in the Psalter (see, e.g., Psalms 35:16; 37:12; 58:6) and lifts the psalm above a limited reference to David.

The description of the tongue of the enemy as a sharp weapon is found elsewhere. (See Psalms 52:2, 4; 64:3.)

David prayed for the exaltation of God, who was identified in the Hebrew Scriptures with His glory (verse 5).[94] This refrain was repeated in verse 11.

The description of his enemies' efforts as preparing a net and digging a pit into which they have fallen further connects this psalm with previous psalms that advance the Psalter's messianic theme (verse 6).[95]

In the face of his enemy's efforts, David had a steadfast heart and a commitment to sing and praise (verse 7).

The word "glory" (*kabod*) may be intended as a synonym for "soul" (verse 8a). It is so translated by the NIV, and there is some evidence for this in the Psalter. (See Psalm 30:12.) The word is frequently used to refer "to the whole human being or existence."[96]

David would use the lute and harp to sing his praises to God (verse 8b). He would arise even before dawn to sing and play his praises (verse 8c).

Verse 9 provides another connection to previous messianic references in the Psalter. The commitment to praise the Lord "among the peoples" and to sing to Him "among the nations" recalls the Messiah's prayer of Psalm 22:22: "I will declare Your name to My brethren; in the midst of the assembly I will praise You." (See Hebrews 2:12.) It also recalls the messianic prayer of Psalm 35:18: "I will give You thanks in the great assembly; I will praise You among many people."

David would praise the Lord because His "mercy reaches unto the heavens" and His "truth unto the clouds" (verse 10). The themes of mercy and truth link verse 10 with verses 1 and 3.

Verse 11 reiterates the sentiments of verse 5.

Although we cannot point to a specific New Testament reference to Psalm 57, the themes it has in common with earlier psalms that are referenced in the New Testament indicate that it represents more here than just David's experiences fleeing from

Saul. It seems intentionally placed here to continue the Psalter's messianic theme. On the one hand, the psalm demonstrates the continued failure of all attempts to frustrate God's messianic purpose through David. On the other hand, the words could be read as a prayer of the Messiah in view of the attempts of His enemies to take His life.

Psalm 58

Psalm 58 is one of seven psalms commonly identified as imprecatory.[97] To say that a psalm is imprecatory means that it includes "an invocation of judgment, calamity, or curse uttered against one's enemies, or the enemies of God."[98] Other psalms commonly identified as imprecatory include Psalms 6, 35, 69, 83, 109, and 137, but Laney rightly enlarges this list to include Psalms 7 and 59.[99] There are, however, imprecatory elements in many of the psalms.[100]

In view of the teaching of the New Testament that believers are to bless and not curse their enemies and that they are not to repay evil for evil,[101] these shocking appeals for judgment upon the enemy have caused some to question the imprecatory psalms.[102] This perceived ethical problem has led to a variety of unsatisfactory solutions: (1) The imprecations were not those of the writer of the psalms against his enemies, but of the enemies of the biblical writer against him; (2) the imprecations were merely David's sentiments; he was not led by the Holy Spirit; (3) the ethical standard of the New Testament was higher than that of the Old Testament; (4) the imprecations were not against human beings, but against spiritual foes; (5) the imprecations were prophetic, describing the fate of the ungodly, so the responsibility was God's, not the psalmist's; (6) as a human being, the psalmist was cut off from the Spirit of God.[103]

That the imprecations must be viewed as authoritative and as part of the inspired text may be seen in that they were quoted in the New Testament. (See Psalms 69:25; 109:8; Acts 1:20.)

Although the New Testament writers may not have used the precise imprecatory formula found in Psalms,[104] there was little difference between the curses pronounced in the New Testament and the imprecatory prayers of the Old Testament. (See Acts 13:10-11; 23:3; I Corinthians 16:22; Galatians 1:8-9; II Timothy 4:14.) The prayer of those who had been slain for the Word of God and for their testimony certainly fit the pattern of the imprecatory psalms. (See Revelation 6:9-10.)

How can it be valid to pray for or to pronounce a curse upon one's enemies or even upon the enemies of God, in view of Jesus' teaching that we are to love our enemies, bless them, do good to them, and pray for them? (See Matthew 5:44.) Indeed, Jesus taught that even the Father is impartial on the evil and on the good, the just and the unjust. (See Matthew 5:45.)

As Laney points out, the basis for cursing lay in the Abrahamic covenant. God said to Abraham, "I will bless those who bless you, and I will curse him who curses you" (Genesis 12:3). This promise extended to Abraham's descendants as well: Those who blessed Abraham's descendants through the promised seed—Isaac and Jacob (see Romans 9:6-13)—would be blessed, and those who cursed them would be cursed. (See Deuteronomy 30:7; Isaiah 14:1-2; Joel 3:1-8; Micah 5:7-9; Haggai 2:21-22; Zechariah 14:1-3; Matthew 25:40-45.)

> On the basis of the unconditional Abrahamic covenant, David had a perfect right, as the representative of the nation, to pray that God would effect what He had promised—cursing on those who cursed or attacked Israel. David's enemies were a great threat to the well-being of Israel! The cries for judgment in the imprecatory psalms are appeals for Yahweh to carry out His judgment against those who would curse the nation—judgment in accordance with the provisions of the Abrahamic covenant.[105]

Six purposes for the imprecatory psalms may be seen: (1) Judgment against evildoers will establish the righteous (Psalm 7:8-9); (2) God is praised by deliverance (Psalms 7:17; 35:18, 28; 58:10); (3) The reward of the righteous will cause men to recognize that God judges the earth (Psalm 58:11); (4) God's judgments demonstrate His sovereignty (Psalm 59:13); (5) Judgment prevents the wicked from enjoying the same blessings as the righteous (Psalm 69:28); (6) Judgment may cause the wicked to seek the Lord (Psalm 83:16-18).[106]

It should be noted, however, that the imprecatory prayers do not reflect a desire for personal vengeance, which certainly would violate the prohibition on taking vengeance into one's own hands. (See Deuteronomy 32:35; Romans 12:19; Hebrews 10:30.) David did not pray that he could take vengeance on his enemies, but that God would do so. (See Psalms 7:6; 35:1; 58:6; 59:5.) This concept is supported not only in the Old Testament, but also in the New Testament. (See Luke 18:1-8.)[107]

As it relates to its placement in the Psalter, Psalm 58 can be read as if David were turning to address the enemies who had pursued him in the previous psalms.[108] The purpose of the psalm is "to set before the reader a vivid picture of God's righteous vindication of the oppressed (v. 10a) and thus to encourage them in the faith that 'there is a God who judges the earth' (v. 11b)."[109] This would be especially meaningful to the Israelites in the days of the Exile and following, as they pondered their captivity in Babylon and its impact on their future.

As with Psalms 57, 59, and 75, this psalm is set to the tune "Do Not Destroy" (superscription). We know nothing about this tune.

The psalm begins with a question that can be read as being directed to those who had tried to destroy David: "Do you indeed speak righteousness, you silent ones? Do you judge uprightly, you sons of men?" (verse 1).[110] As would be expected from the actions of David's enemies as recorded in the previous psalms, the answer was, "No, in heart you [worked] wickedness; you [weighed] out the violence of your hands in the earth" (verse 2). Those who sought to destroy David were not righteous and upright, but wicked and violent.

David's enemies were "estranged from the womb." They went "astray as soon as they [were] born, speaking lies" (verse 3). In interpreting this verse, we must remember that it is poetry. The verse does not mean that some are estranged from the womb and that others are not; nor does it mean that some go astray as soon as they are born and that others do not. Verse 3 is not a comment on the precise nature of the universal fallenness of the human race; it is a poetic description of the thoroughgoing, persistent wickedness of David's enemies.[111]

David compared his enemies to serpents and lions (verses 4-6). The reference to "the fangs of the young lions" connects Psalm 58 thematically with Psalm 22. (See Psalm 22:13, 21.)

David prayed that his enemies would "flow away as waters which run continually" and for the destruction of his enemies' weapons (verse 7). He prayed that his enemies would fade away "like a snail which melts away as it goes" and that they would be like "a stillborn child of a woman, that they may not see the sun" (verse 8).

At verse 9, the psalm changes from a prayer to a prophetic word.[112] The Hebrew text is difficult, leading to a variety of translations:

> Before your pots can feel the thorns, he shall take them away as with a whirlwind, both living, and in his wrath. (KJV)

> Before your pots can feel the burning thorns, He shall take them away as with a whirlwind, as in His living and burning wrath. (NKJV)

> Before your pots can feel the fire of thorns, He will sweep them away with a whirlwind, the green and the burning alike. (NASB)

> God will sweep them away, both young and old, faster than a pot heats on an open flame. (NLT)

> Before your pots can feel [the heat of] the thorns—whether they be green or dry—the wicked will be swept away. (NIV)

However the words are translated, the meaning is not obscure. The destruction of the wicked is imminent. It will come like a whirlwind, and soon: "Before your pots can feel the burning thorns." Thorns were used to provide a fire under cooking pots. (See Ecclesiastes 7:6.) The point seems to be that the destruction of the wicked was so near that heat would have no time to build up under a pot before it happened. Again, this is poetry, and it should not be read as an attempt to predict the precise timing of the destruction. When God was ready to judge the wicked, it would happen without delay. (Compare with Hebrews 10:37.)

When God took vengeance on His enemies, it would be a cause for rejoicing for the righteous (verse 10). The reign of terror would have come to an end, and the righteous would share with God in His victory.[113] The idea of washing one's feet in the blood of the enemy portrays this victory. (See Isaiah 63:1-6; Revelation 14:19-20; 19:13-14.)

As the psalm comes to a conclusion, its purpose is clear: When people saw God's victory over His enemies—a victory shared by the righteous—they would say, "Surely He is God who judges in the earth" (verse 11). These words would offer hope to the people of Israel in their Babylonian oppression and in the bleak days following their return from Babylon.

As seen consistently from the beginning of the Psalter, Psalm 58 reinforces the idea that every attempt to destroy David would be unsuccessful. Thus, every effort to defeat the Davidic covenant would fail. When the Psalter was composed, David was, of course, long dead. But Psalm 58 does not merely point to the past; it points to the future. The same God who preserved David's life in the face of many acts of treachery would preserve the people of Israel. The ultimate judgment would be in the hands of David's greatest Son, the Messiah.

Psalm 59

Like Psalms 57, 58, and 75, this psalm is "set to 'Do Not Destroy'" (superscription). Nothing more is known about this tune.

Laney rightly identifies Psalm 59 as an imprecatory psalm.[114] It is a prayer in which David prays for the judgment of God to come upon his enemies. (See verses 11-13.)

The occasion for the writing of this psalm was "when Saul sent men, and they watched the house in order to kill him" (superscription). Although, as Sailhamer points out, "the details of the specific event shed little light on the sense of the psalm itself,"[115] and our primary concern is how the psalm fits contextually and compositionally in the Psalter, it seems appropriate to consider the circumstances under which the psalm was written. Since the words of the superscription are part of the psalm, they should be considered in efforts to interpret the psalm.

In this case, the event giving birth to the psalm was an occasion when Saul sent men to watch David's house with the intent to kill him. This is recorded in I Samuel 19. Leading up to this event, Saul told his son Jonathan and all of his servants to kill David. Jonathan, however, "delighted greatly in David" (I Samuel 19:1). Jonathan warned David of Saul's intentions, advising him to be on his guard and to hide in a secret place. (See I Samuel 19:2.) Jonathan arranged to talk with his father in the very field where David was hiding (I Samuel 19:3), saying, "Let not the king sin against his servant, against David, because he has not sinned against you, and because his works have been very good toward you. For he took his life in his hands and killed the Philistine, and the LORD brought about a great deliverance for all Israel. You saw it and rejoiced. Why then will you sin against innocent blood, to kill David without a cause?" (I Samuel 19:4-5).

Saul swore, "As the LORD lives, he shall not be killed" (I Samuel 19:6).

Jonathan told David about this and brought David to Saul again. (See I Samuel 19:7.)

Later, in another battle with the Philistines, David fought them "and struck them with a mighty blow, and they fled from him" (I Samuel 19:8).

Following that battle, as David was playing music for Saul, "Saul sought to pin David to the wall with the spear, but he slipped away from Saul's presence; and he drove the spear into the wall. So David fled and escaped that night" (I Samuel 19:9-10).

It was at this point that "Saul also sent messengers to David's house to watch him and to kill him in the morning" (I Samuel 19:11a). David's wife, Michal, was Saul's daughter. "If you do not save your life tonight," she said to David, "tomorrow you will be killed" (I Samuel 19:11b).

Michal helped David escape through a window and laid an image in the bed, covering it with goats' hair to represent David's head. She covered the image with clothing. When Saul's messengers arrived to take David, Michal told them David was sick. (See I Samuel 19:12-15a.) Saul was not to be deterred. He sent the messengers back, saying, "Bring him up to me in the bed, that I may kill him" (I Samuel 19:15b).

When the messengers arrived the second time, they discovered the image in the bed. Saul said to Michal, "Why have you deceived me like this, and sent my enemy away, so that he has escaped?" (I Samuel 19:17a.) Michal responded, "He said to me, 'Let me go! Why should I kill you?' " (I Samuel 19:17b).

David's escape from Saul was successful. (See I Samuel 19:18.)

As Psalm 59 finds it place in the Psalter, it represents yet another attempt on David's life, demonstrating the failure of all efforts to thwart God's messianic purpose through David. In addition, the psalm has close thematic ties to previous messianic psalms.

The psalm opens with a prayer for deliverance from one's enemies (verse 1a). David asked for defense against those "who [rose] up" against him (verse 1b). The first person recorded in the Psalter as rising up against David was his son Absalom, but the theme is a common one. (See Psalms 3:1; 17:7; 18:48; 35:11; 44:5; 74:23; 92:11; 139:21.)

Verse 2 continues the request for deliverance, describing David's enemies as "workers of iniquity" and "bloodthirsty men." Those viewed as enemies were often described as "workers of iniquity" in the Psalter. (See Psalms 5:5; 6:8; 14:4; 28:3; 36:12; 37:1; 53:4; 64:2; 92:7, 9; 94:4, 16; 125:5; 141:4, 9.) To say that they were bloodthirsty describes their iniquity as specifically having to do with violence.

Although David was innocent in his relationship with Saul, these bloodthirsty men lay in wait for his life, gathering for the specific purpose of killing him (verses 3-4).

David prayed for the Lord to awake to his aid, punishing the nations and withholding mercy from "any wicked transgressors" (verse 5).[116]

David compared those who sought his life to dogs, going "all around the city" (verse 6; see also verse 14). This provides a thematic connection with Psalm 22. (See Psalm 22:16, 20.)

The words of the wicked were described as swords (verse 7; compare with Psalms 55:21; 57:4; 64:3).

Verse 8 provides a direct connection with the theme established at the beginning of the Psalter:

> But You, O LORD, shall laugh at them; You shall have all the nations in derision. (verse 8)

> He who sits in the heavens shall laugh; the LORD shall hold them in derision. (Psalm 2:4)

In the midst of the Saul's treachery, David determined to wait for the Lord, his strength and defense (verse 9).[117] He prayed that the God of mercy would come to meet him, letting David see what he desired to happen to his enemies (verse 10).

David prayed that God would not immediately slay his enemies, lest his people miss or quickly forget the danger of opposing God's purposes. Instead, he prayed that God would scatter them and "bring them down" (verse 11).

David's enemies were characterized by pride, which motivated their cursing and lying (verse 12).

As opposed to immediately slaying his enemies, David wanted them to be gradually consumed in such a convincing way that it would be clearly known that "God [ruled] in Jacob to the ends of the earth" (verse 13).

Verse 14 reiterated the words of verse 6. With verse 15, David's enemies were compared to wild dogs. (Compare with Psalm 22:16, 20.) The reference to the dogs returning at evening is a metaphor for affliction; the song of mercy in the morning (verse 16) is a metaphor for deliverance.[118]

Even in the midst of treachery, David sang of God's power and mercy (verse 16a). In the day of his trouble, God was his strength, defense, and refuge (verses 16b-17).

The psalm concludes with the assurance that the prayer with which it opens will be answered. (Compare verses 1 and 17.)

In view of the specific connections between Psalm 59 and previous messianic psalms, and in connection with the larger messianic shape of the Psalter, it may be appropriate to see Psalm 59 as another prayer of the Messiah. (Compare Psalm 2:4 with Psalm 59:8 and Psalm 22:16, 20 with Psalm 59:6, 14-15.) Even though, as originally written, it expressed David's prayer in the face of Saul's attempts to take his life, the words may have been taken up by the Messiah in His prayers in response to the many attempts on His life, even before His crucifixion. Even if Jesus did not pray these words, they flowed with the messianic theme of the Psalter by demonstrating yet another failed attempt on David's life. Regardless of the efforts of any enemy, David would be preserved as the Messiah's ancestor.

Psalm 60

The superscription of Psalm 60 indicates that it is set to the tune of "Lily of the Testimony." Other psalms set to the tune of "The Lilies" include Psalms 45 and 69. Psalm 80 is set to the tune of "The Lilies of the Testimony."[119] The word "covenant" (*'eduth*, translated "testimony" in the NKJV) is significant, for the boundaries established by David in his victory over the territories described in verses 6-8 correspond to the territory God promised Abraham. (Compare verses 6-8 with II Samuel 8:1-14; Genesis 15:18; Deuteronomy 11:24; Joshua 1:4; and I Kings 4:21.)[120] Thus, Psalm 60 connects the Davidic covenant with the Abrahamic covenant. Both covenants are messianic. The Messiah is Abraham's ultimate seed (compare Genesis 13:15; Genesis 22:18; Galatians 3:16) and the greatest Son of David. (See II Samuel 7:12-16; Psalm 132:11; Isaiah 9:6-7; Luke 1:31-33; Acts 2:30; Romans 1:3-4; Revelation 22:16.) The geographical connection between the Abrahamic covenant and David's conquest shows that it is through David that the Abrahamic covenant would be fulfilled. Ultimately, of course, in view of the post-Davidic dispersion of Israel, the Abrahamic covenant will be fulfilled by the Messiah, the greatest representative of the house of David.

The superscription of Psalm 60 indicates that the psalm is "for teaching." In view of the fact that the psalm is a national lament,[121] perhaps on the occasion of an early and temporary defeat of David's army, it may be that this psalm was originally intended to provide instruction to the military as to how to trust God in the midst of battle.[122] Other psalms that may have been originally intended for military instruction include Psalms 144 and 149. (See Psalms 144:1; 149:6.)

The historical event that was the occasion for the writing of this psalm is found in II Samuel 8 and I Chronicles 18. Following the establishment of the Davidic covenant (see II Samuel 7 and I Chronicles 17), David conquered the Philistines and Moab

(II Samuel 8:1-2). He recovered his territory at the River Euphrates by defeating Hadadezer, king of Zobah (II Samuel 8:3-4). Then David conquered the Syrians of Damascus who came to help Hadadezer (II Samuel 8:5-8). David also conquered the Edomites, the Ammonites, and the Amalekites (II Samuel 8:11-14).

Our concern is not so much, however, for the details of the event behind the psalm, but for the purpose the psalm serves in its canonical, post-exilic placement in the Psalter. Why is Psalm 60, reflecting significant territorial expansion of David's kingdom immediately following the establishment of the Davidic covenant, located in the Psalter immediately after Psalm 59, a psalm connected with Saul's attempt to kill David? Psalm 59 is connected thematically with Psalm 2. (Compare Psalm 59:8 with Psalm 2:4.) Just as Psalm 2 addresses the futility of opposing the Messiah, so does Psalm 59.[123] Immediately after this expression of the futility of Saul's desperate effort, the Psalter includes a psalm describing David's victory over his enemies, a victory that expands his territory to include the land promised to Abraham. Psalm 60, then, is a counterpart to Psalm 59. In Psalm 59, Saul has attempted to kill David, but in Psalm 60, David is alive and well, conquering his foes and expanding his kingdom.

Only in Psalm 60 do we discover an apparently early but temporary defeat of David's army as he began the expansion of his kingdom. The indication of this defeat is seen in verses 1-3. It seems that Israel had been cast off and broken down because of God's displeasure. The defeat was so pronounced that David compared it to an earthquake. It was hard to grasp the reason for this event; the people of Israel were as confused as if they were intoxicated. David prayed, "Oh, restore us again!"

The entire psalm was not consumed with lament, however. Verse 4 offered hope: God had "raised a banner to be unfurled against the bow" (NIV) for those who feared Him. The banner designated "a place where the godly may find refuge under the protection of the Divine Warrior."[124] The bow symbolized the attacks of the enemy.[125]

Verse 5 was a prayer for deliverance. The "right hand," a symbol of the power and authority of God,[126] was connected with salvation.[127]

In verses 6-8, God spoke, declaring His victory over the territory He had promised to Abraham, from east (Moab, Edom, Gilead, and the Valley of Succoth) to west (Shechem, Philistia, and Manesseh) and from north (Ephraim) to south (Judah). That God would "divide" Shechem and "measure out" the Valley of Succoth suggested that He would use them for His own purposes. Ephraim was the leading tribe of the northern tribes, representing all of them. To say that Ephraim was "the helmet for My head" (NKJV, but literally "the strength of mine head" [*ma'owz ro'shiy*], as in the KJV) symbolized force.[128] To identify Judah as God's lawgiver followed Jacob's prophetic declaration that the scepter, symbolizing royal rule, belonged to this tribe. (See Genesis 49:10 and Psalm 78:67-72.)

The "washpot" metaphor of verse 8 indicated that Moab, like a servant, would wash God's feet. The Moabites, descendants of the incestuous relationship between Lot and his firstborn daughter (see Genesis 19:37), were consistently seen as enemies of Israel.

That God would cast His shoe over Edom indicated that He was the new owner of the land.

> Casting a sandal was a symbolic, legal gesture employed in those situations where a levir refused to accept his responsibility to a widow. She in turn then removed his sandal, the symbol of ownership and inheritance, and cast it at him. This signified his loss of inheritance rights to the lands of his relative (see Deut 25:9 and Ruth 4:7-8). Land transfers in the Nuzi texts also involved replacing the old owner's foot on the land with that of the new owner. In this verse God aggressively casts a sandal onto Edom as a gesture of conquest or the assumption of ownership of that nation's lands.[129]

The Edomites, descendants of Esau (see Genesis 25:30), were also consistently represented as Israel's enemies. By means of paronomasia,[130] Edom (*'edom*) was sometimes used to represent Adam (*'adam*), a figure for all humankind.[131]

The translation "Philistia, shout in triumph because of Me" (verse 8c) may obscure the meaning. It may be better to translate the phrase something like, "I will shout in triumph over the Philistines" (NLT). The Septuagint supports this kind of translation: "The Philistines have been subjected to me."

In verse 9, David prayed, "Who will bring me to the strong city? Who will lead me to Edom?" He knew his only help was from God—the same God who seemed to have cast them off and who had not gone out with their armies, as indicated in verses 1-3 (verse 10). David knew that human help—as in alliance with other kings—was useless, so he prayed to God for help (verse 11).[132]

The psalm concluded on a quite different note than it had begun: "Through God we will do valiantly, for it is He who shall tread down our enemies" (verse 12). David's defeat was not lasting; God gave him possession of the land promised to Abraham.

Psalm 60 advances the messianic theme of the Psalter by demonstrating that temporary defeat does not mean that God will not fulfill His promises to Abraham and David. The greatest promise God gave these men was not the land, but the Messiah. David enjoyed dominion over the land included in the Abrahamic covenant and passed that dominion on to Solomon. (See I Kings 4:21.) But this dominion was destined to fade away due to the sinfulness of the people of Israel. It will, however, be fully restored when the greatest Son of Abraham and David takes up the scepter to rule the nations with a rod of iron. (See Psalm 2:6-9; Revelation 2:27; 19:15.)

Psalm 61

The superscription of Psalm 61 does not identify it with any historical event. It is a Psalm of David, addressed to the Chief

Musician, to be accompanied on a stringed instrument (*negiynath*). This is the only time in the Hebrew Scriptures that this word—a singular form—appears. The plural "stringed instruments" (*negiynowth*) appears several times in the superscriptions (Psalms 4:1; 6:1; 54:1; 55:1; 67:1; 76:1). It would be speculation to comment on the significance of this.

In the canonical-compositional approach to the Psalter that we are taking, the historical events indicated by the superscriptions are interesting, but they are not critical to discovering the meaning and significance of the psalms as they are located in the present shape of the Psalter.[133]

Psalm 61 begins like a lament, with a cry to be heard by God "from the end of the earth," and with a confession to being "overwhelmed" (verses 1-2). But the prayer of verses 6-7 makes the lament designation difficult, unless the verses are seen as an interpolation.[134] In this case, the form-critical approach seems inadequate to account for the evidence.[135]

The psalm reflected some kind of adversity in David's life. He cried to God "from the end of the earth" (verse 2). The word translated "earth" (*'eretz*) was frequently used to describe the land promised to Abraham, the land just described as having been conquered by David in Psalm 60:6-8. When English readers see "earth," they tend to think that it means "world." But for the ancient Hebrews, *ha'aretz* ("the land") was the Promised Land.[136] Thus, the phrase "from the end of the earth" may refer to David in exile somewhere in the land promised to Abraham, rather than to a location outside of the land. Kidner suggests that the psalm "may have been a cry for help when David was away on campaign . . . or driven out by Absalom."[137] Or, "he could have adapted it during his kingship from an earlier petition made in his years of flight from Saul."[138]

Wherever David was when he uttered this prayer, his heart was overwhelmed (*'ataph*) (verse 2). (See also Psalms 77:3; 142:3; 143:4; Jonah 2:7 where *'ataph* appears.) This could have been an event unknown to us or, as Kidner suggests, it could have been an event that was specified in the superscription of another Psalm. Because of the connection here between Psalms 60 and 61, it could be a reference to the early defeat David's army experienced that was reflected in Psalm 60:1-3. But, again, the historical event behind this psalm is not a critical issue in understanding the psalm's significance in the Psalter. The Psalter was intended to point beyond David and his experiences to a greater someone who, like David, suffered betrayal and danger, but who would not be denied His divinely appointed role as the Messiah, David's greatest Son.

In his weakness, David prayed, "Lead me to the rock that is higher than I" (verse 2). In the natural sense, a high rock is "a metaphor for protection, denoting a fortified or strategic place where one could find refuge."[139] But the context indicates David had something more than a literal rock in mind. In Psalm 62:2, 6-7, David declared that God was his only rock. Because the medieval exegetes read the Psalter as pointing to the Messiah, they interpreted the "rock" of verse 2 as a reference to Christ.[140] This was connected in their minds with I Corinthians 10:4: "For they drank of that spiritual Rock that followed them, and that Rock was Christ." Because the rock from which Israel drank was mentioned twice, forty years apart (Exodus 17:1-7; Numbers 20:1-13), there was a rabbinic legend that a physical rock followed the Israelites through the wilderness.[141] Paul was not, however, denying that the rock that provided water for the Israelites was anything other than a literal rock any more than that the manna was literal food (I Corinthians 10:3). Neither was he suggesting that the literal rock somehow traversed the wilderness, up and down mountains, as alleged by Jewish tradition. When he wrote that the food and the drink were "spiritual," Paul meant that they represented a spiritual reality. Similarly, Paul reported that Jesus said, after the Last Supper, "This cup is the new covenant in My blood" (I Corinthians 11:25). These were figures of speech. Paul meant that "what the rock did for Israel [corresponded] to what Christ did for the Corinthians."[142] Just as the Israelites were given natural life by drinking of the water that flowed miraculously from the rock,[143] so those who believe on Christ receive spiritual life as they drink of the water He provides. (See John 4:10, 13-14; 7:37-38.)

David cried out for deliverance with a history of deliverance: He had already found God to be a shelter and a strong tower protecting him from his enemy (verse 3). David had already found God to be His defense and refuge (Psalm 59:16-17); now he committed to abide in God's Tabernacle forever and to trust in the shelter of His wings (verse 4). Kidner points out that

> God's safekeeping is viewed here in increasingly personal terms, as the aloof ruggedness of the high crag of verse 2 gives place to the purpose-built *tower* of verse 3, and this in turn to the hospitality of the frail *tent* (4) with its implication of safety among friends; and finally the affectionate, parental shelter symbolized by *thy wings*.[144]

The word translated "shelter" (*machaseh*) appears in Psalm 62:7 and 8, where it is translated "refuge" by the NKJV. There, as here, it is closely connected with the idea of a rock being associated with deliverance. Psalm 62:7 clearly points out that God is the rock.[145]

To say that God was "a strong tower from the enemy" (verse 3) followed the military strategy of the day. During a siege, the people could flee to a tower for protection.[146] Here, it was God who was the strong tower; in Proverbs 18:10, the name of the Lord was the strong tower. In this case, the proverb demonstrated equivalency of the "name" of the Lord with the Lord Himself.

David's intention to abide in the Tabernacle forever connects thematically with Psalm 15:1 and 27:5. Immediately, however, this statement lifts the psalm from being merely about David. The only people to which the law of Moses gave access to the Tabernacle were the priests, those of the tribe of Levi. David was from the tribe of Judah. (See Numbers 1:50-51, 53; 8:15; Hebrews 7:13-14.) Even if King David wanted to abide permanently in the

Tabernacle, he could not. When King Uzziah intruded into the Temple, he was guilty of trespass and smitten with leprosy. He spent the rest of his life living in isolation. (See II Chronicles 26:16-23.)

Should the statement "I will abide in Your tabernacle forever" (verse 4) be read as a reference to the Messiah? It should, for reasons we have already explored,[147] but it should also be noted that due to the restrictions of the law of Moses, even Jesus did not qualify for priesthood under its terms. (See Hebrews 7:11-14.[148]) Jesus was from the tribe of Judah. His priesthood was after the order of Melchisedec, who predated the law of Moses. The Messiah's right to dwell in the Tabernacle—and thus in the Temple, including Ezekiel's millennial Temple (see Ezekiel 40-48 and specifically 43:1-7; 44:1-2, 4; 48:35)—was based not on His conformity to the requirements of the law of Moses, but on the fact that He was Yahweh Himself. He was Yahweh in human existence (e.g., Psalm 45:6; 102:25-27 [with Hebrews 1:10-12]; Isaiah 9:6-7; Micah 5:2; John 1:1, 14; I Timothy 3:16). Because the Messiah was not only God, but also a human being, He could communicate with Yahweh as He did in His prayers as recorded in the Gospels and as indicated by a messianic reading of the Psalms.

As Muller suggests, we should not understand the relationship between the Messiah and Yahweh as indicating "independent centers of consciousness, intellect, and will standing over against one another."[149] Instead, this relationship reflects the fullness and genuineness of the Messiah's human existence. If the humanity of the Messiah is compromised in any way so that there is no real communication between Him and Yahweh, Jesus is not God manifest in flesh but in something less than or other than flesh (human existence). On the other hand, if the deity of the Messiah is compromised in any way so that He is something less than or other than Yahweh, the result will be something like Arianism or Sabellianism. In the final analysis, the Incarnation is a mystery (I Timothy 3:16), but it is a mystery that permits the Messiah both to be identified as God and to communicate with God, as a messianic reading of the

Psalter has Him doing here: "I will abide in Your tabernacle forever" (Psalm 61:4a).

The statement, "I will trust in the shelter of Your wings" connects this psalm with Psalm 91:4, where a messianic reading also sees the Messiah as dwelling in the "secret place," the Holy of Holies in the Temple (Psalm 91:1). The "secret" (*sather*) place of Yahweh is identified in the Psalter as the Holiest Place in the Temple.[150] The writer of Hebrews described Jesus' entrance into the true Most Holy Place by means of His own blood. (See Hebrews 9:11-15, 23-24.)

If we read Psalm 61 as having to do only with David, we are at a loss to know the specific vows he made (verse 5a). As it was originally written, there were, of course, specific vows to which David referred. But as the psalm rises above a mere Davidic reference to a messianic reference, it may be that we should understand the vows as being connected with Psalm 40:6-8, where the Messiah declared, "I delight to do Your will, O my God, and Your law is within my heart" (Psalm 40:8). These words were twice placed on the lips of the Messiah by the writer of Hebrews. (See Hebrews 10:5-9.) Thus, the Messiah vowed to do the will of God.

If we read the statement, "You have given me the heritage of those who fear Your name" (verse 5b) as messianic, it connects with the idea that the Son has been appointed heir of all things (Hebrews 1:2) and that He shares His inheritance with people of faith (Romans 8:17).

Verses 6-7 strongly indicate that Psalm 61 has significance beyond David: "You will prolong the king's life, his years as many generations. He shall abide before God forever. Oh, prepare mercy and truth, which may preserve him!" As Kidner points out, whatever the point of these words may have been as they were originally written, they are "fulfilled to overflowing in the person of *the* king, the Messiah."[151] David's life was not prolonged in this sense, or his years to many generations. As Peter pointed out in his use of the psalms on the Day of Pentecost, David was not writing about himself: David was dead and buried (Acts 2:29). What could be true in only a limited sense about David or any other king was true in its fullest sense about the Messiah. Although the Messiah was crucified, His days were prolonged so that He could see His seed. (See Isaiah 53:10.) He was put to death, but His life was also preserved so that He could "abide before God forever" (verse 7a). He was preserved by "mercy and truth" (verse 7b). All of this was made possible by His resurrection from death. (See Psalm 16:9-10; Acts 2:25-28.)

The statement, "I will sing praise to Your name forever" (verse 8) connects Psalm 61 with Psalm 22, where the Messiah said, "I will declare Your name to My brethren; in the midst of the assembly I will praise You" (verse 22). The writer of Hebrews quoted the Septuagint version of this verse as being specifically about the Messiah. (See Hebrews 2:12.) Daily, the Messiah kept His vows. (See comments on verse 5.) He came to do the will of God. As the boy Jesus said to His earthly parents, "Did you not know that I must be about My Father's business?" (Luke 2:49).

Psalm 61 advances the messianic theme of the Psalter. In words that originally had a more limited level of meaning for David, the psalm rises in its context in the Book of Psalms to declare that the Messiah's life will be preserved in the face of His enemy.

Psalm 62

Like Psalm 61, the superscription of Psalm 62 does not provide a link to any specific historical event. It does, however, indicate that the psalm was presented to Jeduthun, who was appointed by David as a chief musician. (See I Chronicles 16:41; 25:1-3.)

The psalm consists of two stanzas, with the first two verses being repeated with slight variation in verses 5-6. Thus, verses 1-2 introduce the first stanza, and verses 5-6 introduce the second stanza. Whatever the historical circumstance that gave birth to the psalm originally,[152] it can readily be seen that Psalm 62 is thematically related to Psalms 39, 61, and 63.[153] These themes can be seen by the following comparisons:

Silence

> Truly my soul silently waits for God. . . . My soul, wait silently for God alone. (Psalm 62:1a, 5a)

> I said, "I will guard my ways, lest I sin with my tongue; I will restrain my mouth with a muzzle. . . . I was mute with silence, I held my peace even from good. . . . I was mute, I did not open my mouth. (Psalm 39:1-2a, 9a)

The Rock

> He alone is my rock. . . . He only is my rock. . . . The rock of my strength, and my refuge, is in God. (Psalm 62:2a, 6a, 7b)

> Lead me to the rock that is higher than I. (Psalm 61:2c)

Lies

> They delight in lies. . . . Men of high degree are a lie. (Psalm 62:4b, 9b)

> But the mouth of those who speak lies shall be stopped. (Psalm 63:11c)

Refuge/Shelter

> The rock of my strength, and my refuge (*machesiy*), is in God. . . . God is a refuge (*machaseh*) for us. (Psalm 62:7b, 8c)

> For You have been a shelter (*machaseh*) for me. (Psalm 61:3a)

Vapor

> Surely men of low degree are a vapor . . . they are altogether lighter than vapor. (Psalm 62:9a, c)

> Certainly every man at his best state is but vapor. . . . Surely every man is vapor. (Psalm 39:5c, 11c)

Riches

> If riches increase, do not set your heart on them. (Psalm 62:10b)

> He heaps up riches, and does not know who will gather them. (Psalm 39:6c)

In addition to these specific parallels, additional parallels, both of vocabulary and theme, may be seen by comparing Psalm 61:2 with Psalm 63:1; Psalm 61:4b with Psalm 63:7b; Psalm 61:6-7 with Psalm 63:11; Psalm 61:8a with Psalm 63:3b and 5b.

The first word in verse 1, *'ak*, also introduces verses 2, 4, 5, 6, and 9. The NKJV translates *'ak* "truly," (verse 1), "only" (verses 4, 6), "alone" (verses 2, 5), and "surely" (verse 9). The word "is an emphasizer, to underline a statement or to point a contrast; its insistent repetition gives the psalm a tone of special earnestness."[154] Demonstrating another link between the two psalms, *'ak* appears four times in Psalm 39, in verses 5, 6, and 11. Although *'ak* appears in several psalms, it appears more frequently in Psalms 39 and 62 than in any other.

As Psalm 62 opened, David declared his intention to wait silently for God. He acknowledged that his salvation (*yeshu'atiy*) came from God (verse 1). The word translated "salvation" was a form of *yeshu'ah*, a word given as the Messiah's personal name.[155] (See Matthew 1:21.[156])

God alone was David's rock and salvation (verse 2a). This connects Psalm 62 with David's prayer in Psalm 61:2c, "Lead me to the rock that is higher than I." It also anticipates verses 6-7. To say that God was David's rock and salvation was another way of saying that He was David's defense (verse 2b). Although in different words, the description of God as a defense provides a thematic connection with Psalm 61:3-4. This anticipates verses 6-8.

Because God was David's rock, salvation, and defense, David would "not be greatly moved" (verse 2c). This anticipates verse 6c and also connects the psalm to Psalms 13:4; 15:5; 16:8; 21:7; 55:22; 66:9; 112:6; and 121:3. As these references pertain to David, they indicated that all attempts to remove him from his throne would be unsuccessful. In their larger significance for the Messiah, they indicated that He would not be denied His right to the throne of David. (See Genesis 49:10-12; II Samuel 7:12-16; 23:1-5; Psalms 2; 89:3-4; 132:10-11; Isaiah 9:6-7; Jeremiah 23:5-6; Luke 1:31-33; Acts 2:30-31; Hebrews 1:8 [with Psalm 45:6-7].)

In verse 3, David addressed his enemies. He asked how long they would attack and assured them that all of them would be "slain . . . like a leaning wall and a tottering fence." It is difficult to see how the slaying of David's enemies would compare to "a leaning wall and a tottering fence." The Hebrew text permits a variety of translations:

> How long will you assault a man? Would all of you throw him down—this leaning wall, this tottering fence? (NIV)

> So many enemies against one man—all of them trying to kill me. To them I'm just a broken-down wall or a tottering fence. (NLT)

The sole purpose of David's enemies was "to cast him down from his high position" (verse 4a). This was a reference to their attempts to remove him from his throne. In their attempt, they delighted in lies (verse 4b). With their mouth, they blessed David, but they cursed him inwardly (verse 4c).

The second stanza of the psalm begins with words very similar to verse 1. In verse 1, David simply stated that his soul waited silently for God; in verse 5, he urged silence upon himself.[157] The "expectation" of verse 5 should be read as a virtual synonym of the "salvation" of verse 1.

Verse 6 continues the restatement of the introduction of the first stanza. The words are virtually identical to verse 2, with the exception that in verse 2 David said he should not be "greatly moved," whereas in verse 6 he said, "I shall not be moved." It seemed as if his confidence had increased with the exercise of waiting silently for God.

Again in verse 7, salvation is connected with God (compare with verses 1-2, 6), and God is seen as the rock (compare with verses 2, 6 and Psalm 61:2). The word translated "refuge" (*machaseh*) is translated "shelter" in Psalm 61:3. The rock and refuge terminology indicates a link between the psalms as they are intentionally placed in the Psalter.

Verse 8 provides thematic linkage all the way back to Psalm 2:12, which states that those who put their trust in the Son are blessed. To pour out one's heart to God is connected with trusting in Him (verse 8b). Again, verse 8 declares that God is a refuge (*machaseh*), as in verse 7 and Psalm 61:3.

Two different words are used for "men" in verse 9. Those men of low degree, who are a vapor (compare with Psalm 39:5, 11), are *'adam*. Those of high degree, who are a lie, are *'iysh*. The Hebrew language has several words commonly translated "man." Here, the two words seem to be used to indicate all of mankind.[158] If all human beings "are weighed on the scales, they are altogether lighter than vapor" (verse 9b). Therefore, there was nothing substantial about those who sought to thwart God's messianic purpose through David.

Those who put their trust in their ability to oppress others, or who hoped to get ahead by robbery, or who trusted in riches, would be disappointed (verse 10). Oppression was an ongoing problem during the times of Israel's spiritual darkness. (See Psalm 73:8; Isaiah 30:12; Jeremiah 6:6; 22:17; Ezekiel 22:7, 12.) So was robbery. (See Leviticus 6:2, 4; Ezekiel 18:12, 16, 18; 22:29.) The danger of trusting riches had always been with the human race, and it was soundly condemned by Jesus (Mark 10:24-25) and Paul (I Timothy 6:5-11).

Verses 11-12 make use of "a Semitic device of a numerical sequence of x and x + 1."[159] In a single oracle of God ("God has spoken once"), David heard two things. The first lesson was "that power [*'oz*] [belonged] to God." The second lesson was that mercy (*chesed*) belonged to God (verse 12). The idea that power belonged to God recalled verse 7, where David declared that God was the rock of his strength (*'oz*). *Chesed*, translated "mercy" in the NKJV, had the idea of "loyal love" and was connected with God's loyalty to the Davidic covenant. (See II Samuel 7:15.) God was both powerful and loving. These two qualities were more than sufficient to counteract any enemy's reliance on lying, cursing, oppression, robbery, or riches.

The final statement of verse 12 ("for You render to each one according to his work") found its way into the New Testament in Matthew 16:27, Romans 2:6, and I Corinthians 3:8. God would reward David for his trust in Him, but He would also reward David's enemies for their attempt to cast David down from his high position (verse 4).

Psalm 62 is connected thematically with the psalms preceding and following it and with the psalms with messianic significance. The psalm offers another example of original significance pertaining to David but has contextual significance pertaining to David's greatest Son, the Messiah. Although there were those who wished to cast the Messiah down from His high position, and those who were liars, oppressors, robbers, and who trusted in their wealth, the Messiah placed His trust in the powerful and loyal God.[160]

Jesus' use of verse 12 to describe what the Son of Man will do at His second coming connects this psalm with the messianic hope and identifies Him as the Lord to whom mercy belongs. (See Matthew 16:27.)

As Sailhamer points out,

> When read within the context of Psalms, David's words point specifically to the future salvation of God's people and the promise of a future Messiah. Its linkage to Pss 61 and 63, which in fact take up the theme of the future promised King, suggests that the composer of Psalms saw in David's words in this psalm an expression of hope in the Messiah.[161]

Psalm 63

According to the superscription, this is a "Psalm of David when he was in the wilderness of Judah." This could be a reference to the time David "stayed in strongholds in the wilderness, and remained in the mountains in the Wilderness of Ziph" (I Samuel 23:14; see I Samuel 23:15; 24:1)[162] or it could refer to the time when Absalom rose up against his father David, forcing David and all the people loyal to him to cross the Brook Kidron "over toward the way of the wilderness" (II Samuel 15:23; see II Samuel 15:28; 16:2). Verse 11 seems to indicate that if the historical event that gave birth to the psalm was one of these two, it was most likely that the reference was to Absalom's rebellion, because David was apparently the king at this time.

The opening words of the psalm could cause us to think of it as a lament, but it quickly moves to expressions of confidence in God.[163] As to its location in the Psalter, Psalm 63 falls within an ABBA arrangement including Psalms 61-64. Psalms 61 and 64 are individual laments, and Psalms 62-63 are psalms of confidence. Thus, "they form a subgroup in the larger Davidic collection which extends from Ps 51 to Pss 70-71."[164] It is interesting to note that in a Qumran psalm manuscript fragment, Psalms 62-63 are joined.[165]

There are numerous parallels or thematic connections between Psalms 61, 62, and 63.

Lies

> They delight in lies. . . . Men of high degree are a lie. (Psalm 62:4b, 9b)

> But the mouth of those who speak lies shall be stopped. (Psalm 63:11c)

Longing for God

> From the end of the earth I will cry to You, when my heart is overwhelmed; lead me to the rock that is higher than I. (Psalm 61:2)

> . . . My soul thirsts for You; my flesh longs for You in a dry and thirsty land where there is no water. (Psalm 63:1)

God's Wings

> I will trust in the shelter of Your wings. Selah. (Psalm 61:4b)

> Therefore in the shadow of Your wings I will rejoice. (Psalm 63:7b)

The King

> You will prolong the king's life, his years as many generations. (Psalm 61:6)

> But the king shall rejoice in God; everyone who swears by Him shall glory. (Psalm 63:11a)

Praise

> So I will sing praise to Your name forever. . . . (Psalm 61:8a)

> My lips shall praise You. . . . And my mouth shall praise You with joyful lips. (Psalm 63:3b, 5b)

Wilcock points out further parallels with Psalms 42-43 and 84 in the Korah collections.[166] He also points out that Psalm 63 is a morning or evening prayer (see verses 1, 6), as are Psalms 3-5 in the first Davidic collection (see Psalms 3:5; 4:4, 8; 5:3)—psalms also reflecting Absalom's rebellion. Thus, Psalm 63 might be "the equivalent, here in the second collection, of those three in the first, as 51 and 56 seem to be the counterparts of 32 and 34."[167]

Psalm 63 is firmly connected with the psalms immediately surrounding it and with the Psalter at large. The psalm begins with a confession that God (*Elohim*) was David's God (*El*) (verse 1). The "emphatic 'O God' signifies essentially the same as Yahweh ("LORD"), the covenant-faithful God."[168] The word translated "early" (*shachar*) (verse 1) does signify looking for dawn, but it also contains within its semantic range the ideas of eagerness and longing.[169]

A vivid picture is drawn in the poetic words, "My soul thirsts for You; my flesh longs for You in a dry and thirsty land where there is no water" (verse 1b). This should not be taken as an attempt to establish a biblical anthropology, including a sharp distinction between the soul and body. The Hebrew view of human existence did not fragment human beings into sharply distinct entities; their view was much more holistic. As Tate observes, the " 'soul-body' merismus of v 2 (equals "my total being") shifts to 'my desire/longing' in v 6 and to 'my life' in v 10."[170] With his total being, David longed for God as a person would long for water "in a dry and thirsty land where there is no water" (verse 1b). This was an appropriate metaphor in view of David's wilderness experience.

In his wilderness experience, David recalled the power and glory of God he had seen in "the sanctuary" (verse 2). The NLT captures the idea: "I have seen you in your sanctuary and gazed upon your power and glory." By "sanctuary" David did not refer, of course, to the Temple. The word translated "sanctuary" is a form of *qodesh*, the essential idea of which is "holiness" or "apartness." The phrase used here (*baqodesh*) can refer to the Temple (e.g., Psalms 68:24; 74:3; Ezekiel 44:27), but the Temple was not built in David's time. In Psalm 46:4, *qodesh* was used in an apparent equation of Jerusalem with the Holy Place. In other words, the city itself could be said to be "the sanctuary." David had seen the power (*'oz*) and glory of God there. This reference to the power of God immediately connects Psalm 63 with Psalm 62 and the declaration in verse 11 that "power belongs to God." If Psalm 63 should be read as a reference to David's flight from Absalom, we may understand this to mean that Absalom, who had temporarily usurped David's throne, thought that he was exercising power in Jerusalem. In reality, the power in Jerusalem belonged to God. Absalom's defeat proved conclusively that he was not Yahweh's anointed.

The word translated "glory" appears several times in the Psalter. The heavens declare His glory (Psalm 19:1). Yahweh's glory dwells in His house (Psalm 26:8). It is above all the earth (Psalms 57:5, 11; 108:5). When Yahweh builds up Zion, He will appear in His glory (Psalm 102:16). His glory endures forever (Psalm 104:31) and is great (Psalm 138:5). His kingdom is glorious (Psalm 145:11). The word translated "glory" (*kabod*) includes within its semantic range the meanings "heavy," "rich," and "honorable." The glory of God is something weighty in significance and value. In connection with the Babylonian captivity, Ezekiel saw the glory of God withdrawing from the Holy of Holies to the threshold of the Temple, then to the mountain to the east of Jerusalem. It would not return to the Temple until a new Temple—the millennial Temple—was built. (See Ezekiel 9:3; 10:4, 18-19; 11:22-23; 43:2, 4, 5; 44:4.)

The word translated "lovingkindness" in verse 3 by the NKJV (*chesed*) referred to Yahweh's "loyal love" connected with the Davidic covenant. (See II Samuel 7:15; II Chronicles 6:42; Isaiah 55:3; Acts 13:34.) Although David was in the wilderness, he knew God would be loyal to him on the basis of the covenant God had established with him. As a consequence, he would praise God with his lips (verse 3b). Although David was in the wilderness and could not offer an animal sacrifice, he could offer the sacrifice of praise. (See Hebrews 13:15.)

As long as David had life, he would bless the Lord (verse 4). He would do this by lifting up his hands in the name of the Lord. (Compare with I Timothy 2:8.) Although the name "Yahweh" did not appear in Psalm 63, this was an allusion to it. Elohim was a title of deity; Yahweh was God's name. (See Exodus 6:3.)

Although he was in the wilderness, David confessed that he would be satisfied with "marrow and fatness" (verse 5). The juxtaposition of the two words used here (*cheleb* and *deshen*) made the meaning something like "fat and fatness." It seems that one word would not suffice to express the degree of emphasis David wanted to express. The NLT captured this in the translation "the richest of foods." Just as a person's appetite is satisfied by rich food, so David was satisfied with God's loyal love. Building on his previous statement in verse 3b, David expressed his intent to praise God "with joyful lips" (verse 5).

A comparison of verses 1 and 6 has led to an identification of Psalm 63 as a morning or evening psalm. In verse 1, David sought God early; in verse 6, he remembered God on his bed and meditated on Him in the night watches.

God was David's help (*'azar*) (verse 7). *'Azar* is used more than twenty times in the Hebrew Scriptures, with the most frequent use in reference to God as our help. The word has to do with a significant help, one that cannot be done without.

The reference to God's wings in verse 7 connects Psalm 63 with Psalm 61:4. (See also Psalm 91:4.)

David refused to distance himself from God, even in the wilderness (verse 8). He found stability at God's right hand. The way God came to the aid of the faithful was often described in the Psalter by the metaphor of His "right hand." (See Psalms 16:11; 17:7; 18:35; 20:6; 44:3; 48:10; 60:5; 73:23; 77:10; 98:1; 108:6; 138:7; 139:10.)

Absalom was one who sought David's life (verse 9). His fate was death (verses 9-10). The phrase "the lower parts of the earth" referred here to death. This was the fate of all of those who opposed God's messianic purpose through David.

Even though David was in the wilderness, he rejoiced in God (verse 11). All those who were loyal to God would praise Him, but liars would be stopped. The reference in verse 11 to liars connects Psalm 63 with Psalm 62:9.

The messianic theme of the Psalter is advanced in Psalm 63 in the same way it was advanced by Psalms 3-7. There would be those, like Absalom, who sought to kill David, thus thwarting God's messianic purpose. They would fail. The king would rejoice.

Psalm 64

Psalm 64 connects thematically with Psalm 63 and reaches back to connect with the tension between the righteous (*tsaddiq*) and the wicked (*rasha*) of Psalm 1 and with the messianic emphasis of Psalm 2. Although the superscription offers no information about the specific historical background of the psalm, the content of the psalm and its connection with Psalm 63 suggest that it reflects the trial David experienced at the hand of his son Absalom. (See Psalms 3-7.)

Wilcock suggests that the superscription "represents a true tradition of authorship, that the conspiracy of verse 2 is Absalom's, and that the psalmist is David. His circumstances could be similar, perhaps identical, to those of Psalm 63."[171] The difference between the psalms is that in Psalm 63, David "and his security in God were in the foreground, and his enemies and their schemes loomed in the background; here in [Psalm] 64 it is the other way round."[172]

The psalm begins with a prayer that seems to flow out of the final verse in Psalm 63, developing the thought that "the mouth of those who speak lies shall be stopped" (Psalm 63:11).[173] It is an individual lament.[174] The Hebrew *siyach* (translated "meditation" by the NKJV) in verse 1 is often translated "complaint."[175] But essentially *siyach* describes a person's "musing on his situation, whether good (104:34), or bad (*e.g* Jb. 10:1)."[176] Here, the idea is something like "troubled thoughts."[177] David was not moaning, "he [was] simply telling God what [was] on his mind."[178]

As is often the case with the lament psalms, David began with a plea for God to hear his voice (verse 1a). (Compare Psalms 5, 25, 28, 141, 142.) He prayed to be preserved from fear of the enemy (verse 1b). From the influence of the Ugaritic cognate of *pachad*, Dahood suggests the literal translation "from the pack of foes" for the phrase *mipachad 'owyeb*.[179] This translation, together with the reference to the "secret plots of the wicked" in verse 2, connects with Psalm 2:1-3: "For the nouns *conspiracy* and [*noisy*] *crowd* we find in Psalm 2:1-2 the corresponding verbs, 'gather together' and 'rage.' This psalm is describing a classic instance of the rebellion against God of which . . . one warned us in the Psalter's preamble."[180] VanGemeren points out that the conspiracy "results from their banding together in their council of war (cf. 2:1)."[181]

The reference to "the secret plots of the wicked" and "the rebellion of the workers of iniquity" (verse 2) described well the scheming rebellion of Absalom and those who identified with him. (See comments on Psalms 3-7.)

One of the most significant weapons used by David's enemies was the tongue: They "[sharpened] their tongue like a sword, and [bent] their bows to shoot their arrows—bitter words" (verse 3). This was one of several places in the Psalter where the words of enemies were described as swords and arrows. (See Psalm 55:21; 57:4; 59:7; 120:3-4.) In this case, "it is Absalom and Ahithophel plotting behind David's back, not Ziba flattering and Shimei cursing him face to face, who are reflected in Psalm 64."[182]

David's enemies had ambushed him; they shot "in secret . . . suddenly they [shot] at him and [did] not fear" (verse 4). (Compare with Psalms 10:8; 17:12.) In the midst of this danger, David declared his innocence: he was blameless. This did not indicate, of course, that he was sinless. (See I Kings 8:46; II Chronicles 6:36.) He was innocent of any wrongdoing in the situation with Absalom. The ambush would "be either the prepared situation which ['framed'] an innocent man, or the shelter of anonymity from which a rumour [could] be launched *without fear*."[183]

David's enemies "[encouraged] themselves in an evil matter; they [talked] of laying snares secretly; they [said], 'Who will see them?'" (verse 5). Absalom plotted secretly under a guise of innocence. (See II Samuel 15:1-12.) The claim that no one would see them revealed the ignorance of David's enemies. It placed them in the category of fools who said, "There is no God" (Psalm 53:1). They would be seen, for "God looks down from heaven upon the children of men, to see if there are any who understand, who seek God" (Psalm 53:2). In retrospect, Psalm 53 seems to describe the character of David's enemies, who "[devised] iniquities" and who said, "We have perfected a shrewd scheme" (verse 6a). Like so many before and after them, Absalom and his henchmen were convinced that they had planned the perfect crime. The NLT translates the final phrase of verse 6, "Yes, the human heart and mind are cunning." The reference to both the heart and the mind indicates that man "is evil through and through."[184]

But, as always happens, the tables would be turned on the wicked: "God shall shoot at them with an arrow; suddenly they shall be wounded. So He will make them stumble over their own tongue" (verses 7-8a). The figure of speech here indicates that God would use the weapons of the enemy against them. Just as the wicked "suddenly" shot at David (verse 4) with their poisonous words, so they would "suddenly" be wounded by God. When they rebelled against God, they decided the terms of their own destruction. As it relates to Absalom, this "law of retribution"[185] is described in terms of the pit (Psalm 7:15-16) as it often is elsewhere in the Psalter. (See Psalms 9:15; 35:7-8; 55:23; 57:6; 94:13.)

As a consequence of God's intervention against David's enemies, "All who see them shall flee away. All men shall fear, and shall declare the work of God; for they shall wisely consider His doing. The righteous shall be glad in the LORD, and trust in Him. And all the upright in heart shall glory" (verses 8b-10). This reference to "all men" lifts the psalm out of any narrow application to Israel alone: "As with the preceding psalm, within the larger context of the entire book, David's words express faith and hope in God's promise of future salvation for 'all mankind.' "[186]

The reference to "the righteous" as those who trust the Lord extends the theme begun in Psalms 1-2. (See Psalms 1:6; 2:12.) The fact that those who are upright in heart will "glory" connects Psalm 64 with Psalm 63:11.

As with all of the psalms that arose out of David's conflict with Absalom, Psalm 64 advances the messianic theme of the Psalter by pointing out that all attempts on David's life would fail. This meant that all attempts to oppose God's messianic purpose through David would come to nothing. Regardless of how clever, well-organized, and ambitious God's enemies may be, they will suffer humiliating defeat. Those who trust the Lord will be rewarded for their faithfulness.

Psalm 65

Psalm 65 is the first of four psalms in a group that not only identify the poem as a psalm (*mizmor*) but also as a "song" (*shiyr*). Although we do not know the significance of this, the use of the dual identification with four psalms in a row at least suggests that

Psalms 65-68 originally formed a small group of related psalms that found its way intact into the Psalter. Thirteen psalms are identified as both psalms and songs in the superscriptions, but this is the largest collected group.[187] Seventeen psalms are identified only as songs in the superscriptions. No psalm identified only as a song is found in isolation from other psalms identified only as songs. First, there is a small collection of two psalms identified as songs.[188] Then, there is a group of fifteen psalms identified as songs.[189] Tate suggests that Psalms 65-68 form "a short collection of . . . hymnic prayers."[190] It may be that Psalm 65:2 serves as an introduction not only to Psalm 65, but also to the entire collection, with Psalm 65:3 functioning more specifically as an introduction to Psalm 65.[191]

Psalm 65 can be divided into three sections. Section one begins with a reference to Zion (verse 1) and concludes with a reference to the Temple (verse 4). Section two begins with a reference to "the ends of the earth" (verse 5) and concludes with a reference to "the farthest parts" (verse 8). The third section begins with a reference to rain (verse 9) and concludes with a reference to fertile pastures and valleys (verse 13). Wilcock labels these sections as follows: (1) God in the Temple; (2) God in the world; and (3) God in the harvest.[192] Kidner suggests: (1) God of grace; (2) God of might; and (3) God of plenty.[193] Tate points out that Psalm 65 "seems to move on two tracks through its three sections. One track is that of *hymnic praise* which sets forth the power of God. . . . The second track in the psalm is that of the *petitions* which seek the activation of the powers of the Hearer of Prayer."[194]

Psalm 65 connects with the theme of God's universal rule over all men—not just over Israel—in Psalm 64:9.[195] Although God's headquarters, so to speak, are in Zion (verses 1-4), His rule extends to "the ends of the earth," "the far-off seas" (verse 5), and "the farthest parts" (verse 8). All flesh will come to Him in Zion (verse 2). These geographical references see Zion as the center of the earth; every point on the globe is located by its proximity to Zion.

The reference to Zion picks up the Zion theology theme that is, together with the Davidic covenant theme, central to the Psalter.[196] Zion is a special place that is chosen by God (Psalms 78:67-68; 132:13). God loves Zion (Psalm 87:2). He dwells in Zion (Psalms 9:11a; 20:2; 50:2; 76:2; 99:2; 132:13; 135:21; 146:10). Zion is holy to God (Psalms 2:6; 48:1-2). It is a place of rejoicing (Psalms 9:14; 149:2). Zion is beautiful (Psalms 48:2; 50:2). God's name is loved there (Psalms 69:35-36; 102:21). God keeps record of those born in Zion (Psalm 87:5). Yahweh's judgments make Zion glad (Psalm 97:8). Yahweh will have mercy on Zion (Psalm 102:13). Zion is protected and blessed by Yahweh (Psalm 147:12-14). Zion is stable (Psalm 125:1). Zion is the place where people appear before God (Psalm 84:7). Zion is worthy of reflection (Psalm 48:12). Those who hate Zion will suffer the consequences (Psalm 129:5). In Babylonian captivity, the people of Israel remembered Zion (Psalm 137:1). God's people would return to Zion (Psalm 126). The walls of the city would be rebuilt (Psalm 51:18). Israel's return from captivity was connected with salvation (Psalms 14:7; 53:6). Blessing is associated with Zion (Psalms 128:5; 133:3; 134:3). The Messiah will rule as King in Zion (Psalms 2:6; 110:1-2).

From a survey of the references to Zion in the Psalter, we can conclude that (1) although the Psalter recognizes the judgment of God upon His holy city due to the sinfulness of its inhabitants, the book is oriented toward a bright future beyond the Babylonian captivity, a future involving the restoration of Zion and the establishment of a literal kingdom governed by the Messiah from His headquarters in Zion [Jerusalem]; (2) from the time of Israel's monarchy, Zion has been the focal point of God's activity on earth. All evidence indicates that this focus has been on the literal city; there is no indication that Zion is to be viewed in a non-literal way; and (3) God's sovereignty is demonstrated by His ability to prevent the sinfulness of Zion's inhabitants from thwarting His purposes as they relate to Zion.

The phrase translated "praise is awaiting You, O God" (*leka dumiyah tehillah 'elohim* [verse 1]) might be better translated something like "stillness praises you, O God." A literal translation would be "to you stillness is praise O God."[197] Although praise is often associated with joyous singing, dancing, and the playing of musical instruments in the Psalter, there is an aspect of praise that is found in waiting silently upon God. Kidner points out that it "may sometimes be the height of worship . . . to fall silent before God in awe at His presence and in submission to His will."[198] In the context here, this may be waiting silently on the answer to prayer (verse 2). Specifically, those who are in Zion praise God by waiting on Him.

The vow in view in verse 1 may also relate to the prayer to which verse 2 refers. In view of the agricultural theme of verses 9-13, A. A. Anderson suggests that "the vows may presuppose a time of trouble . . . or they may allude to promises made by the Israelite farmers at the time of sowing."[199] Tate points out that rain "and a good harvest would be signs of blessing and forgiveness so that the vows could be joyfully fulfilled."[200]

The God who dwells in Zion is a God who hears prayer (verse 2a). All flesh—not just Israelites—will come to Him there (verse 2b). When will this happen? According to Isaiah, it will be after the creation of the new heavens and the new earth. (See Isaiah 66:22-23.)[201]

Verse 3 includes a confession of personal sinfulness: "Iniquities prevail against me." This connects thematically with Psalm 51. (See comments on Psalm 64:4.) The messianic theme of the Psalter rises with great clarity in the words, "As for our transgressions, You will provide atonement for them" (verse 3). The word translated "atonement" (*kafar*) has to do with a ransom paid.[202] In terms of the New Covenant, the Messiah dealt with the sin problem by taking upon Himself the sins of the world. (See Psalms 51:2; 79:9; Isaiah 6:7; 53:5-6, 8-12; Romans 5:11; II Corinthians 5:21; Hebrews 9:14; I John 1:7, 9; 2:1-2.)

The blessing pronounced upon the chosen person in verse 4 calls to mind the blessed man of Psalm 1:1. The word translated "blessing" (*'asheray*) is sometimes translated "happy." It appears twenty-four times in the Psalter, including twice in the imprecatory Psalm 137.[203] As a significant theme, it describes the rewards of walking in the ways of God in contrast to the penalties for walking in one's own way. (See Psalm 1.)

The reference to those whom God causes to approach Him in order to dwell in His courts and be satisfied with the goodness of His house, His holy Temple (verse 4), connects Psalm 65 with the Temple theme that runs through the Psalter, and specifically with Psalms 15 and 24. The person who enjoys the presence of the Lord must meet specific qualifications. (See comments on Psalms 15 and 24.)

How can a psalm of David refer to the Temple? The Tabernacle at Shiloh, long before David's time, was referred to as the *heykal* ("temple"). (See I Samuel 1:9; 3:3.) This was the same word used in verse 4. David used the word "to denote the dwelling of God in its widest sense."[204] (See Psalms 18:6; 29:9.) Here, the context connects the Temple with Zion itself (verse 1).

The second section of the psalm begins in verse 5. The God who hears prayers (verse 2) will answer them "by awesome deeds in righteousness" (verse 5a). The word translated "awesome deeds" (*nora'ot*) is "used for divine acts which both produce fear and terror in God's enemies (cf. Pss 47:3; 76:8; 89:8) and bring forth reverential awe and praise on the part of the faithful (68:35; 96:4; 99:2-3)."[205]

A messianic emphasis may be seen again in verse 5b: "God will be the 'Savior, the hope of all the ends of the earth and of the farthest seas' (v.5)."[206] The Messiah's universal rule is in view here. (See comments on Psalms 22:27-29; 24:1; 45:12; 46:10; 47:7-9; 48:10.)

To the ancient Israelites, mountains represented "the most fixed and stable parts of the world."[207] (See Psalms 30:7; 46:3; 90:2; 96:10; 97:5; 104:5-6.) God, who established the mountains, was greater than the mountains. He was "clothed with power" (verse 6b). The seas were frightening to the ancients (verse 7). (See comments on Psalm 29:3-9.) God was able, however, to still the stormy seas, just as He was able to still "the tumult of the peoples" (verse 7b). The reference to the tumult of the peoples seems to connect with Psalm 2:1-3 and with all of the psalms that describe human rebellion against God. The messianic emphasis of the Psalter makes Jesus' miracle of calming the stormy sea even more significant. (See Matthew 8:23-27.) If it is God who stills the noise of the seas, and if the Messiah calmed the sea, the Messiah must be God.

The universality of the Messiah's rule is seen in verse 8: "They also who dwell in the farthest parts are afraid of Your signs." The signs that will cause all people to fear God are the "awesome deeds" of verse 5. A "spatial reference to the whole world"[208] is seen in the phrase "outgoings of the morning and evening" (verse 8b). In other words, God causes the whole world to rejoice.

The third section of the psalm begins in verse 9 with agricultural references that would have been very meaningful to the ancient Israelites. For them, blessing, health, and wealth were associated with their crops. The blessings of verses 9-13 could be in answer to the confession of sins in verses 2-3. Abundant rain was evidence that God was visiting the earth to water it, enriching it. The rain was called "the river of God." Grain grew as the earth was softened with showers. This was the blessing of God. (See verse 10.) The phrase "Your paths drip with abundance" (verse 11) is a reference to "a richly-laden cart dropping its contents in its track."[209] In this meaningful figure of speech, God drives a cart that is so overloaded with an abundance of produce that it falls off as He drives by. This overabundance drops off on the pastures and hills (verse 12). The evidence of God's blessing is seen in pastures covered with flocks and valleys with grain (verse 13). As a consequence of these rich blessings, the pastures and valleys shout for joy and sing.

By its connection with previous messianic themes, its reference to God's universal reign, and the hope of atonement for sins, Psalm 65 advances the messianic theme of the Psalter. The One who provides the atonement will dwell in Zion, hear prayer, and receive universal homage. He is the One who calms the seas. During His reign, the earth will produce abundantly.

As Paul and Barnabas preached the gospel in Lycaonia and the surrounding region, they attempted to deflect attention from themselves and toward God by declaring, "Nevertheless He did not leave Himself without witness, in that He did good, gave us rain from heaven and fruitful seasons, filling our hearts with food and gladness" (Acts 14:17). It is significant that they would make this appeal in conjunction with preaching the gospel of Jesus Christ. He is the God of whom the rain and fruitful seasons witness.[210]

Psalm 66

Within the group of four psalms identified as both psalms and songs,[211] two are attributed to David (Psalms 65 and 68) and two are anonymous (Psalms 66 and 67). Psalm 66 is divided into two sections. The first section, consisting of verses 1-12, is a call to corporate praise; the second section, consisting of verses 13-20, is the prayer of an individual. Section one is further punctuated into three stanzas by *Selah* at the end of verses 4 and 7; section two is divided into two stanzas by one occurrence of *Selah* at the end of verse 15. Although we do not know for certain the significance of *Selah*, it at least suggests intentional internal structure wherever it appears.[212] The first stanza of section one, verse 1, begins with "an imperative summons to praise."[213] So do the next two stanzas, beginning with verses 5 and 8. In the second section, the first stanza, beginning with verse 13, declares the psalmist's intention to worship in God's house. At the beginning of the second stanza, starting with verse 16, the psalmist calls on the congregation "to hear his account of God's deed for him."[214]

Dahood points out that the first section of the psalm "is a hymn in praise of God's might and his care for his people throughout its history, especially at the Exodus (vss. 5-9) and during the wanderings in the desert (vss. 10-12)."[215] The second section "is the thanksgiving hymn of an affluent individual fulfilling his vows in the temple (vss. 13-15) and recounting the story of his experience."[216] We do not know for certain the historical event behind this psalm,[217] but Wilcock suggests that it "belongs to the days of the Assyrian invasion of 701 BC," pointing out parallels with Isaiah 37.[218]

The first verses of Psalms 66 and 100 are identical in the Hebrew text, except for the use of *Elohim* in Psalm 66:1 and *Yahweh* in Psalm 100:1. The command to "all the earth" (*kal ha'aretz*) to make a "joyful shout to God" connects Psalm 66 with the universal acknowledgement of God seen in the previous two psalms. (See Psalms 64:9; 65:5-8.) Walvoord points out that the "song of the nations worshiping the Lord . . . is a frequent theme of the Old Testament which will be fulfilled . . . in the millennial kingdom as well as in the eternal state."[219] (See also Psalms 2:8-9; 24:1-10; 72:8-12; 86:9; Isaiah 2:2-4; 9:6-7; 66:18-23; Daniel 7:14; Zephaniah 2:11; Zechariah 14:9.) References to the universal worship of God in the Psalter advance the messianic theme of the book, for in the introduction to the Psalter it is the Son who is to be given the nations and the ends of the earth for His inheritance. (See Psalm 2:8-9.)

The command to "sing out the honor of His name" (verse 2a) reflects the theology of the Name seen frequently in the Old Testament. The name

> is an expression of the presence of God. . . . The Name carried something of the essential nature and power of God. To invoke his name was to invoke his presence. The Name theology is especially evident in the Deuteronomic writings. The Israelites were to worship at the place chosen by Yahweh where he would "put his name" (see Deut

> 12:5, 11, 21, passim; also Exod 20:24). The use of the Name to protect both the transcendence and presence of Yahweh is especially present in the Solomonic address to the people and prayer at the dedication of the temple (I Kgs 8:1-66). Yahweh is repeatedly affirmed to be in heaven, but his powerful presence is invoked because his name is in the temple. . . .[220]

The essential idea in "sing out the honor of His name" is to "sing out His honor." The name of God represents God Himself.

The phrase *siymu kabod tehillato*, translated "make His praise glorious" (verse 2b), can be translated in a variety of ways. The RSV translates it as "give to Him glorious praise!" The Douay-Rheims and the LXX read, "Give glory to his praise." The NAB reads, "Give him glorious praise." The NLT, in a kind of paraphrase, reads, "Tell the world how glorious he is." The NJB translates, "Glorify him with your praises." If *kabod* is adverbial, the phrase can be translated, "Set forth gloriously his praise."[221] However the phrase is translated, the verse consists of two imperatives, the commands to sing and to glorify God. These commands are given to "all the earth" (verse 1).

Since *kabod* appears twice in verse 2, once in the construct state with "name," where it is translated "honor of," and since the verse is a form of poetic parallelism, it may be that we are to understand "His praise" as a parallel to "His name." This is not to say that "praise" is a precise equivalent to "name." Rather, the second phrase picks up the idea present in the first phrase and further advances it. As we "make His praise glorious," we are honoring His name.[222]

Verses 3-4 give the actual script for the song and praise commanded in verse 2. All the earth is to say to God, "How awesome are Your works! Through the greatness of Your power Your enemies shall submit themselves to You. All the earth shall worship You and sing praises to You; they shall sing praises to Your name."

The reference to God's awesome works connects Psalm 66 with Psalm 65. (See Psalm 65:5, 8.) The "awesome deeds" of Psalm 65:5 and the "awesome works" of Psalm 66:3 are connected by the common use of a form of *yare'*. The reference to "the greatness of Your power" (verse 3b) also connects the two psalms conceptually; also, different words are used for "power."[223] (See Psalm 65:6b.) Further connection between the two psalms is seen in the reference to the submission of God's enemies to Him (verse 3c). In Psalm 65:8, this is described in terms of the fear that would be experienced by those "who dwell in the farthest parts."

The universal rule of God is seen in verse 4. All the earth will worship Him. This worship will include singing praises to Him, an idea that is further developed in the phrase, "They shall sing praises to Your name." When praises are sung to God's name, they are sung to Him. In a very real sense, as we know God's name, we know Him. Verse 4 is connected with verse 2 by the concept of praising and honoring God's name.

The universal nature of God's rule (see also verse 1) continues a theme seen in Psalms 64:9; 65:2, 5, 8. The Messiah's universal dominion is seen many times in the Psalter, beginning at Psalm 2:8-10, as well as elsewhere throughout the Scriptures. (See Psalms 24:1-10; 72:8-12; 86:9; Isaiah 2:2-4; 9:6-7; 66:18-23; Daniel 7:14; Zephaniah 2:11; Zechariah 14:9.) Those who had victory over the Beast, as seen by John, sang "the song of Moses, the servant of God, and the song of the Lamb, saying: 'Great and marvelous are Your works, Lord God Almighty! Just and true are Your ways, O King of the saints! Who shall not fear You, O Lord, and glorify Your name? For You alone are holy. For all nations shall come and worship before You, for Your judgments have been manifested" (Revelation 15:3-4). Just as the people of Israel sang the song of Moses (Exodus 15:1-21) upon their deliverance from Egypt, so those who had victory over the Beast sang a form of the song—now the song of the Lamb—upon their deliverance. Although the words were not found precisely in the song of Moses, they reflected the sentiments of that song. The song of the Lamb was composed of phrases from the Psalms and Prophets.[224] (See, e.g., Exodus 15:11; Psalm 139:14; Amos 4:13; Deuteronomy 32:4; Jeremiah 10:7; Psalm 86:9.)

In Isaiah 45:22-23, Yahweh said, "Look to Me, and be saved, all you ends of the earth! For I am God, and there is no other. I have sworn by Myself; the word has gone out of My mouth in righteousness, and shall not return, that to Me every knee shall bow, every tongue shall take an oath." Paul saw this as fulfilled in the universal exaltation of Jesus: "Therefore God also has highly exalted Him and given Him the name which is above every name, that at the name of Jesus every knee should bow, of those in heaven, and of those on earth, and of those under the earth, and that every tongue should confess that Jesus Christ is Lord, to the glory of God the Father" (Philippians 2:9-11). To say that Jesus Christ is Lord is to say that He is Yahweh. The New Testament uses *kurios* to translate *Yahweh*. To confess Jesus as Lord is to glorify the Father.

Verse 5 begins the second stanza, with the command, "Come and see the works of God." Again, this command is extended to "all the earth" (verse 1). These awesome works have already been mentioned in verse 3, and they connect with Psalm 65:5. At this point, the specific awesome work the psalmist had in mind was the deliverance of Israel from Egypt in the parting of the Red Sea (verse 6). God's victory over Egypt—the most powerful nation on earth at that time—was an example of His universal dominion: "His eyes [observed] the nations" (verse 7b). Rebellion would not be tolerated.

Verse 8 begins the third stanza, also with a command: "Oh, bless our God, you peoples! And make the voice of His praise to be heard." This continues the universal praise theme of verses 2-4. God is to be praised because He sustains life and provides security for His people (verse 9).

Verses 10-12 seem to refer to Israel's wilderness experience. There they were tested and refined as God brought them "into the net," "laid affliction" on their backs, and caused them to go "through fire and through water." In the end, He brought them out "to rich fulfillment" in the Promised Land. This was similar language to that by "which the prophets [described] the afflictions of the exile (the figure of testing and smelting in Isa. 48:10; Jer. 9:7; Zech. 13:9; Mal. 3:3; the net in Ezek. 12:13; 17:20; and passing through the water and fire in Isa. 43:2)."[225]

In verse 6, it is tempting to view the "sea" as a reference to the Red Sea and the "river" as a reference to the Jordan.[226] But "sea" (*yam*) and "river" (*nahar*) are probably poetic alternatives.[227] The Jordan is never identified as "the river" in the Hebrew text.[228] *Nahar* is used, however, of the sea.[229] (See Jonah 2:3; Psalm 93:3-4.)

The Hebrew perspective is much more holistic and communal, as opposed to the fragmented individualism of the Western world. The statement, "There we will rejoice in Him" (verse 6c) demonstrates that there is a sense in which the people of God of all ages identify with the experiences of the people of God in the past. In a New Testament sense, today's people of faith join those of the first century when they participate in the sacrament of the Lord's Supper. (See I Corinthians 11:23-26.) As often as we eat the bread and drink the cup, we "proclaim the Lord's death till He comes" (I Corinthians 11:26).

Believers should not be surprised to face "fiery trials" (I Peter 4:12).[230] For Israel, Egypt was a "furnace." (See Deuteronomy 4:20; I Kings 8:51.) Their passage through the Red Sea was their trial by water. God "caused men to ride over [their] heads" (verse 12a). (See Isaiah 51:23.) But "faith [was] not faith unless it [had] been tried like silver and gold."[231] When faith proved genuine, it resulted in a rich reward. (See I Peter 1:6-9.)

With verse 13, the psalm moves from corporate praise to individual worship. The psalmist would go into God's house with burnt offerings to pay his vows. This psalm was not attributed to David in the superscription, so there was no reason to think that this reference to God's house was anything other than a reference to the Temple. We do not know the identity of this worshiper. It is often speculated that it was the king, perhaps Hezekiah.[232] Others, reading the Psalter with what may be an extreme form of messianism, see this as a reference to the Messiah.[233]

Whoever the worshiper was in verses 13-20, he made vows to God when he was in trouble (verses 13-14). Apparently, he promised to offer specific sacrifices in response to God's intervention in his situation. These consisted of fat animals, rams, bulls, and goats (verse 15).

The second stanza of the second section of this psalm begins with an imperative in verse 16. (See the imperatives in verses 1, 5, and 8 at the beginning of the three stanzas of the first section.) This was a command for all those who feared God to "come and hear." The psalmist would declare what God had done for him to those who came.

This individual worshiper cried to God with his mouth; he extolled God with his tongue (verse 17). He practiced what he preached. (Compare with verses 1-4.)

He knew God would not hear him if he regarded iniquity in his heart (verse 18). God heard those who walked humbly with Him. (See Micah 6:8.) Thus, it was evident that this worshiper confessed his sins to God. God responded by hearing him (verse 19) and responding to his prayer in mercy (verse 20).

Does Psalm 66 advance the messianic theme of the Psalter? It is fascinating to note that the LXX, in the superscription, identifies the Psalm as "a song of psalm of resurrection." The Vulgate follows suit. This may be based at least in part on seeing the exodus of Israel from Egypt as a type of the redemptive work of Christ in delivering His people from captivity to sin (verse 6).[234]

Whatever the reason for the messianic reading of the LXX may be, Psalm 66 advances the messianic theme of the Psalter by its emphasis on God's universal reign, a reign that is seen in the Psalter and elsewhere to belong uniquely to the Messiah.

Psalm 67

Psalm 67 is the third in a group of four psalms[235] identified as both psalms and songs. Like each of these psalms, it is addressed "to the Chief Musician" in the superscription. Like the second of the group, it is not identified with David. Unlike any of the other three, it is to be performed "on stringed instruments."

The psalm begins with an apparent reference to the Aaronic blessing found in Numbers 6:24-25.

> God be merciful to us and bless us, and cause His face to shine upon us. Selah. (verse 1)

> And the LORD spoke to Moses, saying: "Speak to Aaron and his sons, saying, 'This is the way you shall bless the children of Israel. Say to them: "The LORD bless you and keep you; the LORD make His face shine upon you, and be gracious to you; the LORD lift up His countenance upon you, and give you peace." ' So they shall put My name on the children of Israel, and I will bless them." (Numbers 6:22-27)

Verse 1 may not reflect only the Aaronic blessing, however. As Wilcock points out,

> Our psalmist builds his poem on this text, developing it in the light of the original blessing given centuries before to Abraham: 'I will make you into a great nation and I will bless you; I will make your name great, *and you will be a blessing. . . .* All peoples on earth will be blessed through you' (Gen. 12:2-3).[236]

Kidner agrees with the Abrahamic influence on the Psalm:

> If a psalm was ever written round the promises to Abraham, that he would be both blessed and made a

blessing, it could well have been such as this. The song begins at home, and returns to pause there a moment before the end; but its thought always flies to the distant peoples and to what awaits them when the blessing that has reached 'us' reaches all. . . .

. . . If the spirit of the psalm . . . is that of the Abrahamic hope, its text is the Aaronic Blessing.[237]

As it relates to the messianic theme of the Psalter, the influence of the Abrahamic covenant on Psalm 67 is significant. The Abrahamic covenant, as first given by God, contained the promise, "And in you all the families of the earth shall be blessed" (Genesis 12:3b). From the outset, there was a dimension of the Abrahamic covenant that was not exclusively for Abraham's physical descendants; all the families of the earth, not just his family, would be blessed in Abraham. This was confirmed in the further development of the Abrahamic covenant: "In your seed all the nations of the earth shall be blessed, because you have obeyed My voice" (Genesis 22:18). Isaac, Abraham's promised son, received a new confirmation: ". . . and in your seed all the nations of the earth shall be blessed" (Genesis 26:4). Jacob, Abraham's grandson, also received such a confirmation.[238] According to Paul, the ultimate and final fulfillment of this promise of universal blessing came through Christ.

Now to Abraham and his Seed were the promises made. He does not say, "And to seeds," as of many, but as of one, *"And to your Seed,"* who is Christ. (Galatians 3:16)[239]

The universal dimension of Psalm 67 indicates that more is in view than just the covenant God established with Israel at Sinai. That covenant was not made with any other nation.[240] Psalm 67 is a prayer, not just for the blessing and mercy of God upon the nation of Israel, but for God's salvation to be known "among all nations" (verse 2), for "the nations" to be glad and sing for joy, for God to "govern the nations" (verse 4), and for "all the peoples" to praise God (verse 5). This is the language of the Abrahamic covenant, with its focus on the coming Messiah.

Mays recognizes the influence of the Abrahamic covenant on the theme of universal blessing in this psalm but also points out that there is a universal dimension to God's dealings with the nation of Israel.

> The second tradition [of blessing] is the prophecy of Isaiah 40-55 and its proclamation that the LORD's salvation of Israel will be a revelation to the nations that the LORD reigns and leads the ends of the earth to praise the LORD (e.g., Isa. 40:1-5; 45:20-25; 49:22-26).[241]

This universal dimension is a consequence of the New Covenant.[242]

"God be merciful to us," the initial request in this psalm, connects the psalm with the *chesed* ("mercy" or "loyal love") theme that begins early in the Psalter.[243] Because the general context of the Psalter is about the Davidic covenant[244] with its promise of mercy,[245] this further connects Psalm 67 with that covenant, including its universal dimension.[246]

The appeal for the blessing of God (verse 1) connects Psalm 67 with the first word in the first psalm and the promise of the final verse of the second psalm.

> Blessed is the man who walks not in the counsel of the ungodly, nor stands in the path of sinners, nor sits in the seat of the scornful. (Psalm 1:1)

> Blessed are all those who put their trust in Him. (Psalm 2:12c)

Although different words are used for the concept of blessing,[247] the words have an overlapping semantic range.[248]

The phrase "cause His face to shine upon us" (verse 1) probably reflects the idea that an "Oriental monarch revealed in his facial expression either his pleasure or displeasure with the party that sought an audience with him."[249] Tate explains the use of this metaphor.

> The shining forth of the face of God among his people is a metaphor for his goodwill and blessing (cf. Pss 4:6; 31:16; 44:3; 80:3, 7, 19; 89:15; 119:135). A shining, bright face reveals a person of good disposition and is a sign of inward pleasure. . . . The opposite of God's shining face is his hidden face. When God hides his face, the life of his people is endangered (cf. Pss 10:1; 13:1; 30:7; 44:24; 104:29; Deut 31:17).[250]

As Proverbs 16:15 points out, "In the light of the king's face is life, and his favor is like a cloud of the latter rain."

Verse 1, then, reaches out in several directions to gather together the themes of the Abrahamic, Davidic, and New covenants. These are messianic themes. As Tate points out,

> . . . the psalm invites a messianic perspective which looks forward to an age when the relationship between Yahweh's saving-work in Israel and his blessing-work in all creation will no longer be obscure but will lead the peoples of the world to rejoice and sing of his judgments and guidance (v 5).[251]

VanGemeren agrees.

> . . . the psalm anticipates a glorious messianic era in which Jews and Gentiles share in the glorious presence of God. When God blesses his people, it is with the goal of provoking the nations to jealousy so that they too

might come to know him, share in his blessings, and have reason to praise him.[252]

As Mitchell observes, "Psalm 67 proclaims the ultimate triumph of Yhwh's kingdom over all nations."[253] Indeed, "A later tradition illustrates the messianic conquest theme of Ps. 67. It relates that this psalm was inscribed on David's shield in the form of the *menorah*, and that 'when he went forth to battle, he would meditate on its mystery and conquer.'. . ."[254]

Payne views Psalm 67 as a reference to "the righteousness of the Messiah's future rule"[255] in the Millennium and connects it with David's messianic prophecy in II Samuel 23:3-4.

The reference to God's "way" (*derek*) in verse 2 also connects this psalm to a theme originating in Psalm 1:1. There is one way that is the way of sinners, and there is another way that is the way of God.[256] The prayer includes the request that God's salvation (*yeshu'ah*) would be known among all nations (verse 2). Again, this connects with a theme that runs throughout the Psalter.[257] The Messiah's name, *Yeshua'*, which means "Yahweh is salvation," is related to this word.[258]

This is, of course, poetry, and there is a parallel between God's way and His salvation. His salvation will come to the nations as they walk in His way. In terms of the New Covenant, the first step in this "way" is to put one's faith in the Messiah, *Yeshua'*. The way of *Yeshua'* is the way of salvation, or deliverance.

The prayer continues with an appeal for "the peoples," "all the peoples," to praise God (verse 3). This leads into the central verse of the psalm, which focuses on God's universal reign (verse 4). Wilcock demonstrates the centrality of verse 4 by means of a simple chiasm:

> Bless us, and all the nations (vv. 1-2);
>   may all the peoples praise you (v. 3)
>   for the joy of your universal rule (v. 4)!
>   May all the peoples praise you (v. 5)!
> Bless us, and all the ends of the earth (vv. 6-7).[259]

When the time comes—and this points to the millennial era—when God is governing the nations of the earth and judging the people righteously, the nations will be glad and sing for joy (verse 4). The universal rule of God is a significant theme in the Psalter.[260] But, as the introduction to the Psalter points out, the Lord reigns through His Son.[261]

Verse 5 reiterates the prayer of verse 3. Verses 6-7 capture the content of verses 1-2. The phrase "then the earth shall yield her increase" (verse 6a) ties Psalm 67 together with Leviticus 26:4, where this is one of God's blessings He gives obedient Israel, along with "rain, food, peace, and his presence (Lev. 26:3-13)."[262] The blessing of verses 6-7 is the same blessing as that of verse 1. The "ends of the earth" of verse 7 is a reference to the same universal dimension of God's rule as seen in the reference to "all nations" in verse 2. The phrase "God, our own God" identifies the true God in distinction from the false gods of the nations.[263]

Although Psalm 67 does not specifically mention the Messiah, it advances the messianic theme of the Psalter by its focus on the universal reign of God. References to God's universal reign throughout the Psalter must be read in view of Psalm 2:7-8. The Messiah receives the nations for His inheritance and the ends of the earth for His possession.[264]

Psalm 68

Psalm 68 is the last of the group of four psalms identified as both psalms and songs. All four are addressed "to the Chief Musician." The first (Psalm 65) and last of the group are identified as psalms of David, indicating that the two middle psalms should also be read as psalms of David, even though they are not so identified.

Although Psalm 68 is an interpretive challenge,[265] the content is sufficiently clear to know that it advances the messianic theme of the Psalter. The psalm declares God's victory over His enemies (verses 1-23) and His entry into His sanctuary, where He receives universal worship (verses 24-35). A specific messianic theme appears in verse 18, which Paul saw as being fulfilled in the ascension of Jesus Christ.

> You have ascended on high, You have led captivity captive; You have received gifts among men, even from the rebellious, that the LORD God might dwell there. (Psalm 68:18)

> Therefore He says: *"When He ascended on high, He led captivity captive, and gave gifts to men."* (Ephesians 4:8)

The date and setting of Psalm 68 are uncertain,[266] but Tate says, "The psalm is probably post-exilic in its present form, but certainly contains traditional material from earlier periods."[267] The psalm recalls God's past victories and looks ahead to His future reign; both views would encourage the people of Israel during the time after the Temple was destroyed and Jerusalem decimated. Their situation as vassals of a foreign power was bleak, but it was not permanent.

The psalm begins with a reference to the liturgy accompanying the progress of the ark of the covenant:

> So it was, whenever the ark set out, that Moses said: "Rise up, O LORD! Let Your enemies be scattered, and let those who hate You flee before You." (Numbers 10:35)

> Let God arise, let His enemies be scattered; let those also who hate Him flee before Him. (Psalm 68:1)

The use of this theme at the opening of the psalm suggests that the entire psalm reflects God's victorious journey from Sinai to Zion.[268]

The phrase "let God arise" picks up a theme seen throughout the Psalter. This is a plea for Him to rise from His throne to conquer His enemies.[269] The plea for Him to arise means that He is seated on His throne in the heavens, ruling in spite of human rebellion. This idea is initiated in Psalm 2:4: "He who sits in the heavens shall laugh; the LORD shall hold them in derision."

God's enemies are as nonthreatening to Him as drifting smoke and melting wax (verse 2a). The wicked perish at His presence (verse 2b). This reference to the "wicked" (*resha'im*) continues a theme that begins at Psalm 1:1 and reaches all the way to Psalm 147:6, with nearly seventy occurrences all together.[270]

The contrast between the righteous (*tsadiqim*) and the wicked, which begins in Psalm 1:5 and reaches to Psalm 146:8 with a total of nearly forty occurrences, continues here.[271] As in Psalm 1:4-6, the wicked perish. But as implied in Psalm 1:2-3, and 6, the righteous are glad and rejoice before God. Even though different Hebrew words are used to represent the prosperity of the righteous (*tsalach* in Psalm 1:3 and *kosharah* in Psalm 68:6), the semantic idea seems to be the same. The wicked perish; the righteous prosper.

The identification of God with His name is seen in the parallelism of verse 4a: "Sing to God, sing praises to His name." This is an imperative. The God who "rides on the clouds" is to be extolled (verse 4b). To the Israelites, this meant that it was the God of Israel and not Baal who made "the rain clouds his chariot and [rode] across the heavens to aid the defenseless."[272] God is to be extolled by His name YAH, an abbreviation for Yahweh (verse 4c). This underscores the importance of identifying the true God by His name.

God is concerned for the welfare of the fatherless and widows (verse 5).[273] He sets the fatherless and widows in families (verse 6a).[274] The connection here of the fatherless and widows with those who are bound, but who are brought into prosperity (verse 6b), suggests that this is a reference to the Exodus: "That deliverance was the classic provision for the homeless, liberation for the prisoners and chastening for the rebels."[275] Those who are bound are brought into prosperity; those who are rebellious dwell in a dry land (verse 6c). In view of verse 7, this is an apt description of the circumstances surrounding the Israelites and the Egyptians.

Verse 7 picks up the idea of Israel's journey through the wilderness as they followed the ark of the covenant, an idea suggested in verse 1. The journey began at Sinai, where the presence of God caused the earth to shake and the heavens to produce rain (verse 8). At this point, the psalm borrows poetic language from the song of Deborah and Barak describing Sisera's defeat:

> LORD, when You went out from Seir, when You marched from the field of Edom, the earth trembled and the heavens poured, the clouds also poured water; the mountains gushed before the LORD, this Sinai, before the LORD God of Israel. (Judges 5:4-5)

> O God, when You went out before Your people, when You marched through the wilderness . . . the earth shook; the heavens also dropped rain at the presence of God; Sinai itself was moved at the presence of God, the God of Israel. (Psalm 68:7-8)

The thunder and lightning that accompanied the giving of the law at Sinai was described in Exodus 20:18. In Hebrews 12:18, this was depicted as a "tempest."

The appearance of *Selah* at the end of verse 7, apparently in the middle of a sentence, is unusual. *Selah* ordinarily appears at the end of a sentence. There appear to be only three exceptions: Psalms 67:1; 68:7, 32. This may indicate that in the original use of the psalms, *Selah* indicated a point in the psalm at which "some relevant section of the story alluded to would be recited."[276] Here, it would be "some account of the exodus from Egypt, the crossing of the sea, and the leading of Yahweh through the wilderness and on to Sinai. . . ."[277]

In his discussion of the " 'spiritual' or second sense"[278] of the psalms, C. S. Lewis pointed out the use of Psalm 68:8 on Whitsunday (Pentecost):

> Verse 8, "The earth shook and the heavens dropped at the presence of God, even as Sinai also was moved," was, no doubt, for the original writer a reference to the miracles mentioned in *Exodus*, and thus foreshadows that very different descent of God which came with the tongues of fire.[279]

It may at first seem strange to see Psalm 68 as foretelling the events of Pentecost in the language of the giving of the law at Sinai, but the justification for this is the use of verse 18 by Paul in Ephesians 4:8.[280] Paul seemed to understand verse 18 as being fulfilled in some way on Pentecost, where the Spirit was poured out (Ephesians 4:4). He specifically connected verse 18 with the grace that was given to each of us "according to the measure of Christ's gift" (Ephesians 4:7). On Pentecost, Peter put it this way:

> Therefore being exalted to the right hand of God, and having received from the Father the promise of the Holy Spirit, He poured out this which you now see and hear. (Acts 2:33)

Rain was a symbol of blessing,[281] and verse 9 continued this idea in a description of the entrance of the people of Israel into the Promised Land. God confirmed His inheritance to Israel with plentiful rain upon the land. The word "weary" referred to the congregation—the people—not to the land (verse 9). The people of Israel were "poor," but God provided for them from His goodness (verse 10). To say that Israel was "poor" reflected the idea that the land did not actually belong to them; it belonged to God.[282]

Verse 11 refers to a "word" given by the Lord, a "word" or "message" that had to do with His victory over rebellious kings and their armies.[283]

> The psalm recalls the battle in which the land was gained. The recollection is evoked in allusive language that speaks of the flight of kings and their armies, women who brought the tidings of victory and shared in the spoils when the Almighty scattered kings.[284]

The word translated "those who proclaimed it" (*hamebasserot*) is a feminine plural participle, indicating that those who gave the proclamation were women.[285] Some translations recognize this.

> The Lord gives the command; The women who proclaim the good tidings are a great host. (NASB)

> The Lord doth give the saying, The female proclaimers are a numerous host. (YLT)

> The Lord announces victory, and throngs of women shout the happy news. (NLT)

Women were often the ones who proclaimed God's victories, including His victory over Pharaoh (Exodus 15:20-21) and Israel's enemies in the days of Saul and David (I Samuel 18:6-7). This idea is also seen in verse 25.

In view of the connection between Psalm 68 and Christ's resurrection and ascension, it seems significant that the first to herald the good news that Jesus was risen were women.[286] The Septuagint uses *euangelizō* for the phrase "those who proclaimed it." This is, of course, the word that is transliterated into English in the word "evangelize." It is related to *euangelion*, which means "good news" and is often translated "gospel."

C. S. Lewis also saw a connection between verse 11 and Pentecost.

> Verse 11 is a beautiful instance of the way in which the old texts, almost inevitably charge themselves with the new weight of meaning. The Prayer Book version gives it as "The Lord gave the word, great was the company of the preachers". The "word" would be the order for battle and its "preachers" (in a rather grim sense) the triumphant Jewish warriors. . . . The verse really means that there were many to spread "word" (i.e. the news) of the victory. This will suit Pentecost quite as well. But I think the real New Testament authority for assigning this Psalm to Whitsunday appears in verse 18. . . . According to the scholars the Hebrew text here means that God, with the armies of Israel as his agents, had taken huge masses of prisoners and received "gifts" (booty or tribute) from men. St. Paul, however (Ephesians 4, 8) quotes a different reading: "When He ascended up on high He led captivity captive and gave gifts to men." This must be the passage which first associated the Psalm with the coming of the Holy Ghost, for St. Paul is there speaking of the gifts of the Spirit (4-7) and stressing the fact that they come after the Ascension. After ascending, as a result of ascending, Christ gives these gifts to men, or receives these gifts . . . from His Father "for men", for the use of men, in order to transmit them to men. And this relation between the Ascension and the coming of the Spirit is . . . in full accordance with Our Lord's own words, "It is expedient for you that I go away, for if I go not away the Comforter will not come unto you" (John 16, 7); as if the one were somehow impossible without the other, as if the Ascension, the withdrawal from the space-time in which our present senses operate, of the incarnate God, were the necessary condition of God's

presence in another mode. There is a mystery here that I will not even attempt to sound.[287]

If the psalms are interpreted as merely historical documents, no connection could be seen between them and future events. But that was not how they were interpreted by Jesus and the New Testament church. These poems, which in their original form prior to the final shaping of the Psalter were largely, if not exclusively, about historical events, were arranged in such a way as to point ahead. The historical events recorded in them came to represent future events. That such a marvelous thing could be possible was due to the influence of the Holy Spirit not only in the original composition of the individual psalms, but in their final composition as a new integrated work.

In this psalm, the historical journey of Israel from Sinai to Zion (Jerusalem)[288] became a symbol of the journey from the Old Covenant to the New Covenant. As the writer of Hebrews put it, "For you have not come to the mountain [Sinai] that may be touched and that burned with fire, and to blackness and darkness and tempest. . . . But you have come to Mount Zion and to the city of the living God, the heavenly Jerusalem, to an innumerable company of angels, to the general assembly and church of the firstborn who are registered in heaven, to God the Judge of all, to the spirits of just men made perfect, to Jesus the Mediator of the new covenant, and to the blood of sprinkling that speaks better things than that of Abel" (Hebrews 12:18, 22-24).

| A Comparison Between Sinai and Pentecost ||
Sinai	*Pentecost*
Old Covenant	New Covenant
Given on Sinai (Exodus 19:20)	Given on Zion (Luke 24:49; Acts 1:12-13)
The mountain burned with fire (Exodus 19:18)	Tongues of fire (Acts 2:3)
Tempest (Hebrews 12:18)	Sound as of a rushing mighty wind (Acts 2:2)

Verse 12 apparently refers to the Canaanite kings who fled with their armies before the advancing Israelite army.[289] In the larger messianic context of the Psalter, this may have anticipated the victory of the Messiah over His enemies.[290] The spoils of victory were divided with "she who [remained] at home." This reference to a woman who shared in the spoils even though she remained at home may have been influenced by the connection between this psalm and the account of the victory of Deborah and Barak over Sisera. The song of Deborah and Barak included a taunt against the tribe of Reuben for its failure to participate in the battle.

> The princes of Issachar were with Deborah and Barak. They followed Barak, rushing into the valley. But in the tribe of Reuben there was great indecision. Why did you sit at home among the sheepfolds—to hear the shepherds whistle for their flocks? In the tribe of Reuben there was great indecision. (Judges 5:15-16, NLT)

> Though you lie down among the sheepfolds . . . (Psalm 68:13a)

The translation of verse 13 is notoriously difficult. A comparison of the following attempts demonstrates the point.

> Though ye have lien among the pots, yet shall ye be as the wings of a dove covered with silver, and her feathers with yellow gold. (KJV)

> Though you lie down among the sheepfolds, you will be like the wings of a dove covered with silver, and her feathers with yellow gold. (NKJV)

> Though ye do lie between two boundaries, wings of a dove covered with silver, and her pinions with yellow gold. (YLT)

Though they lived among the sheepfolds, now they are covered with silver and gold, as a dove is covered by its wings. (NLT)

Even while you sleep among the campfires, the wings of my dove are sheathed with silver, its feathers with shining gold. (NIV)

When you lie down among the sheepfolds, you are like the wings of a dove covered with silver, and its pinions with glistening gold. (NASB)

The opinions here are so diverse and the translation so difficult that I will not attempt to resolve the problems. I will, however, make some observations based on the context, the evident connection of this text with the victory over Sisera in Judges, and the messianic focus of the Psalter.

First, those who proclaimed the message given by the Lord were women (verse 11). Second, the woman who remained at home during the battle was privileged to share in the booty (verse 12). The connection between Psalm 68 and Judges 4-5 suggests that the woman in view may have been Jael, who killed Sisera when he fled to her tent.[291] Although she had remained at home, she participated in the victory and thus had a right to the spoil. Third, the men of the tribe of Reuben, on the other hand, avoided the battle. They did not deserve to share in the spoils. Fourth, there is no Hebrew text to support any translation like "you will be" to indicate a relationship between those who avoided the battle and "the wings of a dove."[292]

The difficulties continue with the reference to the silver-colored wings of a dove with yellow-gold feathers. Did this "dove" represent the warriors returning from battle laden with gold and silver? Or is the dove a Canaanite cult object captured in battle? Was it a symbol of Yahweh's revelation at Sinai? Was it something involved in covenant-making ceremonies?[293] Or perhaps the dove was a symbolic reference to the prosperity of Israel, the enemy in flight, or the glory of the Lord manifested in battle.[294] Kidner has another suggestion: Perhaps it depicted the women of verse 12 "preening themselves in their new finery: peacocking around. . . ."[295] Gaebelein understands the dove as symbolic of Christ and Israel.

> The dove, as a sacrificial bird, is a type of Christ. However, in Solomon's Song the dove is used as a type of Israel, for the Lord addresses Israel as "O my dove." The dove then applies to both, Christ and Israel. Silver stands for redemption and the green gold for glory. Christ has purchased redemption and glory. Under His wings Israel, once lying indifferent and unredeemed, has now found redemption and glory. Then God on account of Israel redeemed scatters kings, the kings which come against Israel's land at the close of the times of the Gentiles.[296]

There is obviously great uncertainty here, so perhaps no harm will be done if I suggest yet another possibility. If we are influenced by verse 18 to read the entire psalm as a reference to the victorious Messiah, perhaps we should see verse 11 as foreseeing the Messiah's command to the women to herald His resurrection. The fleeing kings of armies of verse 12 may represent Christ's victory over His enemies by means of His resurrection.[297] The woman who remained at home but was privileged to share in the spoils, who may, in a look to the past, be represented by Jael, may, in a look to the future, be represented by Mary, the mother of Jesus, who contributed to the victory over God's enemies by bringing the Messiah into the world.[298] As Jael delivered a crushing blow to Sisera's head, so Mary made possible the bruising of Satan's head.[299] She, along with other women, was there in the upper room in Jerusalem to "share in the spoil" of Christ's victory, so to speak.[300] Those who "[lay] down among the sheepfolds" may have represented those who rejected the Messiah, refusing to participate in the declaration of the gospel. They would not share in the spoil. And, finally, could it be that the reference to the silver-winged dove anticipated the anointing of the Messiah, upon whom the Holy Spirit descended in the form of a dove?[301]

Admittedly, this is all very speculative, and the best interpretation of verse 13 may be yet to come. Whatever the meaning, it is couched in a context that seems to clearly portray the journey of Israel from Sinai to Zion as a journey from the Old Covenant to the New Covenant. The historical events of the journey take on new significance in the context of the Psalter.

God is identified in verse 14 as the Almighty (*Shaddai*). The translation of this verse is also difficult, as is illustrated by the following attempts:

> When the Almighty scattered kings in it, it was white as snow in Salmon. (KJV)

> When the Almighty scattered the kings in the land, it was like snow fallen on Zalmon. (NIV)

> When the Almighty scattered the kings there, it was snowing in Zalmon. (NASB)

> When the Mighty spreadeth kings in it, it doth snow in Salmon. (YLT)

> The Almighty scattered the enemy kings like a blowing snowstorm on Mount Zalmon. (NLT)

Zalmon means "black mountain."[302] Judges 9:48 referred to a Zalmon near Shechem, which was located in the narrow valley between Mount Gerizim and Mount Ebal about sixty-five kilometers north of Jerusalem.[303] Many commentators think this Zalmon refers to the lava-covered Jebel Druze, an extinct volcano in Transjordan on the borders of Bashan. This mountain has peaks more than six thousand feet high and gets snowfall in winter.[304] Tate thinks, however, that its use here is more literary than geographic, with the intention of heightening the contrast between "Black Mountain" and the white snow.[305]

Regardless of the location of the mountain, there remains uncertainty as to the meaning of the verse. As Kidner points out,

> Whether the rout of the kings there was caused by a blizzard, or whether the battlefield was "snowed" with weapons and garments (or, later, with bones), or the fleeing armies compared to driven snowflakes, we cannot tell.[306]

Wilcock's comment may be helpful: "In spite of the puzzles with which verses 11-14 tantalize us, they are clearly about Israel's conquest of *the kings in the Land*."[307] We may be uncertain about the meaning of some details in this text, but the overall picture is clear: God conquers His foes.

Verses 15-16 contrast the mountain of Bashan with the mountain in which God desires to dwell. Although it is possible to translate *har elohim* as "a mountain of God," it is equally possible to translate the phrase as "a mighty mountain" or something similar.

> The mountains of Bashan are majestic mountains; rugged are the mountains of Bashan. (NIV)

> The majestic mountains of Bashan stretch high into the sky. (NLT)

A translation like this may be preferable in view of the fact that it is often Zion that is identified as the mountain of God.[308] In comparison with the many-peaked, majestic mountain of Bashan—perhaps still a reference to Zalmon (verse 14)—the mountain in which God desires to dwell is of modest height. But the fact that God has chosen Zion makes other mountains "fume with envy."

The idea in verse 17 is that the chariots of God are without number.[309] This is a reference to His angelic host.[310] The Lord is in the midst of this host, now in the Holy Place on Zion, as He was in Sinai.

It is at this point, in verse 18, that we have a specific connection with the New Testament. Paul saw this verse as having to do with the ascension of Christ and the gifts He gave in conjunction with His ascension:

> But to each one of us grace was given according to the measure of Christ's gift. Therefore He says: *"When He ascended on high, He led captivity captive, and gave gifts to men."* (Ephesians 4:7-8)

The statement "therefore He says" indicates that Paul saw the ascension of Christ as fulfilling verse 18. He did not see it as a mere application of the verse, nor did he see only a similarity between the ascension of God to Zion and the ascension of Christ into heaven. Whatever historical events were portrayed in Psalm 68 as it was originally written, they came to represent future and even greater events connected with the Messiah in their new context in the Psalter. The ascension of God up to Zion became the ascension of Christ into heaven.

Even here there was a connection with the song of Deborah and Barak:

> Awake, awake, Deborah: awake, awake, utter a song: arise, Barak, and lead thy captivity captive, thou son of Abinoam. (Judges 5:12, KJV)

In the literary structure of the Hebrew Scriptures, the victory of Deborah and Barak over Sisera anticipated the victory of God over His enemies and His ascension to Zion, which in turn anticipated the victory of the Messiah over death and His ascension into heaven.

Wilcock's comments are helpful:

> When Paul refers to half a verse from this psalm, we should not imagine that he is lifting a dozen words out of their context to suit his own purposes. On the contrary, that one sentence distils the entire psalm, which is what the apostle has in mind in quoting it. Its quotation brings together not only Ephesians 4:8 and Psalm 68:18, but Judges 5:12 as well. . . . Our chief interest, however, is on the lines on either side of it, not drawn from Judges, about ascension and gifts.
>
> Here, as elsewhere, something clear stands along something obscure. God the King, represented by the ark, and David his viceroy, are going up to the holy mountain in their victory procession (v. 24). Paul takes the event to be a foreshadowing of the great going up, the ascension of Christ after his victory on the cross.[311]

Why, though, did Paul say Christ "gave gifts to men" (Ephesians 4:8) when Psalm 68 said God "received gifts among men"? There is really no disagreement here, as Wilcock points out:

> If Ephesians 4 understands the whole sweep of the psalm, from Egypt to Zion, as a picture of the saving work of Christ, then both phrases are equally true. All, friend and foe alike, pay tribute to the great Old Testament victor: naturally his people also will be enriched by his conquests, but the psalm focuses on what they give to him. All God's people will be blessed by the triumph of the greater King: of course all will give him their tribute too, but the New Testament passage focuses on what he gives to them.[312]

Even though verse 18 does not specifically indicate that the Lord gave gifts, that idea is found in verse 19. He "daily loads us with benefits," benefits all of which are bound up with the gift of salvation. It seems that verse 19 anticipates Paul's emphasis on Christ as a giver of gifts. These are grace gifts,[313] and they include the apostles, prophets, evangelists, pastors, and teachers given "for the equipping of the saints for the work of the ministry, for the edifying of the body of Christ" (Ephesians 4:11-12). For Israel, "salvation" had to do with deliverance from their enemies. But as this text is read with a look to the future, "salvation" involves the gifts Christ gives to His church, gifts that are a consequence of His victory over His enemies.

Verses 20-23 are concerned with "the rescuings and bringings out achieved by God's victory" and "are bound to involve destruction as well as salvation."[314] In verse 20, the words translated "salvation" (*mosha'ot*) and "escapes" (*totsa'ot*) are plural, "which is a way of indicating their repeated occurrences, and probably their richness and range."[315] God repeatedly delivered the Israelites, and He delivered them in a variety of ways.

The statement that "God will wound the head of His enemies" (verse 21) seems to echo the initial messianic promise of One who would bruise the head of the serpent.[316] All of God's enemies are those who have chosen in some way to identify themselves with His first enemy. The certainty of the defeat of that first enemy is the certainty of the defeat of all enemies.

The "hairy scalp" of God's enemy "may allude to a practice of leaving the locks unshorn in the hope that wholeness and strength would be thereby preserved."[317] If so, this may provide another conceptual link with Judges 5. Although many translations render the first two words of Judges 5:2 something like "when leaders lead in Israel," it is also possible to translate them as having to do with leaders or warriors in Israel unbinding their hair by removing their turbans. The first word (*para'*) has to do with letting go or letting loose, as unbinding the head.[318] The second word (*pera'*) has to do with long hair of the head, or locks.[319] Although it is possible to translate these words as having to do with leaders leading, interpreting the words in a metaphorical sense as having to do with those who are the "top" or the "head," a more literal translation would be something like, "When locks of hair grow long in Israel"[320] or, as in the NJB, "That the warriors in Israel unbound their hair." In view of the substantial connections between Psalm 68 and Judges 5, the idea in Psalm 68:21 may have been that, just as the warriors of Israel "unbound their heads" for battle, so did the warriors of Sisera. But God wounded the head of the hairy scalp of His enemy. In the specific case of Sisera, God wounded his head by means of Jael, who drove the tent peg through Sisera's temple, nailing his head to the earth.[321]

Although verse 22 does not specify who it was that God would "bring back from Bashan" and "from the depths of the sea," verse 23 indicates that they were Israel's enemies. The idea here is that "God can and will defeat his enemies whether they flee to the heights of Mount Bashan or to the depths of the sea; God will give his people participation in his victory."[322] The enemies of Yahweh "cannot escape from Yahweh regardless of the remote places to which they may flee."[323] A similar idea is expressed in Amos 9:2-4.

Verses 24-27 describe the victory procession of God into His sanctuary in the Temple at Jerusalem.[324] God was identified as the king. Taken with Psalm 2:6, this suggested the deity of the Messiah. This procession involved singers and musicians surrounded by maidens playing timbrels.[325] Throughout the psalm, women were seen to be as involved as men in obtaining victory over God's enemies, proclaiming the good news of victory, and celebrating the victory.[326]

Verse 26 is a command, apparently to the singers, musicians, and timbrel-playing maidens to bless the Lord God. Although some translations (e.g., KJV) take no note of it, the word "Lord" here represents the Hebrew *Yahweh*. To be consistent with the practice of most English translations, it should be rendered "LORD," as in the NLT and NASB. Israel was to be a fountain of blessing to the Lord God.

Verse 27 is the soundtrack of "what the narrator hears from the singers and leaders of the procession."[327] They sing, "There is little Benjamin, their leader, the princes of Judah and their company, the princes of Zebulun and the princes of Naphtali." Why are these tribes mentioned and not the rest of the tribes of Israel? The mention of Benjamin first may further connect Psalm 68 with Judges 5. Benjamin took the lead in the battle against Sisera.[328] The mention of these four tribes may be intended to represent all of the tribes of Israel: "The tribal names are samples of the whole: two each of the southernmost and of the northernmost."[329]

Verses 28-31 "call on God finally to subdue the nations that oppose his will."[330] Isaiah 60 develops this idea more fully.

Verse 28 should probably be translated somewhat like it is in the NLT: "Summon your might, O God. Display your power, O God, as you have in the past." When the Lord subdues all of His enemies, the kings of the earth will pay homage to Him by bringing presents to Him at His Temple in Jerusalem (verse 29). The "beast [singular] of the reeds" (verse 30) probably represents Egypt, and the "herd of bulls with the calves" represents other nations that are hostile to God.[331] God will rebuke these nations with such finality that they will submit "with pieces of silver" (verse 30). That is, they will acknowledge their submission by paying tribute. War will be a thing of the past, for those who love war will be scattered. They will be unable to organize opposition to God. In this sense, they will be like the scattered population of the earth following the confusion of tongues at Babel.

Verse 31 seems to reiterate the idea expressed in symbolic language in verse 30. Envoys from Egypt represent the entire nation in paying homage; Ethiopia will "quickly stretch out her hands to God." The word "Ethiopia" here should not be thought to be limited to the modern nation of Ethiopia. The Hebrew word is *kush*, representing Nubia or North Sudan.[332]

Verses 32-35 call on all the nations of the earth to pay homage to God. Egypt and "Ethiopia" are mere representatives of all the nations of the world. The "kingdoms of the earth" are commanded to sing praises to the Lord God (verse 32). God is the one who "rides on the heaven of heavens" and who "sends out His voice, a mighty voice" (verse 33). He is God not only on earth, but also throughout the universe. His "voice" represents God Himself.[333] The God of Israel is strong and excellent (verses 34-35). Although His holy places are awesome, He is more awesome than they are (verse 35a). Not only is He a strong and powerful God, but He also gives strength and power to His people (verse 35b).

Although Psalm 68 traces the historical journey of Israel from Sinai to Zion, the psalm has significance beyond its account of past events. Those events, often described in terms of the victory of Deborah and Barak over Sisera, portray future events. Specifically, Psalm 68 anticipated the ascension of the Messiah and the gifts He gives to His church. With its contextual connection with Psalm 69—a psalm that clearly anticipates the Messiah[334]—Psalm 68 participates in the development of the messianic theme of the Psalter.

Psalm 69

The rich vein of messianic prophecy found in Psalm 69 was mined frequently by the writers of the New Testament. Together with Psalms 22 and 110, Psalm 69 "is one of the three psalms most often quoted in the New Testament."[335] The following verbal connections may be readily seen:

> Those who hate me without a cause are more than the hairs of my head. . . . (verse 4a)

> But this happened that the word might be fulfilled which is written in their law, *"They hated Me without a cause."* (John 15:25)

> Because zeal for Your house has eaten me up. . . . (verse 9a)

Then His disciples remembered that it was written, *"Zeal for Your house has eaten Me up."* (John 2:17)

And the reproaches of those who reproach You have fallen on me. (verse 9b)

For even Christ did not please Himself; but as it is written, *"The reproaches of those who reproached You fell on Me."* (Romans 15:3)

They also gave me gall for my food, and for my thirst they gave me vinegar to drink. (verse 21)

. . . they gave Him sour wine mingled with gall to drink. . . . Immediately one of them ran and took a sponge, filled it with sour wine and put it on a reed, and offered it to Him to drink. (Matthew 27:34a, 48)

Let their table become a snare before them, and their well-being a trap. Let their eyes be darkened, so that they do not see; and make their loins shake continually. (verses 22-23)

And David says: *"Let their table become a snare and a trap, a stumbling block and a recompense to them. Let their eyes be darkened, so that they do not see, and bow down their back always."* (Romans 11:9-10)

Let their dwelling place be desolate; let no one live in their tents (verse 25).

For it is written in the book of Psalms: *"Let his dwelling place be desolate, and let no one live in it. . . ."* (Acts 1:20a)

In addition to these verses, which are specifically connected in the New Testament with the person of Christ or with the affairs of His kingdom, there are other statements in Psalm 69 that may not be quoted by the writers of the New Testament but that are conceptually related to the Messiah, His experiences, or His kingdom. For example:

> I am weary with my crying; my throat is dry; my eyes fail while I wait for my God. (verse 3)

> And about the ninth hour Jesus cried out with a loud voice, saying, "Eli, Eli, lama sabachthani?" that is, *"My God, My God, why have You forsaken Me?"* (Matthew 27:46)

> After this, Jesus, knowing that all things were now accomplished, that the Scripture might be fulfilled, said, "I thirst!" (John 19:28)

> Because for Your sake I have borne reproach; shame has covered my face. (verse 7)

> . . . looking unto Jesus, the author and finisher of our faith, who for the joy that was set before Him endured the cross, despising the shame, and has sat down at the right hand of the throne of God. (Hebrews 12:2)

> I have become a stranger to my brothers, and an alien to my mother's children. (verse 8)

> His brothers therefore said to Him, "Depart from here and go into Judea, that Your disciples also may see the works that You are doing. . . . For even His brothers did not believe in Him. (John 7:3, 5)

> When I wept and chastened my soul with fasting, that became my reproach. I also made sackcloth my garment; I became a byword to them. (verses 10-11)

> Then Jesus was led up by the Spirit into the wilderness to be tempted by the devil. And when He had fasted forty days and forty nights, afterward He was hungry. (Matthew 4:1-2)

In addition to these conceptual links, we will see that there are other thematic indications that Psalm 69 should be read as pointing ahead to the Messiah. Opinions regarding the connections between Psalm 69 and the New Testament range from those who see Psalm 69 as specifically about Christ[336] to those who deny this specificity but nevertheless grasp the significance of Psalm 69 to the New Testament writers.

> This is not to say that the Psalms are predictions of Jesus, but the laments certainly do testify to and instruct us about a God whose presence in the depths would ultimately be expressed by the death of God's Son on a cross. Not surprisingly, the Gospel writers could not narrate the story of Jesus' suffering apart from the Psalms, especially Psalms 22 and 69. . . . Crucial events and aspects of Jesus' life—birth, baptism, temptation, teaching, and ministry—are not remembered nor fully understood without recourse to the Psalms.[337]

> Because of its relation to the pattern and the correspondence of the life of Jesus to it, Psalm 69 was used repeatedly in the New Testament for christological and theological purposes. . . . Psalm 69 cannot be read directly as the prayer of Jesus or as an intentional prophecy of his sufferings. But it does provide a context for reflection on the passion of one who bore reproach

for the sake of his God and by the way he bore it and by the vindication of his resurrection gave hope to the lowly and promise that God's saving will for his servants will be completed. Jesus is the consummate and correcting example of the kind of person for whom the psalm was composed.[338]

Though we can appreciate these insights into the significance of Psalm 69 for the New Testament, they seem to fall short of the fact that the New Testament sees Psalm 69 as specifically fulfilled in the life, experiences, and kingdom of Christ. Jesus Himself considered verse 4 to be fulfilled in His own experiences.[339] This, together with Jesus' broader statements about the nature of messianic prophecy, lifts texts such as Psalm 69 above the level of mere generic instruction.[340] If we read the Old Testament as the New Testament does, we will see these texts as specifically anticipating the Messiah and the events of His life and kingdom. When Jesus cleansed the Temple, it caused His disciples to remember Psalm 69:9a.[341] Paul saw Christ's selflessness as having been anticipated in Psalm 69:9b.[342] He also saw the consequences of Jewish rejection of the Messiah as having been foreseen in Psalm 69:22-23.[343] Peter appealed to Psalm 69:25 for support in the need to replace Judas.[344] As Wilcock points out, "the New Testament relates [Psalm 69] directly to Christ."[345]

In view of the nature of the use of Psalm 69 in the New Testament, the larger view of Jesus and the New Testament church concerning the messianic focus of the Old Testament, and the influence of the messianic context of the Psalter, we will read Psalm 69 as a psalm that specifically points to the person of Christ, to His experiences, and to the affairs of His kingdom. Like Psalm 22, Psalm 69 could well be one of the prayers of Jesus, the entire content of which is not revealed in the New Testament.

Like fifty-four other psalms, Psalm 69 is addressed "to the Chief Musician." Like seventy-three other psalms, it is connected in some way with David. But the fact that Psalm 69 is set to the tune, "The Lilies," distinguishes it from all but three other psalms.[346] Commentators frequently refrain from any attempt to determine the significance of this tune, but Mitchell sees eschatological significance. Commenting on the Septuagint translation of *'l shoshannim* ["Set to 'The Lilies' "] as *huper tōn alloiōthēsomenōn* ["for those who will be changed"] in Psalms 45, 69, and 80, and as *tois alloiōthēsomenois eti* ["for those who shall yet be changed"] in Psalm 60, Mitchell makes the following point.

> At first glance this seems to be no translation at all. But there is an underlying idea that links *lilies* and *the transformation (of the year)*—the idea of springtime, when lilies bloom. So this may be an interpretation rather than a departure from the Hebrew. And there may be eschatological implications. For the idea of the transformation of the earth in spring connotes the image-complex of Passover, new creation and resurrection, for which lilies are an ancient symbol.[347]

If we accept Mitchell's suggestion, it may further strengthen the idea that Psalm 69 is specifically messianic: It points ahead to the Messiah, whose sufferings—so vividly described in the psalm—result in new life for those who believe on Him. That the psalm includes the promise of new life for those who trust in the Messiah may be seen in verse 32: "The humble shall see this and be glad; and you who seek God, your hearts shall live."

The parallels between Psalms 69 and 22 further indicate the messianic focus of Psalm 69.

> It is not that the wording of one psalm often appears in the other also. Here in 69, verse 3 recalls 'my tongue sticks to the roof of my mouth' (22:15), verse 19 recalls 'scorned by men and despised by the people' (22:6), and verse 32 recalls 'the poor will eat and be satisfied; they who seek the LORD will praise him—may your hearts live

for ever!' (22:26); but that is practically all. No; it is much more a matter of a common theme. There are two poems each of which is a heartfelt cry to God from someone in great distress, the object of general scorn, yet confident in the end of an outcome which will bring praise to God. . . .

There is a further correspondence, of a different kind. In 22 we noticed a feature which suggested a sensible way of dividing the psalm. It started with 'me' and 'my groaning'; 22:3 began 'Yet you . . .'; 22:6, 'But I . . .'; and 22:9, 'Yet you. . . .' To-ing and fro-ing of this kind was observable at least down to 22:21, and possibly further. We find that in 69 the psalmist's attention shifts in the same way, and the alternation gives this psalm also a satisfying shape. On this basis, it has five sections, beginning successively with the words *Save me* (v. 1), *You know* (v. 5), *But I pray* (v. 13), *You know* (v. 19), *I will praise* (v. 30).[348]

So both the structure and content of Psalm 69 echo Psalm 22, another psalm rich in messianic content.

It is not difficult to read Psalm 69 as a prayer of the Messiah in the midst of His suffering. The prayer begins with a plea for deliverance (verse 1). The danger is described metaphorically as deep mire and waters that make it impossible to stand (verses 1-2). The Messiah had cried to the point of exhaustion; His throat was dry. The combination of tears and dehydration hindered His eyesight (verse 3). Lest we think this is too dramatic a description, we must remember that the New Testament described the Messiah's prayers as "vehement cries and tears" (Hebrews 5:7).

As He described His solidarity with the Father, a solidarity so complete that those who hated Jesus hated His Father also, Jesus said, "But this happened that the word might be fulfilled which is written in their law, *'They hated Me without a cause'*" (John 15:25). This was, of course, a reference to Psalm 69:4: "Those who hate me without a cause are more than the hairs of my head. . . ."[349] Moyise offers interesting insight on Jesus' use of this psalm.

> This verse is remarkable in that John has Jesus introduce a scriptural quotation with the words, 'It was to fulfil the word that is written in *their* law' (see also 8.17; 10.34). Not only does this make Jesus sound like a non-Jew, it also seems to set a chasm between John and the Jewish scriptures. And since the following verses speak of the Holy Spirit coming to reveal truth, it could be seen as an antithesis—they have the scriptures, we have the Spirit.[350]

But, as Moyise notes, Jesus' use of Psalm 69:4 could be understood otherwise. Daly-Denton points out,

> The recourse to a scriptural antecedent is intended to encourage a community now experiencing persecution to see a parallel between their situation and the events of Jesus' hour which were also foretold in scripture. It does this by giving them a sense of having a superior insight into the scriptures to that of their opponents and an entitlement to claim as their own the heritage which their persecutors would wish to deny them.[351]

The idea here and in John 8:17 and 10:34 may be that, when the Old Testament is read without a Christ-centered consciousness, it becomes a book other than what God intended. Jesus did not say, "As it is written in *our* law," or even, "As it is written in *the* law." Suddenly, the "law" became the law as it was identified with and owned by the unbelieving Jewish leaders who rejected the central theme of the law: the Messiah. This was not God's law; it was their law. The words were the same, but the words—stripped of the meaning intended by God—were no longer His; they were theirs.

The enmity of the religious leaders who—had they been able—would have killed Jesus is bound up with the words of verse 4. They were numerous ("more than the hairs of my head") and mighty.[352] The wrongfulness of their enmity was captured in the words, "Though I have stolen nothing, I still must restore it" (verse 4). Wilcock observes that we "do not know in what sense the psalmist was *forced to restore what [he] did not steal,*"[353] but this could be a reference to the view of Jesus' unbelieving enemies that He had "stolen" the messianic claim. They did not believe it was rightfully His, so they demanded that He "restore it." Even if this was not the point, the statement indicates that their claims—whatever they were—were false.

Verse 5 is the only one in the psalm that may seem to prohibit us from reading the text as a reference to the Messiah: "O God, You know my foolishness; and my sins are not hidden from You." If this is indeed a necessary reference to the foolishness of the speaker and to sins he has personally committed, the verse cannot refer to the Messiah. In that case, if we view the psalm as an integrated unit, we shall have to deny that it has any reference to the Messiah. But the psalm's use in the New Testament does not allow this position. Perhaps we could agree with Wilcock that although much of the psalm has to do with the Messiah, some of it does not.[354] But we have previously taken a position similar to Dodd's, who sees quotations from the psalms as carrying their context with them.[355] If the individual psalms are integrated units within which some words are attributed to the Messiah, and if there is no change of speaker within the psalm, the entire psalm must be attributed to the Messiah.

But what are we to do with the statement, "O God, You know my foolishness"? As Mays points out, verse 5

> can be read two ways. It is either a further claim of innocence ("If I had committed folly, you, God, would know") or it is a statement that what folly he has done is known by God and not a cause for those who hate him and seek to destroy him (v. 4).[356]

Even if, as it was originally written, the psalm referred to the folly of David or someone else, it need not refer to the folly of the speaker in its new messianic context in the Psalter. And the second half of verse 5 ("and my sins are not hidden from You") can be understood in the same way as the sin references in previous messianic psalms.[357] That is, the reference is not to personal sins committed by the Messiah, but to His role as a sin-bearer. In this case, the word *'ashmah*, translated "sins," has within its semantic range the meaning "trespass-offering."[358] If the verse is read this way, the meaning is similar to that of II Corinthians 5:21: "For He made Him who knew no sin to be sin for us. . . ." The fact that *'ashmah* is plural in verse 5 may seem to be a problem for understanding the verse this way (i.e., is it appropriate to think of the Messiah's redemptive work in terms of trespass *offerings*?). But this would not be the only place in Scripture where the concept of Christ's offering for sins is described with a plural word: "Therefore it was necessary that the copies of the things in the heavens should be purified with these, but the heavenly things themselves with better sacrifices than these" (Hebrews 9:23).

> That the heavenly things are cleansed with "better sacrifices" does not mean that the one sacrifice of Christ is insufficient. In view of the author's insistence that Christ's singular sacrifice was sufficient (9:28; 10:10, 14), we should understand the word "sacrifices" as a generic plural that, still in the language of the old covenant, states the necessity of sacrifice to deal with the sin problem. The focus is not on how many sacrifices are necessary under the new covenant, but on the need for something superior to the blood of animals to cleanse the heavenly things.[359]

If we read *'ashmah* as a reference to the Messiah bearing the sins of the people as in Isaiah 53, the plural form poses no problem. If we read it as a reference to the trespass-offering made by Christ in His death, with the plural form picking up the language of the Old Covenant, no problem is posed. There is but one sacrifice for sin, but that one sacrifice fulfills the prophetic significance of all of the sacrifices for sin offered under the law of Moses.

Verse 6 was the Messiah's plea that none who waited for the Lord God (i.e., those who trusted Him) would be ashamed or confounded because of Him. This prayer was certainly answered, as were all of Jesus' prayers. No person of genuine faith found Christ to be a stumbling block. But He was a stumbling block to those who lacked faith.[360]

The Messiah bore the reproaches of those who reproached the Lord God (verses 7, 9b).[361] He was so closely identified with God in these reproaches that He was rejected even by His siblings (verse 8).[362] In the context of bearing God's reproaches, the Messiah was consumed with zeal for the purity of God's house (verse 9a).[363] The Messiah was reproached for His weeping and fasting (verses 10-11a). Although we do not read a specific reference in the New Testament reflecting this, we do read that Jesus' fasting experience was for the purposes of being tempted by the devil.[364]

The Messiah became a byword, the object of verbal opposition, and the subject of drinking songs (verses 11b-12). Some of this may be seen in the claims that Jesus was a Samaritan who was possessed of a devil, that He was born of fornication, and that He was empowered by Beelzebub.[365]

In the face of opposition, the Messiah prayed (verse 13a). He prayed that at the right time (verse 13b), on the basis of His mercy (verse 13c), God would hear Him (verse 13d) and deliver Him "out of the mire," a metaphor for those who hated Him (verses 14-15). The description of His dangerous circumstances as a "pit" connects with a theme reaching all the way back to Psalm 7:15.[366]

In verse 16, the words of the Messiah's prayer echoed the words of David's prayer in Psalm 51:1. This may reflect the purpose of Psalm 69 as originally written; perhaps it was a prayer of David in the midst of dire but unspecified circumstances.

The identification of the supplicant as God's "servant" in verse 17 connects with the Messiah's identification as His "servant" elsewhere.[367]

The prayer for redemption in verse 18 does not require the idea of redemption from sin, although it certainly could have that meaning in the right context. But if this was a prayer of the Messiah, it could simply have been a plea for deliverance from His enemies. The word translated "redeem" (*ga'al*) was also used, for example, for the deliverance or redemption of Israel from bondage in Egypt.

The Messiah referred again to His reproach, shame, and dishonor (verses 19-20a). He had no human comforters (verse 20). Indeed, all of His disciples forsook Him and fled.[368]

Verse 21 anticipated Jesus' experience on the cross when He was given vinegar laced with gall—a poison—to drink.[369]

Verses 22-23 anticipated the consequences of rejecting the Messiah for unbelieving Israelites.[370] It is significant that these verses follow immediately on the heels of a verse (verse 21) that described Jesus' experience on the cross. Their rejection of Jesus came to its ultimate expression in His crucifixion; its consequence was spiritual blindness. The "table" was a symbol of blessing. Because of their rejection of the Messiah, the covenant God had made with the nation of Israel became a snare and trap for them. Because their eyes were darkened so they could not see the truth, they focused on the law of Moses rather than on the Messiah to whom the law pointed.[371] Metaphorically, the nation experienced continual shaking of the loins. That is, they had no peace, no stability, no relief from suffering. As the Septuagint put it—and as quoted by Paul—their backs are always bowed down.

The prayer that those who rejected Him would experience God's indignation and anger (verse 24) indicated the severity and magnitude of the nation's sin.[372] As Jesus warned the Israelites who rejected Him, it would be more tolerable for unbelieving

Gentiles—including Sodom—in the day of judgment than for unbelieving Israelites who were recipients of special revelation and who had every reason to believe.[373]

Although verses 25-28 refer in the plural to those who persecuted others who were stricken by God, Peter interpreted verse 25 to refer to one specific person—Judas—who betrayed Jesus.[374] The fate of Judas was the fate of all those who rejected the Messiah.

The plural references in verses 25-28 suggest that in its original form, before it was placed in its context in the Psalter, Psalm 69 had other referents. But in its context here, the plural referents can be read as generic plurals; they are collapsed down to one whose dwelling place would be desolate, to one who persecuted, to one who had iniquity added to his iniquity, to one who would not come into God's righteousness, to one who would be blotted out of the book of the living: Judas. The plurals are also collapsed down to One was stricken by God,[375] One who was wounded:[376] Jesus.

The Messiah confessed to His poverty and sorrow, praying for God's salvation to set Him "up on high" (verse 29). As Isaiah put it, the Messiah was "a Man of sorrows and acquainted with grief" (Isaiah 53:3). Paul described the richness of the Christian experience as a consequence of the Messiah's poverty (II Corinthians 8:9).

The Messiah promised to "praise the name of God with a song" and to "magnify Him with thanksgiving" (verse 30). This connects with Psalm 40:3, where the Messiah had a "new song." Verse 30 is one of those places where the name of God represents God Himself in poetic parallelism.

As in Psalm 51:15-17, verse 31 sees sincere worship as being better than animal sacrifices. This, together with the Messiah's zeal for the Temple in verse 9, seems to point to a day when the Temple would not feature sacrifices that were efficacious for sin. In other words, a Temple was standing in Psalm 69. This may indicate a post-exilic date for the psalm, since there was no

Temple during David's reign. But, on the other hand, the Tabernacle was also referred to as a temple.[377] But the psalm's messianic focus, and its reference to an offering more pleasing to God than animal sacrifices, may have pointed ahead to the Temple described by Ezekiel. Although sacrifices will be offered at that Temple—and they are referred to as sin offerings—they may serve as memorials.[378] There is no ark in the Holy of Holies upon which to sprinkle blood; the Messiah occupies that most sacred place as His throne room.[379]

Verse 32 reprises Psalm 34:2: The humble (i.e., people of faith) rejoiced at heartfelt worship. These were people who sought God; they would live. If we read the superscription of the psalm as does the Septuagint, with an eschatological reference to those who will be changed, the idea connects with the promise of life found in verse 32.

It is certain that those who sought God would live, for "the LORD [heard] the poor, and [did] not despise His prisoners" (verse 33). The concept of believers being God's "prisoners" was picked up by Paul.[380] As Kidner points out, the term "His prisoners" is an expression that "reveals what touches God particularly closely . . . and brings out the contrast between Him and the grasping gods of heathendom; namely our relationship to Him, and our need."[381]

Universal praise is called for in verse 34, in view of the fact that "God will save Zion and build the cities of Judah, that they may dwell there and possess it" (verse 35). This connects with the Zion theology theme that began in Psalm 2:6. The psalm expresses "the fervent desire of the psalmist for God's salvation of Zion and the establishment of his kingdom (vv. 34-36)."[382] It looks "back to God's promise to David (cf. Ps 2:7; 2 Sa 7:16) and eagerly await[s] its fulfillment in Zion."[383]

The land promised to Abraham, Isaac, and Jacob will be inherited by their descendants; those who occupy it will be those who love God's name (verse 36).

Psalm 69 certainly advances the messianic theme of the Psalter. It is one of the psalms relied on most heavily by the writers of the New Testament to describe and interpret the events of the Messiah's life.

Psalm 70

The first thing we notice about Psalm 70 is the close similarity of the psalm with Psalm 40:13-17.

> Be pleased, O LORD, to deliver me; O LORD, make haste to help me! (Psalm 40:13)

> Make haste, O God, to deliver me! Make haste to help me, O LORD! (Psalm 70:1)

> Let them be ashamed and brought to mutual confusion who seek to destroy my life; let them be driven backward and brought to dishonor who wish me evil. (Psalm 40:14)

> Let them be ashamed and confounded who seek my life; let them be turned back and confused who desire my hurt. (Psalm 70:2)

> Let them be confounded because of their shame, who say to me, "Aha, aha!" (Psalm 40:15)

> Let them be turned back because of their shame, who say, "Aha, aha!" (Psalm 70:3)

> Let all those who seek You rejoice and be glad in You; let such as love Your salvation say continually, "The LORD be magnified!" (Psalm 40:16)

> Let all those who seek You rejoice and be glad in You; and let those who love Your salvation say continually, "Let God be magnified!" (Psalm 70:4)

> But I am poor and needy; yet the LORD thinks upon me.
> You are my help and my deliverer; do not delay, O my God.
> (Psalm 40:17)
>
> But I am poor and needy; make haste to help me, O God! You are my help and my deliverer; O LORD, do not delay. (Psalm 70:5)

These similarities have given rise to a great deal of speculation about the relationship between these psalms. Kidner puts the "duplication" down to "the compiling of separate collections of psalms."[384] Many commentators think that verses 13-17 of Psalm 40 originally formed a separate psalm that was incorporated with other material to form the current Psalm 40.[385] According to this view, it could be that Psalm 70 was the original psalm that was adapted for use in Psalm 40. Mays writes,

> Whether Psalm 70 is a fragment of Psalm 40 or a composition used in Psalm 40 is difficult to determine with certainty. The literary completeness of Psalm 70 favors the latter possibility.[386]

In response to Cragie's view that Psalm "40 is a psalm for the king during the monarchical period" and his suggestion that Psalm "70 is a 'salvaged psalm' for use in a time after the monarchy, during the exile or later," Tate responds,

> This may be correct, but it seems to me that the differences between 40 and 70 can be explained better as adaptation of material from 70 to 40 . . . , or they are two versions of common poetic material. Ps 70 forms a complete unit, which appears to have been adapted to the context of Ps 40.[387]

For our purposes, speculation about the reason for the similarities between the two psalms is of little help. What is helpful is to examine the contextual relationship of the psalms with the psalms around them and to be alert to themes connecting the psalms with other psalms or with the entire Psalter. Why are verses 13-17 included in Psalm 40, and why was Psalm 70 placed where it is? What is the relationship between Psalms 69 and 71?

In our comments on Psalm 40, we noted that it is one of the psalms specifically quoted in the New Testament as a reference to the Messiah.[388] In Hebrews 10:5-7, Psalm 40:6-8 is tied to the Incarnation. The messianic focus of Psalm 40 suggests, apart from any other evidence, a messianic focus for Psalm 70, since Psalm 70 is virtually identical to the final five verses of Psalm 40. The connection between these psalms would require clear, compelling contextual evidence from the psalms around Psalm 70 before we would reject the idea that Psalm 70 is messianic in its focus. As we shall see, the situation is just the reverse: The context in which Psalm 70 is found supports the idea that it should be read as pointing to the Messiah.

First, Psalm 70 with its appeal for hasty deliverance is positioned to read as a virtual conclusion to Psalm 69, a clearly messianic psalm.[389] It "puts in a nutshell what [Psalm] 69 has said at length."[390]

Second, although Psalm 70 includes a superscription, Psalm 71 does not. From Psalm 3 through Psalm 89 the only psalms lacking a superscription are Psalms 10, 33, 43, and 71.[391] In "each case there is manuscript evidence for combining each of the psalms . . . with the psalm which precedes it."[392] As we shall see, Psalm 71 continues the messianic focus of the Psalter.

Third, Psalm 70 is thematically connected with Psalm 35, "especially the latter part of that fearsome, much longer, prayer (vv. 17-28)."[393]

> They also opened their mouth wide against me, and said, "Aha, aha! Our eyes have seen it." (Psalm 35:21)

> Let them be turned back because of their shame, who say, "Aha, aha!" (Psalm 70:3)

As we noted in our comments on Psalm 35, it is clearly a messianic psalm, intended to be read as a prayer of the Messiah. Its thematic connections with Psalm 22 are striking.[394] There also is a verbal connection between Psalm 35 and Psalm 69.

> Let them not rejoice over me who are wrongfully my enemies; nor let them wink with the eye who hate me without a cause. (Psalm 35:19)

> Those who hate me without a cause are more than the hairs of my head. . . . (Psalm 69:4a)

Jesus saw this theme as being fulfilled by those who rejected Him: "But this happened that the word might be fulfilled which is written in their law, *'They hated Me without a cause'* " (John 15:25).[395] Since Psalms 35 and 69 point ahead to the Messiah, the connections between Psalm 70 and these psalms indicates that it carries a messianic focus.

Fourth, Psalm 70 "brings to mind . . . the ultimate suffering of [Psalm] 22."[396]

> But you, O LORD, do not be far from Me; O My Strength, hasten to help Me! (Psalm 22:19)

> Make haste, O God, to deliver me! Make haste to help me, O LORD! . . . Make haste to me, O God! You are my help and my deliverer; O LORD, do not delay. (Psalm 70:1, 5)

Sailhamer's observations are helpful:

> This psalm serves as a fitting request for a speedy answer to David's call for salvation in Ps 69. . . .

By itself, in isolation from its context within the book of Psalms, this psalm is a simple call for help in an unnamed emergency. When read as a follow-up to Ps 69 and as a prelude to Pss 71-72, it is a call for God's swift return to establish his universal kingdom and to send his eternal King.[397]

But even more than that, Psalm 70 can be read as the Messiah's prayer for deliverance from His enemies.[398]

The superscription of Psalm 70 addresses the psalm to "the Chief Musician." It is one of fifty-five psalms so addressed. It is also identified as "a Psalm of David." A total of seventy-three psalms are identified with David in their superscriptions. But Psalm 70 is one of only two psalms with *lehazkir* ("to bring to remembrance") in the superscription. Only Psalms 38 and 70 use this word.

Like Psalm 38, Psalm 70 is a prayer for deliverance from enemies. Psalm 38 is a prayer of David; Psalm 70 may have, in its original form, isolated from its present context in the Psalter, been a prayer of David. But as it is placed here, it reads, with Psalm 69, as a prayer of the Messiah. As we have already noted, it may even be read as a conclusion to the prayer of Psalm 69. Although there are similarities between the two psalms,[399] there is also an important difference. In Psalm 38, David confessed his sinfulness.[400] There is no such confession in Psalm 70. Psalm 38 cannot, therefore, be pressed into service as a messianic prayer while Psalm 70 can.

Lehazkir may indicate that as it relates to their original purpose, Psalms 38 and 70 were prayers to be offered to God in connection with the memorial (*'azkarah*) offering.[401] On the other hand, they may have been intended "to remind Yahweh of the distress of the worshiper."[402] Although it is possible that Psalm 38 could have been recited by David or others as they offered a memorial sacrifice, "the idea of 'bring to remembrance' . . . seems more appropriate for Ps 70. . . ."[403] The

Septuagint translates the superscription, "For the end, by David for a remembrance, that the Lord may save me." The idea here is that "with God to remember is to act. . . ."[404] The point is that "this word speaks of laying before Him a situation that cries out for His help."[405] The phrase "to bring to remembrance" may "mean simply a personal plea like that of the thief on the cross, 'Jesus, remember me.' "[406] When God remembers, He acts.[407] In biblical thought, remembering is connected with doing.[408]

So Psalm 70 begins with a plea for God to act on behalf of One who is suffering. Verses 1 and 5 form an inclusion, a chiasm, with their plea for hasty help.[409] Sandwiched between these pleas is a prayer concerning enemies (verses 2-3) and a prayer for those who seek God (verse 4). The chiasm may be seen as follows:

> A   Make haste, O God, to deliver me! Make haste to help me, O LORD!
> > B   Let them be ashamed and confounded who seek my life; let them be turned back and confused who desire my hurt. Let them be turned back because of their shame, who say, "Aha, aha!"
> > B'   Let all those who seek You rejoice and be glad in You; and let those who love Your salvation say continually, "Let God be magnified!"
>
> A'   But I am poor and needy; make haste to me, O God! You are my help and my deliverer; O LORD, do not delay.

A comparison of Psalm 70 with Psalm 40:13-17 demonstrates that in Psalm 70 "there is a tightening of the language" to "emphasize the urgency of the matter."[410] It is not difficult to read Psalm 70 as a prayer of the Messiah. In the face of His enemies who plotted to kill Him,[411] the Messiah prayed that God would make haste to deliver Him. Like other messianic prayers in the Psalter, this brings to mind Hebrews 5:7-8:

> who, in the days of His flesh, when He had offered up prayers and supplications, with vehement cries and tears to Him who was able to save Him from death, and was heard because of His godly fear, though He was a Son, yet he learned obedience by the things which He suffered.

But the Messiah prayed not only for deliverance from His enemies; He also prayed that those who sought God would "rejoice and be glad" in Him (verse 4a). He prayed that those who loved God's name would continually say, "Let God be magnified!" (verse 4b). One prayer of the Messiah for His disciples may be seen in John 17. Jesus did pray for those who sought God and loved His salvation, and it seems that Psalm 70 was one of those prayers.

The Messiah's reference to His poverty and neediness in verse 5 is not unique to Psalm 70.[412] Paul captured this idea in II Corinthians 8:9: "For you know the grace of our Lord Jesus Christ, that though He was rich, yet for your sakes He became poor, that you through His poverty might become rich."

Psalm 70, by its content, its connection with other messianic psalms, and its immediate context in the Psalter, advances the messianic theme of the Book of Psalms. In view of this, it is appropriate that the Common Lectionary appoints Psalm 70 as the psalm for Wednesday of Holy Week.

> When read in this context, the psalm in verse 3 echoes the scornful "Aha!" addressed to the crucified Jesus (Mark 15:29). It is reread, as it has been for centuries, as the prayer of Jesus in his passion and of the church in its neediness.[413]

Psalm 71

The first thing we notice about Psalm 71 is the lack of a superscription. From Psalm 3 through Psalm 89 the only psalms lacking a superscription are Psalms 10, 33, 43, and 71. In "each case there is manuscript evidence for combining each of the psalms . . . with the psalm which precedes it."[414] In the final shaping of the Psalter, the placement of psalms lacking superscriptions was apparently intentional. They are to be read as continuing the theme of the previous psalm, or as one with the previous psalm, or as in some other way vitally connected with the previous psalm.

The relationship between Psalms 70 and 71 can be seen as follows:

First, it is possible to read directly from the end of Psalm 70 into the beginning of Psalm 71 with no interruption in the flow of thought.

> But I am poor and needy; make haste to me, O God! You are my help and my deliverer; O LORD, do not delay. (Psalm 70:5)

> In You, O LORD, I put my trust; let me never be put to shame. Deliver me in Your righteousness, and cause me to escape; incline Your ear to me, and save me. (Psalm 71:1-2)

Second, both psalms address the threat of death.

> Let them be ashamed and confounded who seek my life; let them be turned back and confused who desire my hurt. (Psalm 70:2)

> For my enemies speak against me; and those who lie in wait for my life take counsel together. (Psalm 71:10)

Third, both psalms cry for haste.

> Make haste, O God, to deliver me! Make haste to help me, O LORD! . . . But I am poor and needy; make haste to me, O God! You are my help and my deliverer; O LORD, do not delay. (Psalm 70:1, 5)

> O God, do not be far from me; O my God, make haste to help me! (Psalm 71:12)

Since the word translated "make haste" (*hushah*) appears only seven times in the Psalter,[415] it seems significant that three of these occurrences are grouped so closely together in these two psalms. Two of the previous appearances of "make haste" are in psalms that are actually quoted in the New Testament in reference to the Messiah. (See Psalm 22:19; 40:13). One of the previous appearances, though not in a prayer of the Messiah, is in a prayer of David that is messianic in its focus. (See Psalm 38:22.)

Fourth, both psalms call for enemies to be confounded.

> Let them be ashamed and confounded who seek my life; let them be turned back and confused who desire my hurt. (Psalm 70:2)

> Let them be confounded and consumed who are adversaries of my life; let them be covered with reproach and dishonor who seek my hurt. . . . For they are confounded, for they are brought to shame who seek my hurt. (Psalm 71:13, 24b)

The final verse in Psalm 71 suggests that it is to be read as the answer to the prayer first offered in Psalm 70:2.

The next thing we notice about Psalm 71 is its relationship to psalms further removed from its immediate context in the Psalter. There are so many similarities between Psalm 71 and other psalms that Wilcock describes the psalm as "largely a mosaic of allusions to or even quotations from others."[416]

Wilcock points out that if "71 is related to 70, it is by the same token related to 40, of whose closing verses 70 is practically a duplicate."[417] Psalm 40 was quoted by the writer of Hebrews as the words of the Messiah.[418]

The relationship between Psalm 71 and Psalm 31 should be noted.

> In You, O LORD, I put my trust; let me never be ashamed; deliver me in Your righteousness. Bow down Your ear to me, deliver me speedily; be my rock of refuge, a fortress of defense to save me. For You are my rock and my fortress. . . . (Psalm 31:1-3a)

> In You, O LORD, I put my trust; let me never be put to shame. Deliver me in Your righteousness, and cause me to escape; incline Your ear to me, and save me. Be my strong refuge, to which I may resort continually; You have given the commandment to save me, for You are my rock and my fortress. (Psalm 71:1-3)

This connection is significant in view of the fact that Jesus quoted from Psalm 31 as part of His prayer on the cross.[419] If Psalm 31 was a prayer of the Messiah, it would be reasonable—unless there is strong evidence otherwise—that Psalm 71 is as well.

A connection between Psalm 71 and Psalm 22 may be seen in that the thoughts of Psalm 71:4-6 "run parallel with those of 22:9ff, though they are differently expressed."[420]

> But You are He who took Me out of the womb; You made Me trust while on My mother's breasts. I was cast upon You from birth. From My mother's womb You have been My God. Be not far from Me, for trouble is near; for there is none to help. (Psalm 22:9-11)

> Deliver me, O my God, out of the hand of the wicked, out of the hand of the unrighteous and cruel man. For You are my hope, O Lord GOD; You are my trust from my youth. By You I have been upheld from birth; You are He who took me out of my mother's womb. My praise shall be continually of You. (Psalm 71:4-6)

Jesus prayed from Psalm 22 on His cross.[421] The conceptual link between the two psalms suggests that Psalm 71 was also a prayer of the Messiah.

A further connection between Psalms 22 and 71 may be seen:

> Be not far from Me. . . . But You, O LORD, do not be far from Me; O My Strength, hasten to help Me! (Psalm 22:11a, 19)

> O God, do not be far from me; O my God, make haste to help me! (Psalm 71:12)

Still another link between Psalms 22 and 71 may be seen.

> I will declare Your name to My brethren; in the midst of the assembly I will praise You. . . . A posterity shall serve Him. It will be recounted of the Lord to the next generation, they will come and declare His righteousness to a people who will be born, that He has done this. (Psalm 22:22, 30-31)

> Until I declare Your strength to this generation, Your power to everyone who is to come. (Psalm 71:18b)

There is close affinity between Psalm 35:4, 26, Psalm 71:13, and Psalm 109:29.

> Let those be put to shame and brought to dishonor who

seek after my life; let those be turned back and brought to confusion who plot my hurt.... Let them be ashamed and brought to mutual confusion who rejoice at my hurt; let them be clothed with shame and dishonor who exalt themselves against me. (Psalm 35:4, 26)

Let them be confounded and consumed who are adversaries of my life; let them be covered with reproach and dishonor who seek my hurt. (Psalm 71:13)

Let my accusers be clothed with shame, and let them cover themselves with their own disgrace as with a mantle. (Psalm 109:29)

The reference to God as a "rock" and "fortress" (verse 3) is first seen in the Psalter in Psalm 18:2, a psalm in which David is cast "as a figure of the promised messianic King, God's 'anointed' (v. 50), seeing in his own divinely wrought victories a portrait of his eternal descendant (v. 50b)."[422] When Psalm 18 is read in its context, in view of its use in the New Testament, in view of its themes that appear elsewhere in the Psalter and in the New Testament in reference to the Messiah, and in view of its poetic description of the events surrounding the crucifixion and resurrection of Jesus Christ, it seems certain that the psalm is intended to advance the messianic theme of the Psalter. In that case, the "rock" and "fortress" parallel may extend that theme to Psalm 71.

Because Psalms 22 and 31 "both are used in telling the passion story, Psalm 71 has also been associated with the passion of Jesus and the services of Holy Week. In the Common Lectionary and others it is the psalm set for Tuesday of Holy Week."[423]

In addition to virtually identical verses and conceptual parallels, Psalm 71 is linked with the messianic theme of the Psalter by key motifs. This includes trust in God (verses 1, 5), first commended in Psalm 2:12. It also includes God as a refuge (verses 3, 7), an idea first introduced in Psalm 9:9.

Verses 20-21 can be read as a reference to the resurrection of the Messiah.

> You, who have shown me great and severe troubles, shall revive me again, and bring me up again from the depths of the earth. You shall increase my greatness, and comfort me on every side.[424]

There seems to be only one significant obstacle to reading Psalm 71 as a prayer of the Messiah. Two of the verses refer to the speaker's old age.

> Do not cast me off in the time of old age; do not forsake me when my strength fails. . . . Now also when I am old and grayheaded, O God, do not forsake me, until I declare Your strength to this generation, Your power to everyone who is to come. (Psalm 71:9, 18)

Since we know that Jesus was crucified as a young man, do these verses nullify Psalm 71 as a prayer of the Messiah?

On the basis of these verses, many Bibles identify Psalm 71 as "a prayer for old age." It has, no doubt, been prayed with profit by many people of faith in their advancing years. Even if the psalm cannot be read as a prayer of the Messiah, Sailhamer sees it advancing the messianic theme of the Psalter.

> This is the last prayer of David; Ps 72 is by Solomon. In it David, now as an old man (vv. 9, 18), looks back over a lifetime of God's faithfulness (vv. 5-6, 17). . . .
>
> As David's last words about himself and God's promised Messiah, this psalm plays an important role in the strategy of Psalms. Just as this section began in Ps 3 with an expression of David's trust in God's promise (Ps 2; cf. 2 Sa 7), so now it concludes with a similar statement of trust. It can hardly be accidental

> that this psalm, with David's reflective glance over his long life, was placed at the conclusion of his prayers.[425]

Certainly it does seem appropriate and significant that this psalm is placed at the conclusion of the prayers of David.[426] As the psalm was originally written, it may very well have been David's reflection over a long lifetime of experiencing God's faithfulness, even though he continued to face the threat of enemies at that point in his life.

But how is the psalm to be read in its context in the Psalter? If Psalm 70 is to be read as a prayer of the Messiah, are the connections between Psalm 70 and Psalm 71—as well as the connections between Psalm 71 and other messianic psalms—negated by the age of the speaker in Psalm 71?

> The psalmist speaks as one who is elderly (vv. 9, 18) and looks back on a long life (vv. 6, 17). So the psalm has been a favorite of the old through the centuries. But we must not overlook how plastic the idioms of psalmic language are. The prayers for help use every resource to describe trouble. Old age means declining powers and can be read as a metaphor for neediness.[427]

This is poetry. Metaphorical language is a feature of poetry. When the Messiah prayed that He had been surrounded by bulls, we understand that He was speaking of humans, using a figure of speech.[428] The same is true when He said He was surrounded by dogs.[429] When He prayed for deliverance from the mouth of a lion and from the horns of wild oxen, we do not think of literal animals.[430] When the Messiah prayed to be pulled out of a net, we understand this as a metaphor for some kind of trap.[431] Likewise, when the Messiah celebrated His deliverance from a "horrible pit" filled with "miry clay," we read this as a description of His deliverance from his enemies.[432]

Although, as it was originally written, Psalm 71 no doubt expressed David's gaze back over a long life, there is nothing to prevent it from being a prayer of the Messiah, if we read it according to its context and its links with other psalms that are messianic prayers.

Since Psalm 71 has so much in common with other psalms, what are its distinctives?

First, though it is a prayer for help, Psalm 71 "majors in assertions of trust, so much so that confidence in God outweighs the concern with trouble."[433] Ten verses in some way allude to the need for help, but sixteen verses express trust in God.[434]

Second, the "psalmist speaks as one who is elderly (vv. 9, 18) and looks back on a long life (vv. 6, 17)."[435] Although this may be taken as poetic metaphor if the psalm is applied to the Messiah, it is unique among the Davidic psalms. The only other references to the old age of the psalmist are found in Psalms 32:3 and 37:25, neither of which are prayers of the Messiah. There are two other references in the Psalter to old age. Psalm 92:14 refers to those who bear fruit in their old age, and Psalm 148:12 refers to old men praising the Lord.

Third, "more than most prayers for help, this one is focused on praise."[436] Eleven verses address in some way the psalmist's praise to God. (See verses 6, 8, 14-19, 22-24.) This is not unusual in a messianic prayer. Nor is it unusual in a messianic prayer for the Messiah to declare that He will sing His praises.[437] That these are indeed references to the Messiah's singing of praise is demonstrated by the use made of this concept by Paul and the writer of Hebrews.[438] But what is unusual is that Psalm 71:22 describes the speaker as praising with the lute and the harp. Since we do not think of the Messiah playing a musical instrument, we may tend to ascribe this exclusively to David. But at the conclusion of the Last Supper, Jesus did sing a hymn with His disciples.[439] In this case, the word *humneō* is used, which has to do with singing praises, rather than *psalmos*, which includes the playing of a stringed instrument. But this does not exclude the possibility that Jesus may actually have played a lute or harp as He and His disciples, in keeping with Jewish tradition, sang a paschal hymn from the "great Hallel."[440] In

Hebrews 2:12, Psalm 22:22 is quoted in reference to the Messiah singing praise. The writer of Hebrews, like Matthew and Mark, used *humneō*. But Psalm 22 is a "psalm [*mizmor*] of David." The Septuagint translates *mizmor* as *psalmos*.[441] This suggests that a sharp distinction is not to be drawn between the use in the New Testament of *humneō* and *psalmos*. Though there may be some difference of meaning,[442] that difference may not extend to the use of a musical instrument. Though *psalmos* specifically includes the use of a musical instrument, *humneō* does not exclude it.

Fourth, the psalmist prayed, "I have become as a wonder [*mophēt*] to many" (verse 7). *Mophēt* includes in its range of meaning the ideas of "a wonder, as a special display of God's power," and "a sign or token of a future event."[443] However it is read here, it is unique in the Psalter. As it is read in its immediate context in verses 6-13, it could be a reference to the way the Messiah displayed God's power in His life and even in the face of His death, a sign that was ultimately displayed in His resurrection (verse 20). Mays points out that when "Psalm 71 is read during Holy Week the line 'I have been like a portent to many' announces that the suffering of Jesus calls for understanding and response."[444]

In Psalm 71, then, the Messiah prayed, putting His trust in the Lord and asking never to be put to shame (verse 1). In some ways, this reminds us of His prayer in Gethsemane. Although Jesus prayed to be spared the cup, He was willing to drink it.[445] Likewise, although He prayed to be spared shame, He was willing to bear it.[446]

The Messiah prayed for deliverance and escape (verse 2). This deliverance came, not by being spared death, but by His resurrection from the dead.[447]

Picking up a theme first seen in Psalm 18, Psalm 71 has the Messiah referring to God as His rock and fortress (verse 3).[448] God was also His refuge, an idea first seen in Psalm 14:6.

The wicked one (*rasha'*) surfaces again in verse 4. He is first seen in Psalm 1:1. The tension between the righteous and the wicked runs throughout much of the Psalter.

The Messiah confessed that God was His hope (verse 5). This theme first appeared in Psalm 16:9 in a verse quoted by Peter as being specifically about the Messiah.[449] The Messiah also confessed again His trust in God, as in verse 1.

The Messiah acknowledged God's care for Him from His mother's womb and stated His intention to continually praise God (verse 6). This idea was expressed in the Messiah's prayer in Psalm 22:9-11.

The Messiah was "a wonder to many."[450] Again, He confessed God to be His refuge, as in verse 3 (verse 7).

The Messiah wished His mouth to be filled with God's praise and glory continually (verse 8).

He prayed not to be cast off "in the time of old age" nor forsaken when His strength failed (verse 9). It may be that the reference to "old age" should be read as a poetic metaphor.[451]

The Messiah's enemies spoke against Him and lay in wait for His life, taking counsel together (verse 10). This connects with Psalm 2:2, where "the rulers take counsel together, against the LORD and against His Anointed."

In this case, the Messiah's enemies claimed that God had forsaken Him, so that they could pursue and take him (verse 11). This seems to be conceptually linked to Psalm 22:8, fulfilled in Matthew 27:43. Jesus' enemies were convinced that God would not deliver Him.

Verse 12 seems to be conceptually linked to Psalm 22. In Psalm 22:1, the Messiah prayed, "Why are You so far from helping Me?" Here, He prayed, "O God, do not be far from me." Verse 12 "seems to be the pivot verse in the psalm which focus [sic] toward both vv 1-11 and vv 13-24."[452]

The Messiah prayed that His enemies would be "confounded and consumed," "covered with reproach and dishonor" (verse 13). This links with Psalm 35:4, 26, a messianic prayer.

The prayer continues from verses 14 through 17 with an exclusive focus on hope and praise. Verse 18 includes another plea not to be forsaken, coupled with the intention to declare

God's strength and power. Like verse 9, verse 17 refers to old age, which may be taken as a metaphor for weakness.[453]

In verse 19 the Messiah declared God's exalted righteousness. God had done great things; there was none like Him.

Verse 20 seems to anticipate the resurrection of the Messiah. Although He had seen "great and severe troubles," He would be revived again and brought up "from the depths of the earth."

In conjunction with the Resurrection, the Messiah's "greatness" would be increased, and He would be comforted "on every side" (verse 21). The idea of greatness "is normally used of God or of princes and people in high positions."[454]

The Messiah would praise God, singing and playing a lute or harp (verse 22).[455] His singing would be with great rejoicing; He would sing with His soul, which God had redeemed (verse 23). The Hebrew word translated "redeemed" here (*padah*) does not necessarily involve the idea of redemption from sin. It is used to speak of deliverance from Egypt and from exile. The Messiah's soul was delivered by the Resurrection.[456]

Verse 24 connects with verse 8. The Messiah's talk "all the day long" was of God's righteousness. The conclusion of the psalm at this point seems intended to be read as the answer to the Messiah's prayer first uttered in Psalm 70:2:

> Let them be ashamed and confounded who seek my life; let them be turned back and confused who desire my hurt. (Psalm 70:2)

> For they are confounded, for they are brought to shame who seek my hurt. (Psalm 71:24)

By its connections with Psalm 70 and with other messianic psalms and themes, Psalm 71 is positioned to be read as a prayer of the Messiah. Thus, it advances the general messianic theme of the Psalter. David's prayer in old age became the Messiah's prayer in the face of weakness and opposition. His prayer was answered by His resurrection from the dead. Because of His resurrection, He was "a wonder to many."

Psalm 72

The placement of Psalm 72 is quite significant for the structure of the Psalter as a whole. We notice two things immediately: First, this is identified in the superscription as "a psalm of Solomon." The psalm is one of only two in the Psalter connected with Solomon.[457] Second, the psalm concludes with an apparently intentional sectional marker: "The prayers of David the son of Jesse are ended" (verse 20). This conclusion follows the ending that is typical for each of the books within the Psalter except the final book, which provides an equivalent of this ending in the final psalm.[458] Thus, the conclusion found in Psalm 79:20 apparently embraces the first two books of the Psalter, identifying both books as the prayers of David with the exception of Psalms 1-2, which introduce the entire Psalter. The "amen" conclusions to each of the books—except the final book, which does not need an "amen" since it is obviously final—suggest some kind of earlier, smaller collections that found their way into the final collection that we now know as the Book of Psalms. The reference to the conclusion of David's prayers suggests not only that this larger collection, composed of books one and two, is a later development, but it also suggests editorial or compositional purpose in grouping the two previous books together as one. Sailhamer observes,

> One can see evidence of a literary strategy in the composition of the book of Psalms in the way Pss 2 and 72 are linked. Just as Ps 2 provided a vivid reminder to the reader of God's messianic promise (2 Sa 7), so Ps 72 returns to a restatement of that promise. Furthermore, just as the superscription of Ps 3 provided the historical setting for these psalms by placing them within the con-

text of the rebellion of David's son Absalom (3:1), so the superscription of Ps 72 returns the reader to David's son Solomon, another likely heir to the promise. . . .

The last verse in this psalm (v. 20) belongs to the composer of the book of Psalms. It ties together the entire first half of the book, from Ps 3 through 72, and shows that all these psalms are to be read as prayers on behalf of God's promise of a Messiah. Psalm 72 thus fits within this group because it also focuses on the divine promise. It is important to note that the next group of psalms are [sic] not by David. There are only scattered Davidic psalms or groups of psalms in the remainder of the book (Pss 86; 101; 103; 108-110; 138-145).[459]

Although editorial or compositional evidence in the Psalter is clear, Whybray points out that

there is no direct evidence (except Ps. 72:20), internal or external, about the process by which the Psalter received its shape. All hypotheses about this basic question are purely speculative, based on inferences drawn from textual data that can be . . . interpreted in quite different ways by different scholars. . . . All that can be said with reasonable certainty about the process is that it was extremely complex, took place over a considerable time, and was influenced at its various stages by different editorial policies. . . .[460]

Scholarly curiosity about the process by which the Psalter arrived at its final shape is appropriate, but a high view of inspiration provokes a greater concern with the final shape itself, not the process that led to the final shape. We are more concerned with the Psalter as we have it, which is itself as much a result of inspiration as the original manuscripts. Although the original psalms written by David were inspired when he wrote them,

David did not live to arrange them and compile them with other psalms into our present Psalter. Whoever did this final compositional work also labored under the direction of the Holy Spirit, so that it is not just the individual psalms that are inspired, but the entire book, including the arrangement of the psalms and their connections with each other. As the individual psalms are connected with the psalms before and after them, they take on an inspired significance even greater than the individual psalms when first written or than the smaller, earlier collections of psalms indicated by the division of the Psalter into five books.

At least three facts indicate that this is the correct view: First, the Psalter as we now have it was the Psalter from which Jesus read and quoted. Jesus' use of the Psalter indicated His acceptance of its present content and order. Nothing about His use of the psalms suggests that the Psalter needed correction.[461] Second, the use made of the Psalter by the apostles and the first-century believers indicated the authority of its present content and order.[462] Third, Paul's claim that "all Scripture is given by inspiration of God" (II Timothy 3:16) gave apostolic and divine authority to the Old Testament as it was in the first century.

Although the order of the books was rearranged in the Septuagint, the integrity of the books themselves was not violated. Inspiration extended to the context within each book, so that to reorder the contents would be to disturb the inspired shape of the book. From a human perspective, two books may contain precisely the same words, but the order in which those words are found may result in completely different meanings. The Book of Psalms is unlike any other book in that it consists entirely of individual poems originally written without regard for any larger context than that of the poem itself. But under the guidance of the Holy Spirit, these individual poems were collected into another context, forming one new book. In this new context, the poems took on meaning beyond, but not in contradiction to, their original meaning. It is the nature of literary construction that this is so. Any smaller piece of literature will take on new and larger significance when placed within a larger piece of literature.

Summarizing his discussion of the shaping of the Psalter, Mitchell writes,

> Detailed investigation of the MT [Masoretic Text] Psalter reveals internal evidence that suggests it is more than a collection of songs for use as a temple or synagogue hymnbook. Instead it seems to be a purposefully crafted 'scripture' with some kind of inbuilt message about the Davidic *malkut* [kingdom]. It bears evidence of this at both small- and large-scale levels. Thematic and linguistic links exist between adjacent psalms. Larger psalms-groups appear to have been deliberately placed. Books I-III are a carefully crafted sub-unit, skilfully linked to Books IV and V. Royal psalms occur at structurally significant points. The five-book division is intrinsic to the final shaping.[463]

In his brilliant work that sprang from his doctoral research, Mitchell points out that although

> current theories have major strengths, rightly noting the centrality of Davidic kingship and the importance of Ps. 89, they also fail to fit the evidence in a number of details. What these theories have in common is that they propose that the sequence of psalms principally reflects historical events. However, there is internal evidence, particularly in the placing of royal and eschatological psalms, that the Psalter was designed to refer to eschatological events.[464]

Mitchell's contribution is that he combines these two approaches, "investigating the Psalter's arrangement in terms of an eschatologically oriented editorial agenda" and sketching "the outline of a programme of eschatological events in the Psalter that makes sense of both heading and content of the individual psalms, the sequence of the psalms, the arrangement of internal collections and the five-book arrangement."[465]

From our study to this point, it seems evident that the historical background of the individual psalms is significant, but this significance is not limited to the original circumstance that gave birth to each psalm; it extends to the application of that circumstance to the messianic promise and person. This alone gives an eschatological orientation to the Psalter. But this eschatological orientation is further confirmed by the relationships between and among the psalms and, as Mitchell points out, the relationships between the Psalter and other eschatological texts like Zechariah 9-14.

In our attempt to interpret Psalm 72, we will discuss the obvious questions first: What is the significance of this psalm being connected with Solomon, and what is the significance of the psalm serving as the conclusion of the prayers of David?

Not counting the first two introductory psalms, fifty-five of the first seventy psalms are associated in some way with David. If we include Psalms 10, 33, and 71 with the Davidic psalms due to their connection with the Davidic psalms that immediately precede them, fifty-eight of the first seventy psalms are associated with David. In view of Korah's connection with David, Psalms 42-49 could also be viewed as reflecting the affairs of David's kingdom,[466] and so could Psalm 50 because of Asaph's connection with David. This leaves only Psalms 66-67 in question due to the fact that they are not connected with any person in the superscription. Psalm 65 is a psalm of David, however, and this may influence Psalms 66-67 to be read the same way.

The overwhelming impression gained by reading the first two books of the Psalter is that they are about David and the affairs of his kingdom. We have also seen, of course, that David serves as a messianic figure, pointing ahead to the greater and ultimate David: the Messiah.[467] Now, however, we come upon what seems to be an abnormality. We suddenly have a psalm that does not immediately seem to be about David. Although it could be said that it is about the affairs of David's kingdom, it seems more properly to be about his successor, Solomon, who moved the story beyond David to his own future, an idealized future brighter than anything ever enjoyed by David even at the height of his reign. (See verses 7-11, 17.)

So what does it mean to say that this is a psalm "of Solomon" (*lishlomoh*)? The preposition *le*, here, as in all of the psalms said in their superscriptions to be *ledavid* (commonly translated "of David"), permits a wide variety of translations. *Lishlomoh* could be translated "to Solomon," "for Solomon," "in regard to Solomon," "in reference to Solomon," "by Solomon," or even "for the use of Solomon." How should it be read here? Is this a psalm written by Solomon, or is it—as could possibly be suggested by verse 20—a prayer of David for Solomon on behalf of the blessings of the Davidic covenant, or could it even be a prayer written by David for use by Solomon?

It is Sailhamer's view that Psalm 72 focuses on Solomon as a likely heir to God's messianic promise to David as found in II Samuel 7.[468] From this perspective, Solomon wrote the psalm, and the "fact that it was written by Solomon rather than David shows that Solomon was not the fulfillment of the promise. Like his father David, Solomon looked forward to the time when God would fulfill his promise and send the Messiah. That is the theme of Ps 72."[469]

It is Whybray's view that the

> whole psalm—apart from the doxology in vv. 18-19—is a prayer for the king and may have been written for his coronation. The hyperbolic language of some verses, especially vv. 5-11, which express a wish for the king's eternal reign (v. 5; not the eternal reign of the dynasty but of the individual named in v. 1 as *melek* [king] and *ben-melek* [son of a king]), for life-giving influence like

> that of the rain falling on the earth (v. 6), and above all for universal dominion (vv. 8-11), is such as to point beyond the present to a future savior-figure. . . .[470]

Whybray does not speculate as to the identity of the psalm's author, but in his view "the psalm's present position suggests that this pre-exilic 'messianism' was adopted and given prominence by editors of a later period."[471]

While Wilcock suggests that this could be a psalm by Solomon, perhaps for Rehoboam, his successor, he thinks it more likely that it is for Solomon by his father David.[472]

Kidner's view is that *lishlomoh* should be translated "of Solomon," just as *ledavid* is regularly translated "of David."[473] This begs the question as to whether *ledavid* should indeed be consistently translated "of David."

The Septuagint translates *le* with the preposition *eis*, making the psalm "for Solomon." This is followed by the KJV. This accords with the views of Gerald Wilson and Brevard Childs. Wilson "views Psalm 72 as one of the Psalter's strategically placed royal psalms. He maintains that the psalm functions in the story of the Psalter as David's 'attempt to transfer the blessings of his covenant with YHWH to his descendents.' "[474] It is Childs's view that "the canonical placement of Psalm 72 indicates strongly that the psalm 'is "for" Solomon, offered by David.' It brings to the minds of its readers/hearers the covenant that YHWH made with David in 2 Samuel, chapter 7, and which YHWH renewed with Solomon in I Kings 9:5."[475]

Our attempt to determine the identity of the author of Psalm 72 is bound up with our discussion of the significance of verse 20: "The prayers of David the son of Jesse are ended." It seems reasonable to conclude that verse 20 influences the translation of the superscription, so that the psalm is a prayer by David "for Solomon." Sailhamer's point is well-taken that the "psalm begins with a request for justice and righteousness on behalf of the King (vv. 1-4) and is reminiscent of Solomon's own request for wisdom to rule God's people (1 Ki 3:9)."[476] But a thematic connection between Psalm 72 and Solomon's prayer does not require that Psalm 72 is a prayer by Solomon. It is conceivable, at least, that Solomon could have been influenced in his remarkable prayer by the prayer of his father David for him.

Although we may never know with finality the significance of *lishlomoh* and of verse 20 for this psalm, we will read it as a prayer of David on behalf of Solomon. But although David may have prayed this prayer for Solomon or written the prayer for use at Solomon's coronation, Solomon did not live up to the ideal of the king described in the psalm. As Mays points out,

> In the light of the story of Solomon, it is evident how incompletely the vocation materialized in him. The prayer has a dimension and reach that transcend Solomon and all the kings of Judah. Within the Old Testament, it prays for what is not yet—a king whose person and practice bring the people of God and the nations of the earth into the time of the reign of God.[477]

Mays further observes,

> The prayer calls for divine government to inhabit human rulers. The model of kingship is far more than a challenge and goal; it is, if taken in ultimate seriousness, as the prophets surely did, a prescription for failure. It creates a tension out of which come prophecies of "one to come," as in Isaiah 11:1-9. By the time Psalm 72 became part of Scripture it was probably being understood by some as a prayer for the coming of the Messiah.[478]

Although as David penned this psalm he appears to have hoped—on the basis of God's promise to him in II Samuel 7:12-16—that Solomon would be the son through whom his house, kingdom, and throne would be established forever, this was not to be. God did renew the Davidic covenant with Solomon, but that renewal was conditioned upon perfect obedience to His commandments and statutes. (See I Kings 9:3-9.) However fervent David's prayer may have been, Solomon's disobedience prevented its fulfillment.

Why, then, is the psalm included in the Psalter? If there can be no fulfillment of this psalm, it seems that its placement here serves only to remind us of what could have been. In this case, we discover, much to our disappointment, that there could have been a righteous and just king who would break in pieces all those who oppressed the poor and needy; there could have been a king whose universal dominion would usher in world peace and prosperity. How would such a regrettable situation foster faith and hope?

But the psalm is included to point ahead to "a greater than Solomon" (Matthew 12:42). Indeed, Jesus' identification of Himself as "greater than Solomon" in the context of the queen of Sheba's visit to Solomon may have been an allusion to Psalm 72:10, where it is declared that the "kings of Sheba and Seba will offer gifts" to the king. These gifts will include the "gold of Sheba" (verse 15). The fact that Solomon's visit was from the queen of Sheba rather than the kings of Sheba may further suggest that Solomon was not the fulfillment of Psalm 72. Surely it was a substantial honor to receive homage from the queen of Sheba, but the king must pay the ultimate homage. Jesus' rebuke of the unbelieving scribes and Pharisees was appropriate: The queen of Sheba acknowledged Solomon's greatness when Solomon was a mere shadow of the idealized "Solomon" of Psalm 72. In contrast, the scribes and Pharisees would not acknowledge the greatness of Jesus, although He was the "Solomon" in view in David's prophetic prayer.

The messianic focus of Psalm 72 is indicated by a number of direct references to messianic texts found in other books.

> He shall come down like rain upon the grass before mowing, like showers that water the earth. (Psalm 72:6)

> And he shall be like the light of the morning when the sun rises, a morning without clouds, like the tender grass springing out of the earth, by clear shining after rain. (II Samuel 23:4)

David's reference was not to any merely human king of his lineage (II Samuel 23:5) but to the Messiah.[479] The poetic description of these verses was not appropriate for any Davidic king before the Messiah.

> He shall have dominion also from sea to sea, and from the River to the ends of the earth. (Psalm 72:8)

> Ask of Me, and I will give You the nations for Your inheritance, and the ends of the earth for Your possession. (Psalm 2:8)

> I will cut off the chariot from Ephraim and the horse from Jerusalem; the battle bow shall be cut off. He shall speak peace to the nations; His dominion shall be from sea to sea, and from the River to the ends of the earth. (Zechariah 9:10)[480]

Although there may have been in David's mind a reference here to the initial promise God made to Israel of dominion from the Red Sea to the sea of the Philistines (the Mediterranean) and from the desert to the Euphrates River,[481] Psalm 72:10-11 extends the dominion beyond this vast but limited tract of land to "all kings" and "all nations." Of all the Davidic kings prior to the Messiah, Solomon most closely fulfilled the prayer of Psalm 72. He "reigned over all kingdoms from the River to the land of the Philistines, as far as the border of Egypt. They brought tribute and served Solomon all the days of his life" (I Kings 4:21). Indeed, "men of all nations, from all the kings of the earth who had heard of his wisdom, came to hear the wisdom of Solomon" (I Kings 4:34).

But upon Solomon's death we learn that he had ruled with a "heavy yoke" (I Kings 12:4), a political policy that resulted in the division of the kingdom. Those who brought tribute and served him as long as he lived did so apparently because of Solomon's political might, not because of personal loyalty to him. And it was one thing for the kings of the earth at that time to come to hear his wisdom; it will be quite another thing for all kings to fall down before the Messiah, serving Him. Solomon reigned only forty years (I Kings 11:42); the king of Psalm 72 will reign "as long as the sun and moon endure, throughout all generations" (verse 5). This king will live (verse 15) and "His name shall endure forever; His name shall continue as long as the sun. And men shall be blessed in Him; all nations shall call Him blessed" (verse 17). Although Solomon's reign was great and most closely approximated the Messiah's reign, it did not measure up to the prophetic significance of Psalm 72. In Wilcock's words, "The historical reality never quite measured up to the vision of the poem; the final reality will far surpass it."[482]

> Those who dwell in the wilderness will bow before Him, and His enemies will lick the dust. (Psalm 72:9)

> So the LORD God said to the serpent: "Because you have done this, you are cursed more than all cattle, and more than every beast of the field; on your belly you shall go, and you shall eat dust all the days of your life." (Genesis 3:14)[483]

This suggests that the king in Psalm 72 "is identified as the one who will defeat the serpent of Genesis 3."[484]

> The kings of Tarshish and of the isles will bring presents; the kings of Sheba and Seba will offer gifts. (Psalm 72:10)

> Surely the coastlands shall wait for Me; and the ships

> of Tarshish will come first, to bring your sons from afar, their silver and their gold with them, to the name of the LORD your God, and to the Holy One of Israel, because He has glorified you. (Isaiah 60:9)[485]

The One to whom Tarshish brings its gifts is "the Holy One of Israel." This precludes Psalm 72 from having its ultimate fulfillment in Solomon.

> Yes, all kings shall fall down before Him; all nations shall serve Him. (Psalm 72:11)

> Then the kingdom and dominion, and the greatness of the kingdoms under the whole heaven, shall be given to the people, the saints of the Most High. His kingdom is an everlasting kingdom, and all dominions shall serve and obey Him. (Daniel 7:27)

The only One who deserves universal homage is the Most High.

> And men shall be blessed in Him; all nations shall call Him blessed. (Psalm 72:17b)

> I will make you a great nation; I will bless you and make your name great; and you shall be a blessing. I will bless those who bless you, and I will curse him who curses you; and in you all the families of the earth shall be blessed. (Genesis 12:2-3)

Sailhamer points out that the "king in Psalm 72 is the seed in which all nations are blessed in the covenant with Abraham in Genesis 12:3."[486] Paul seemed to understand this concept: "Now to Abraham and his Seed were the promises made. He does not say, 'And to seeds,' as of many, but as of one, *'And to your Seed,'* who is Christ" (Galatians 3:16).

The connections between Psalm 72 and other specifically messianic texts, the context in which Psalm 72 is found in the Psalter, and the content of the psalm itself all indicate that the psalm is to be read as pointing to an "idealized" Solomon, someone beyond the immediate son of David whose reign, though significant, fell short of the psalm's ideal. The psalm does point toward a Son of David, but a Son who is introduced in Matthew 1:1, not Matthew 1:6.

The psalm begins with a prayer for One is who both a king and a king's Son (verse 1). Although this description would fit Solomon, it fits the Messiah more perfectly, in that He is not only the king's Son, as a descendant of David, but in that He is also the King of kings and Lord of lords.[487] The psalm exalts the high calling of the King so far beyond what is humanly attainable "as to suggest for its fulfilment no less a person than the Messiah, not only to Christian thinking but to Jewish. The Targum at verse 1 adds the word 'Messiah' to 'the king', and there are rabbinic allusions to the psalm which reveal the same opinion."[488] This King's reign will be characterized by justice and righteousness (verse 2). God's concern with social justice is seen frequently in the Old Testament.[489]

As a consequence of the king's righteous judgment, peace (*shalom*) would come to the people (verse 3 [see also verse 7]). *Shalom* has to do with wholeness in "the political, economic, social, and spiritual dimensions of life."[490] Although the word is a common greeting among those who speak Hebrew today, it means much more than "hello." *Shalom* is about wholeness and well-being in every aspect of life. *Shalom* will characterize the Messiah's rule. Although there was the absence of military conflict during Solomon's reign, it could not truly be said that *shalom* characterized his rule, for he was personally flawed by his love for strange women who drew his heart away from the true God. This provoked God's anger with Solomon and resulted in the kingdom being torn.[491]

In the process of bringing justice to the poor and needy, the Messiah would "break in pieces the oppressor" (verse 4, 12-14).

This picks up the language of Psalm 2:9 and anticipates Isaiah 11:4, both messianic texts.

A textual variant should be noted in verse 5. The reading followed by the KJV and NKJV indicates that the Messiah will be feared "as long as the sun and moon endure, throughout all generations." The Septuagint is joined by some translations that apply eternality to the Son Himself. Solomon could fulfill neither reading.

The Messiah fulfilled the refreshing poetic description of rain upon the grass, a description with its roots in David's inspired prophecy of II Samuel 23:4 (verse 6). The idea is that He brought life and abundance.

The righteous would flourish during the Messiah's peaceful reign, a reign that would outlast the moon (verse 7).

His dominion would be universal, including but extending beyond the boundaries promised to Abraham and Israel (verses 8-11).[492]

The Messiah would live (verse 15). Solomon died. Not only would the gold of Sheba[493] be given to Him (see also verse 10); prayer would be made for Him continually and He would be praised daily (verse 15). It may at first seem strange to think of prayer being made for the Messiah, in view of the fact that He is God, but this, like His prayers, underscores the reality of the Incarnation; He was also human. Jesus invited the prayerful watchfulness of His disciples as He prayed in Gethsemane.[494]

The Messiah's reign would be characterized by abundance, both in the countryside and in the cities (verse 16).

His reign would be forever (verse 17). Although the Messiah's millennial reign would endure for one thousand years, it would flow into His eternal reign, still characterized by the obedience of the nations.[495]

The psalm—and Book II of the Psalter—concludes with a vision of the Messiah's universal kingdom (verses 18-19).

It should come as no surprise that Psalm 72 has been interpreted, by both the Jewish and Christian communities, to be about the Messiah's future reign. The Peshitta[496] declared

Psalm 72 to be a "Psalm of David, when he had made Solomon king, and a prophecy concerning the advent of the Messiah and the calling of the Gentiles."[497] David Kimhi, a mediaeval rabbi, interpreted Psalm 72 as referring to the Messiah.[498] Ibn Ezra wrote that Psalm 72 was a "prophecy of David or one of the [temple] singers about Solomon or about Messiah."[499] Justin Martyr cited Psalm 72 as a messianic proof-text.[500] Bucer, the reformer who produced the first full commentary on Psalms, regarded Psalm 72 as containing messianic prophecy.[501] J. P. Peters, perhaps the most original thinker on the Psalter in the first quarter of the twentieth century, viewed Psalm 72 as

> not a liturgy for a sacrifice, but an ode, like Ps. 2, to depict the glories of the kingdom of the ideal king of David's line, the Messiah or Christ that was to be, and appears to have been designed for the conclusion of the collection of the Psalms of David, as Ps. 2, a much more militant treatment of the same theme, was for the commencement of that volume.[502]

Isaac Watts, in his book *The Psalms of David, Imitated in the Language of the New Testament*, paraphrased Psalm 72 to begin with the words, "Jesus shall reign where'er the sun Does his successive journeys run."[503]

We are certainly in good company to read Psalm 72 as a prayer/prophecy concerning the Messiah's coming kingdom. But we are in the company not only of ancient and modern interpreters, both Jewish and Christian. We are also in the company of those Old Testament prophets who—though they may have never seen Psalm 72—expressed their hopes for the Messiah in virtually identical words. As Kidner points out, the "picture of the king and his realm is so close to the prophecies of Isaiah 11:1-5 and Isaiah 60-62 that if those passages are messianic, so is this."[504]

Kimhi interpreted verse 20 to mean that when the messianic kingdom described in the psalm was in place, the prayers of David would be fulfilled. This would make verse 20 not so much an editorial comment about the collection of psalms, but a fitting conclusion to the prayer of Psalm 72.

> And if it is [interpreted] concerning the King Messiah, Ibn Ezra interprets it as follows. When all these consolations will be completed, then *Fulfilled are the prayers of David ben Jesse*. It does not say 'Fulfilled are the songs' or 'fulfilled are the hymns,' but *Fulfilled are the prayers of David*, in relation to atonement and deliverance. For when everything is completed, that Israel go forth from the exile and are in their land, and the King Messiah ben David rules over them, nothing will be lacking, neither atonement, nor deliverance, nor prosperity, for everything will be theirs. And then *Fulfilled are the prayers of David ben Jesse*.[505]

Book Two of the Psalter concludes with a dramatic and appropriate messianic psalm. The Messiah has come and Israel is restored. Through that restored nation the Messiah rules over the earth.[506] But Book Three of the Psalter begins with the plaintive cry of disappointment over the apparent prosperity of the wicked and the delay of the messianic kingdom.

APPENDIX 1

Canonical-Compositional Hermeneutics

By the term "canonical-compositional hermeneutics," I mean the hermeneutic that views the final shape of the TaNaK as intentional and informative.[1] As it pertains to the Psalter, this is the view that the order of the psalms and other evidence of post-exilic composition—sometimes referred to as redaction—are part of the process of inspiration and are therefore vital to meaning.

There is no consensus as to the definition of canonical criticism.[2] But it is agreed by most scholars working in this field that "the context of the final canon is *more important* than the original author."[3] Common emphases of canonical criticism include the following: Since the church has received the Bible as authoritative in its present form, the focus should be on that canonical form rather than on a search for the sources behind the text; the text must be studied holistically to determine how it functions in its final form; the theological concerns of the final editor(s) must be explored; in later texts, the canon provides interpretive clues in the use of earlier biblical texts.[4]

Brevard Childs, a leading proponent of canonical criticism, asserts that "the lengthy process of the development of the literature leading up to the final stage of canonization involved a profoundly hermeneutical activity on the part of the tradents."[5] In his view, the canon "was shaped in order to provide means for its continuing appropriation by its subsequent hearers."[6]

As it relates to the Book of Psalms, Childs holds that the Psalter makes use of reinterpreted imagery.

> Israel continued to celebrate the righteous rule of its king long after the institution of kingship had been destroyed because the earthly king from the line of David had become a type of God's Messiah. Especially in Ps. 2 the psalm has been given an eschatological ring by emphasizing the kingship of God which God's anointed ruler merely represents.... Pss. 45 and 72 continue to function in the Psalter because it is the rule of God which is being celebrated by means of reinterpreted imagery. The eschatological dimension emerges clearly in Pss. 89 and 132 where the promise of Nathan concerning David is actually cited.[7]

Thus the psalms that had to do with David in their original form, devoid of any context beyond the psalm, now have to do with the Messiah in their new canonical context.

Bruce K. Waltke argues "for a canonical process approach in interpreting the psalms, an approach that does justice both to the historical significance(s) of the psalms and to their messianic significance."[8] He further argues that

> ... from a literary and historical point of view, we should understand that the human subject of the psalms—whether it be the blessed man of Psalm 1, the one proclaiming himself the son of God in Psalm 2, the suffering petitioner in Psalms 3-7, the son of man in Psalm 8—is Jesus Christ.[9]

By canonical process approach, Waltke means "the recognition that the text's intention became deeper and clearer as the parameters of the canon were expanded."[10] Waltke distinguishes his approach from Childs's as follows: (1) Childs does not distinguish the changes that took place through literary activity in the development of the text from those that took place through scribal copying. In Waltke's view, the development of the text and canon was a product of inspiration; (2) Childs looks to a vague process of historical criticism—with the possible denial of supernatural activity—to trace the development of the tradition. Waltke affirms God's supernatural intervention in Israel's history; (3) Childs emphasizes the authority of the Jewish text of AD 100. Waltke emphasizes the meaning of the Hebrew Scriptures in their New Testament context.[11]

In contrast to the majority view of scholars who are involved in canonical criticism, Waltke holds that "the original authorial intention was not changed in the progressive development of the canon but deepened and clarified."[12] Further, "the canonical process approach does not divorce the human authorial intention from the divine intention."[13] Still, Waltke sees that there were four points "in that winning of the clearer and deeper significance of older texts through the discernment of the stages in the development of the canon. . . ."[14] They are as follows:

> (1) the meaning of the psalm to the original poet, (2) its meaning in the earlier collections of psalms associated with the First Temple, (3) its meaning in the final and complete Old Testament canon associated with the Second Temple, and (4) its meaning in the full canon of the Bible including the New Testament with its presentation of Jesus as the Christ.[15]

In defense of his view that the order of the books in the canon is "revelatory of a divinely-intended pattern,"[16] Lubeck points to two important clues for hermeneutics.

> The first is intratextual: how later biblical texts used earlier texts teaches us about how we should view these texts. The second is sequential: how the books were arranged serves as a very early "commentary" on the relationships

> between books as understood at a very early stage in the history of their reception and interpretation. . . . And at least the tripartite structure of the TaNaK also appears to bear the imprimatur of N.T. sanction.[17]

Lubeck thinks the "sequentiality in the arrangement of the Psalms provides a microcosmic picture of the identical issues we are dealing with at the macrostructural level of the TaNaK."[18]

John H. Sailhamer, a leading proponent of compositional hermeneutics, urges "the consideration of a return to the notion that the literal meaning of the OT may . . . be linked to the messianic hope of the pre-Christian, Israelite prophets."[19]

> By paying careful attention to the compositional strategies of the biblical books themselves, we believe in them can be found many essential clues to the meaning intended by their authors—clues that point beyond their immediate historical referent to a future, messianic age. By looking at the works of the scriptural authors, rather than at the events that lie behind their accounts of them, we can find appropriate textual clues to the meaning of these biblical books. Those clues . . . point to an essentially messianic and eschatological focus of the biblical texts. In other words, the literal meaning of Scripture . . . may, in fact, be the spiritual sense . . . intended by the author, namely, the messianic sense picked up in the NT books.[20]

Sailhamer's compositional approach is quite similar to Childs's canonical approach. Although Waltke distinguishes between his view of canonical process and *sensus plenior*, he does acknowledge that his view is similar to *sensus plenior* "in that it recognizes that further revelation [brings] to light a text's fuller or deeper significance."[21] In Childs's view, to see the Messiah in the psalms is reinterpretation. To Sailhamer, it is interpretation, without any appeal to *sensus plenior*. In

Sailhamer's view, the psalmist was describing himself, but as a prophet, he was looking to the messianic King.[22]

In my reference to canonical-compositional hermeneutics, I am combining features of Childs's, Waltke's, and Sailhamer's views. The individual psalms were inspired as originally written. In their original form, they had to do with the person identified in the superscription,[23] but the Holy Spirit intended that person to represent, in some way, the ultimate Son of David, the Messiah. It is suggested by II Samuel 23:1-7 that David knew he was writing about the Messiah.[24] This was certainly Peter's view.[25] The final composition of the Psalter was also inspired, so that the final shape of the book gives us an inspired interpretation of the psalms. Evidence of composition includes those portions of the Psalter that could not have been written until after the Exile and those that indicate intentional shaping of the book.[26]

APPENDIX 2

The Use of Psalms in the New Testament

During His last meeting with His followers, Jesus said, "These are the words which I spoke to you while I was still with you, that all things must be fulfilled which were written in the Law of Moses and the Prophets and the Psalms concerning Me" (Luke 24:44). It was traditional to view the Hebrew Scriptures, our Old Testament, in these three categories.[1] By referring to the Scriptures in this way, Jesus endorsed the entirety of the written Scriptures as they existed at that time.

Jesus' statement was extremely significant, in that it identified Him as the central theme of written revelation. In his account of Jesus' last moments on earth, Luke followed these words from Jesus by writing, "And He opened their understanding, that they might comprehend the Scriptures" (Luke 24:45). The idea here is that it is possible to understand the Old Testament only to the extent that one sees the Messiah as its central idea. (See also Luke 24:25-27; II Corinthians 3:14-17.)

The significance of Jesus' statement is further seen in its connection to the great commission: "Thus it is written, and thus it was necessary for the Christ to suffer and to rise from the dead the third day, and that repentance and remission of sins should be preached in His name to all nations, beginning at Jerusalem" (Luke 24:46-47). The phrase "thus it is written" refers back to Christ's previous words about the theme of messianic prophecy running through the entire Old Testament. We may be sure, therefore, that the Hebrew Scriptures inform us of the sufferings of the Messiah and His resurrection from the dead. They also inform us that the only proper response to the gospel of Jesus Christ is repentance, that the result of obedient faith is remission of sins, that the preaching of the gospel would originate in the Jewish community at Jerusalem, and that it would extend beyond that to all the Gentile nations of the world.

Unfortunately, we do not know everything that Jesus said to His followers when "He opened their understanding, that they might comprehend the Scriptures" (Luke 24:45). It is certain that at least some of what He said found its way into the preaching, teaching, and writing of the New Testament community. The church existed for something like fifteen years without any New Testament Scriptures. During this time, therefore, the only scriptural authority was what we know today as the Old Testament. We can learn a great deal about the messianic theme of the Old Testament from the New Testament documents, but there is no indication that their exploration of the messianic theme was exhaustive. It may very well be that there were elements of messianic preaching and teaching that never found their way into the New Testament, even though they may have been well known among first-century believers. This is one reason why it is profitable to study the Old Testament carefully with an awareness of its messianic theme; untold depths of christological riches wait to be mined there.

Jesus' Use of the Psalms' Messianic Theme

Even though the writers of the New Testament may not have been exhaustive in their treatment of the messianic content of the Old Testament, their exploration of this central theme is rich and revealing. For our purposes, we will look specifically at how selected New Testament texts reveal Christ to be the theme of the Psalms.

In an exchange with the Pharisees, Jesus asked, "What do you think about the Christ? Whose Son is He?" (Matthew

22:42a). They answered, "The Son of David" (Matthew 22:42b). Jesus responded, "How then does David in the Spirit call Him *'Lord,'* saying: *'The LORD said to my Lord, "Sit at My right hand, till I make Your enemies Your footstool" '*? If David then calls Him *'Lord,'* how is He his Son?" (Matthew 22:43-45). The Pharisees were unable to answer, and this terminated their questions. (See Matthew 22:46; Mark 12:35-37; Luke 20:41-44).

Jesus' appeal here to Psalm 110:1 as a messianic text was quite significant. First, it revealed that the Jewish scholars of the first century understood the messianic theme of the Hebrew Scriptures. One of David's descendants would actually be the Messiah. (See Acts 2:29-31; II Samuel 7:12; Psalm 132:11.) Second, Jesus' use of Psalm 110:1 endorsed David as the author of the psalm, as indicated in the first line of the psalm in the Hebrew text.[2] (See II Samuel 23:1-2; Acts 1:15-16.) Third, Psalm 110:1 indicates that although the Messiah was David's Son—a human being—He was also in some way David's Lord, requiring the Messiah to be more than a human being.

Peter's Use of the Psalms' Messianic Theme

In quotes from two psalms, Peter indicated on the Day of Pentecost that these psalms were messianic. First, in reference to the resurrection of Jesus from the dead, Peter said, "For David says concerning Him: *'I foresaw the LORD always before my face, for He is at my right hand, that I may not be shaken. Therefore my heart rejoiced, and my tongue was glad; moreover my flesh also will rest in hope. For You will not leave my soul in Hades, nor will You allow Your Holy One to see corruption. You have made known to me the ways of life; You will make me full of joy in Your presence'* " (Acts 2:25-28). In this quote from the Septuagint translation of Psalm 16:8-11, Peter identified the Messiah as the theme of Psalm 16.[3] In Psalm 16 we do not merely have a general principle that is applied to the Messiah; Peter said, "David says concerning Him." What David said was specifically about the Messiah.

Further, David knew that he was writing about the Messiah. It was not that David thought he was writing about someone else, or that he was setting forth general principles that the Holy Spirit intended—without David's knowledge—to apply to the Messiah. Peter put it this way: "Men and brethren, let me speak freely to you of the patriarch David, that he is both dead and buried, and his tomb is with us to this day. Therefore, being a prophet, and knowing that God had sworn with an oath to him that of the fruit of his body, according to the flesh, He would raise up Christ to sit on his throne, he, foreseeing this, spoke concerning the resurrection of the Christ, that His soul was not left in Hades, nor did His flesh see corruption" (Acts 2:29-31). David was a prophet. He knew that the Messiah would physically descend from him and that the Messiah would sit on his throne (i.e., that the Messiah would exercise the royal authority of the Davidic lineage). David foresaw the resurrection of the Messiah and spoke specifically concerning His resurrection when he wrote, "For You will not leave my soul in Hades, nor will You allow Your Holy One to see corruption" (Acts 2:27).[4]

Then, just as Jesus did in Matthew 22:43-44, Peter appealed to Psalm 110:1 as a messianic text: "For David did not ascend into the heavens, but he says himself: 'The Lord said to my Lord, "Sit at My right hand, till I make Your enemies Your footstool"'" (Acts 2:34-35). When Jesus referred to this text, it was to inquire as to the Pharisees' understanding of the significance of David calling the Messiah his Lord. But Peter's use of the text indicated its connection to the Resurrection. In other words, Psalm 110:1 does not describe the situation as it was when David wrote, but as it would be in the future upon the resurrection and ascension of the Messiah, Jesus. This is why David referred to God as LORD (*Yahweh*) and the Messiah as Lord (*Adonai*).[5] Elsewhere, the Messiah is identified as "LORD." (See Hebrews 1:10-12; Psalm 102:25-27.[6])

By definition, the Messiah is God as He is manifested in genuine and full human existence. (See I Timothy 3:16; John 1:14.) The Messiah certainly is *Yahweh*, but when a distinction is to be made, as in Psalm 110:1, between *Yahweh* and *Adonai* (when *Adonai* refers to the Messiah), that distinction is due to the human persona *Yahweh* assumed in the Incarnation. The humanness of the Messiah is not swallowed up or obliterated by His divine nature. Therefore, the Messiah and God (*Yahweh*) can have conversations, and the Messiah can pray to God. This recognizes a distinction introduced by the Incarnation, but it does not radically separate God and the Messiah into two "persons," as we think of the word "person." The Messiah is just as much *Yahweh* as God is, but the Messiah is *Yahweh* in human existence. It may seem strange to think of *Yahweh* communicating with *Yahweh*, but if this were not possible the humanness of Jesus would be less than real, or the Incarnation would mean that all that there is to God is now limited to a human existence and that God does not exist outside of Jesus. Psalm 110:1 is not about the first person in the Godhead speaking to the second person in the Godhead. It is about the transcendent God—as He exists above and beyond the Incarnation—speaking to God incarnate in conjunction with His ascension, which had not yet occurred when David wrote.[7]

For David to refer to the Messiah as *Adonai* did not suggest inferiority to *Yahweh*; it recognized the humanness of the Messiah and the superiority of the Messiah to David, even though the Messiah was human. The theological purpose of Psalm 110:1 was not to inform us about the relationship between persons in the Godhead, but to inform us that David's human descendant was in some way his Lord, who—although He shared in humanity to such an extent that He could be addressed by *Adonai*—was exalted to the place of greatest dignity and majesty in anticipation of the subjugation of the entire created realm to Him. (See Hebrews 2:5-9.) In Psalm 110:4, further evidence of the Messiah's humanity was seen in His identification by *Yahweh* as "a priest forever according to the order of Melchizedek." In order for the Messiah to be a priest, He had to stand in solidarity with those He represented to God. He had to be a human being representing other human beings to God.[8]

It was not only on the Day of Pentecost that Peter appealed to the messianic theme of the Psalms as justification for preaching Jesus as the Messiah. Following the healing of the lame man at Gate Beautiful, Peter explained his actions to the Sanhedrin with these words: "Rulers of the people and elders of Israel: If we this day are judged for a good deed done to a helpless man, by what means he has been made well, let it be known to you all, and to all the people of Israel, that by the name of Jesus Christ of Nazareth, whom you crucified, whom God raised from the dead, by Him this man stands here before you whole. This is the *'stone which was rejected by you builders, which has become the chief cornerstone.'* Nor is there salvation in any other, for there is no other name under heaven given among men by which we must be saved" (Acts 4:8-12).

The phrase "stone which was rejected by you builders, which has become the chief cornerstone" is a reference to Psalm 118:22. The author of Psalm 118 was not identified in the Old Testament or by Peter. The messianic theme was evident not only in verse 22 (see also Matthew 21:33-46; Mark 12:1-11; Luke 20:9-19; Romans 9:33; Ephesians 2:20; I Peter 2:4, 6), but also in verses 25 and 26, which were quoted by the people who greeted Jesus as He rode into Jerusalem on a donkey. (See Matthew 21:9; Mark 11:9; Luke 19:38-40.[9]) To identify Jesus, the Messiah, as the chief cornerstone was quite significant in the Jewish milieu of the first century. The term "chief cornerstone was . . . used to refer to the stone placed on the summit of the Jerusalem temple. Thus Peter used the phrase to point out that when the people rejected Jesus Christ, they rejected the One who completed the plan of God for humankind."[10]

To use these verses from Psalm 118 to refer to the Messiah was not the mere application of general principles. These verses had to do specifically with the Messiah, and it would have been inappropriate to use them in reference to others. The messianic content of these verses was divinely intended to point to Jesus Christ.

The Apostolic Community's Use of the Psalms' Messianic Theme

After their release by the Sanhedrin, Peter and John shared with their companions what the chief priests and elders had said. In response, the community of believers prayed, "Lord, You are God, who made heaven and earth and the sea, and all that is in them, who by the mouth of Your servant David have said, *'Why did the nations rage, and the people plot vain things? The kings of the earth took their stand, and the rulers were gathered together against the LORD and against His Christ.'* For truly against Your holy Servant Jesus, whom You anointed, both Herod and Pontius Pilate, with the Gentiles and the people of Israel, were gathered together. . ." (Acts 4:24-27).

It is evident from their use of Psalm 2:1-2 in their prayer that the earliest believers viewed the psalm as a specific prophecy concerning the Messiah. Although the Hebrew text did not identify the author, the New Covenant community assigned the psalm to David. It was possible that the words of Psalm 2, identified as a royal psalm, were used upon the ascension of David's descendants to his throne, but that was not the reason they were found in the inspired Scripture. Psalm 2 was included in the text specifically as a messianic psalm, a song about the coming Messiah, Jesus. The use of the psalm by the first believers identified Jesus as the anointed One of *Yahweh*, Herod and Pilate as included in the "kings of the earth" and "rulers" who rebelled against *Yahweh* and His Messiah, and "the Gentiles and the people of Israel" as included in "the nations [that] rage" and "the people [who] plot vain things."

Paul's Use of the Psalms' Messianic Theme

Even though the content of Paul's preaching was not influenced by any human teacher—it was revealed directly to him by Jesus Christ—his use of the messianic theme of Psalms was virtually identical to Peter's use. (See Galatians 1:11-12, 15-18; 2:1-10.) Of course this was not surprising; the Holy Spirit inspired both men.

On his first missionary journey, Paul's preaching at a synagogue in Antioch was deeply influenced by David's role as the Messiah's physical ancestor and by the prophetic implications of the Psalms. "He raised up for them David as king, to whom also He gave testimony and said, *'I have found David the son of Jesse, a man after My own heart, who will do all My will.'* From this man's seed, according to the promise, God raised up for Israel a Savior—Jesus" (Acts 13:22-23). (See Psalm 89:20.)

According to Paul, the Jewish community at Jerusalem and its religious leaders had condemned Jesus "because they did not know Him, nor even the voices of the Prophets which are read every Sabbath" (Acts 13:27). He made a connection between not knowing Jesus and not understanding the messianic content of the Prophets. In their ignorance, the unbelieving Jews had fulfilled the Scriptures even while rejecting their message. (See also Acts 13:29.)

The resurrection of Jesus was the fulfillment of "that promise which was made to the fathers" (Acts 13:32). As evidence that God had promised the fathers that the Messiah would be resurrected, Paul offered these words from Psalm 2:7: "You are My Son, today I have begotten You" (Acts 13:33). Here, Paul was in harmony with the believing Jewish community in Jerusalem in seeing Psalm 2 as a specific messianic prophecy. (See Acts 4:24-28.)

As further evidence of the prophetic declaration of the resurrection of the Messiah in the Psalms, Paul quoted Psalm 16:10: "Therefore He also [said] in another Psalm: *'You will not allow Your Holy One to see corruption'*" (Acts 13:35). These words had already been used by Peter to point out that the Psalms foretold the resurrection of the Messiah. (See Acts 2:25-28, especially 27.) Like Peter, Paul was careful to point out that David was not talking about himself, for David was still in his tomb and had seen corruption. (Compare Acts 13:36-37; 2:29-35.)

In his letter to the believers at Rome, Paul appealed to Psalm 69:9 as a messianic text: "For even Christ did not please Himself; but as it is written, *'The reproaches of those who reproached You fell on Me'* " (Romans 15:3).[11] This indicated that Paul saw this psalm of lament as having to do specifically with the Messiah.

Later in Romans 15, Paul pointed out that Psalm 18:49 indicated that the Jewish Messiah would also be worshiped by Gentiles: "Now I say that Jesus Christ has become a servant to the circumcision for the truth of God, to confirm the promises made to the fathers, and that the Gentiles might glorify God for His mercy, as it is written: *'For this reason I will confess to You among the Gentiles, and sing to Your name'* " (Romans 15:8-9).[12]

Paul saw the messianic implications even of Psalm 117, using it in a contextual reference to Jesus Christ: "And again: *'Praise the LORD, all you Gentiles! Laud Him, all you peoples!'* " (Romans 15:11). (See Psalm 117:1; Romans 15:8, 12.)

In a discussion of the events that would occur after the second coming of Christ, Paul wrote, "For *'He has put all things under His feet.'* But when He says 'all things are put under Him,' it is evident that He who put all things under Him is excepted" (I Corinthians 15:27). Paul, like the writer of Hebrews (see Hebrews 2:6-8), saw Psalm 8 as a messianic psalm. It was not just a generic psalm about human beings that seemed to fit certain events in the life of Jesus. Under inspiration, it was placed in the Psalter for the specific purpose of indicating that the Messiah would be a human being, made a little lower than the angels, but crowned with glory and honor and given dominion over the entire created realm. Paul saw the subjugation of all things under the Messiah as evidence of His resurrection. (See I Corinthians 15:3-8, 12-30.) If He did not rise from the dead, Psalm 8 would never be fulfilled.

Paul interpreted Psalm 68:18 as having to do specifically with the Messiah: "But to each one of us grace was given according to the measure of Christ's gift. Therefore He says: *'When He ascended on high, He led captivity captive, and gave gifts to men.'* (Now this, *'He ascended'*—what does it mean but that He also first descended into the lower parts of the earth? He who descended is also the One who ascended far above all the heavens, that He might fill all things.)" (Ephesians 4:7-10).[13] Psalm 68, then, foretold the ascension of the Messiah following His resurrection.

The Use of the Psalms' Messianic Theme in the Book of Hebrews

It is significant that the Book of Hebrews, written to Jewish believers in danger of defecting from their New Covenant faith in Christ, appealed repeatedly to a variety of psalms to assert that Jesus was the true Messiah, the fulfillment of all Jewish messianic hopes.[14] Psalm 2:7 was appealed to, to indicate both the superiority of the Messiah over the angels (Hebrews 1:5) and His high priesthood (Hebrews 5:5).

The deity of the Messiah was asserted by a quote from Psalm 45:6-7 (Hebrews 1:8). He was identified as *Yahweh*, the Creator, by a quote from Psalm 102:25-27 (Hebrews 1:10-12).

Psalm 110:1, also used by Jesus (Matthew 22:44-46) and Peter (Acts 2:34-35) as a messianic reference, was seen in Hebrews 1:13 as further evidence of the Messiah's superiority over the angels. It was also seen to refer to the Messiah as "a priest forever according to the order of Melchizedek" (Hebrews 5:6, 10; 7:17, 21). (See Psalm 110:4.)

The writer of Hebrews joined Paul in viewing Psalm 8 as having to do with the incarnation and exaltation of the Messiah. (See Hebrews 2:6-8; Psalm 8:4-6; I Corinthians 15:27.)

Psalm 22, claimed by Jesus as His own on the cross (Matthew 27:46), was identified as a reference to the Messiah in Hebrews 2:12. (See Psalm 22:22.)

The Messiah's willingness to surrender to the will of God in providing Himself as the atonement for sin was seen in Psalm 40:6-8, according to Hebrews 10:5-9.

In the inspired attempt to convince wavering Jewish believers to retain their faith in Christ, the writer of Hebrews could find no richer resource than the messianic psalms. These were the Scriptures the original readers of Hebrews believed without question, the words their ancestors had long clung to in hopes of deliverance: They were fulfilled in Jesus Christ.

The Use of the Psalms' Messianic Theme in the Revelation

Jesus, the Son of God, claimed Psalm 2:7-9 as a reference to His authority in Revelation 2:26-27: "And he who overcomes, and keeps My works until the end, to him I will give power over the nations—*'He shall rule them with a rod of iron; they shall be dashed to pieces like the potter's vessels'*—as I also have received from My Father." He thus authenticated the view of the early believers (Acts 4:24-27), Paul (Acts 13:33), and the writer of Hebrews (Hebrews 1:5; 5:5) that Psalm 2 was about the Messiah.

The Gospel "According to the Scriptures"

In view of the rich pattern of appeal to the Book of Psalms to establish the messianic teaching of the New Testament, it was no wonder that Paul described the gospel as the teaching that "Christ died for our sins according to the Scriptures, and that He was buried, and that He rose again the third day according to the Scriptures" (I Corinthians 15:3-4).

The good news was "according to the Scriptures"; that is, the Old Testament. And a major part of that good news was found in the Book of Psalms, a collection of writings largely intended to communicate the promise and hope of the coming Messiah.

APPENDIX 3

David's Explanation of the Psalms

In his last words, David wrote:

> Thus says David the son of Jesse; thus says the man raised up on high, the anointed of the God of Jacob, and the sweet psalmist of Israel: The Spirit of the LORD spoke by me, and His word was on my tongue. The God of Israel said, the Rock of Israel spoke to me: 'He who rules over men must be just, ruling in the fear of God. And he shall be like the light of the morning when the sun rises, a morning without clouds, like the tender grass springing out of the earth, by clear shining after rain.' Although my house is not so with God, yet He has made with me an everlasting covenant, ordered in all things and secure. For this is all my salvation and all my desire; will He not make it increase? But the sons of rebellion shall all be as thorns thrust away, because they cannot be taken with hands. But the man who touches them must be armed with iron and the shaft of a spear, and they shall be utterly burned with fire in their place. (II Samuel 23:1-7)

These last words of David were significant, for they expressed the inspiration and content of his psalms and the certainty of the Davidic covenant.

David asserted the inspiration of his words when he wrote, "The Spirit of the LORD spoke by me, and His word was on my tongue. The God of Israel said, the Rock of Israel spoke to me...." The inspiration of David's words was confirmed by Jesus: "For David himself said by the Holy Spirit..." (Mark 12:36). Peter understood the psalms of David to be inspired: "Men and brethren, this Scripture had to be fulfilled, which the Holy Spirit spoke before by the mouth of David concerning Judas, who became a guide to those who arrested Jesus" (Acts 1:16). The first-century church understood the words of David to be the words of God: "So when they heard that, they raised their voice to God with one accord and said: 'Lord, You are God, who made heaven and earth and the sea, and all that is in them, who by the mouth of Your servant David have said...'" (Acts 4:24-25). They made no distinction between the Lord God and the Holy Spirit as the actual Author of David's words.

The content of David's psalms was messianic, as may be seen in his words, "He who rules over men must be just, ruling in the fear of God. And he shall be like the light of the morning when the sun rises, a morning without clouds, like the tender grass springing out of the earth, by clear shining after rain" (II Samuel 23:3b-4). In this description of a just ruler, David was not talking about himself or any of his merely human descendants: "Although my house is not so with God..." (II Samuel 23:5).

In the psalms, the Messiah was frequently associated with banishing darkness by bringing light. (See Psalms 4:6; 18:28; 27:1; 30:5; 36:9; 37:6.) His rule was noted by justice. (See Psalms 7:6; 9:7-8, 16; 25:9; 33:5; 35:23; 37:6, 28; 72:2.)

Further evidence that David wrote intentionally and knowingly about the Messiah may be seen in an examination of the Hebrew text of II Samuel 23:1 and in a survey of the history of the interpretation of the text.

Young's Literal Translation (1862/1898) renders II Samuel 23:1: "And these are the last words of David:—'The affirmation of David son of Jesse—And the affirmation of the man raised up—Concerning the Anointed of the God of Jacob, And the Sweetness of the Songs of Israel.' " The word translated "on high" (*'al*) by the KJV and many modern English translations may also be translated "concerning." The Douay-Rheims, following the Latin Vulgate, renders the verse: "Now these are David's last words. David the son of Isai said: The man to whom it was appointed concerning the Christ of the God of Jacob, the excellent psalmist of Israel said."

The difference in meaning between the two translations is that to translate *'al* "on high" makes David "the anointed of the God of Jacob," or the messianic person. To translate *'al* "concerning" makes the Messiah someone other than David and the subject of David's words. The phrase "anointed of the God of Jacob"[1] contains the word that finds its way by transliteration into the New Testament as a reference to Christ: *Meshiyach* becomes "Messias" or "Messiah." The meaning is the same as the Greek *Christos*. Both words mean "anointed."

That *'al* should be translated "concerning" and not "on high" is indicated not only by the contextual reference to the Messiah in II Samuel 23:3-4, but also by the history of the interpretation of the text. With the finalization of the form of the Hebrew text by the Masoretic ("traditionalist") scribes in about AD 1000, there arose a series of Jewish commentators who determined the meaning of the Hebrew text for the Jewish communities. One of the most influential of these commentators was Rashi, who was born in about AD 1040. Rashi did not believe that the Messiah had come. During this time of the Crusades, European Jews were being forced to convert to Christianity. Rashi's mission was to give the Jewish people a biblical ground to resist conversion to Christianity. The way he chose to do this was to take passages that could be understood messianically and to explain them in light of some historical figure. He identified messianic prophecies as being fulfilled by David or Solomon. Rashi did this by introducing glosses in the margins of the Hebrew text with these interpretations. Rashi's interpretation was called the *Peshat*, the Hebrew word that means "simple."

According to Erwin Rosenthal, a leading Rashi scholar of the twentieth century, Rashi was willing to sacrifice messianic hope to resist Christian interpretation.[2]

The Septuagint, a Greek translation of the Hebrew Scriptures dating from about 250 BC, was much more messianic than the Masoretic text of AD 1000. The Septuagint saw II Samuel 23:1 as indicating that David wrote about the Messiah. The Septuagint was in common use in first-century Jewish communities and became the Bible of the first-century Christian church. Because of the use of this Greek translation by the followers of Jesus, the non-messianic Jewish communities gradually turned from the Septuagint.

Martin Luther and John Calvin, with their desire to minimize the influence of Roman Catholic interpretation, championed the turn from the Latin Vulgate to the Hebrew text. At that time, no Christian commentaries had been written on the Hebrew text, so Luther and Calvin went to Rashi, viewing his interpretation as the "original historical" meaning. Rashi's interpretation was, however, non-messianic.

The influence of the reformers on current Christian interpretation may be seen in the view that the messianic texts were first about some historic person or persons in ancient Israel and only by application, reinterpretation, or fuller meaning (*sensus plenior*) about the Messiah.[3]

II Samuel 23 indicated the certainty of the Davidic covenant in spite of the unfaithfulness of David's descendants in the statement, "Although my house is not so with God, yet He has made with me an everlasting covenant, ordered in all things and secure" (II Samuel 23:5a). Ultimately, the Messiah will sit on David's throne, fulfilling the promise God made to David. (See II Samuel 7:4-16; I Kings 6:11-13; 11:9-13; Isaiah 55:1-4; Luke 1:32-33; Acts 2:30-36; Psalm 132:10-18.)

II Samuel 23 indicated that David was aware of the prophetic nature of the psalms. Their messianic content was not hidden from him. Although the events and persons he described were rooted in actual history, they were intended by him to represent the coming Messiah. When Peter declared that David was a prophet who spoke knowingly about the Messiah and who foresaw messianic events, he intended his words to be taken literally. (See Acts 2:25-31.) Rather than the messianic content of the psalms being a result of reinterpretation by the first-century church or of "fuller meaning," it was the result of David's intention.

Notes

Introduction

[1] See also Acts 26:27.
[2] Robert G. Bratcher, *Old Testament Quotations in the New Testament* (New York: United Bible Societies, 1984), 81-88.

Chapter 1. The Book of Psalms

[1] Much of the information in the introductory section of this work is adapted from unpublished class notes from the course "The Messiah in the Psalms and Daniel," taught by John H. Sailhamer, Summer 2000, at Western Seminary, Portland, Oregon.
[2] Paul J. Achtemeier, gen. ed., *Harper's Bible Dictionary* (San Francisco: Harper & Row, 1985), s.v., "Ethan" and "Jeduthun."
[3] This explanation of a poem from John Ciardi is cited by John H. Sailhamer in his unpublished notes for the course "The Messiah in the Psalms and Daniel," offered at Western Seminary, Summer 2000. This section follows Sailhamer.
[4] The information on synthetic parallelism, climactic parallelism, and emblematic parallelism follows Earl D. Radmacher, gen. ed., *The Nelson Study Bible*, New King James Version (Nashville, Tenn.: Thomas Nelson Publishers, 1997), 876.
[5] The smaller collections consisted of "the psalms associated with the sons of Korah (42-49; 84-85; 87-88), with Asaph (50; 73-83), the second Davidic psalter (51-71), and the Hallelujah psalms (146-50). The larger collections consisted of the psalms associated with David (3-41; cf. 72:20) and the Elohistic psalter (42-83)—itself a collection of smaller collections; the Korahite (42-49) and Davidic (51-71) psalms; the Asaphite psalter (73-83); and the Songs of Ascent (120-34)." Willem A. VanGemeren, in Frank E. Gaebelein, gen. ed., *The Expositor's Bible Commentary*, vol. 5 (Grand Rapids: Zondervan Publishing House, 1991), 20.
[6] But the final verse of Psalm 72 concludes: "the prayers of David the son of Jesse are ended" (Psalm 72:20), suggesting that there was an earlier collection of the prayers of David for another purpose that included

some of the psalms prior to this. That this collection did not include all of the psalms up to this point is suggested by the fact that not all of the psalms up to this point are prayers and that Psalm 72 is a psalm of Solomon and not of David.

[7] This discussion of the various views of the structure of the Psalter follows Sailhamer's unpublished class notes.

[8] Psalm 1, for example, addresses the individual, not the community. The Psalter is not merely a hymnbook for post-exilic Israel: "It was . . . a *collection* of individual prayers from which one would make a selection for reading in everyday life. . . . The Psalter thus preserved a variety of prayers/praises and assured a certain spontaneity of prayers/praises for the individual. The individual, by choosing his prayers and praises from the Psalter, is made to identify his own troubles with the troubles of others before him and in the context of the past acts of God on Israel's behalf. The individual is thereby given a hope in God's help for his own troubles and, in the end, pointed back to the community as the context for his praises." John H. Sailhamer, unpublished notes, 56-57.

[9] These three points follow Sailhamer, unpublished notes, 57.

[10] Sailhamer, 57.

Chapter 2. Book One, Psalms 1-41

[1] The discussion of the themes in Psalms 1-2 follows John H. Sailhamer, *NIV Compact Bible Commentary* (Grand Rapids: Zondervan Publishing House, 1994), 315.

[2] "Egyptian kings celebrated their rule by writing the names of their enemies on pots and symbolically smashing them. These are referred to as the execration texts. Assyrian kings likewise used the metaphor of smashed pottery to assert their supremacy over enemies." John H. Walton, Victor H. Matthews, Mark W. Chavalas, *The IVP Bible Background Commentary, Old Testament* (Downers Grove, IL: InterVarsity Press, 2000), 519.

[3] VanGemeren, 75.

[4] Ibid.

[5] Walton, et al., 517-518.

[6] Ibid., 80.

[7] See discussion in Ibid., 81.

[8] Ibid., 84.

[9] The Hebrew theology of the name of the Lord made this mean that he loved the Lord Himself. The name of the Lord represents the Lord. In Hebrew thought, name and person are identical.

[10]Psalm 6:5 should not be taken as a denial of life after death or of consciousness after death. The context was not a discussion of the state of the dead, but of whether David would survive Absalom's rebellion. The Old Testament put "the emphasis on the present life as the most important stage in a man's relationship with God. The psalmist [believed] that there [was] *still* life to live and that there [was] therefore still time to praise the Creator!" (VanGemeren, 99).

[11]The word "man" in the first line is singular, as is the pronoun "him." Grammatically, the question is not "what is mankind that you are mindful of them," but "what is a man, that you are mindful of him." The second line identifies the man in view: the Son of Man. This is preserved in the translation of Hebrews 2.

[12]Sailhamer, 316. The KJV translates *'l* as "upon," but it can be translated "concerning."

[13]Absalom's rebellion was in principle against the promised Son. His attempt to dethrone David was an act of rebellion against the ultimate Son of David.

[14]In this case, the acrostic begins with the second verse and continues with every other verse, except where it is interrupted by references to "the wicked one" (*rasha*). In Psalm 9, verse 2 begins with *aleph*, verse 4 with *beth*, and verse 6 with *gimel*. Verse 6 includes a reference to "the wicked one," and the acrostic is interrupted in verses 7-9. In verse 10, the acrostic continues with *waw*. Verse 12 begins with *zayin*, verse 14 with *heth*, and verse 16 with *teth*. Verse 17 includes a reference to "the wicked one," and the acrostic continues in a somewhat irregular fashion with the *yod* beginning verse 18 and the *kaph* beginning verse 19. Psalm 10:1 begins with *lamed*. Verses 2-4 contain references to "the wicked one," and the acrostic picks back up in verse 7, which begins with the *pe*. The third line in verse 8 begins with the *ayin*. [This order for the *pe* and *ayin* reflects an earlier form of the Hebrew alphabet.] Verse 12 begins with the *qoph*, verse 14 with the *resh*, and verse 15, which includes a reference to "the wicked one," with the *shin*. Verse 17 begins with the *tau*.

[15]Notice in Psalm 9:1-2 how the name of the Lord represents the Lord Himself. (See comments on Psalm 5:11.)

[16]Again, notice the connection between knowing the name of the Lord and trusting Him in Psalm 9:10.

[17]For a full discussion of these verses in Hebrews, see Daniel L. Segraves, *Hebrews: Better Things*, Vol. 1 (Hazelwood, MO: Word Aflame Press, 1996).

[18]See the discussion in VanGemeren, 132.

[19] The Hebrew text reads "with a heart and a heart." This implies insincerity.

[20] Verse 7 has been misunderstood, especially by advocates of KJV Onlyism (the belief that only the King James Version faithfully transmits the Scriptures in English) to mean that the Lord will keep and preserve His words "from this generation forever." The grammar of the Hebrew text will not allow this meaning. The words translated "poor" and "needy" in verse 5 are masculine. The word translated "words" in verse 6 is feminine. The words translated "them" in verse 7 are masculine, requiring that the pronoun "them" refer back to the "poor" and "needy" of verse 5, not to the "words" of verse 6.

[21] See comments on Psalm 53.

[22] Israel was not in captivity when David wrote this psalm.

[23] VanGemeren, 148.

[24] VanGemeren, 156-157.

[25] Sailhamer, *NIV Compact Bible Commentary*, 318.

[26] For New Testament references to the prayers of Jesus, see Luke 3:21; Mark 1:35; 6:46 (compare Matthew 14:23); Luke 9:18, 28-29; 11:1; Matthew 11:25-26 (compare Luke 10:21); 19:13; Luke 22:31-32; John 11:41-42; 12:28; 17:1-26; Mark 14:35-42 (compare Matthew 26:36-46; Luke 22:39-46); Luke 23:34, 46; Matthew 27:46.

[27] VanGemeren, 163.

[28] See the discussion in VanGemeren, 166.

[29] If the Hebrew text of verse 14 is translated literally, it reads something like this: "your hidden will be full—their—belly sons will have plenty; and will leave their remains to your children" (VanGemeren, 166). The verse requires a dynamic equivalence that gives full regard to the context.

[30] See the discussion of II Samuel 23 in Appendix 3.

[31] Sailhamer, *NIV Compact Bible Commentary*, 318.

[32] See comments on Psalm 17.

[33] Compare the angel's appearance as lightning with Psalm 18:14: "He sent out His arrows and scattered the foe, lightnings in abundance, and He vanquished them."

[34] Sailhamer, *NIV Compact Bible Commentary*, 319.

[35] Ibid.

[36] In this case, the "name" of the Lord represented the works of the Lord in raising the Messiah from the dead.

[37] The broad outline of Psalm 22 presented here follows Sailhamer, *NIV Compact Bible Commentary*, 319.

[38] See the references to Matthew and John at the beginning of the discussion of Psalm 22.

[39] Notice the contextual connection between the death of Jesus and the words of Psalm 22:22 in Hebrews 2:9-12.

[40] VanGemeren, 201.

[41] When Jesus said "our fathers," He acknowledged His solidarity with the people of Israel. This was attributable to the genuineness and fullness of His human existence.

[42] The statement "I am a worm, and no man" was certainly not intended to deny Christ's humanity, any more than it was intended to be literally understood to mean that He was a worm.

[43] Walton, Matthews, and Chavalas, 523.

[44] VanGemeren, 205.

[45] Walton, Matthews, and Chavalas, 524.

[46] The Masoretic text reads, "My hands and my feet are like a lion" instead of "They pierced My hands and My feet." This results from reading *ka'ariy* as a noun formed from the preposition *ke* ("like") and the word *'areyh* ("lion") rather than as a verb formed from *karah*, meaning to "pierce" or "dig." It may be that the reading "like a lion" arose from attempts like those of Rashi to minimize the messianic content of the Hebrew text. (See comments under "David's Explanation of the Psalms" in Appendix 3.) Some Hebrew manuscripts do read "pierced," as do the Septuagint, Syriac, and Vulgate translations. In view of the fact that this is a messianic psalm and that the hands and feet of Jesus were pierced, it seems that the reading that should be accepted as original is "pierced." If the reading is "like a lion," there is no satisfactory way to explain its meaning.

[47] See footnote 9.

[48] Derek Kidner, *Psalms 1-72* (Downers Grove, IL: InterVarsity Press, 1973), 41-42.

[49] See Mark 16:9.

[50] VanGemeren, 217.

[51] Ibid., 219.

[52] Sailhamer, *NIV Compact Bible Commentary,* 320.

[53] Ibid.

[54] See the discussion of Psalm 24:3, 7-10 in the comments on Psalm 27.

[55] See discussion in Sailhamer, *NIV Compact Bible Commentary,* 320.

[56] VanGemeren, 226.

[57] This prosperity is not to be defined in terms of the materialism of the Western world in the twenty-first century. It has to do with the covenant promises, like inheriting the land, as seen in verse 13.

[58] See discussion in Sailhamer, *NIV Compact Bible Commentary,* 320-321.

[59] The "glory" of God is periphrastic for God Himself.

[60] Through Psalm 27, references to the "enemy" or "enemies" so far in the Psalter include 3:7; 5:8; 6:7, 10; 7:4-6; 8:2; 9:3, 6; 10:5; 13:2, 4; 17:9; 18: superscription, 3, 17, 37, 40, 48; 21:8; 23:5; 25:2, 19; 27:2, 6, 11, 12.

[61] See marginal note in the New King James Version (Nashville, Tenn.: Thomas Nelson, Inc., 1982).

[62] See discussion in Sailhamer, *NIV Compact Bible Commentary*, 321.

[63] The concept of the Lord as a rock to the faithful is a rich thread in Psalms. In addition to the references noted above, the idea is found in 31:2, 3; 40:2; 42:9; 61:2; 62:2, 6, 7; 71:3; 78:35; 89:26; 92:15; 94:22; 95:1.

[64] See comments on Psalms 1:1, 5-6; 3:7; 7:9; 9:17; 11:6; 12:8; 17:9; 26:5.

[65] See comments on Psalms 5:10; 7:6; 9:19-20; 10:2, 15; 12:3; 25:3.

[66] See Psalms 3:3; 5:12; 18:35.

[67] See Psalms 18: superscription, 1, 2, 32, 39; 19:14; 20:6; 21: superscription; 22:19; 27:1.

[68] See Psalms 2:12; 4:5; 5:11; 7:1; 9:10; 11:1; 16:1; 17:7; 18:2, 30; 20:7; 25:2, 20.

[69] See Psalms 7:17; 9:2; 13:6; 18:49; 21:13; 27:6.

[70] See Psalms 2:11; 5:11; 9:2, 14; 13:5; 14:7; 20:5; 21:1.

[71] Sailhamer, *NIV Compact Bible Commentary*, 321.

[72] Ibid.

[73] VanGemeren, 252-253.

[74] For a brief discussion of the theology of the Name, see Segraves, *Hebrews: Better Things*, Vol. 1, 40-41.

[75] See discussion in VanGemeren, 254, n. 2. If the reference is to attire, it is difficult to see how this would be a meaningful command to angels.

[76] Similarly, the phrase "praises of Israel" is a poetic description of the ark of the covenant (Psalm 22:3).

[77] Quoted by VanGemeren, 253.

[78] C. I. Scofield, ed., Arthur L. Farstad, consulting editor, 1989 ed., *The New Scofield Study Bible, New King James Version* (Nashville, TN: Thomas Nelson Publishers, 1989), 1267.

[79] Sailhamer, *NIV Compact Bible Commentary*, 321.

[80] VanGemeren, 257.

[81] See Ezra 5:12; Jeremiah 20:4-6; 21:4, 7, 10; 22:25; 25:9, 11; 27:6, 8-9, 12, 14, 17.

[82] See Jeremiah 25:11-12; 27:22; 29:10-14.

[83] Mount Moriah is also known as Mount Zion. (See II Samuel 5:7; I Kings 8:1; Psalm 2:6; 9:11; 48:2; 74:2; 76:2; Isaiah 8:18; 18:7; Jeremiah 31:6.

[84] The phrase "will the dust praise You" should not be read as meaning that the dead are unconscious. The psalm is not addressing the state of the dead.

[85] VanGemeren, 262.

[86] See comments on Psalm 22.

[87] Note how *padah* is used in Job 33:28 and Psalm 55:18.

[88] Texts may sometimes be translated in more than one way. In such cases, translators may be influenced by their theology. The most important influences should be, however, context and biblical theology, or the perspective that arises from a broad overview of biblical teaching. In the case of Psalm 31, there is good reason in the context to view the psalm as messianic, both within the psalm and the Psalter, and the fact that Jesus used the words as His own on the cross indicates that it is appropriate to read the psalm as messianic.

[89] Compare with Psalm 22:1, 14-17; Isaiah 52:14; 53:3-8, 10-12; II Corinthians 8:9.

[90] Sailhamer, *NIV Compact Bible Commentary,* 321.

[91] For trust as a theme to this point in the Psalter, see Psalms 4:5; 5:11; 7:1; 9:10; 11:1; 13:5; 16:1; 17:7; 18:2, 30; 20:7; 21:7; 22:4-5, 8; 25:2, 20; 26:1; 28:7; 31:1, 6, 14, 19; 32:10.

[92] For the "righteous" as a theme to this point in the Psalter, see Psalms 1:5-6; 5:12; 7:11 (KJV); 11:3, 5; 14:5; 31:18.

[93] For the "upright" as a theme to this point in the Psalter, see Psalms 7:10; 11:2, 7; 18:23, 25; 19:13.

[94] In Romans 4:1-3, Paul also offered Abraham as an example of justification by faith. Paul's purpose here was apparently to show that both before the law of Moses and during the law of Moses, justification was by faith.

[95] Before the cross, animal sacrifices were offered in anticipation of the cross; during the Millennium, they will apparently be offered in memory of the cross. (See Ezekiel 40:38-43; 43:18-27.) See John F. Walvoord, "The Doctrine of the Millennium—Part II: Spiritual Life in the Millennium," *Bibliotheca Sacra* 115: 458 (April 1958): 103-08; Clive A. Thomson, "The Necessity of Blood Sacrifices in Ezekiel's Temple," *Bibliotheca Sacra* 123: 491 (July 1966): 237-48. For another view of the purpose for the millennial sacrifices that harmonizes with dispensationalism see Jerry M. Hullinger, "The Problem of Animal Sacrifices in Ezekiel 40-48," *Bibliotheca Sacra* 152: 607 (July-September 1995): 279-89.

[96] See comments on Psalm 25:4, 8, 10, 12; 27:11; 31:3, 8.

[97] See comments on Psalms 9-10.

[98] The theme of "the righteous" begins in Psalm 1:5-6 and continues to Psalm 33:1.
[99] Sailhamer, *NIV Compact Bible Commentary*, 322.
[100] For a New Testament perspective, see Ephesians 5:19 and Colossians 3:16.
[101] See Daniel 2:21 and Acts 17:26.
[102] F. F. Bruce in Gordon D. Fee, gen. ed., *The Epistle to the Hebrews*, rev. ed., *The New International Commentary on the New Testament* (Grand Rapids: William B. Eerdmans Publishing Company, 1990), 137, n. 5.
[103] Ibid., 145, n. 40.
[104] See II Corinthians 8:9.
[105] Radmacher, gen. ed., *The Nelson Study Bible*, 910. For a general discussion on the imprecatory psalms, see comments on Psalm 58.
[106] See comments on Psalm 22.
[107] The KJV translates *yechiydatiy* ("my precious life," NKJV) as "my darling."
[108] See also Psalm 69:4 and the comments there. Jesus may actually have quoted from Psalm 69, but the theme is the same as here.
[109] C. H. Dodd has pointed out that "the principal Old Testament quotations in the New Testament are not isolated proof-texts, but carry their contexts with them by implication." See F. F. Bruce, *The Epistle to the Hebrews*, rev. ed., 82.
[110] Further connections between Psalm 35:1-8 and previous psalms can be seen by comparing references to the Lord as a shield (3:3; 5:12; 18:35; 28:7; 33:20; 35:2) and buckler [a small shield] (18:2, 30; 35:2) and requests for the Lord to arise [stand] and deliver (3:7; 7:6; 9:19; 10:12; 12:5; 17:13; 35:2).
[111] Radmacher, *The Nelson Study Bible*, 913.
[112] For a discussion of "the way," see comments on Psalms 1:1, 6; 2:12; 25:4, 9; 27:11; 32:8.
[113] See also John 3:19-21; 8:12; 9:5; 12:35-36, 46; Acts 26:23; II Corinthians 4:4, 6; Ephesians 5:14; I Thessalonians 5:5; I Peter 2:9; II Peter 1:19; I John 1:5, 7; 2:8; Revelation 21:23; 22:5.
[114] Sailhamer, *NIV Compact Bible Commentary*, 322.
[115] Radmacher, 914.
[116] For a New Testament perspective on possible connections between sin and physical illness, see I Corinthians 11:29-32 and James 5:14-16.
[117] See the previous references to the idea of David's enemies "rejoicing" over him in Psalms 30:1; 35:19, 24.

[118]Sailhamer, *NIV Compact Bible Commentary,* 322-323.

[119]See Psalm 2:10-12 and compare Psalm 102:25-27 with Hebrews 1:10-12.

[120]Sailhamer, *NIV Compact Bible Commentary,* 322.

[121]For a New Testament perspective on possible connections between sin and physical illness, see I Corinthians 11:29-32 and James 5:14-16.

[122]VanGemeren, 313.

[123]Sailhamer, *NIV Compact Bible Commentary,* 323.

[124]A handbreath was "one of the smallest units of measurement in ancient Israel. It was equivalent to 'a couple of inches' " (VanGemeren, 314). Specifically, it was "less than three inches" (VanGemeren, 315).

[125]Note that each reference to man as "vapor" is followed by *Selah* (see verses 5 and 11). Although we are not certain as to the meaning of *Selah*, this seems to place intentional emphasis on the brevity of life in the psalm.

[126]On the brevity of life, compare with Psalm 90:3-12 and James 4:14.

[127]Sailhamer, *NIV Compact Bible Commentary,* 323.

[128]For a treatment of the entire context in Hebrews 10, see Daniel L. Segraves, *Hebrews: Better Things,* Vol. 2 (Hazelwood, MO: Word Aflame Press), 1997.

[129]Contrary to some interpreters (e.g., Sailhamer, 323), the phrase "My ears You have opened" does not seem to be a reference to the practice of driving an awl through the ear of a slave who chooses loyalty to his master over freedom (see Exodus 21:6). To dig out the orifice for the ear is not the same thing as piercing the ear. The word translated "bore" or "pierce" in Exodus 21:6 is *ratsa'*. The word translated "opened" in Psalm 40:6 is *karah*.

[130]Segraves, *Hebrews: Better Things,* Vol. 2, 67.

[131]See comments on Psalm 31:5, 10.

[132]Here, the KJV translates *'avon* as "iniquity," but it was not the iniquity of the city Lot was urged to escape; it was the punishment for iniquity.

[133]Robert Jamieson, A. R. Fausset, David Brown, *Commentary Critical and Explanatory on the Whole Bible* (Expanded Electronic Edition, 1871).

[134]Spurgeon, Charles H. "Commentary on Psalms 40:12." "The Treasury of David." <http://bible.crosswalk.com/Commentaries/TreasuryofDavid/tod.cgi?book=ps&chapter=040&verse=012>. 1865-1885.

[135]Northrup.awwwsome.com/Christin%20sheol.htm.

[136]This is in contrast to the author's understanding of the entire

psalm in *Hebrews: Better Things,* Vol. 2, 61.

[137]To see how the people of Israel should have responded to the law of Moses with its sacrificial system, see Paul's personal response in Romans 7. The law aroused sinful passions in him (verse 5), producing all manner of evil desire (verse 8), and resulting in spiritual death (verses 9-11). The law enhanced Paul's sinfulness (verse 13), causing him to cry out in desperation for deliverance (verses 14-24). He found his deliverance through Jesus Christ (verse 25). Rather than recognizing their desperate need of deliverance from sin, available only by faith in God, the people of Israel at large sought to attain righteousness by the works of the law, which included the sacrificial rituals. (See Romans 9:30-33.)

[138]M. J. J. Menken, "The Translation of Psalm 41.10 in John 13.18," JSNT 40 (1990), pp. 70-71.

[139]See comments on Psalms 3-7.

[140]For another example, compare Hosea 11:1 with Matthew 2:15.

[141]The word translated "evil" in the phrase "evil disease" is *belial,* a word commonly associated with Satan.

[142]See comments on Psalms 3-7.

Chapter 3. Book Two, Psalms 42-72

[1]For a discussion of the various theories concerning the significance of the division of the Psalter into five books, see "The Structure of the Book of Psalms," pages 21-24.

[2]Eighteen out of the thirty-one psalms in Book Two are attributed to David (Psalms 51-65, 68-70), and one psalm that is not attributed to anyone, Psalm 71, is apparently written by David.

[3]Psalms 42, 44-49 are attributed to the sons of Korah.

[4]Psalm 50 is attributed to Asaph.

[5]Psalm 72 is attributed to Solomon.

[6]The anonymous psalms include Psalms 43, 66-67, 71.

[7]Psalm 71 is apparently by David.

[8]Sailhamer, *NIV Compact Bible Commentary,* 331.

[9]Those attributed to David are Psalms 86, 101, 103, 108-110, 122, 124, 131-133, 138-144.

[10]Walton, Matthews, and Chavalas, 527.

[11]VanGemeren, 333, n. 5.

[12]Ibid., 330.

[13]See comments on Psalm 23:6 and Psalms 24-31, 36:8.

[14]See the discussion concerning the sons of Korah in the comments on Psalms 42-43.

[15] Sailhamer, *NIV Compact Bible Commentary,* 324.

[16] VanGemeren, 337.

[17] In verses 5 and 8, the identification of God with His name may be seen. This reflects the theology of the Name seen throughout the Scriptures. In a very real sense, the name of God represents God Himself.

[18] The poetic connection between "soul" and "body" in verse 25 indicates that both words represent the entire human existence. This is typical of the holistic view of anthropology found in the Hebrew Scriptures.

[19] Compare especially Deuteronomy 28:25 with Psalm 44:9-10; Deuteronomy 28:32 with Psalm 44:12; Deuteronomy 28:33 with Psalm 44:10b; Deuteronomy 28:37 with Psalm 44:13-14; Deuteronomy 28:64 with Psalm 44:11.

[20] Sailhamer, *NIV Compact Bible Commentary,* 324.

[21] Some commentators, on the view that the people of Israel were innocent in this instance, "argue in favor of a dating to the period of Hezekiah or Josiah, when Judah had experienced some form of spiritual revival." VanGemeren, 337.

[22] This assumes that Psalm 43 is to be read as a continuation of Psalm 42.

[23] For a discussion of the possible eschatological significance of this tune, see the comments on the superscription of Psalm 69.

[24] Sailhamer, *NIV Compact Bible Commentary,* 324.

[25] VanGemeren, 343.

[26] Sailhamer, *NIV Compact Bible Commentary,* 324.

[27] The NIV translates the phrase, "You are the most excellent of men."

[28] VanGemeren, 345.

[29] http://www.bible.org/cgi-bin/netbible.pl#note_14.

[30] Luke recorded Jesus' physical descent through Mary; Matthew recorded his legal descent through Joseph. Joseph's father was Jacob. (See Matthew 1:16.) Joseph was Mary's husband, but he was not the physical father of Jesus. The words "of whom" (*ex hes*) require Jesus to be born of Mary, but not of Joseph. *Hes* is the feminine singular pronoun. Luke's genealogy from Abraham to David is identical to Matthew's genealogy from Abraham to David. (Compare Matthew 1:2-6 with Luke 3:31-34.) The difference between the genealogies begins with David's descendant. In Matthew, it is Solomon (Matthew 1:6). In Luke, it is Nathan (Luke 3:31). In Luke, the father of Joseph is not Jacob, but Heli (Luke 3:23). It was customary in Jewish genealogies not to list the mother as the final ancestor, but the father. Luke pointed out that Jesus was only "supposed" to be the son of Joseph (Luke 3:23). Heli was Joseph's father-in-law.

[31]VanGemeren, 343.

[32]See the use of *habar* in Exodus 36:10; 39:4; Psalm 119:63; Proverbs 28:24. See the use of various forms of *metochous* in Luke 5:7 and II Corinthians 6:14.

[33]See comments on Hebrews 1:9 in Segraves, *Hebrew: Better Things,* Vol. 1, 52-53.

[34]http://www.bible.org/cgi-bin/netbible.pl#note_26

[35]See I Kings 9:28; 10:11; 22:48; I Chronicles 29:4; II Chronicles 8:18; 9:10; Job 22:24; 28:16; Isaiah 13:12.

[36]VanGemeren, 347.

[37]Radmacher, 924.

[38]Sailhamer, *NIV Compact Bible Commentary,* 324.

[39]The word translated "white" (*lampros*) by the KJV includes within its range of meaning "shining, brilliant, splendid, magnificent."

[40]VanGemeren, 354-357.

[41]Ibid., 354.

[42]Sailhamer, *NIV Compact Bible Commentary,* 325.

[43]VanGemeren, 350.

[44]This assumes that Psalm 43 is to be read as a continuation of Psalm 42.

[45]Abridged BDB Lexicon, 763. Referenced in BibleWorks 4, copyright 1992-1999 *BibleWorks,* L.L.C., programmed by Michael S. Bushell and Michael D. Tan.

[46]VanGemeren, 350.

[47]Sailhamer, *NIV Compact Bible Commentary,* 325.

[48]The *New Living Translation* renders Psalm 47:9: "The rulers of the world have gathered together. They join us in praising the God of Abraham. For all the kings of the earth belong to God. He is highly honored everywhere."

[49]The "sides of the north" should not be understood in a geographical sense. The psalmist borrowed "the imagery and not the theology" of the Canaanites (VanGemeren, 363). The Hebrew word translated "north" is *zaphon*. The Canaanites believed that the chief God lived on Mount Zaphon. Actually, Mount Zion was the dwelling place of the chief and only God, the great King. When Lucifer rebelled against God, he wished to "sit on the mount of the congregation on the farthest sides of the north [*zaphon*]" (Isaiah 14:13).

[50]See comments on Psalm 5:11.

[51]VanGemeren, 365.

[52]Ibid., 367.

[53]VanGemeren, 372.

[54]Sailhamer, *NIV Compact Bible Commentary*, 325.
[55]Ibid.
[56]See Psalms 2:6; 9:11, 14; 14:7; 20:2; 48:2, 11-12 and especially the comments on Psalm 46.
[57]Note the conceptual connections between Psalm 50:9-10, 23 and Psalm 51:15-17.
[58]VanGemeren, 373.
[59]VanGemeren, 375.
[60]For a discussion of Hebrews 13:15-17, see Segraves, *Hebrews: Better Things*, Vol. 2, 239-244.
[61]VanGemeren, 380.
[62]Ibid., 381.
[63]Earl S. Kalland, in Frank E. Gaebelein, gen. ed., *The Expositor's Bible Commentary*, vol. 3 (Grand Rapids: Zondervan Publishing House, 1992), 140.
[64]See discussion in VanGemeren, 381.
[65]See discussion in VanGemeren, 384.
[66]See comments on Psalm 50:2.
[67]For biblical evidence of the Tabernacle's first location and the subsequent destruction of Shiloh, see Joshua 18:1; Judges 18:31; I Samuel 1:3, 9, 24; 4:3-4; Psalm 78:60; Jeremiah 7:12-14; 26:6, 9.
[68]Sailhamer, *NIV Compact Bible Commentary*, 326.
[69]See comments on Psalm 14.
[70]The Septuagint translation of Psalm 14:3 reads, *"Pantes exeklinan, hama echreiothesan, ouk esti poion chrestoteta, ouk estin heos henos."* Psalm 53:3 reads, *"Pantes exeklinan, hama echreiothesan, ouk esti poion agathon, ouk estin heos henos."* Romans 3:12 reads, *"Pantes exeklinan, hama echreothesan: ouk estin ho poion chrestoteta, ouk estin heos henos."* The Greek Majority Text is in precise conformity to the Septuagint translation of Psalm 14:3: *"Pantes exeklinan, hama echreiothesan: ouk esti poion chrestoteta, ouk estin heos henos."* The most significant variant under consideration here is that Psalm 14:3 and Romans 3:12 use *chrestoteta* [kindness]; Psalm 53:3 uses *agathon* [good]. It is interesting to note that the Hebrew text has *tov* [good] in both psalms, but Paul followed the Greek translation of Psalm 14. This suggests intent on his part. His intent in Romans 3 was to demonstrate the universal sinfulness of the Jewish people (see Romans 3:19). Therefore, he quoted from Psalm 14 with its Jewish context rather than Psalm 53 with its Gentile context.
[71]Verse 6 was apparently an inspired post-exilic addition to the psalm. Israel was not in captivity when the psalm was originally written by David.

[72] Wilcock, 196.

[73] Dahood is of the opinion that Psalm 54 "distinctly emerges as the supplication of a king for deliverance from his foreign enemies." (See Mitchell Dahood, *The Anchor Bible, Psalms II 51-100* [Garden City, NY: Dubleday & Company, Inc., 1968], 23.) Although Ziph belonged to the tribe of Judah (Joshua 15:20-24), it is possible that Gentiles remained in the area and that they were the ones who betrayed David to Saul.

[74] See comments on Psalm 14.

[75] VanGemeren, 143.

[76] Or, like, Doeg, the Ziphites may have been Gentile inhabitants of Ziph. David called them "strangers." See Dahood, *Psalms II 51-100*, 23-24.

[77] See comments on Psalms 3 and 41.

[78] VanGemeren, 392.

[79] Ibid.

[80] Radmacher, 932.

[81] C.H. Spurgeon, *Treasury of David*, available at http://www.botcw.com/bible/treasury/55.html.

[82] See the discussion under "David's Explanation of the Psalms."

[83] See comments on Psalm 34.

[84] See comments on Psalm 2:12.

[85] VanGemeren, 37.

[86] Paul J. Achtemeier, gen. ed., *Harper's Bible Dictionary* (San Francisco: Harper & Row, Publishers, 1985), s.v. "En-gedi."

[87] John H. Sailhamer, *The Books of the Bible* (Grand Rapids: Zondervan Publishing House, 1998), 36.

[88] Ibid.

[89] VanGemeren, 401.

[90] See comments on Psalm 2:12.

[91] VanGemeren, 123.

[92] See Psalms 7:17; 9:2; 21:7; 46:4; 47:2; 50:14; 56:2; 77:10; 78:17, 56; 82:6; 83:18; 91:1, 9; 92:1, 8; 107:11.

[93] See also Psalms 35:17; 58:6.

[94] For a discussion of the identification of the glory of God with God Himself, see Daniel L. Segraves, *James: Faith at Work* (Hazelwood, MO: Word Aflame Press, 1995), 77-78.

[95] See Psalms 7:15; 9:15; 10:9; 25:15; 31:4; 35:7-8; 40:2; 69:15; 140:5. See especially the comments on Psalm 35.

[96] VanGemeren, 262.

[97] Ibid., 405.

[98] J. Carl Laney, "A Fresh Look at the Imprecatory Psalms," *Bibliotheca Sacra* 549 (1981): 35.

[99] Ibid., 36.
[100] Ibid.
[101] See Romans 12:14, 17, 19-20.
[102] Psalm 137:8-9 is an example: "O Babylon, you will be destroyed. Happy is the one who pays you back for what you have done to us. Happy is the one who takes your babies and smashes them against the rocks!" (NLT).
[103] For a response to each of these views, see Laney, 37-40.
[104] Laney defines an imprecation as being a prayer or address to God containing the request for the judgment and punishment of the enemies of Yahweh or of the writer (J. Carl Laney, "A Fresh Look at the Imprecatory Psalms," *Bibliotheca Sacra* 549 [1981]: 35).
[105] Laney, 42.
[106] This list of six purposes for the imprecatory psalms follows Laney, 41.
[107] For additional insight on the appropriateness of the imprecatory prayers, see Laney, 42-43.
[108] Sailhamer, *NIV Compact Bible Commentary*, 327.
[109] Ibid.
[110] The KJV translates *'elem* as "congregation." The NKJV translates the word "silent ones." The Masoretic Text's *'elem* may not fit the context, however. The NIV follows the emendation *'elim*, translating the word as "rulers." The Septuagint, Syriac, and Vulgate support a reading other than *'elem*. (See VanGemeren, 406.) This would harmonize Psalm 58 with Psalm 82:1, 6.
[111] Paul pointed out that unborn children have done no good or evil (Romans 9:11). Jesus declared that it was necessary to "become as little children" in order to enter the kingdom of heaven. (See Matthew 18:1-6.)
[112] VanGemeren, 408.
[113] Ibid. 408-409.
[114] See comments on Psalm 58.
[115] Sailhamer, *NIV Compact Bible Commentary*, 327.
[116] References to "the nations" in this psalm (see also verse 8) cause some to view Psalm 59 as a community lament rather than an individual lament. (See VanGemeren, 409.)
[117] The Masoretic Text reads "his strength," but some Hebrew manuscripts, along with the Septuagint, Targum, and Vulgate, read, "My strength." The different readings would be a matter of vowel pointing.
[118] VanGemeren, 413.
[119] For a discussion of the possible eschatological significance of this tune, see the comments on the superscription of Psalm 69.

[120] See the discussion in Ronald F. Youngblood, in Frank E. Gaebelein, gen. ed., *The Expositor's Bible Commentary*, Vol. 3 (Grand Rapids: Zondervan Publishing House, 1992), 908-09.

[121] VanGemeren, 414.

[122] Radmacher, 937.

[123] See comments on Psalm 59.

[124] VanGemeren, 415. Although "truth" is included in the range of meaning for *qoshet*, so is "bow." The battle context suggests "bow" would be a better translation than "truth." The Septuagint translates *qoshet* with *toxou*, "bow."

[125] Ibid.

[126] See comments on Psalm 110:1.

[127] Verses 5-12 are virtually identical with Psalm 108:6-13. We will leave the significance of this for our study of Psalm 108.

[128] VanGemeren, 416.

[129] Walton, Matthews, and Chavalas, 536.

[130] A wordplay or pun.

[131] See concluding comments on Psalm 52.

[132] VanGemeren, 417.

[133] By "canonical-compositional," I mean the approach to interpreting the Psalter that sees the meaning to be rooted in the present shape of the book as it was composed of individual psalms in the post-exilic period. This approach sees significance in the order of the psalms and in how they relate to each other. For further explanation, see Appendix 1.

[134] See the discussion in Dahood, *Psalms II 51-100*, 83-84 and in VanGemeren, 417-18.

[135] See the summary of form criticism in John H. Sailhamer, *Introduction to Old Testament Theology: A Canonical Approach* (Grand Rapids, MI: Zondervan Publishing House, 1995), 91-92.

[136] See the discussion in John H. Sailhamer, *Genesis Unbound: A Provocative New Look at the Creation Account* (Sisters, OR: Multnomah Publishers, Inc., 1996). VanGemeren suggests that " 'from the ends of the earth' may denote a geographical distance away from the land" (VanGemeren, 418) and offers Psalm 46:9 and Deuteronomy 28:49 as examples. But these texts may not prove the point. Psalm 46:9 may be read as a reference to the cessation of war within the boundaries of the Promised Land, and Deuteronomy 28:49—which may indeed use "earth" as a reference to land beyond the borders of the Promised Land—further qualifies the word by declaring that the nation that will come against Israel "from the end of the earth" is coming "from afar." In this case, to say that the nation is coming "from afar" may redefine the "earth." VanGemeren

also points out that "from the end of the earth" could be "a metaphor for despair, alienation, and spiritual distance from the Lord" (Ibid.).

[137] Derek Kidner, *Psalms 1-72* (Downers Grove, IL: InterVarsity, 1981), 219.

[138] Ibid.

[139] VanGemeren, 418.

[140] See William L. Holladay's review of W. H. Bellinger, Jr., *A Hermeneutics of Curiosity and Readings of Psalm 61* (Macon, GA: Mercer University Press, 1995) in *The Catholic Biblical Quarterly* 58/3 (July 1996): 500.

[141] See Charles Caldwell Ryrie, *The Ryrie Study Bible*, King James Version (Chicago: Moody Press, 1978), 1632; Craig S. Keener, *The IVP Bible Background Commentary New Testament* (Downers Grove, IL: InterVarsity Press, 1993), 473; Leland Ryken, James C. Wilhoit, Tremper Longman III, gen. eds., *Dictionary of Biblical Imagery* (Downers Grove, IL: InterVarsity Press, 1998), 447; Ronald B. Allen, in Frank E. Gaebelein, gen. ed., *The Expositor's Bible Commentary*, vol. 2 (Grand Rapids: Zondervan Publishing House, 1990), 867. One of the Jewish legends, according to John Gill, was that the rock took the form of a beehive and rolled along after the Israelites. Another said it took the form of a sieve. (See John Gill, "Commentary on 1 Corinthians 10:4" in "John Gill's Exposition of the Bible," accessed at http://bible.crosswalk.com/Commentaries/GillsExpositionoftheBible/ on August 16, 2002.)

[142] Keener, 473.

[143] The rock may be legitimately said to have followed them in that they drank from a rock at two widely differing times and places. As far as the actual experience was concerned, it was the same. In this sense, Mark 16:20 declares that miraculous signs followed the believers. This does not mean that a specific miracle followed the believers, but that wherever they went, miracles occurred. Similarly, the Israelites had two occasions, some forty years apart, when they drank from a rock that miraculously provided water.

[144] Kidner, 219.

[145] *Machaseh* is also translated "refuge" in Psalm 46:1.

[146] VanGemeren, 419.

[147] See comments on Psalm 23:6.

[148] For a discussion of Hebrews 7:11-14, see Segraves, *Hebrews: Better Things*, Vol. 1.

[149] See Richard A. Muller, in John D. Woodbridge and Thomas E. McComiskey, *Doing Theology in Today's World* (Grand Rapids: Zondervan, 1991), 85.

[150] See comments on Psalm 27, specifically verses 4-5. See also Psalm 31:20.

[151] Kidner, 220.

[152] It has been suggested that Psalm 62 and Psalm 4 both reflect Absalom's rebellion. (See VanGemeren, 420.)

[153] Ibid., 421.

[154] Kidner, 221.

[155] Note Simeon's understanding of Jesus as the Lord's "salvation" in Luke 2:30 and compare Luke 2:25-38 with Isaiah 52:9-10, 13-15.

[156] For a discussion of the Hebrew and Greek forms of the Messiah's name, see Daniel L. Segraves, *The Messiah's Name: JESUS, not Yahshua'* (Kearney, NE: Morris Publishing, 1997).

[157] Kidner, 222.

[158] VanGemeren, 424 and Kidner, 223.

[159] VanGemeren, 424. See also Dahood, 94.

[160] The Pharisees, who as a group were Jesus' enemies, were lovers of money (Luke 16:14). The false witnesses at his "trial" were liars (Matthew 26:60-61). The false messiahs who came before Jesus were thieves and robbers (John 10:8, 10).

[161] Sailhamer, *NIV Compact Bible Commentary*, 328.

[162] See Psalm 54.

[163] See discussion in Marvin E. Tate, *Word Biblical Commentary*, vol. 20, Psalms 51-100 (Dallas, TX: Word Books, Publisher, 1990), 125.

[164] Ibid.

[165] Ibid.

[166] Michael Wilcock, *The Message of Psalms 1-72*, The Bible Speaks Today, J. A. Motyer, OT series ed. (Downers Grove, IL: InterVarsity Press, 2001).

[167] Ibid., 222-223.

[168] VanGemeren, 425.

[169] BDB, 1007.

[170] Tate, 125. See also Kidner, 224-25 and VanGemeren, 425, n. 1.

[171] Wilcock, 224.

[172] Ibid.

[173] See Dahood, 104.

[174] Ibid.

[175] See NASB, NLT, NIV.

[176] Kidner, 227.

[177] Ibid.

[178] Wilcock, 225.

[179] Dahood, 89-90.

[180] Wilcock, 225. The translation to which Wilcock refers is the NIV.
[181] VanGemeren, 430.
[182] Wilcock, 225.
[183] Kidner, 228.
[184] VanGemeren, 430.
[185] Ibid., 431.
[186] Sailhamer, *NIV Compact Bible Commentary*, 328.
[187] The psalms identified both as psalms and songs include Psalms 30; 48; 65; 66; 67; 68; 75; 76; 83; 87; 88; 92; 108.
[188] Psalms 45 and 46.
[189] Psalms 120-134.
[190] Tate, 174.
[191] Ibid., 139.
[192] Wilcock, 226-228.
[193] Kidner, 230-232.
[194] Tate, 143-144.
[195] Sailhamer, *NIV Compact Bible Commentary*, 329.
[196] In New Testament terms, Zion represents the New Covenant; Sinai represents the Old Covenant. (See Galatians 4:21-31; Hebrews 12:18-24.)
[197] Tate, 137.
[198] Kidner, 230.
[199] Quoted by Tate, 140.
[200] Tate, 140.
[201] For a discussion of the new heavens and the new earth, see Daniel L. Segraves, *Second Peter and Jude* (Hazelwood, MO: Word Aflame Press, 2000), 168-170.
[202] BDB, 497.
[203] See Psalms 1:1; 2:12; 32:1, 2; 33:12; 34:8; 40:4; 41:1; 65:4; 84:4, 5, 12; 89:15; 94:12; 106:3; 112:1; 119:1, 2; 127:5; 128:1; 137:8, 9; 144:15; 146:5.
[204] Michael Wilcock, *The Message of Psalms 73-150*, The Bible Speaks Today (J. A. Motyer, OT series ed.; Downers Grove, IL: InterVarsity Press, 2001), 257.
[205] Tate, 142.
[206] Sailhamer, *NIV Compact Bible Commentary*, 329.
[207] Tate, 142.
[208] Ibid.
[209] Kidner, 232.
[210] For the suggestion that Psalm 65 has a historical referent in the events surrounding the Assyrian assault on Jerusalem in 701 BC see Wilcock, 228.

[211] See comments on the superscription of Psalm 65.

[212] See the concluding comments on Psalm 3.

[213] James L. Mays, *Interpretation: A Bible Commentary for Teaching and Preaching, Psalms* (Louisville, KY: John Knox Press, 1994), 221.

[214] Ibid.

[215] Dahood, 119.

[216] Ibid.

[217] Ibid.

[218] Wilcock, 231.

[219] John F. Walvoord, *The Prophecy Knowledge Handbook* (Wheaton, IL: Victor Books, 1990), 595.

[220] Tate, 47.

[221] Ibid., 144-145, n. 2.a.

[222] Robert Alter points out the inadequacy of the view that biblical parallelism is synonymity. It seems more accurate to say, with Herder, that "the two [parallel] members strengthen, heighten, empower each other." See Robert Alter, *The Art of Biblical Poetry* (N.P.: BasicBooks, 1985), 9-11.

[223] Psalm 66:3 uses *'oz*; Psalm 65:6 uses *geborah*.

[224] See Alan F. Johnson, in Frank E. Gaebelein, gen. ed., *The Expositor's Bible Commentary*, vol. 12 (Grand Rapids: Zondervan Publishing House, 1981), 547.

[225] Mays, 223.

[226] Kidner, 234, and Wilcock, 230.

[227] Dahood, 121.

[228] Tate, 148.

[229] Ibid., 149.

[230] For a discussion of the place of suffering in the believer's life, see Daniel L. Segraves, *I Peter: Standing Fast in the Grace of God* (Hazelwood, MO: Word Aflame Press, 1999).

[231] VanGemeren, 438.

[232] Wilcock, 231.

[233] See Arno Clemens Gaebelein, *The Book of Psalms* (New York: Our Hope Publications, 1939), 262-63.

[234] See further possible connections in Tate, 153.

[235] The group includes Psalms 65-68.

[236] Wilcock, 66-67.

[237] Kidner, 236.

[238] See Genesis 28:14.

[239] The development of the Abrahamic covenant may be seen by comparing Genesis 12:1-3; 13:14-18; 15:1-21; 17:4-8; 22:15-24; 26:1-5; 28:10-15.

[240] See Exodus 34:10; Deuteronomy 4:7-8; Psalm 147:19-20.

[241] Mays, *Interpretation: Psalms*, 224-225.

[242] See Isaiah 40:3-5, fulfilled by John the Baptist as he prepared the way for the Messiah. (See Matthew 3:3.) Also see Isaiah 45:23, which was applied by Paul to Jesus. (See Philippians 2:10-11.)

[243] See Psalm 4:1.

[244] See Psalm 2:6-7.

[245] See II Samuel 7:12-16.

[246] See Psalm 2:8.

[247] In Psalms 1:1 and 2:12, the noun *'esher* is used; in Psalm 67:1 the verb *barak* appears.

[248] For the use of *'esher* as blessing in the Psalter, see Psalms 32:1, 2; 33:12; 34:8; 40:4; 41:1; 65:4; 84:4, 5, 12; 89:15; 94:12; 106:3; 112:1; 119:1-2; 127:5; 128:1; 144:15; 146:5. For the use of *barak* as blessing in the Psalter, see Psalms 3:8; 21:3, 6; 24:5; 45:2; 118:26; 132:15; 147:13.

[249] VanGemeren, 440.

[250] Tate, 157.

[251] Ibid., 159.

[252] VanGemeren, 442.

[253] Mitchell, 253.

[254] Ibid.

[255] J. Barton Payne, *Encyclopedia of Biblical Prophecy* (New York: Harper & Row, Publishers, 1973), 270.

[256] Various forms of *derek* are used to describe the way of rebellion against God (see Psalms 1:1, 6; 2:12; 10:5; 35:6; 36:4; 37:7; 49:13; 119:29, 59; 139:24) and God's way or the way of faithfulness to God (see Psalms 1:6; 5:8; 18:21, 30, 32; 25:4, 9; 27:11; 37:5, 34; 39:1; 50:23; 51:13; 67:2; 77:13, 19; 86:11; 91:11; 103:7; 119:1, 5, 26, 27, 30, 32, 33, 168; 139:3; 143:8; 145:17).

[257] *Yeshu'ah* appears in various forms in Psalms 3:2; 14:7; 18:50; 28:8; 42:5, 11; 43:5; 44:4; 62:1; 67:2; 68:19; 69:29; 70:4; 74:12; 88:1; 89:26; 96:2; 98:2-3; 116:13; 119:155; 140:7.

[258] See BDB, 221, 448.

[259] Wilcock, 233.

[260] See Psalms 58:11; 82:8; 94:2; 96:13; 98:9.

[261] Psalm 2:2-9.

[262] VanGemeren, 443, n. 6. In Leviticus 26:4 the phrase is *wenatenah ha'arets yeblah*. In Psalm 67:6 the words are rearranged as *'eretz natenah yibulah*.

[263] Some scholars are of the opinion that the psalm in its original form read *Yahweh, our God*. See Tate, 154.

[264] See Revelation 19:11-21.

[265] Tate declares that the "difficulties in interpreting Ps 68 are almost legendary" (170).

[266] Ibid., 174.

[267] Ibid.

[268] This idea is strengthened by verses 7, 16-17, 24, 29.

[269] See Psalms 3:7; 7:6; 9:19; 10:12; 12:5; 17:13; 44:23, 26; 74:22; 82:8; 102:13; 132:8.

[270] See Psalms 1:1, 5, 6; 3:7; 7:9; 9:5, 16, 17; 10:2, 3, 4, 13, 15; 11:6; 12:8; 17:9; 26:5; 28:3; 31:17; 34:21; 36:11; 37:10, 12, 14, 16, 17, 20, 21, 28, 32, 34, 35, 38; 39:1; 45:7; 55:3; 58:3; 68:2; 71:4; 73:3; 75:10; 82:2, 4; 84:10; 91:8; 92:7; 94:3; 97:10; 101:8; 106:18; 109:2, 6, 7; 112:10; 119:61, 95, 110, 119; 129:4; 139:19; 140:4, 8; 141:10; 146:9; 147:6.

[271] See Psalms 1:5, 6; 5:8; 7:9, 11; 11:3, 5, 7; 14:5; 31:18; 32:11; 33:1; 34:15, 19, 21; 37:17, 25, 28, 29, 39; 52:6; 58:10; 64:10; 69:28; 72:7; 75:10; 92:12; 94:21; 97:11; 112:6; 118:15, 20; 119:137; 129:4; 140:13; 141:5; 142:7; 145:17; 146:8.

[272] Tate, 176.

[273] See James 1:27.

[274] See Matthew 19:29; Mark 10:30.

[275] Kidner, 239.

[276] Tate, 177.

[277] Ibid.

[278] C. S. Lewis, *Reflections on the Psalms* (New York: Harcourt, Brace & World, Inc., 1958), 120.

[279] Ibid.

[280] See the discussion in Lewis, *Reflections*, 126.

[281] See Leviticus 26:4; Deuteronomy 11:14, 17; 28:12.

[282] See Leviticus 25:23.

[283] Tate, 178.

[284] Mays, 226.

[285] Kidner, 240 and Wilcock, 237.

[286] See Matthew 28:1-10.

[287] Lewis, *Reflections*, 125-126.

[288] See verses 8, 29.

[289] VanGemeren, 447 and Wilcock, 237.

[290] Compare with Psalm 2 and Revelation 19:11-21.

[291] See Judges 4:17-24.

[292] For a discussion of the difficulties involved in the text and the various conclusions, see VanGemeren, 448.

[293] VanGemeren, 448.
[294] Kidner, 240.
[295] Ibid., 241.
[296] Gaebelein, 269.
[297] See Colossians 2:15.
[298] A comparison of Judges 5:24 with Luke 1:28, 42 may suggest that Jael is in some way a type of Mary. These are the only three references in the entire Bible to include the words "blessed" and "women" in the same verse other than Ruth 4:14, where it is the women saying, "Blessed be the LORD. . . ."
[299] See Genesis 3:15.
[300] See Acts 1:14.
[301] See Luke 3:22.
[302] Tate, 166, n. 15.d.
[303] Http://www.robibrad.demon.co.uk/shechem.htm. Accessed December 6, 2002.
[304] Tate, 166, n. 15.d., Dahood, 142, and http://www.jewishencyclopedia.com/view.jsp?artid=31&letter=P, Accessed December 6, 2002.
[305] Tate, 166, n. 15.d.
[306] Kidner, 241.
[307] Wilcock, 237.
[308] See Isaiah 2:3; Joel 3:17; Micah 4:2.
[309] Tate, 166, n. 18.a.
[310] Kidner, 241, n. 5.
[311] Wilcock, 238.
[312] Ibid.
[313] Ephesians 4:7.
[314] Wilcock, 237.
[315] Kidner, 243.
[316] See Genesis 3:15.
[317] Kidner, 243.
[318] BDB, 828.
[319] Ibid.
[320] Herbert Wolf, in Frank E. Gaebelein, gen. ed., *The Expositor's Bible Commentary*, Vol. 3 (Grand Rapids: Zondervan Publishing House, 1992), 408.
[321] See Judges 4:17-22; 5:24-27.
[322] Mays, *Interpretation*, 227.
[323] Tate, 182.
[324] See verse 29.
[325] Kidner, 243.

[326] See also verses 11-12.
[327] Tate, 183.
[328] Judges 5:14.
[329] Kidner, 243-244.
[330] Wilcock, 238.
[331] Kidner, 244 and Wilcock, 238.
[332] Kidner, 244.
[333] See Psalm 29:3-9.
[334] See Psalm 69:4, 9, 21-23, 25.
[335] Wilcock, 239.
[336] See A. T. Hanson, *The Living Utterances of God: The New Testament Exegesis of the Old* (London: Darton, Longman & Todd, 1983).
[337] J. Clinton McCann, Jr., *A Theological Introduction to the Book of Psalms* (Nashville, TN: Abingdon Press, 1993), 87-88, 166.
[338] Mays, *Interpretation*, 232-233.
[339] See John 15:25.
[340] See Luke 24:25-27, 44-48.
[341] See John 2:17.
[342] See Romans 15:3, and note how Paul connected this quote from Psalm 69 with the fact that "whatever things were written before were written for our learning" in the next verse (Romans 15:4a). The point seems to be that when we read the Scriptures messianically, "we through the patience and comfort of the Scriptures might have hope" (Romans 15:4b).
[343] See Romans 11:9-10.
[344] See Acts 1:20.
[345] Wilcock, 241.
[346] See Psalms 45, 60, and 80.
[347] Mitchell, 19-20.
[348] Wilcock, 240.
[349] See also Psalm 35:19 and the comments there.
[350] Steve Moyise, *The Old Testament in the New: An Introduction* (London and New York: Continuum, 2001), 69.
[351] M. Daly-Denton, *David in the Fourth Gospel*. The Johannine Reception of the Psalms (Leiden, Netherlands: Brill Academic Publishers, 2000), 207-08, quoted by Moyise, 69.
[352] See Matthew 26:4; Luke 4:28-29; 22:2; John 5:18; 7:1, 19, 25; 8:37, 40.
[353] Wilcock, 241.
[354] Ibid.
[355] Moyise, 12.

[356] Mays, *Interpretation*, 230.
[357] See comments on Psalm 31:10; 40:12.
[358] BDB, 80.
[359] Segraves, *Hebrews: Better Things*, Vol. 2, 48-49.
[360] See Isaiah 8:14; Romans 9:33; Galatians 5:11; I Peter 2:8.
[361] See Romans 15:3.
[362] See John 7:3-5.
[363] See John 2:17.
[364] See Matthew 4:1.
[365] See Matthew 12:24; John 8:41, 48.
[366] See also Psalms 9:15; 28:1; 30:3, 9; 35:7; 40:2; 55:23; 57:6.
[367] See Isaiah 42:1; 52:13; Zechariah 3:8.
[368] See Matthew 26:56; Mark 14:50.
[369] See Matthew 27:34.
[370] See Romans 11:9-10.
[371] See Romans 9:30-33.
[372] For a discussion of the imprecations in the Psalter, see the comments on Psalm 58.
[373] See Matthew 10:15; 11:22, 24.
[374] See Acts 1:20.
[375] See Isaiah 53:4, 8.
[376] See Isaiah 53:5.
[377] See I Samuel 1:9; 3:3.
[378] See Ezekiel 40-47 and comments on Psalm 51:5.
[379] See Ezekiel 43:1-7.
[380] See Ephesians 3:1; Philemon 1:1, 9.
[381] Kidner, 248-249.
[382] Sailhamer, *NIV Compact Bible Commentary*, 330.
[383] Ibid.
[384] Kidner, 249.
[385] Norman Whybray, *Reading the Psalms As a Book,* Journal for the Study of the Old Testament Supplement Series 222 (eds. David J. A. Clines and Philip R. Davies; Sheffield, England: Sheffield Academic Press, 1996), 101.
[386] Mays, *Interpretation*, 233.
[387] Tate, 204.
[388] See comments on Psalm 40.
[389] See comments on Psalm 69:4, 7, 8, 9, 21, 22, 23, 25 and the superscription.
[390] Wilcock, 244.
[391] In Books 1 and 2 of the Psalter, these are the only psalms without

superscriptions, except Psalms 1 and 2, which are introductory to the entire Psalter. There is also evidence for joining Psalms 1-2 (see Mitchell, *The Message of the Psalter*, 29).

[392]Tate, 206. See also McCann, *The Shape and Shaping of the Psalter*, 119.

[393]Wilcock, 245.

[394]See comments on Psalm 35.

[395]See comments on Psalm 69:4.

[396]Wilcock, 245.

[397]Sailhamer, *NIV Compact Bible Commentary*, 330.

[398]Other texts in the Psalter that seem to be prayers of the Messiah include Psalms 16; 17; 18:1-19; 22:1-22; 31; 35; 40; 55; 57; 59; 69.

[399]See Psalm 38:21-22.

[400]See Psalm 38:1-10, 18.

[401]See Leviticus 2:2, 9, 16; 5:12; 6:15; 24:7; Numbers 5:26.

[402]Tate, 203, n. 1.c.

[403]Ibid.

[404]Kidner, 153.

[405]Ibid.

[406]Wilcock, 134.

[407]See, e.g., Genesis 9:15-16; Leviticus 26:42, 45.

[408]See, e.g., Numbers 15:40.

[409]Wilcock, 244 and Dahood, 168-169.

[410]Kidner, 250.

[411]See comments on Psalm 69:4.

[412]See also Psalms 40:17; 69:29.

[413]Mays, *Interpretation*, 234.

[414]Tate, 206. See also McCann, *The Shape and Shaping of the Psalter*, 119 and Mitchell, *The Message of the Psalter*, 29.

[415]See also Psalms 22:19; 38:22; 40:13; 141:1.

[416]Wilcock, 245.

[417]Ibid., and see comments on Psalm 70.

[418]See Psalm 40:6-8 and Hebrews 10:5-7.

[419]Compare Psalm 31:5 with Luke 23:46.

[420]Kidner, 251.

[421]Compare Psalm 22:1 with Matthew 27:46.

[422]Sailhamer, *NIV Compact Bible Commentary*, 318.

[423]Mays, *Interpretation*, 234.

[424]Although there is some manuscript evidence for plural forms in verse 20 ("Though you have made us see troubles—many hurtful troubles—will you let us live again? And from the depths of the earth bring

us up again?" [Tate, 208]), many English translations follow the singular forms. But even if the plural forms are followed, they "do not nullify the validity of the prayer for an individual" (Tate, 216).

[425] Sailhamer, *NIV Compact Bible Commentary*, 330.

[426] See Psalm 72:20.

[427] Mays, *Interpretation*, 235. Andrew A. Bonar wrote, "It will be asked how Christ could use such verses as verses 9 and 18, since these look forward apparently to the frailty of age. The reply to this difficulty is, that these expressions are used by Him in sympathy with His members, and in His own case denote the state equivalent to age. His old age was, ere he reached three and thirty years. . . ." Quoted in Charles Haddon Spurgeon, David Otis Fuller, ed., *Psalms* (Grand Rapids: Kregel Publications, 1968), 305.

[428] See Psalm 22:12.

[429] See Psalm 22:16.

[430] See Psalm 22:21.

[431] See Psalm 31:4.

[432] See Psalm 40:2.

[433] Mays, *Interpretation*, 234.

[434] On the need for help, see verses 1, 2, 3, 4, 9, 10, 11, 12, 13, 18; on trust, see verses 1, 3, 5, 6, 7, 8, 14, 15, 16, 17, 19, 20, 21, 22, 23, 24.

[435] Mays, *Interpretation*, 235.

[436] Ibid.

[437] See Psalms 18:49; 22:22; 61:8.

[438] See Romans 15:8-9; Hebrews 2:12.

[439] See Matthew 26:30; Mark 14:26.

[440] The "great Hallel" included Psalms 113-118, 136.

[441] Like the Greek *psalmos*, the Hebrew *mizmor* means "a song sung with musical accompaniment." John H. Sailhamer, "Notes on the Psalms," Summer 2000, unpublished. Sailhamer references Hans-Joachim Kraus, BK, xix.

[442] See Ephesians 5:19; Colossians 3:16.

[443] BDB, 68-69.

[444] Mays, *Interpretation*, 235-236.

[445] See Matthew 26:39-42.

[446] See Hebrews 12:2.

[447] See Hebrews 5:7.

[448] See Psalm 18:2, 31, 46.

[449] See Acts 2:26.

[450] See comments above.

[451] See comments above.

[452]Tate, 214.
[453]See comments above.
[454]Tate, 216.
[455]See comments above.
[456]See Psalm 16:10.
[457]See Psalm 127:1.
[458]Compare Psalms 41:13; 72:19; 89:52; 106:48; and Psalm 150.
[459]Sailhamer, *NIV Compact Bible Commentary,* 330-331.
[460]Whybray, 119.
[461]See Matthew 22:42-45; Mark 12:36; Luke 20:41-44; 24:44-47; John 10:34.

[462]See the discussions under "Peter's Use of the Psalms' Messianic Theme," "The Apostolic Community's Use of the Psalms' Messianic Theme," "Paul's Use of the Psalms' Messianic Theme," and "The Use of the Psalms' Messianic Theme in the Book of Hebrews," pages 333-341.

[463]Mitchell, *The Message of the Psalter,* 88.
[464]Ibid.
[465]Ibid., 88-89.

[466]This would include Psalm 43 because of its connection with Psalm 42.

[467]On the idea of David as a messianic figure, see Jeremiah 23:5-6; 30:9; Ezekiel 34:11, 15, 23-24; 37:24-25; Hosea 3:4-5. In Ezekiel 34:11, 15, *Yahweh* identifies Himself as Israel's shepherd, but the shepherd is named as David in Ezekiel 34:23-24. This suggests that the shepherd is the Messiah, Jesus Christ, ruling on David's throne. Hosea was written 207 years after the death of David, but the prophet declared that after many days without a king, Israel would seek David. The Messiah was "the David of the time, ruling on David's throne" (Leon J. Wood, in Frank E. Gaebelein, gen. ed., *The Expositor's Bible Commentary*, vol. 7 [Grand Rapids: Zondervan Publishing House, 1985], 183).

[468]Sailhamer, *NIV Compact Bible Commentary,* 330.
[469]Ibid., 331.
[470]Whybray, 92.
[471]Ibid.
[472]Wilcock, 249.
[473]Kidner, 254.

[474]Quoted by Nancy L. deClaissé-Walford, *Reading From the Beginning,* 71.

[475]Ibid., 71-72.
[476]Sailhamer, *NIV Compact Bible Commentary,* 331.

[477] Mays, *The Lord Reigns,* 104.
[478] Mays, *Interpretation,* 238.
[479] See the discussion of II Samuel 23:1-7 under "David's Explanation of the Psalms" in Appendix 3.
[480] Evidence that this text is messianic may be seen by comparing Zechariah 9:9-10 with Genesis 49:10-11 and Matthew 21:1-9.
[481] See Exodus 23:31 and Kidner, 256.
[482] Wilcock, 252.
[483] See also Micah 7:15-17.
[484] Sailhamer, "Notes on the Psalms," unpublished class notes, Summer 2000, 61.
[485] Evidence that this text concerns the Messiah's future reign may be seen by comparing Isaiah 60:3, 5-6, 9, 11-12 with Revelation 21:22-27.
[486] Sailhamer, "Notes on the Psalms," unpublished class notes, Summer 2000, 61.
[487] See I Timothy 6:15; Revelation 17:14; 19:16.
[488] Kidner, 254.
[489] See Isaiah 1:12-17; Amos 5:14-15, 24.
[490] Tate, 225.
[491] See I Kings 11:1-13.
[492] See Genesis 13:14-15; 15:18-21; 17:8; 26:3; 28:4, 13.
[493] Sheba refers to the "South Arabic Saba, an area known for its wealth (Isa 60:6; Jer 6:20; Ezek 27:22-25)"; Seba "is either an Arabian kingdom, perhaps located in modern Yemen, or a Sabean colony in North Africa. See Gen 10:7; Isa 43:3; 45:14; Joel 3:8; 1 Chr 1:9" (Tate, 221, n. 10.c. and n. 10.d., 221).
[494] See Matthew 26:36-46; Mark 14:32-42; Luke 22:39-46; John 18:1.
[495] See Revelation 20-22, and especially Revelation 21:24-26; 22:2.
[496] The Peshitta was an early fifth-century translation into Syriac that served as the standard version for the Syriac church (Achtemeier, *Harper's Bible Dictionary,* 1047).
[497] Mitchell, 21.
[498] Ibid., 32.
[499] Ibid., 33.
[500] Ibid., 36.
[501] Ibid., 40.
[502] Quoted by Mitchell, 49.
[503] Wilcock, 249.
[504] Kidner, 254.
[505] Quoted by Mitchell, 68.
[506] See Zechariah 8:13, 20-23.

Appendix 1. Canonical-Compositional Hermeneutics

[1] This section on canonical-compositional hermeneutics is taken from my Th.M. thesis, "An Application of Canonical-Compositional Hermeneutics to Psalms 14 and 53" (Western Seminary, 2003).

[2] Ray Lubeck, "An Introduction to Canonical Criticism," *Evangelical Theological Society Papers* 1995 (Portland, OR: Theological Research Exchange Network), 3.

[3] Ibid., emphasis in original.

[4] Ibid., 1-2. Some practitioners of canonical criticism add other emphases, but these are pertinent for our purposes.

[5] Brevard S. Childs, *Biblical Theology of the Old and New Testaments: Theological Reflection on the Christian Bible* (Minneapolis, MN: Fortress Press, 1992), 70. The idea here is that those who were involved in the preservation of the literary tradition shaped the text in such a way that the shape influences interpretation. The word "tradent" refers to someone who studies or preserves tradition and is increasingly used by scholars in place of "traditionist." This may be due to possible confusion between "traditionist" and "traditionalist."

[6] Ibid., 71.

[7] Ibid., 193-94.

[8] Bruce K. Waltke, "A Canonical Process Approach to the Psalms," in John S. and Paul D. Feinberg, eds., *Tradition and Testament: Essays in Honor of Charles Lee Feinberg* (Chicago, IL: Moody Press, 1981), 7.

[9] Ibid.

[10] Ibid.

[11] Ibid., 7-8.

[12] Ibid., 8.

[13] Ibid.

[14] Ibid.

[15] Ibid., 9.

[16] Ray Lubeck, "An Apologetic for Canonical Shaping of the Old Testament (TaNaK)," *Evangelical Theological Society Papers* 2000 (Portland, OR: Theological Research Exchange Network), 3.

[17] Ibid., 3-4.

[18] Ibid., 6.

[19] Sailhamer, *Introduction to Old Testament Theology*, 154.

[20] Ibid.

[21] Waltke, 8.

[22] These observations are based on notes taken from Sailhamer's comments in the course "The Messiah in the Psalms and Daniel,"

offered at Western Seminary during the summer 2000 semester. The notes were taken by the author.

[23] The superscription is the first verse in the Hebrew text.

[24] Sailhamer, *Introduction to Old Testament Theology*, 204-05 and *NIV Compact Bible Commentary*, 247-248.

[25] Acts 2:25-36.

[26] Evidence of composition includes features like the final verses of Psalms 14 and 53. These verses refer to a return from captivity, suggesting they were written during the Exile. The evidence also includes the use of Aramaic rather than Hebrew, as in Psalm 2:12, where *bar* instead of *ben* is used for "son." It also includes verses like Psalm 72:20 ("The prayers of David the son of Jesse are ended") that suggest earlier collections of psalms.

Appendix 2. The Use of Psalms in the New Testament

[1] The law of Moses includes Genesis, Exodus, Leviticus, Numbers, and Deuteronomy. The Prophets include Joshua, Judges, Samuel, Kings, Isaiah, Jeremiah, Ezekiel, Hosea, Joel, Amos, Obadiah, Jonah, Micah, Nahum, Habakkuk, Zephaniah, Haggai, Zechariah, and Malachi. The Psalms, also referred to as "the writings," include Psalms, Job, Proverbs, Ruth, Song of Solomon, Ecclesiastes, Lamentations, Esther, Daniel, Ezra, Nehemiah, and Chronicles. These three categories comprise the entire Old Testament, although in the Hebrew Bible the order and division of the books differ from the English Old Testament, which follows the arrangement of the Septuagint.

[2] Although it is common to reject the superscriptions of the Psalms as being of later origin and uninspired, they are actually included in the Hebrew text as the first verse of the psalm.

[3] The writers of the New Testament frequently quoted from the Septuagint rather than from the Hebrew text. In a sense, the Septuagint was the Bible of the first-century church. In fact, ". . . the majority of the Old Testament quotations rendered by the New Testament authors are borrowed directly from the Septuagint . . . the vocabulary and style of the Septuagint is reflected in the theological terms and phraseology chosen by the New Testament writers. . . . It is not surprising—due to its early widespread use and enduring influence in the Church—that the order of the Biblical Books in the Septuagint, rather than that of the Hebrew O.T., became the accepted order" (Sir Lancelot C.L. Brenton, *The Septuagint With Apocrypha: Greek and English* [Peabody, MA: Hendrickson Publishers, Originally published by Samuel Bagster & Sons, Ltd.,

London, 1851], Preface). Brenton also pointed out that the apostles "used it [the LXX] more often than not in making citations from the Old Testament. . . . Besides the direct citations in the New Testament in which the Septuagint is manifestly used, there are not a few passages in which it is clear that the train of expression has been formed on words and phrases of the Septuagint" (p. iv). By actual count, the "Index of Quotations" found in Kurt Aland, et al., *The Greek New Testament*, Third corrected edition (Stuttgart: German Bible Society, 1983) attributes nearly 21 percent of Old Testament quotations in the New Testament to the Septuagint, but this does not represent the full use of the Septuagint in the New Testament. *The Greek New Testament* indicates the Septuagint only where it differs from the Hebrew. (See p. xlvii.) The most significant consideration on this issue is not where the Septuagint is used where it differs from the Hebrew, or where it is used when it is substantially the same as the Hebrew, but where the Hebrew is used where it differs from the Septuagint. It is at these points where the writers of the New Testament indicated that the translation offered in the Septuagint was not adequate to their inspired purposes. Regardless of the precise statistics, the fact that the New Testament uses the Septuagint indicates the widespread use of the Greek language among both Gentiles and Jews in the first century and the fact that the Hebrew language was not so widely known or used at that time.

[4]Based on the English translation alone, one might think that the word "foreseeing" (seeing . . . before [KJV]) refers back to Acts 2:30, so that what David foresaw was only that the Messiah would descend from him. But the word translated "foreseeing" (*proidon*) is an aorist active participle, serving as an adverbial modifier of "spoke" (*elalesen*), an aorist active indicative verb. The idea is something like "when foreseeing this ["this" is not in the Greek text; it is supplied for stylistic reasons], he spoke" or "after foreseeing this, he spoke." In other words, what David said was a result of his foresight concerning the resurrection of the Messiah.

[5]It is not *Yahweh* who referred to the Messiah as *Adonai*, but David.

[6]For a full discussion of Psalm 102:25-27 in Hebrews 1:10-12, see Segraves, *Hebrews: Better Things*, Vol. 1, 54-58. At this point, Hebrews follows the Septuagint. The Hebrew text does not have LORD (*Yahweh*) in Psalm 102:25, but it is *Yahweh* who is being addressed throughout the Psalm. (See verses 1, 12, 15, 16, 18, 19, 21, 22.) Therefore, whether or not *Yahweh* appears in verse 25, we know that verse 25 does address *Yahweh*, and the inspired writer of Hebrews quoted this verse as a reference to the Messiah.

[7] The trinitarian perspective would suggest that Psalm 110:1 is a conversation between the first and second persons of the Godhead. But if this conversation occurs between two divine persons who are ontologically equal, it seems impossible to take the words at face value. Why is one person identified as *Yahweh* and the other as *Adonai*? Why does one sit at the right hand of the other? Why is it necessary for one to conquer the enemies of the other? Trinitarianism attempts to resolve these problems with the claim that the second person is functionally subordinate, not ontologically subordinate. In other words, the second person functions as if he were subordinate, but he is not actually subordinate. Although it will forever be beyond human ability to understand and explain everything about God and all the nuances of the Incarnation, it seems better to understand texts like this as reflecting the significance of the Incarnation. A mystery is at work here that no one can satisfactorily explain.

[8] For further discussion of the relationship between the humanity of the Messiah and His Melchizedekian priesthood, see the comments in Segraves, *Better Things*, Vol. 1 on Hebrews 5:6, 10; 6:20; 7:1, 10-11, 15, 17, 21.

[9] The Hebrew words translated "save now" are transliterated "hosanna."

[10] Radmacher, 1822.

[11] The first time Jesus cleansed the Jerusalem Temple, the event brought to the mind of His disciples the first phrase of Psalm 69:9: "Because zeal for Your house has eaten me up." (See John 2:17.)

[12] Psalm 18 is virtually identical to the psalm found in II Samuel 22:2-51. Compare Psalm 18:49 with II Samuel 22:50.

[13] The phrase "the lower parts of the earth" should not be taken to mean that Christ descended into an earthly abyss. Nor does it mean that He went to the place where unbelievers await final judgment. Although it could be a reference to His tomb, the phrase most likely is simply a reference to His descent to the earth in His incarnation. The words translated "the lower parts of the earth" (*ta katotera mere tes ges*) may be translated something like "the lower parts, the earth." In this case, "the earth" (*tes ges*) forms a genitive of apposition. As compared to His previous existence in heaven, the Incarnation involved the Messiah coming to the "lower parts."

[14] For a full treatment of the Book of Hebrews, see Segraves, *Hebrews: Better Things*, Vol. 1 and *Hebrews: Better Things*, Vol. 2.

Appendix 3. David's Explanation of the Psalms

[1]The Hebrew phrase transliterates as *meshiyach 'elohey ya'akov*.
[2]See the discussion in Sailhamer, *Introduction to Old Testament Theology*, 132-142.
[3]Waltke, 3-18 and Philip E. Satterthwaite, Richard S. Hess, and Gordon J. Wenham, *The Lord's Anointed: Interpretations of Old Testament Messianic Texts* (Grand Rapids: Baker Publishing Group, 1995).